On 22 August 1914, on a battlefield one hundred kil[ometres]
to the River Meuse, two French and two German arm[ies]
collectively as the Battle of the Ardennes. On that day 27,000 young French soldiers died, the bloodiest day in the military history of France, most of them in the Ardennes, and yet it is almost unknown to English-speaking readers. There has never been an operational study of the Battle of the Ardennes, in any language; at best a single chapter in a history of greater scope, at least a monograph of an individual tactical encounter within the overall battle. This book fills a glaring gap in the study of the opening phase of the First World War - the Battles of the Frontiers - and provides fresh insight into both French and German plans for the prosecution of what was supposed to be a short war.

At the centre of this book lies a mystery. In a key encounter battle one French army corps led by a future Minister of War, General Pierre Roques, outnumbered its immediate opposition by nearly six-to-one and yet dismally failed to capitalise on that superiority. The question is how, and why. Intriguingly there is a six-hour gap in the war diaries of all General Roques' units; it smacks of a cover-up. By a thorough investigation of German sources, and through the discovery of three vital messages buried in the French archives, it is now possible to piece together what happened during those missing hours and show how Roques threw away an opportunity to break the German line and advance unopposed deep into the hinterland beyond. The chimera of a clean break and exploitation, that was to haunt the Allied High Command for the next four years in the trenches of the Western Front, was a brief and tantalising opportunity for General Roques.

The final part of this book seeks to answer the question "why?" The history of both French and German pre-war preparation reveals the political, economic and cultural differences that shaped the two opposing national armies. Those differences, in turn, predicated the behaviour of General Roques and his men as well as that of his German opponent. With a clear understanding of those differences, the reader may now understand how the French lost their best opportunity not only to stymie the Schlieffen Plan, but to change the course of the rest of the war.

Simon J. House is an independent military historian, and *Lost Opportunity* is his first book. It is the book of his doctoral thesis, gained at King's College London in May 2012 under the supervision of Professor William Philpott (*Bloody Victory* and *Attrition*) and examined by Professor Sir Hew Strachan and Professor David Stevenson.

Despite a life-long passion for military history, Simon came to the profession late in life, having fitted in a thirty-two year career as an accountant and senior executive at British Telecom before retiring in 2001 to pursue other interests. One of those interests was of course military history, which took him to the reading rooms of the Imperial War Museum. There he used his French and German language skills to research the Battles of the Frontiers. Whilst translating the French Official History's version of the Battle of the Ardennes, his eye was drawn to a copy of the German History - *Der Weltkrieg* - which when translated gave a very different story of the battle. There followed nearly ten years of painstaking research to unearth the truth about this little-known and misunderstood battle.

Simon is now a 72 year-old widower living in retirement in Dorchester, Dorset. He is actively working on a sequel to *Lost Opportunity*, with the provisional title of *To Die in White Gloves*, and which will be a history of the French Army during the Battles of the Frontiers in August 1914. A third study, *Red Trousers: the development of the French Army from 1870 to 1914* may yet see the light of day. Simon's weakness for the counterfactual still leads him to continue his research into the 'tipping points' of the Second World War.

LOST OPPORTUNITY

The Battle of the Ardennes 22 August 1914

Simon J. House

Helion & Company

Helion & Company Limited
Unit 8 Amherst Business Centre
Budbrooke Road
Warwick
CV34 5WE
England
Tel. 01926 499 619
Email: info@helion.co.uk
Website: www.helion.co.uk
Twitter: @helionbooks
Visit our blog http://blog.helion.co.uk/

Published by Helion & Company 2017. Reprinted in paperback 2023
Designed and typeset by Mary Woolley, Battlefield Design (www.battlefield-design.co.uk)
Cover designed by Paul Hewitt, Battlefield Design (www.battlefield-design.co.uk)

Text © Simon J. House 2016
Present-day battlefield photographs © Simon J. House. Contemporary photographs open source
unless noted otherwise.
Maps drawn by George Anderson © Helion & Company 2016

Front cover: "En avant, mes enfants, vive la France!" - Virton, the morning of 22 August 1914.
Watercolour by Nestor Outer, reproduced with the kind permission of the Musée gaumais, Virton.
Rear cover: "In retreat". Watercolour by Nestor Outer, reproduced with the kind permission of the
Musée gaumais, Virton.

ISBN 978-1-804514-68-9

For details of other military history titles published by Helion & Company Limited, contact the
above address, or visit our website: http://www.helion.co.uk. We always welcome receiving book
proposals from prospective authors.

Contents

List of Illustrations

List of Maps in Map Book

List of Abbreviations

France

CA	*Corps d'armée*	Army corps
CAC	*Corps d'armée coloniale*	Colonial army corps
CC	*Corps de cavalerie*	Cavalry Corps
DC	*Division de cavalerie*	Cavalry Division
DI	*Division d'infanterie*	Infantry division
DIC	*Division d'infanterie colonial*	Colonial Infantry Division
DIR	*Division d'infanterie de reserve*	Reserve Infantry Division
RI	*Régiment d'infanterie*	Infantry Regiment
RAC	*Régiment d'artillerie de campagne*	Field Artillery Regiment

Germany

AK	*Armeekorps*	Army Corps
RAK	*Reserve Armeekorps*	Reserve Army Corps
HKK	*Höhe Kavallerie Kommando*	Independent Cavalry Command
KK	*Kavallerie Korps*	Cavalry Corps
ID	*Infanterie-division*	Infantry Division
RID	*Reserve Infanterie-division*	Reserve infantry Division
KD	*Kavallerie division*	Cavalry Division
IR	*Infanterie-regiment*	Infantry Regiment
RIR	*Reserve Infanterie-regiment*	Reserve Infantry Regiment
FAR	*Feld-artillerie regiment*	Field Artillery Regiment

Foreword

On August 18, the German 4th and 5th Armies began advancing into the Ardennes Forest, part of the massive enveloping movement known as the Schlieffen Plan. The pace was limited by a thin road network, broken terrain, and high humidity. Three days later General Joseph Joffre countered by sending his 3rd and 4th Armies into the Ardennes from the other direction. The French generalissimo, by now aware of the massive German concentration in Belgium, reckoned with relatively weaker opposition in the center, and expected to disrupt the enemy offensive by disrupting its hinge.

The result was a misbegotten, murderous, now almost forgotten encounter battle in the Ardennes. Better expressed, it was a series of separate battles, head to head, corps against corps, that added up to a French debacle that remained conveniently buried in the official records. Everywhere the Germans dominated tactically. The signature combat took place around Rossignol, where the French Colonial Corps was outflanked and broken, taking almost 12,000 casualties. In other sectors entire divisions disintegrated under German artillery, broken men fleeing in all directions. August 22 remains the single bloodiest day in the history of the French army—27,000 dead, thousands more wounded or missing, and most of the latter dead as well.

Until now this debacle has been generally presented as a fiasco from first to last, an endeavor rendered hopeless above all by a tactical doctrine emphasizing "offensive to the limit" at all times and all cost, a doctrine regarding a rifle as something on which to fix a bayonet. Simon House presents a far more nuanced picture. Operationally he describes the French achieving a complete surprise that enabled the concentration of significantly superior force at two critical points.

These opportunities to inflict a stinging defeat, perhaps disrupting the entire German plan, were not moreover squandered by heedless frontal attacks. The strength of this work is its painstaking, pitiless demonstration of French structural weaknesses, and the way they came together in the Ardennes. Command above the regimental level was uneven, ranging at best from mediocre to incompetent. The French counterpart to German "mission tactics" was individual ability and charisma - a matrix better suited to Austerlitz or the Crimea than a modern high-tech battlefield. Orders were treated as suggestions. Intelligence was random, communications unreliable. In short, for a professional framework for a citizen army, France's cadres were highly unprofessional.

That characteristic extended to troop levels as well. French doctrines were uncertain. Too many revisions to too many manuals in too short a time frame made combat behavior unpredictable. Training fell well short of even the minimum requirements of 1914 - in good part due to a chronic shortage of officers and NCOs. The artillery was slow to engage and slow to react, German gunners consistently neutralized the technically superior French 75s, leaving the infantry to demonstrate their dash and valor without the fire support called for by "offensive to the limit." In practice that meant the men in the ranks were left to be ground down by an enemy who understood that successful battlefield improvisation depended on systematic peacetime preparation.

House appropriately emphasizes the misunderstood and wasted opportunities for at least tactical breakthroughs. But he demonstrates even more convincingly that the spectrum of institutional flaws generated by French prewar systems and methods positioned those opportunities solidly in the realm of theory - at least in August. French learning curves were high even in these early days. But the victory on the Marne would reflect German operational and strategic deficiencies rather than French institutional improvements. And Simon House deserves full marks for this model case study of an often overlooked commonplace: that failure on peacetime training grounds and in peacetime educational institutions costs blood in war—a LOT of blood, and most of it wasted.

Professor Dennis Showalter
University of Colerado

Acknowledgements

This book is avowedly the book of my thesis, and my thesis was the product of my retirement. A thirty-two year career as an accountant with British Telecom culminated in 2001 with a mutual decision between my lifelong employer and me to part company on good terms. That life-changing event allowed me to spend more time on my two hobbies, gardening and military history. Thus it was that I found myself in the Reading Rooms of the Imperial War Museum, translating a passage from Volume One of the French Official History of the First World War (as you do) in an attempt to track down the story behind one fact - that 27,000 French soldiers had been killed on 22 August 1914, an event so monumental that I was shocked that no-one I spoke to knew anything about it. Following a trail, I ended up at a small village called Nevraumont, and a general called Roques: standing on a hill, commanding an army corps that in one key spot outnumbered his opponent by six to one, doing nothing. At that moment, sitting in what had been the chapel of the old Hospital of Bethlehem (Bedlam), I looked up from my study of the French history; my eye caught the title of a book on the shelf above me - *der Weltkrieg*. Curiosity and a rudimentary understanding of German naturally led me to find out what the Germans had to say about Roques' lack of endeavour. A thesis was born. Two things, no, three things became clear: that on 22 August 1914 at Nevraumont the French had had no idea of the state of affairs 'on the other side of the hill'; that consequently what had been written in the French Official History was not accurate, being one-sided; and that the true story of the 'Lost Opportunity' had to be written. So I would like to thank my former employers at British Telecom for setting me free. And I would like to thank all the staff past and present at the Reading Rooms of the Imperial War Museum for their help, advice and guidance in the embryonic research towards this book.

Following my discovery of a potential story in the 'Lost Opportunity', the question arose as to what to do with my knew-found knowledge. I wanted to publish something; I wanted to know if I could write. I am therefore very much indebted to my friend George Karger for introducing me to the Military History Department of Kings College London. Without you, George, I would not have put even a first foot on the ladder. Thank you, and thanks also for your friendship and for the excellent Polish cuisine at the Gay Hussar.

George took me to have coffee with a man called Bill Philpott, who worked at Kings. Bill, who had taken the time to read my ten-page synopsis of the 'Lost Opportunity', basically told me that my writing was dreadful; but with his unerring eye for a good topic and his instinct for spotting potential he also said that I should apply to take a PhD research degree. Bill (now Professor William Philpott, specialist on Anglo-French military history in the First World War and author of those excellent works 'Bloody Victory' and 'Attrition') turned out to be at that time a senior lecturer at Kings. With his help and guidance I was accepted and enrolled at Kings, and Bill became my supervisor. Bill, twelve years on, twelve years older and wiser, I can honestly say that as a military historian I am what you have made me - and what that is, good, bad or ugly - my readers may judge for themselves.

I want to thank all the staff at Kings College London, and the Institution itself, for their part in the making of my thesis. I want to thank my friends and colleagues of Bill's military operations study group (the 'Coal Hole Club') for their help, support, analytical advice and beer. I want to thank the convenors and members of the Military History Seminar at the Institute of Historical Research for giving me a platform and sounding-board for my ideas. Professor Dennis Showalter has been kind enough to advise me and to write a Foreword to this book. And I want to thank the two examiners of my thesis, Professor Sir Hew Strachan and Professor David Stevenson, for subjecting my work to such rigorous scrutiny that it surely will withstand any further test.

Turning a thesis into a book is no easy task. The first major publisher to whom I offered it demanded such an extensive rewrite that I balked at the task. I am therefore eternally grateful to Duncan Rogers and Helion for finding me, for having faith in my original work, and allowing it to see the light of day. And for the freedom to do maps, maps, maps, which give life to dry words.

Introduction

On 22 August 1914, on a battlefield one hundred kilometres wide, stretching from Luxembourg in the south–east to Dinant on the river Meuse in the north–west, two French and two German armies clashed in a series of encounters known collectively as the Battle of the Ardennes. The battle came about as a result of an offensive ordered by General Joffre under the overall strategic umbrella of the French *Plan XVII,* an offensive designed to counter the developing German threat to the French left flank. The outcome was a clear tactical defeat for the French, whose armies retreated first to their start–line and then, in accordance with the general strategic situation, deep into the hinterland of France. By 23 August, the day on which the British Expeditionary Force (BEF) met the German 1st Army at Mons, the focus of the war had already shifted to the west bank of the Meuse and the broad open Belgian plain.

Maps 1 & 2

On 22 August, about twenty–seven thousand French soldiers were killed and many more men wounded and missing in action.[1] Overall German casualties have never been published, but individual regimental histories and eye–witness accounts give sufficient evidence to suggest that they were similarly high in the combatant units. However, the French retreated, defeated; the Germans advanced, victorious. French losses for so little gain and the unanticipated failure of their offensive strategy had to be explained: over time the myth of the 'Cult of the Offensive' arose. Overlaid with the ensuing four years of savage and unheard–of casualties on the Western Front, the legend of gallant but suicidal French attacks gained credence amongst many historians. In 1930 Liddell Hart wrote: 'The troops attacked blindly with the bayonet and were mown down by machine guns'[2]; and in 2005 Doughty could still write: 'Tragically for France, many casualties suffered in the attacks from August 14 to 23 were unnecessary and came from foolish bayonet charges against an entrenched enemy'.[3]

In fact the French Ardennes counter–offensive had had the strategic potential to change the course of the war, by cutting the lines of communication of the three powerful German right wing armies (*Schwenkungsflügel*)[4] which were seeking to execute the 'Schlieffen Plan'. Indeed the mission and role of the two German central armies in the Ardennes was to prevent just such a move. The French failure, following as it did their earlier defeats at Sarrebourg and Morhange on 20 August (which battles were the main French attack towards the German frontier in Alsace–Lorraine), surrendered the strategic initiative to the Germans and dictated the pattern of events leading to the Battle of the Marne, the 'race to the sea' and stalemate in the trenches.

Map 3

The first compelling reason for writing this book is that there has not yet been an operational study of the Battle of the Ardennes as a complete, unitary military campaign, in any language. Sewell Tyng's excellent book *The Campaign of the Marne,* written in 1935, devotes one chapter

---

1   H. Contamine, *La Victoire de la Marne* (Eds. Gallimard. Paris, 1970), p.120.
2   B.H. Liddell Hart, first published as *The Real War 1914-1918* in 1930, but this quotation taken from *A History of the First World War* (Faber & Faber, London, 1930), p.82.
3   R.A. Doughty, *Pyrrhic Victory* (Harvard University Press, Harvard MA, 2005), p.75.
4   H.H. Herwig, *The Marne, 1914* (Random House, New York, 2009), p.50: translated as 'pivot wing'.

from forty–three to the French perspective of the offensive in the Ardennes;[5] Terence Zuber's *The Battle of the Ardennes, 1914* claims to be merely a tactical comparative study and even then focuses predominantly on German tactical performance in individual encounters, giving the French side much less attention.[6] Apart from Tyng's and Zuber's works, the battle has so far either been hastily summarised in general histories of the Great War, in which it necessarily takes but a small part in a general survey of the Battles of the Frontiers, or it has been treated piecemeal with individual encounter-battles being analysed in detail. In the first instance, the general histories attempt to draw out the essence of the campaign, identify themes and find vignettes that succinctly exemplify the points to be made. The danger in this approach is that the diversity of the Ardennes campaign defies such brief encapsulation. Conversely, the study of an individual encounter-battle may do justice to the one event but will fail to capture the overall operational context.

During the research for this book, it was discovered that, unbeknownst to most previous historians, the French had lost a great opportunity to defeat the Germans in the Ardennes. Had they inflicted a tactical defeat on their enemy, as indeed they might have done, and had they followed it up with further operational manoeuvres, the strategic consequences might have been enormous for the future conduct of the war. There is evidence, for example, that a French victory in the Ardennes would have stopped von Hausen's Third German Army from crossing the Meuse on 23 August, with incalculable impact on the course of the Marne Campaign. The new research surrounding the 'Lost Opportunity' provides a central theme for this book.

Map 4

The French offensive on 22 August came as a complete operational surprise to the German High Command. Marching north from the river Semoy in a typically thick morning mist, the bulk of the French Fourth Army remained undiscovered by German reconnaissance for five vital hours as they advanced into the weak centre of their opponent's defensive screen. When the fog lifted and aircraft were able to fly again, the extent of the French advance was revealed. Duke Albrecht von Württemberg, commanding the German Fourth Army, was himself in no doubt as to the effectiveness of the initial French moves:

> he received an air–reconnaissance report at about midday which blindingly illuminated to him the extremely dangerous situation into which [the German] Fourth Army had fallen... The short, but significant report showed that Fourth Army was facing an immediate and serious crisis: strong enemy forces were slipping past them in a northerly direction and in the very near future superior forces would also strike their centre. The fighting might even have already begun. The priority now for Fourth Army was to protect the left flank of Third Army. Only when this was guaranteed could Third Army cross the Maas [Meuse] in order to help the right wing armies deliver the decisive blow; otherwise a substantial part of Third Army might have to be diverted south. And for the time being Fourth Army only had its two central corps available to oppose the attack.[7]

In contrast to this pessimistic near–contemporary German assessment, English–speaking historians have typically dismissed the French Ardennes offensive as 'an imaginary *coup de grace*[8] a 'failure to

---

5   S. Tyng, *The Campaign of the Marne* (Longmans, Green & Co., London, 1935).

6   T. Zuber, *The Battle of the Ardennes, 1914* (Tempus, Stroud, 2007) .

7   *Der Weltkrieg 1914 bis 1918, Die Militärischen Operationen zu Lande, Erster Band (Weltkrieg 1)* (Reichsarchiv, E.S. Mittler & Sohn, Berlin, 1925), p.316.

8   Liddell Hart, op. cit., p.82.

anticipate the strength of the enemy'[9] and 'a multiple disaster',[10] if indeed they mention the battle at all. But the fact remains that at two separate locations on that hundred–kilometre front and for the whole of the day's fighting on 22 August, the French outnumbered their opponents by odds of between four– and six–to–one in men, supported by an overwhelming superiority in artillery and machine guns.

The facts, as revealed in the research performed for this book, demonstrate that the French had on the one hand a clear opportunity to turn the open right flank of the German Fourth Army and on the other an equally clear chance to break through the centre of that same army into the open and undefended hinterland. A strategically important railway junction and Duke Albrecht's forward command–post, both at Libramont, within ten kilometres of the fighting, were two potentially early and easy prizes. Ironically, all of the above remained unknown to the French generals involved. Their ignorance of their own tactical situation and of opportunities for operational manoeuvre testifies to the poor quality of the French commanders involved.

The magnitude of the French opportunity has not yet been brought to light. The German role in thwarting French strategic and operational ambitions in the Ardennes has similarly not been properly addressed in the history of the opening phase of the Great War, whilst certain misconceptions – for example about parity of numbers and equipment differences – need to be corrected.

Examination of the causes of and reasons for the French failure to grasp these fleeting opportunities and deliver tactical and possibly operational defeat of the Germans in the Ardennes forms the third major theme of this book. As a result of operational failures the Battle of the Ardennes became a series of loosely connected tactical encounter-battles between individual corps, divisions, and on at least one occasion, brigades. Each encounter-battle had its own unique characteristics of terrain, timing and tactics; each presented individual opportunities and problems for the use of specific weapons and pieces of equipment; and each gives us today a different example how both French and German pre–war doctrines worked out in practice and under pressure of battle.

Much has been written about French pre–war military doctrine. Colonel de Grandmaison and his supposed championship and dissemination of the so–called doctrine of *offensive* à *outrance* and élan has been widely blamed for the early French defeats and the enormity of their losses. For example Doughty has written of 'the notion of the *offensive* à *outrance* as articulated by Lieutenant Colonel Louis Loyseau de Grandmaison', claiming that 'had Michel remained chief of staff of the army, his reservations about Grandmaison and the *offensive* à *outrance* might have limited some of its pernicious effects'.[11] But Contamine wrote that the French failure was one of execution rather than doctrine.[12] In this book we will examine Grandmaison's role, and test Contamine's assertion, firstly by a thorough examination of the differences between the military doctrines of both sides and what actually happened on the battlefield, and secondly by an examination of pre–war training and preparation.

Although issues of doctrine and training have been cited by historians as key reasons for French failure in the Ardennes, issues concerning the type, number and quality of various items of equipment on each side have also been highlighted as possible causes. Questions arise for which this book will provide fresh answers. For example: what is the truth of Churchill's and Liddell Hart's

---

9   Doughty, op. cit., p.72.
10   D. Stevenson, *1914–1918* (Allen Lane, London, 2004), p.53.
11   Doughty, op. cit., p.10 and p.26.
12   H. Contamine, *La Revanche 1871-1914* (Berger-Levrault, Paris, 1957), p.237.

assertion of French bayonets against German machine guns? [13] Were the German field howitzers really the decisive battlefield factor that several historians have claimed?[14] Was the absence of French heavy artillery a pivotal mistake?[15] Were the Germans waiting, entrenched, for the French to attack, as many have claimed?[16] What role did aircraft on each side play in the battles? These questions and answers are central to the analysis of the battle, and the second part of this book will compare pre-war preparations with performance in the Battle of the Ardennes in order to throw new light on the reasons why the Germans defeated the French in all the opening battles until that of the Marne.

The consequences not so much of the French defeat but of their failure to grasp two fleeting chances of victory were far–reaching. The French were the attackers, the Germans the defenders (in strategic and operational terms at least); the French had to win, the Germans had simply to avoid losing; this strategic difference is crucial to an understanding of the outcome of two encounters in particular, at Maissin–Anloy where the French failed to turn the German left flank, and at Neufchâteau where they conspicuously missed a potentially decisive opportunity to break through the German centre.

Just as the Germans were under no illusions at the time as to the seriousness of the threat posed to them by the surprise French advance on the morning of 22 August, so they fully appreciated the importance of having avoided defeat:

> The serious crisis which had threatened not only the [Fourth] Army itself but the whole front of the German wheeling right wing was seen to have been favorably overcome thanks to the prudent and methodical leadership and heroic devotion of the troops… Somewhat later news came in from Third Army that it would assault across the Meuse on 23 August.[17]

It is useless to speculate upon what might have happened in the event of a French victory, there are too many random variables influencing possible future alternative decisions and actions. Nevertheless a successful German defence in the Ardennes was evidently so crucial to the continued evolution of the German 'Schlieffen Plan' that a fresh interpretation of events in the Ardennes and analysis of the causes of French failure is needed to properly understand the outcome of the Battles of the Frontiers, of which the Ardennes offensive was a crucial part.

The scope of the book includes the activity of the French Third and Fourth Armies and that of their opponents the German Fourth and Fifth Armies. The role of the French Third Group of reserve divisions originally allocated to Ruffey's Third Army will be touched upon, even though Joffre removed them from Third Army command on the eve of the battle. These reserve divisions formed the core of Maunoury's new Army of Lorraine, whose mission was to protect Verdun and the Meuse Heights against a German sally from Metz. They are included in this history, briefly, because of the issues raised by their unexpected absence from Ruffey's battle–line.

The activity of the French Fifth Army and the British Expeditionary Force (BEF) is specifically excluded from this history; it has been extensively studied in both French and English–speaking historiographies, partly because it constituted the Allied reaction to the 'Schlieffen Plan' which has become the dominant feature of the opening phase of the War, partly because the British naturally concentrate on their own contribution while the French prefer to discuss the victory on the Marne

13   W.S. Churchill, *The World Crisis* (Odhams, Watford, 1938), pp.215-219; and Liddell Hart, op. cit., p.82.
14   For example: H. Strachan, *The First World War Volume 1: To Arms* (Oxford University Press, Oxford, 2001), p.229.
15   M. Goya, *La Chair et l'Acier: l'invention de la guerre moderne (1914-1918)* (Tallandier, Paris, 2004) pp.155-162.
16   For example: P. Miquel, *La Grande Guerre* (Librarie Arthème Fayard, Paris, 1983) pp.130, 132.
17   *Weltkrieg 1*, p.334.

rather than the defeat in the Ardennes. It is useful to redress this balance with an in–depth analysis of the Ardennes campaign, the western boundary of which was the river Meuse.

Also excluded on the French side are the twin battles of Sarrebourg and Morhange. These, the high–water marks of the main French offensive under *Plan XVII*, were very different in nature from the Ardennes battles, being firstly Joffre's pre–emptive attempt to gain the strategic initiative and secondly a set–piece offensive in relatively open (if constricted) terrain.[18] The Battle of the Ardennes was by contrast a counter–offensive in reaction to German moves and a scrappy, uncoordinated, somewhat unexpected series of encounter–battles.

On the German side, the activity of the German *Schwenkungsflügel* – their First, Second and Third Armies – has been excluded from this history, except insofar as the march across the Belgian Ardennes of Third Army, and its mission to cross the Meuse either side of Dinant, impacted upon the activity of Fourth Army, part of whose mission was to secure Third Army's right flank from French attack.

The key primary sources used for the operational and battle analysis in this book have been taken from (on the French side) the military archives at Vincennes (*Service historique de l'armée de terre*) and (on the German side) the military archives at Freiburg (*Bundesarchiv-Militaerarchiv*). Both archives contain a variety of source material, ranging from unit daily journals (*journaux de marche et opérations* or JMOs in French) to casualty returns, medical journals, intelligence reports and occasionally individual battlefield documents such as scribbled notes from officers' pocket books (where collected archive material has survived pruning and weeding). Unfortunately for historians, the original German archive in Potsdam was heavily bombed by the RAF in the Second World War, and many important documents destroyed. Others were taken back to Russia by the conquering Soviet troops in 1945, and are only now coming back into the public domain. To supplement the rather sparse remaining records on the German side, the Imperial War Museum's rich collection of German regimental histories, often written by former commanding officers and containing eye–witness testimony, has added valuable detail. On the French side, their Official History covering the period in question, *Les armées françaises dans la grande guerre, premier tome, premier volume*, contains over a thousand annexes – orders, battle reports, intelligence reports and intelligence briefings – many of which duplicate the originals in the archive and some of which represent surviving documents which have been weeded from the archive.

Further French primary source material can be found in the published works of Commandant Grasset, works which are themselves important secondary sources.[19] But not only did Grasset take part in one of the Ardennes encounter-battles (at Ethe as a sub-lieutenant in 7 Infantry Division (DI)) but after the war he became Commandant of the *Service historique de l'armée de terre*, responsible for collecting and codifying archive material. In this latter capacity, he had access to the recollections of very many eye–witnesses, whose testimony is woven into his text. His book on *Neufchâteau* also includes copies of relevant interrogation reports of German prisoners.[20] Grasset's own personal account of the encounter at Ethe, *Vingt Jours de Guerre aux Temps Héroïques*, contains valuable commentary on the process of mobilisation, concentration and of the period of *couverture*

18   The Vosges Mountains in the east and the fortified zone of Metz in the west contained the space available for the advance of the French First and Second Armies into a front only 140 kilometres wide, sub–divided into the 'Sarrebourg' and 'Morhange' sections by a swampy, flooded lake area known as *Les Étangs*. The terrain itself is open, forested, rolling hills, but there is limited space for deployment.

19   Commandant A. Grasset, *Un combat de rencontre, Neufchâteau, 22 août 1914* (Berger-Lavrault, Paris, 1923), *La Guerre en Action: le 22 août 1914 au 4e Corps d'Armée: Ethe* (Berger-Levrault, Paris, 1924), *Virton* (Berger-Levrault, Paris, 1925).

20   Grasset, *Neufchâteau*, pp.104–107.

leading up to the battle.[21]

Other eye–witnesses have published their own accounts of the encounter in which they took part. On the German side, for example, there is Herman Kaiser, who was an artillery subaltern at Bertrix, and who wrote an account which was translated into English and published in *The Journal of the Royal Artillery* in 1935.[22] On the French side, Colonel (later General) Paloque was the senior officer commanding the French divisional artillery massacred at Bertrix and later published a pamphlet in defence of his own performance.[23] The diary of Commandant Moreau, chief of staff of 3 Colonial Infantry Division (DIC), has recently been found and published, giving a fascinating insight into the minds of the senior officers of that division, as well as a first–hand account of the battle at Rossignol.[24]

In a wider context, contemporary accounts of the events of August 1914 are still available: three in particular have provided valuable background for this study: J. Simonin was *Médecin–Inspecteur* in the 7 DI which fought at Ethe, and wrote his account of the opening weeks of the war, *de Verdun à Mannheim*, in 1917;[25] two priests, le Chanoine Jean Schmmitz and Dom Norbert Nieuwland, published their account of the invasion of Belgium, *L'Invasion Allemande dans les provinces de Namur et de Luxembourg*, in 1924. Volume VII deals specifically with the battle of Neufchâteau and of Maissin [sic] as seen from a civilian perspective;[26] and Fernand Engerand, whose interest in the lost provinces of Alsace–Lorraine and the Briey iron–ore deposits led him to become *rapporteur* at the Briey Commission of Enquiry in 1919, wrote a book, *Le secret de la Frontière 1815–1871–1914*, which contains a chapter on the offensive in the Ardennes, an interesting if biased interpretation of events.[27]

The official histories of the Great War, written by French and German appointed historians and archivists, are the base secondary source material for this study. The first volume of the French official history was published in 1922 and revised in 1936;[28] the German official history was published in 1925.[29] Both are essentially factual, descriptive accounts drawn from the vast array of then available primary sources. Of the two histories, the German contains slightly more analytical content. It says for example:

> Thanks to the excellent telephone links with all corps, the [Fifth] Army Command which had moved forward from its Headquarters at Diedenhofen to its Command Post at Esch, was constantly informed about the situation on the battlefront and whenever the situation required it could take energetic, balanced and supportive action; in particular it provided for fast exchange of news between the individual corps, thus ensuring co–ordination of actions.[30]

21   Commandant A. Grasset, *Vingt Jours de Guerre aux Temps Héroïques* (Berger–Levrault, Paris–Nancy, 1918).

22   H. Kaiser, *Deutsche und Französische Artillerie in der Schlacht bei Bertrix, 22 August 1914* (Waisenhaus–Buchdruckerei, Hanau, 1937).

23   Général Paloque, *Bertrix 1914* (Charles–Lavauzelle & Cie, Paris, 1932).

24   J. Moreau, *Rossignol, 22 août 1914, Journal du commandant Jean Moreau, chef d'état-major de la 3e division Coloniale*, (re-transcribed and with commentary by Éric Labayle et Jean-Louis Philippart, Anvoi, Parçay-sur-Vienne, 2002).

25   J. Simonin, *De Verdun à Mannheim: Ethe et Gomery (22, 23, 24 Août 1914)* (Pierre Vitet, Paris, 1917).

26   Le Chanoine Jean Schmitz et Dom Norbert Nieuwland, *L'Invasion Allemande dans les provinces de Namur et de Luxembourg, Sixième Partie, (Tome VII) La bataille de Neufchâteau et de Maissin* (G. Van Oest & Cie., Librarie Nationale d'Art et d'Histoire, Bruxelles/Paris,1924).

27   Fernand Engerand, *Le Secret de la Frontière 1815–1871–1914, Charleroi* (Éditions Bossard, Paris, 1918).

28   *Les armées françaises dans la grande guerre, Tome premier, Premier Volume* [AFGG I/1] (Ministère de la Guerre, État-major de l'armée, service historique, Imprimerie Nationale, Paris, 1923 and 1936).

29   Reichsarchiv, *Der Weltkrieg 1914 bis 1918, Die militärischen Operationen zu Lande, Erster Band, Die Grenzschlachten im Westen* [*Weltkrieg 1*], (E.S. Mittler & Sohn, Berlin, 1925).

30   *Weltkrieg 1*, p.324.

The French history is very much more factual, giving so much detail, particularly of local geography, that the reader is pressed to distinguish the wood from the trees:

> Only at about 14.30 did the (French) Fourth Army commander learn that the head of 2 CA had reached the vicinity of Tintigny, whilst the following division had clashed with the enemy at Meix–devant–Virton and Villers–La–Loue. Still in ignorance of the fact that 2 CA had found itself embroiled with the enemy at Bellefontaine and that the other Corps were in their turn halted, General de Langle, as has been seen, had invited General Gérard to establish the bulk of 4 DI as flank guard of the army in the region of Tintigny and to attack vigorously south of the woods at Meix whilst linking on its right with 4 CA of Third Army.[31]

Overall, both official histories provide an authoritative high level account written close to the events they record by people who had access to first–hand witnesses and first– hand accounts.

The first and still most authoritative account in English of the Ardennes campaign is that contained within Sewell Tyng's *The Campaign of the Marne*, written in 1935.[32] Drawing extensively on contemporary accounts in France, Germany and England, including (with reference to the Ardennes) Grasset, the sixteen pages devoted to the offensive in the Ardennes remain even today the best overview of events. Tyng's incisive and insightful commentary demonstrates a depth of knowledge indicating extensive research: for example, Tyng acknowledges the temporary nature of German field entrenchments at Longwy, dug whilst the German infantry was 'awaiting daylight before launching their attack',[33] a point which has been lost on many historians who have followed him.

Tyng cites amongst his sources the first six volumes of General Palat's , *La Grande Guerre sur le Front Occidental*, probably the earliest detailed account of the war by a French historian, the first three volumes of which were written before the end of 1918.[34] Palat's first two volumes give an essential background to the opening phases of the war, while volume three provides the most detailed account so far of the Battle of the Ardennes as a whole, as seen from the French point of view. But he wrote too soon after events for any German material to be available to allow a truly balanced account.

After Palat, Grasset is arguably the most influential French secondary source for the Battle of the Ardennes. His books on the encounters at Ethe, Virton, Rossignol and Neufchâteau, serialised in the *Revue Française Militaire,* have been used as sources for several English–speaking historians' accounts of the overall Ardennes offensive.[35] The drawback is that the encounter battles which he did not cover (Maissin, Anloy, and particularly Roques's 12 CA at Nevraumont) have received little or no attention as time goes by.

Other important secondary sources include articles written during the 1920s and 1930s for military journals and publications, notably the *Revue Française Militaire* and the British *The Fighting Forces* and the *Journal of the Royal Artillery*; the authors drew on archive material and eye–witness accounts which have not necessarily survived. Two of Grasset's books – *Ethe* and *Virton* – were used as the basis for articles written in English by Major A.H. Burne and published in *The Fighting*

31   AFGG I/1 (1922), p.405.
32   Tyng, op. cit., pp.75–91.
33   Ibid., p.83.
34   Général Palat, *La Grande Guerre sur le Front Occidental* (Librairie Chapelot, Paris): *I Les* élements *du conflit* (1917), *II Liége, Mulhouse, Sarrebourg, Morhange* (1917), *III Batailles des Ardennes et de la Sambre* (1918) [*Grande Guerre III, Ardennes*].
35   For example the following authors all quote Grasset in their bibliographies: Cyril Falls, *The First World War* (Longmans, London, 1960); Barbara Tuchman, *The Guns of August* (Ballantine, New York, 1994); Hew Strachan, *The First World War Volume 1: To Arms* (Oxford University Press, Oxford, 2001).

Forces journal during the 1930s.[36] The encounter battle at Bertrix has received particular attention, from Herman Kaiser, cited above, and an English article in response by an anonymous officer (A.G.M)[37], as well as General Paloque's apologia, cited above; perhaps this accounts for the fact that that the Bertrix encounter has been given a modern reappraisal by Bruce Gudmundsson.[38] In France, Commandant Pugens published a long two–part article on Neufchâteau in *Revue Française Militaire*.[39] Dr E. Bircher's *Die Schlacht bei Ethe–Virton* (1930) is a rare example of a German account of two of the Ardennes encounters, the more useful because Bircher took part in his capacity as commander of 12 Infantry Brigade.[40] Similarly, Erhard Mutius, a captain in 7 Grenadier Regiment at the time, wrote *Die Schlacht bei Longwy* in 1919.[41]

Detailed examination from both sides of the eight encounter-battles that together make up the Battle of the Ardennes reveals a very different picture of French tactics, and of the application of their pre-war Doctrine than that which has previously been painted by historians. There seems to be a gap between what actually happened on the battlefield and what historians think ought to have happened based on their reading of French Doctrine. Consequently, fresh primary research has been done into the writings of Colonel de Grandmaison, in order to illuminate his true role in the genesis of the so–called *offensive à outrance*.[42] The conclusions of that research have subsequently been broadly confirmed by the findings of Dimitry Queloz in his new book, *De la Manoeuvre Napoléonienne à l'offensive à outrance*.[43]

On the subject of 'Doctrine', as well as Queloz's detailed research, general studies such as Barry Posen's *The Sources of Military Doctrine*[44] and Azar Gat's *A History of Military Thought*[45] provide a thorough backdrop into which one can place performance in the Ardennes campaign. With regard to armaments, David Stevenson's *Armaments and the coming of War*[46] and David Herrmann's *The Arming of Europe*[47] together provide a comprehensive and authoritative background to the whole question of why and how the comparative state of armament in August 1914 came about. The subject of training does not seem to have been addressed yet as a single issue in its own right, and an overall picture for this history has been assembled from a variety of works, including Joffre's *Mémoires*,[48] Douglas Porch's *The March to the Marne*[49] and Erich Dorn Brose's *The Kaiser's Army*.[50]

36   Major A.H. Burne, 'The Battle of Rossignol' (*The Fighting Forces, Vol. VIII*, Nr 3, October 1931) and 'The Battle of Virton' (*The Fighting Forces, Vol. VIII*, 1931).
37   'AGM', 'Bertrix 1914, seen from the German side' (*Journal of the Royal Artillery* Vol. LXIV 1937–8).
38   B. I. Gudmundsson, 'Unexpected Encounter at Bertrix' (in *The Great War*, ed. Robert Cowley (Pimlico, London, 2004).
39   Commandant A. Pugens, 'The Genesis of Neufchâteau' (*Revue Militaire Française* Nrs.96 & 97, July 1929).
40   Dr E.Bircher, *Die Schlacht bei Ethe–Virton am 22 August 1914* (Verlag R. Eisenschmidt, Berlin, 1930).
41   G. von Mutius, *Die Schlacht bei Longwy* (Volume three of a compilation *Der Grosse Krieg in Einzeldarstellungen* , Verlag von Gerhard Stalling, Oldenburg, 1919).
42   Colonel de Grandmaison, *Deux Conférences faites aux officiers de l' État-Major de l'Armée (février 1911)* (Berger-Levrault, Paris, 1911); Colonel de Grandmaison, *Dressage de l'Infanterie en vue du Combat Offensif* (Berger–Levrault, Paris, 1912).
43   D. Queloz, *De la manoeuvre Napoléonienne* à *l'offensive* à *outrance* (Economica, Paris, 2009).
44   B. R. Posen, *The Sources of Military Doctrine: France, Britain, and Germany between the World Wars* (Cornell University Press, London, 1984).
45   A. Gat, *A History of Military Thought from the Enlightenment to the Cold War* (Oxford University Press, Oxford, 2001).
46   D. Stevenson, *Armaments and the Coming of War: Europe 1904–1914* (Clarendon Press, Oxford, 1996).
47   D. Herrmann, *The Arming of Europe and the Making of the First World War* (Princeton University Press, Princeton NJ, 1996).
48   J. Joffre, *Mémoires du Maréchal Joffre (1910-1917), Tome 1* (Librarie Plon, Paris, 1932).
49   D. Porch, *The March to the Marne: The French Army 1871–1914* (Cambridge University Press, Cambridge, 1981).
50   E. D. Brose, *The Kaiser's Army: The Politics of Military Technology in Germany during the Machine Age, 1870 –1918* (Oxford University Press, Oxford, 2001).

Looking at the general histories of the war as a whole written since the 1920s, one finds a number of attempts to encapsulate the Ardennes campaign into a few short paragraphs, sometimes sentences. The campaign defies such brief encapsulation, and most of the myths – of French red trousers and German machine guns, for example – and false interpretations of, say, the doctrine of *offensive à outrance* can be traced to these secondary sources. Winston Churchill published his first edition of *The World Crisis* in 1923.[51] General Hofacker followed closely in 1928 with his *Der Weltkrieg*, and Liddell Hart published the first version of his history of the First World War in 1930. These early writers share a common trait and a common objective: to endorse and justify their own nation's role in the recent conflict, if necessary at the expense of the others. They also all pay scant attention to the Battle of the Ardennes, including it in their overall synopsis of the battles of the Frontiers in a few short, pithy sentences. Nevertheless they represent at a high level their nations' general appreciation of the opening phase of the war. Churchill in particular has influenced generations of English–speaking people with his image of the French army as a Napoleonic anachronism in colourful uniforms throwing itself blindly at entrenched Germans who massacred them with massed machine guns.[52] In short, the first generation of general histories were mostly short on detail and lacked objectivity.

One thread that links the early English general histories with those of the next generation is the emergence of the myth of French *offensive à outrance* and the 'cult of the offensive'. From Churchill and Liddell Hart (quoted above) there is a direct link to Cyril Falls who wrote in 1960: 'Artillery support was hardly taken into account by this high–minded and selfless but crack–brained seer [Grandmaison]. It is impossible to calculate how many men were sent to their deaths through his agency'.[53] And thence to modern scholars such as Professor Herwig, who wrote in 2009 of the encounter battle at Rossignol that 'one furious frontal bayonet charge after another, accompanied by lusty cries of "*En Avant!*," was mowed down by murderous artillery and machine gun fire'.[54]

On a more general note, in the second–generation histories the interpretation at least moved on from regarding the Ardennes offensive as an 'imaginary *coup de grace*' to something more substantial.[55] Cyril Falls in 1960 was the first to acknowledge the serious strategic purpose behind the Ardennes operation: 'Their mission was to strike the marching columns of the enemy in the flank, cut through them, and rout them'.[56] He also referred to the closeness of the result: 'Yet the Germans themselves acknowledge that they had been in a critical situation, threatening the whole of their wheeling wing'.[57] But he then curiously described the French defeat as 'inevitable', attributing their failure to poor intelligence and inferior cavalry, assertions which will be tested in this study.

French analysis has developed in a similar way to that of the English–speaking historians. In 1957, Henry Contamine made an important revisionist step forward with his book *La Revanche*, examining French preparations and early performance with great objectivity and clarity.[58] He asserts, for example, that French tactical weaknesses increased the chances of a German strategic success and that those tactical weaknesses were the overall decisive factor, an opinion that this study broadly confirms.[59]

51   W.S. Churchill, *The World Crisis* (Thornton Butterworth Ltd., 1923).
52   Ibid., pp. 263–266 and (Odhams, Watford, 1938), pp.215–219.
53   Falls, op.cit., p.16.
54   Herwig, op.cit., p.150.
55   Liddell Hart, op. cit., p.82.
56   Falls, op.cit., p.26.
57   Ibid., p.27.
58   Contamine, *La Revanche*.
59   Ibid., Chapter XVII *La Marche à la Bataille 14 –18 août 1914*, pp.222–233 and Chapter XVIII *La Première*

In 1980, Pierre Rocolle produced his work *L'Hécatombe des Généraux*, in which he examined the state of the French senior officer corps and highlighted individual instances of generals who failed the ultimate test under fire and who were removed from their posts.[60] Rocolle's work has made a valuable contribution to the study of the Battle of the Ardennes, particularly because many of the failed generals were in charge of units that took part in the Ardennes encounter–battles. But he also made at least one important factual mistake: Rocolle stated that the French 12 CA at Neufchâteau was faced by a brigade from the German 21 ID which fought additionally at Ochamps and Bertrix.[61] In fact, as this study will show, the encounter between those two units did not take place until the morning of 23 August, and on 22 August the French 12 CA was faced with no more than part of a weak brigade of reservists from 21 RAK. Rocolle's mistake of fact has inadvertently helped to conceal until now the extent of the lost opportunity at Neufchâteau, because it seriously understates the weakness of the opposition faced by Roques.

In Professor Strachan's first volume of his history of the Great War, the Battle of the Ardennes inevitably forms but a small part in the overall picture, just over two pages of analysis. Professor Strachan's thesis regarding the French offensive in the Ardennes is that the French High Command did not expect the Germans to join battle in the forests, 'but would be found on the further side'.[62] This suggests an issue over the gathering and use of French intelligence. He goes on to cite failings in French cavalry and reconnaissance and the absence of mobile field howitzers as major reasons for the French defeat. All these judgements will be tested in this study. The danger of using a single vignette in a concise summary of the Ardennes campaign is highlighted by Strachan's use of the case of 87 Brigade of 2 CA to suggest that the French infantry were exhausted even before the battle began. Putting this case into its operational context shows that 2 CA had been asked to change its orientation and narrow its front in order to accommodate 4 CA of Third Army on its right and CAC on its left, when Joffre changed front from north–east to north and announced a northerly axis for his attack; 2 CA thus suffered more than any other on 21 August from 'marching, counter-marching, orders and counter-orders,' although to be fair there was a high degree of poor staff work and control which exacerbated the situation.[63]

The latest significant addition to French historiography is Michel Goya's *La chair et l'acier*.[64] In Chapter V (*L'Épreuve du feu* – baptism of fire) he uses the action of the French Fourth Army to exemplify the points which he wants to make. He drills down in great detail into a number of specific incidents. But even the five pages which he devotes to description and analysis of the encounters in the Ardennes are insufficient to cover the totality of events, merely a judiciously selected number of highlights. The result is a fair and balanced high–level assessment which correctly identifies the main issues and demonstrates a grasp of detail and factual accuracy which is yet to be found in the British lexicon, whilst leaving scope for an overall detailed study of the campaign. But Goya dismisses the whole of the French Third Army's role in a single sentence: 'This vicious check is similar to that of Third Army, which had been given the same mission further east'.[65] This statement is inadequate to describe the unique contribution of Ruffy's men to the battle; the specific and different role of Third Army will be exposed in this history.

Of the most recent general works that include coverage of the offensive in the Ardennes, Robert Doughty's *Pyrrhic Victory* adds significantly to our overall understanding of the operations of the

Bataille, stratégie et tactique – 18–23 août 1914, pp.234–250.
60   P. Rocolle, *L'Hécatombe des Généraux* (Editions Laranzelle, Paris–Limoges, 1980).
61   Ibid., p.143 and map, p.136.
62   Strachan, op. cit., p.218.
63   General Cordonnier, *Une Brigade au Feu (Potins de Guerre)* (Henri Charles-Lavauzelle, Paris, 1921), passim.
64   Goya, op.cit., p.178.
65   Ibid.

French army.[66] Regarding Doughty's short treatment of the Ardennes, his cited sources are Grasset, and certain GQG instructions and reports (*compte rendu*). But the five pages which Doughty devotes to the Ardennes are insufficient to allow him to get to the heart of the matter. For example, Doughty accepts the official account of Roques's 12 CA action, concluding that that unit 'was, as reported by Fourth Army, in a « good » situation at the end of the day' and its withdrawal was a result of 5 Colonial Brigade uncovering its flank.[67] This study will show how much more there was to that pivotal encounter.

Below the operational level, Terence Zuber's book, *The Battle of the Frontiers: Ardennes 1914*, published in 2007, is a comprehensive tactical study of the whole campaign, seen from the German perspective, but a study which somehow misses its mark.[68] One cannot fault Zuber's research, and his selective conclusions are often eminently supportable. But one is left with the impression that Zuber starts from the premis that the German army of 1914 was near–perfect, and that certain facts have been selected to support that argument; furthermore the argument that the German Army of 1914 was inevitably the best in the world is over–sold. More comprehensive research on the French side, and a more objective approach, would have allowed Zuber to make a more balanced judgement.

With Sewell Tyng's 1935 study remaining the best overall description of the offensive in the Ardennes, the subject is overdue for a fresh interpretation. By returning to primary sources on both the French and German sides, and by setting events into a context of how the two armies prepared for war, this book will not only reinterpret events but also present new and challenging arguments as to why those events transpired as they did.

The book is in three parts, each one dealing with one of the three objectives described above. The first part is the operational study: because of the diversity and complexity of what actually occurred, it will start with a high–level overview of the whole campaign, detailing the strategic intent of the two sides, the intelligence gathered and how it was used, the relevance of the terrain and the key issues at high–command level. Then the study descends to the detail of army command, taking each of the four armies in turn and examining the mission, objectives, plans and instructions of the four army commanders. To complete this analysis, the thesis studies battlefield operational command and control in action, to see how strategic and operational intent was executed, and how events deteriorated into a series of unconnected and uncoordinated encounter battles.

The second part of the book examines the 'Lost Opportunity' - the two encounter battles at Neufchâteau and Maissin–Anloy in which it will be explained how the French missed two chances to beat the Germans at a tactical level and possibly achieve operational success. Two other better known encounters – Bertrix and Rossignol – are also examined in order to put the lost opportunities into the context of de Langle's whole Fourth Army operation. Defeats at those two latter places overshadowed the lost opportunities both at the time and since. Those defeats will also be shown to have been major factors in denying de Langle his chance of operational success. Chance, guesswork and luck came into play on both sides; timing and (for the Germans) serendipity combined to ensure that the French defeats – one at least of which can be shown to have been a completely unnecessary, self–inflicted disaster – took precedence over the French opportunities. It will be shown how it could easily have been different, if with incalculable results.

The third and final part steps back from the action and analyses the reasons for the outcomes

---

66   R. Doughty, *Pyrrhic Victory: French strategy and Operations in the Great War* (Harvard University Press, Harvard MA, 2005).

67   Doughty, op. cit., pp.67–68.

68   T. Zuber, *The Battle of the Frontiers: Ardennes 1914* (Tempus, Stroud, 2007).

described. In a series of chapters, the key issues of doctrine, training and armament are considered in the light of the outcomes analysed in the study. The intention here is not necessarily to conduct fresh research – although certain aspects of French doctrine have necessitated a certain amount of additional investigation – but to use existing scholarship to set a sufficiently firm context in which to frame the activity in the battles.

In summary, this book adds a full operational study to the historiography of the opening phase of the Great War, the phase known as the Battles of the Frontiers. It will identify for the first time the extent of the opportunity for tactical and operational victory foregone by the French on 22 August; and it will analyse through comparative study the reasons for the French failure and German success. This integrated analysis of operations, individual encounter–battles and the underlying causes which led to the outcomes of those battles, together produce a fresh interpretation of the Battle of the Ardennes, and explains why France missed vital opportunities to potentially reverse the outcome of the Battle of the Frontiers.

Part One

The Operational Study

1

Operational Overview

On 3 August 1914, Germany declared war on France, followed a few hours later by a French reciprocation, declaring war on Germany; Great Britain deliberated for a further twenty-four hours or so, issuing an ultimatum on 4 August that expired, unacknowledged, at one hour before midnight. In fact both the French and the Germans had already commenced mobilization before their mutual declarations.[1] The French held their forces at least ten kilometres back from their frontier, a purely political decision, in order not to appear provocative; their opponents were not so scrupulous and there were many border violations by German patrols. The first soldier killed in the Great War actually died in such a skirmish before the war officially started: on 2 August, Corporal Peugeot of 44 régiment d'infanterie (RI) was killed by Leutenant Mayer, an officer of *5 Jäger Regiment zu Pferde*, leading a German cavalry patrol near Jonchery on the French side of the Alsace border.[2] On the Ardennes front, German troops invaded the Duchy of Luxembourg on 2 August and French guns in the fortress at Longwy fired on German troops seen in nearby Aumetz.

Each side had its war plan. That of Germany was the so–called 'Schlieffen Plan' in which the bulk of their forces on the Western Front, their First, Second and Third armies with over a million men in a *Schwenkungsflügel*[3], were to cross the river Meuse between Liège and Dinant and march in a wide encircling movement across the Belgian plain towards Paris. In this plan, Sixth and Seventh armies were to defend the common Franco-German border between Switzerland and their central fortified zone – the *Moselstellung* – around Metz and Diedenhofen (Thionville[4]), while Fourth and Fifth armies were to defend the ground between Metz and the Meuse at Dinant, which included the Belgian Ardennes. The mission of these two armies was to secure, at all costs, the link between the *Schwenkungsflügel* and the *Moselstellung*.

The French Plan, Plan XVII, had been written in 1913 and implemented in the spring of 1914. It differed from its predecessor (Plan XVI, March 1909) in that it was more offensive in nature, recognising the greater threat from the north. However these principles had to a great degree been anticipated in the two variants to Plan XVI, issued in September 1911 and April 1913 respectively.[5] Plan XVII was actually a plan for the mobilisation and concentration of the French armies, not a plan of campaign. The chosen concentration areas of the main French armies were of course based upon certain expected operations, but General Joffre reserved the right to alter his pre–conceived ideas to fit the circumstances at the time. His strategy, to launch his major offensive

1   AFGG I/1 (1936), p.114; and *Weltkrieg 1*, p.35.
2   P. Creuzinger, *Königlich Preussischen Jaeger Regiments zu Pferde nr.5*, (Sporn, Zeulenroda, 1932) pp.22–24 and *Revue Historique de l'Armée* (Vol 3, July-Sept 1950): *Première Victoire de la Grande Guerre, Altkirch 7 août 1914*, p.37.
3   Literally translated as: "Turning or wheeling" (*Schwenkung*) "Wing" (*Flügel*).
4   In Alsace and Lorraine, disputed territories between France and Germany for hundreds of years, most towns and cities had both German and French names.
5   AFGG I/1 (1936), pp.33–91.

across the common frontier into Alsace-Lorraine, was to remain unchanged, but the details of that and of all French operations were contained in general and specific instructions issued from Joffre's *Grand Quartier Général* (GQG). Under Plan XVII, Fifth and Third armies were deployed along the northern frontier from Sedan to Verdun, whilst First and Second armies assembled between Nancy and Belfort for the great offensive into Alsace–Lorraine. Fourth Army was held back in reserve around Bar–le–Duc, from where it could intervene either due east between Verdun and Nancy or due north, west of Verdun.

The Germans held pretty well to their original plan throughout the opening phase of the war, although the enormity of their defensive success in Alsace–Lorraine on 20 August did for a while offer the tempting illusion of a classic double–envelopment. In the central Ardennes sector, the original mission for Fourth and Fifth Armies was executed unchanged at the strategic level.

Joffre, however, started tinkering with his original dispositions from the very first days of the war. Surprisingly, given the common perception in early histories that his main offensive in Alsace–Lorraine was 'wild and premature',[6] he started to move his troops around as early as 8 August, when he transferred 2 CA from Fifth to Fourth Army. He was even then building up Fourth Army into his prospective counter-attack force; and his very early change to the deployment area of that army – on 2 August, to a more northerly–facing front – indicates where, even then, he was contemplating using it.[7]

On 16 August Fifth Army lost another corps – 11 CA – to Fourth Army but on 18 August gained 18 CA from Second Army. Also on 18 August, Joffre gave Fourth Army its third additional corps – 9 CA – again from Second Army.[8] So even before he launched his main attack into Alsace-Lorraine, Joffre had weakened his attacking armies there by two corps, over 20% of their original strength. And in the Ardennes sector, by 20 August, the day he launched his main attack in Alsace-Lorraine and two days before he launched his counter–attack, he had doubled the size of Fourth Army from three to six regular corps so that his total left wing (Fourth and Fifth Armies together) was some 25% stronger than at the outset. These were not the actions of a commander–in–chief fixated inflexibly on a single *offensive à outrance*.

The task of protecting the frontier during mobilisation lay with permanent, full–strength units of each regular army. The French called this force *La Couverture*, the Germans *Grenzschutztruppen*. During the mobilisation and concentration period no major attack was expected by either side – except in the case of an *attaque brusquée*: a swift surprise attack by full–strength units of the standing frontier force. The French had for a long time feared an immediate pre–emptive German attack, directly across their common border between Metz and the Vosges Mountains, against the fortress line of Belfort, Toul, Épinal, Nancy and Verdun, launched before their mobilisation was complete.[9] And although in recent years this strategic option had been replaced as the primary threat by an expected attack in northern Belgium towards Sedan and Charleroi-Mézières, it remained a possibility.[10] So the French concentrated their forces further back behind their fortress zone. The Germans, on the other hand, relied upon an elastic defence between their heavily fortified places at Metz and Strasbourg, preferring to guard the Rhine and suck any French attack into a dangerous salient by temporarily ceding territory in Alsace and Lorraine. All the while their strategy never

6   C.R.M.F. Crutwell, *A History of the Great War 1914-1918* (Clarendon Press, 1934), p.16.
7   AFGG I/1, Annex 33: *GQG, Paris, 2 août, 19.30: IVe armée, variante à la concentration.*
8   AFGG X/1: Order of Battle of Second Army (p.88), Fourth Army (p.204) and Fifth Army (p.266) in August 1914.
9   Palat, *La Grande Guerre, II*, p.10.
10   G. Krumeich, *Armaments and Politics in France on the Eve of the First World War* (transl. Stephen Conn, Berg Publishers, Leamington Spa, 1984), pp.45-47.

deviated from delivering their own main attack into central Belgium.

On the Ardennes sector, the French cover for the concentration of Ruffey's Third Army between Verdun and Metz was provided by 6 CA supported by *7 division de cavalerie* (DC); while for de Langle's Fourth Army between Sedan and Verdun cover was provided by 4 DI of 2 CA and 9 DC. On the German side, the common border with France either side of Metz was protected by 16 and 8 AK from their bases around Diedenhofen (Thionville to the French), whilst von Richthofen's *1 Kavaleriekorps* (KK) and two mixed infantry brigades were deployed rapidly to the north on the Luxembourg and Belgian borders between Diedenhofen and the Eifel mountains.[11]

In August 1914 Verdun was the cornerstone of the French frontier defence, as it was to be two years later. A strong bastion in the north–eastern corner of the country, it stood at the top of the eastern frontier, which ran down to the Swiss border and the French fortress of Belfort, and at the eastern end of the northern frontier, which ran west to the Belgian border and the fortress of Sedan. Frontier defence has nearly always been about rivers, and high ground; Verdun has both. The river Meuse flows almost due north from its source near the Vosges mountains and bends at Verdun to flow north–westwards up to Sedan and beyond. The Meuse heights east and north of Verdun are now legendary; in August 1914 they were that cornerstone of the frontier defence. North of Verdun, just a little more than the prescribed ten kilometres behind the actual border, the river Othain, which the French chose as their main defence line, runs north–west for forty kilometres before flowing into the river Chiers at Montmédy.

Map 5

The river Chiers also figures prominently in the Ardennes campaign, primarily because it flows through the fortress town of Longwy on its way down to Montmédy and thence on to join the Meuse at Sedan. And at Longuyon, some ten kilometres south of Longwy, the river Crusnes flows into the Chiers. The German High Command chose the line of the Crusnes–Chiers rivers as the limit for the advance of their Fifth Army on 22 August, and it lay directly in the path of Ruffey's advancing Third Army. From the Othain to the Crusnes valley is a mere fifteen kilometres.

The French fortress at Longwy requires description, given its pivotal role in the campaign. It had been built by that great engineer, Vauban, for King Louis XIV in the seventeenth century, on the edge of the mighty cliffs above the town of Longwy, which nestled in the valley of the Chiers river below. For three hundred years it had dominated the route into France from the north–east, forcing an approaching enemy to swing west into the bad terrain of the Argonne forest or east towards the fortresses of Verdun and Metz. But it had not been updated to cope with modern weaponry after the technological advances of the late nineteenth century, and was in August 1914 very much a second–rate fortification. It had the additional disadvantage of being too close to the border for the French to use as part of their main line of defence. Nevertheless, with a wartime garrison of two battalions, six 155mm heavy guns and supplies for a month, it was an obstacle that the Germans needed to remove from their path, especially at a time when modern French heavy artillery was scarce.[12]

Another river, the Alzette, was used by the central group of German armies for frontier protection in August 1914. It springs, coincidentally, from the same range of hills as the Crusnes, about five kilometres further north, and flows north rather than west. It became part of the German frontier barrier as it passed through Luxembourg city, from whence it flows some seventy kilometres due north, in the Duchy of Luxembourg but parallel to the German border, before emptying into the Sauer, a tributary of the Moselle, at Ettelbruck. The river Alzette was a convenient defence line for

11   *Weltkrieg 1*, p.103.
12   AFGG I/ 1 (1936), pp.538–539.

the Germans. The high ground on the right bank gave good defensive positions along most if not all of its seventy–kilometre length. It ran through the middle of the Duchy, so any French attack would have to take place on Luxembourg territory. It was also sufficiently far back from the Meuse to be beyond the immediate concern of French intelligence, and yet it was only two days' march from the central Ardennes and the open terrain around Neufchâteau. When, day after day, French flyers reported no enemy movement through the central Ardennes, it was because the Germans were waiting patiently behind the Alzette for the moment to advance. And at its southern reaches, south of Luxembourg, the Alzette linked seamlessly to the static defences of the *Moselstellung*. But the Alzette was a strictly east–west barrier, and the Germans were determined to take some pre–emptive actions in order to secure for themselves the Duchy of Luxembourg, which would require a south–facing defence. *16 Infanterie Division* (ID) of 8 AK (one of the two *Grenzschutztruppen* units in the central sector) started moving in on 2 August.[13] It had completely occupied the Duchy by 18.00 on 3 August, only twelve hours after the war officially started. Luxembourg had been in the German sphere of economic influence for decades, and some might say it was a client state. Occupation would give Germany an extended defensive front in a westerly salient whose southern border conveniently faced Verdun.

OHL also recognised that the town of Arlon in Belgium was an important strategic asset – it was a major railway hub and stood protectively at the eastern (upper) end of the 'Étalle corridor', an anticipated invasion route for the French up the valley of the river Semoy from Florenville and their major bases at Sedan and Charleville–Mézières directly towards the *Moselstellung*. On 12 August a mixed detachment from 16 AK (the second of the two *Grenzschutztruppen* units) moved into and took possession of the town. From that moment the French effectively lost (or gave up) one of their strategic options. Their chosen defensive line was well back, along the river Othain. Consequently they lost control of the Briey basin and the iron ore deposits in the surrounding region and lost the use of the fortress of Longwy as a *point d'appui* (strongpoint) for their defence. The French deployment also conceded to Germany the use of Arlon as their own *point d'appui*: something that Crown Prince William's Fifth Army was quick to seize upon. As a result Ruffey's Third Army had to be given the objective of capturing it when Joffre finally launched his offensive on 22 August.

Plan XVII envisioned that the mobilisation and concentration of the French armies would be completed at some time between midday on the eleventh day (14 August) and the evening of the thirteenth day (16 August) when the reserve divisions arrived in their zones; the regular divisions were expected to be in place by evening on the ninth or tenth day (12 or 13 August).[14] The opening moves on the French side did not wait for full mobilisation, but began on 7 August with a foray into upper Alsace by elements of the *couverture*.[15] This was followed by Joffre's main attack into Lorraine on 14 August, which came to grief on 20 August at the twin battles of Morhange and Sarrebourg, when a German counter–attack comprehensively defeated the French and threw them back beyond their starting line. But by that time, Joffre was already contemplating his next move, his own counter–attack into the Ardennes. In the north, the Belgian fortress–zone of Liège had finally fallen completely into German hands on 16 August.[16] So on that day, OHL issued orders for its main offensive to commence on the morning of 18 August. In the Ardennes, Fourth and Fifth Armies started to move forward to cover the left flank of the main advance. It was time for

13   AFGG I/ 1 (1936), p.114; and *Weltkrieg 1*, p.105.
14   AFGG I/1 (1936), p.50.
15   AFGG I/1 (1936), p.129 & p.137.
16   *Weltkrieg* 1, p.120.

Joffre to finalise his embryonic ideas for the deployment of his Third and Fourth Armies into a full–blown operational plan. But to do that, he needed firm intelligence as to the position, strength and intention of enemy forces in the central Ardennes. And to counter him, von Moltke needed to make his own strategic reconnaissance. The two opponents had very different approaches and consequently executed this important task in contrasting ways.

Between 7 and 10 August, Germany launched her strategic reconnaissance missions, using both aerial and ground forces. In the air, Germany preferred to use her Zeppelin fleet for strategic missions. She had five such airships, all under OHL command, and all capable of long–range missions of several hundred kilometres.[17] One such mission was recorded by a French soldier who observed a dirigible surveying the Verdun defences on 9 August.[18]

On the ground, German doctrine prescribed that the advance of each major group of armies would be preceded by a strong advance guard of reinforced cavalry whose dual mission was both security and reconnaissance.[19] There were two such units initially allocated to the Ardennes sector, von Richthofen's 1 KK and von Hollen's 4 KK, each of two cavalry divisions complete with horse artillery, mobile machine gun companies, light wireless sets, telephone and telegraphic units and their own integral Jaeger infantry battalions. Whilst operating in this strategic reconnaissance role, these cavalry corps were given independent status as *Höhe Kavallerie Kommando* or HKK, reporting direct to OHL.

On 7 August, the two divisions of von Hollen's 4 HKK, consisting of 3 *Kavalerie–Division* (KD) and 6 KD, advanced south beyond Longwy to seek the French. Their mission included small long–distance reconnaissance patrols sent south towards Verdun and St Mihel (6 KD) and west towards Mézières and Sedan (3 KD).[20] But they were stopped short by the strong French defensive screen provided by 6 CA's infantry and artillery and could make no further progress.[21] On 10 August, 4 HKK was ordered to broaden the scope of its reconnaissance, seeking the flank of the French line, and went west to Longuyon, and thence towards the river Othain. Again they encountered firm French resistance. There was a major skirmish at Mangiennes, between the Othain and Loison rivers, on 10 August, after which 3 KD, having failed to break through the French protective screen but having assessed its strength, moved yet again, up to Arlon and the Étalle corridor, leaving 6 KD as security in front of the Crown Prince's assembling Fifth Army. The main French defence had been clearly identified on the line of the Othain river, and it could not be forced by cavalry alone; the Germans settled in on this front to complete their own deployment and to await an expected French attack towards Metz.[22]

Also on 10 August, OHL released von Richthofen's 1 HKK (Garde and 5 KDs) from its assembly positions in north Luxembourg to perform long–range reconnaissance due west up to the river Meuse on a line Namur–Givet–Mézières. Scouting squadrons preceded the general advance of 1 HKK. By 14 August von Richthofen's main force had reached Dinant. Having established the presence there of two French cavalry divisions (1 and 6 DCs), Richthofen proceeded to try to seize the fortress at Dinant by a *coup de main* on 15 August, without success. However his troops did succeed in identifying the presence of major French forces on the left bank (1 and 2 CAs). The German reconnaissance had found the French Fifth Army. But with de Langle de Cary's assembling

Map 8

17   Ibid., pp.126–127.
18   J. Simonin, *De Verdun à Mannheim* (Pierre Vitet, Paris, 1917), p.12.
19   *Bundesarchiv-Militärarchiv*, Freiburg, [BA–MA], PH 3/641: Standing Orders for Army Staff Officers, sections B (Standing Orders for HKK) and C (Standing Orders for cavalry divisions).
20   M. von Poseck, *The German Cavalry in Belgium and France, 1914* (E.S. Mittler & Sohn, Berlin, 1923, translated by Captain Alexander C. Strecker, US Cavalry, and printed by US War Office [IWM Collection]), p.41.
21   *Weltkrieg 1*, pp.123–125.
22   *Weltkrieg 1*, pp.124–5.

Fourth Army remaining firmly on the defensive, well back to the south between Mézières and Sedan, von Richthofen's cavalry missed it, and the intelligence gathered served to focus the German High Command on a possible French advance across the Meuse from west to east. This option – of throwing Fifth Army across the Meuse onto the right bank into the central Ardennes – was indeed being considered by Joffre at that time.[23] The idea was only given up between 13 and 15 August when the strength of the German threat west of the Meuse was re-evaluated.[24] It is worth bearing this fact in mind when considering the strategic surprise achieved by the French through the final decision to direct their attack on 22 August due north from the river Othain.

The other important point to note about von Richthofen's mission was that his deployment in front of both Third and Fourth Armies along the German frontier became necessarily focused on Third Army and Dinant, to the detriment of Fourth Army's southern flank, as the frontage to be covered widened beyond 1 HKK's capability to police it. So Duke Albrecht's army was effectively the only major German operational unit without its own strong independent protective screen, another calculated risk and one that contributed greatly to de Langle's achieving operational surprise on 22 August. From 15 August onwards, 1 HKK was concentrated around Dinant and focused on crossing the Meuse in support of Third Army. The outcome of the absence of a German strategic cavalry screen in the southern Ardennes was noted by French historian Commandant Pugens, who wrote in 1929 about the situation around Neufchâteau: 'The German cavalry did not seem to have tried to get intelligence for the High Command whilst the French 4 and 9 cavalry divisions had despite everything obtained important results'.[25]

France also used dirigibles for long–range strategic reconnaissance, deploying ten craft, divided into two types – *croiseurs*, of which there were six, and four *éclaireurs*.[26] One such mission, by dirigible 'Fleurus' (the name of the captain of one of the *croiseurs*), flew over the railway yards at Trèves, Sierck and Luxembourg on the night of 10–11 August, reporting that there was very little activity on the lines.[27]

On the ground, Joffre issued orders at 19.00 on 5 August for his own strategic reconnaissance mission. Sordet's independent cavalry corps (CC) of three divisions was launched into the Ardennes on 6 August from positions around Charleville.[28] His mission was to establish the position of the enemy on the eastern border of Belgium, to 'note the size and importance of the gaps between different enemy groupings, to delay the enemy's marching columns, to clear the region of enemy cavalry' and 'spread the rumour that the whole French army is following.'[29] Had Sordet achieved his mission, the campaign would have taken a totally different course. But the way in which he executed his orders, dictated in part by doctrine, in part by natural and cultural inclination, meant that he and his huge force achieved almost nothing of import. For ten days his three cavalry divisions roamed the countryside of the central Ardennes looking for signs of German activity in the very same region where, on 22 August, the battles were to take place.[30]

Map 9

23   General Lanrezac, *Le Plan de Campagne Français, et le premier mois de la guerre (2 août – 3 septembre 1914)* (Payot, Paris, 1920), pp.67–78.
24   AFGG I/1 (1936), pp.452–458 and Annex 103: *GQG, Vitry–le–François, 8 août, 07.00:Instruction générale Nr.1*; and Annex 232: *GQG, 13 août, Instruction particulière Nr.6 aux commandants des IIIe, IVe et Vearmées*; and Annex 307: *GQG, 15 août, 20.00: Instruction particulière Nr.10 aux commandants des IVe et Vearmées et du corps de cavalerie*.
25   Commandant A. Pugens, 'The Genesis of Neufchâteau' (*Revue Militaire Française* Nr.97 July 1929), p.109.
26   AFGG I/1 (1936), Appendix 1 v: *Aéronautique*, p.520.
27   AFGG I/1 (1936), p.153.
28   AFGG I/1, Annex 59: *GQG, 5 août,, 19.00:Commandant en chef à commandant corps de cavalerie, à Charleville*.
29   Ibid., *répandre le bruit que toutel'armée française suit*.
30   AFGG I/1, Annex 99: *GQG, 7 août, 09.55: Communication téléphoniqued'Offagne (par Bouillon). Corps de cavalerie*; and Annex 100: *GQG, 7 août, 20.30: reçu du corps de cavalerie à 20.30*; and Annex 195: [Cavalry Corps] *de Givet, 11 août, 15.00: message téléphoné. Corps de cavalerie à commandant en chef*.

But because the German Fourth and Fifth Armies were still firmly dug in on the frontier behind the river Alzette awaiting the order to advance, Sordet achieved nothing except the exhaustion of his troops and especially their horses. The intelligence which he did gather – of unit designations and locations around Liège – helped GQG's *Deuxième Bureau* (intelligence) to form a reasonably accurate picture of the German Second Army and part of Third Army (what French intelligence called the 'northern group' of German forces), but thus had the unfortunate side effect of directing the eyes of Joffre's staff to the north rather than to the east. The central Ardennes was empty of enemy troops, and when that reality changed, the perception lingered. Had Joffre instructed Sordet to set up a protective screen in the German style across the Ardennes from, say, Bastogne to Neufchâteau, much vital intelligence might have been gained when the Germans eventually commenced their advance. But such an action was not part of French strategic doctrine.[31] The German opinion of Sordet's activity has been scathing:

> The presence of this horde of horsemen of eighteen cavalry regiments with thirty–six guns in the area between the Semois, Ourthe and Maas (Meuse) [rivers] had no palpable result. It was a patrol ride by cavalry divisions. At one point, when the cannons thundered at Dinant, this 1st Cavalry Corps (sic) crossed the Maas instead of attempting to clarify the situation by an advance in force to reconnoitre the sector.[32]

It is clear, but for different reasons, that the strategic cavalry reconnaissance on both sides failed to offer anything of substance regarding the Ardennes region. But there were other sources of intelligence, including information from spies and informers about German mobilisation movements, which informed Joffre in preparation for his offensive.

By 9 August, GQG's Intelligence Bureau believed that it had identified seventeen German corps in the west and four corps in the east, with five still to be identified.[33] The French were not counting reserve formations, only regular or *aktiv* ones, which was realistic at this time, given that the reserve corps could only mobilise in a second phase, after the regular army had relinquished use of the depots and trains. They posited five groupings: (i) An 'Army of the Meuse', grouped around Aachen   Map 10 and St Vith, made up of five or six corps; (ii) a group around Luxembourg made up of about four corps: the French believed that they had positively identified 8 and 18 AK here along with the Saxon 11 AK; (iii) a group at Metz, made up of four corps, including 16 AK; (iv) a group around Strasbourg, of about three corps; (v) finally at Freiburg, across the Rhine in south Germany, the French believed there was one corps.

As an initial count and location of the concentration of Germany's twenty–six regular army corps, the French 9 August briefing was remarkably accurate. For example, two of the three regular corps of Fourth Army (8 AK and 18 AK) were correctly identified in their concentration areas. In the context of the Ardennes campaign, the important features of the 9 August briefing were these: firstly Joffre and his staff began to target the northern group (provisionally called in the report the 'Army of the Meuse') as a possible opportunity for counter–attack; and in this context the next group (Luxembourg) would have to be masked by Third Army to allow the counter–attack to go ahead unhindered. Secondly, French intelligence was grouping these identified units according to their concentration areas rather than by knowledge of each German army's order of battle. So there was no clear identification of the German Fifth Army at Diedenhofen as opposed to Fourth

31   See Chapter 7.
32   Von Poseck, *German Cavalry*, pp.42–43, quoting one Colonel Egli who had written to the author with this opinion.
33   AFGG I/1, Annex 125: *GQG, 9 août, 08.00: Groupement connu des forces allemandes actives.*

Army stretching north towards von Hausen's Third Army, which was patently in the 'northern grouping'. Overall at this stage there were five corps which remained undetected; one (6 AK) was to play a crucial part in the Ardennes battle. Having initially concentrated on the Eastern Front in Silesia, it was then moved by rail to the West and was not picked up by the French intelligence gatherers.[34] It appeared unannounced on the battlefield in the Ardennes on 22 August, augmenting the 'Luxembourg' group, which included elements of Fourth Army, and upsetting Joffre's calculations with devastating effect. And lastly, by not counting reserve corps (which in any case were still largely in transit on 9 August), GQG fundamentally underestimated the numbers of troops in the Ardennes theatre.

By 11 August, GQG had identified not five but nine regular corps in the northern grouping, five around Liège and four further south.[35] Now the prime strategic focus of Joffre's intelligence staff would remain firmly on what was happening between Liège and Namur. It is important to note, in the context of how GQG's and Joffre's writings have been subsequently interpreted, that compared to the build–up of this huge German force in the north, a grouping of two or three corps in the central Ardennes appeared relatively insignificant at the strategic level.

Over the next two days (13–14 August) GQG's strategic intelligence picture polarised. Around Liège the 'northern grouping' of German army corps continued to cause concern, whilst a report stated that in the south 'important enemy forces have arrived in the Arlon region, pushing elements up to Virton and Longuyon'.[36] But between those two regions, air reconnaissance reports indicated that the area around Recogne, Neufchâteau and Florenville – Fourth Army's prospective zone of operations – were 'absolutely empty'.[37] This was true, because Duke Albrecht's forces were still behind the Alzette and would be for four more days. But it becomes easier to understand how this polarisation between Liège and Arlon and the cumulative reports of an empty central zone between them could seduce French intelligence and operations staff officers into coming up with a plan to strike north.

By 18 August, Joffre's staff believed that they had enough intelligence to allow them to proceed with their plan. By their reckoning, there were about seven or eight corps in the 'northern' grouping (there were in fact eleven plus five reserve corps, making sixteen); between Bastogne and the *Moselstellung* at Diedenhofen (French called it Thionville), they estimated six or seven corps (when there were actually six plus five reserve corps, making eleven).[38]

What is interesting about this data is that, even by their own optimistic analysis (counting regular corps only), the French High Command intended to attack up to eight corps in the north with ten of their own (five in Fifth Army to fix and hold, five in Fourth Army to turn their flank); but in the south, Ruffey's Third Army was expected to defend the flank of the attack with just three corps against what was thought to be six or seven. It was generally believed that the defender could resist odds of two–to–one for twenty–four hours (and indeed the Germans were to prove this point), so perhaps that was the logic behind the French plan, although there is little evidence on which to base any opinion as to GQG's rationale. Perhaps, and this will be explored briefly below, Joffre was at this stage thinking of using his reserve divisions in a defensive role; but it is by no means clear.

---

34   *Weltkrieg 1*, p.132, note (2).
35   AFGG I/1, Annex 177: *GQG, 11 August, 06.00: Compterendu de Renseignements Nr.32.*
36   AFGG I/1, Annex 266: *GQG,14 août, 06.00: Compterendu de renseignements Nr.38.*
37   AFGG I/1, Annex 267: *GQG, 14 août, 20.00: Compterendu de renseignements Nr.39.*
38   AFGG I/ 1, Annex 450: *GQG, 18 août, 08.00: Instruction particulière Nr.13, aux commandants des IIIe, IVe et Ve armées)*; and *Weltkrieg 1*, p.69.

It is interesting to note that German intelligence was similarly flawed. After a break in flying due to bad weather, observers overflew the French lines between Sedan and Verdun on 18 and 19 August. Their report stated that the region Sedan–Montmédey (de Langle's Fourth Army concentration zone) was 'full of troops...estimated at two or three corps' (in fact there were five). From Montmédey south to Verdun, the fliers reported a strong French presence as before, but were unable to come up with firm numbers. The official historian concluded: 'No clear picture of enemy intentions could be gained from these reports'.[39]

The weather was a very important factor in intelligence gathering, the more so because of the fragility and low engine–power of the early types of aircraft which would cause them to be grounded by conditions of wind and rain and fog that would be considered normal for improved machines only a year later. Duke Albrecht had hoped to use his aircraft on 21 August to help determine his enemy's most likely axis of advance, north or east. At 09.00 on 21 August, a report indicated that three French columns, estimated at about two divisions, were concentrating between Stenay and Montmédy – but there was no clue as to their intentions. By 11.00 cloud cover had grounded his aircraft and no further information was forthcoming.[40]

Joffre's early and necessarily vague concept of a counter–attack through the southern Ardennes took shape and form as the intelligence picture developed and sharpened. Joffre's hope and intention   Map 3 was to place Fourth Army on and behind the left flank of what his intelligence reports called 'the northern group' of German armies. Lanrezac's Fifth Army and the BEF, operating against those German units which had crossed over to the west bank of the Meuse, were to fix and hold the German advance while Fourth Army executed its flank attack. Fourth Army's own right flank, vulnerable to a German counter–stroke out of the *Moselstellung*, would be masked and protected by Ruffey's Third Army. Once the left flank of the German 'northern group' had been located and engaged (by de Langle's own left–wing units), the centre and right of Fourth Army would sweep up and round the German flank and drive it back, trapping the bulk of the 'northern group' between the Ourthe and Meuse rivers. The Germans would effectively have been cut off from their lines of communication with their backs to the major obstacle of the Meuse.

If one looks at the French Plan but with actual German dispositions rather than those provided by French intelligence, a challenging scenario emerges: for his plan to work, Joffre had to ensure that de Langle's army envelop the whole German right wing (First, Second and Third Armies) and push it away from its lines of communication. And he needed to ensure that Ruffey's Third Army stopped all German forces coming from the east from attacking de Langle's flank, which meant getting far enough north to intercept Fourth Army as well as Fifth Army. The errors in French analysis of intelligence, outlined above, meant that GQG did not appreciate how much greater was the task they were setting themselves. And it will be demonstrated how far short of this objective Ruffey and his troops fell.

Having underestimated the strength of the German 'northern group', the operational execution of Joffre's strategic plan was conceptually flawed and it would have been interesting to see how it might have worked out. In the event, due to the early intervention of the German Fourth Army from the east against the flank of de Langle's army, an entirely different scenario unfolded, in the shape of a series of smaller–scale encounter battles, unexpected in time and place by both sides. To achieve the desired result, that of trapping the German 'northern group' against the Meuse, Joffre's two army commanders had to ensure that each corps of both Third and Fourth armies achieved

39   *Weltkrieg 1*, p.226.
40   Pugens, op. cit.,p.107.

its assigned and very specific march objectives on 22 August. The result would have been a strong line, anchored in the south on the modern fortress zone of Verdun and (to a lesser but nevertheless important extent) on the obsolete fort at Longwy, and stretching north–westwards to the mouth of the 'Étalle corridor' at Étalle itself. This line, held by Third Army, would have provided flank protection for Fourth Army from any counter–offensive out of the *Moselstellung*. Having achieved the first day's march objectives, the line was to be extended by Fourth Army, through Neufchâteau further north–westwards to the village of Maissin. The remaining gap between Maissin and the Meuse, some twelve kilometres further west, was a band of rugged terrain which genuinely lived up to the name of the 'impenetrable Ardennes', and which could be covered by light forces. This was where de Langle positioned his cavalry. To the rear, the river crossings over the Meuse and Semoy were strongly guarded by reserve formations.

Map 11

So the French operational orders required de Langle's Fourth Army to march on the first day (22 August) unopposed, due north, through the bands of forest in front of them and occupy the open terrain beyond. On the second and subsequent days they would deploy and advance to find and engage the left wing of the enemy 'northern group'. The supporting advance of Third Army, to achieve the defensive line described above, necessitated a northerly march also, albeit across less wooded and more open terrain and in closer proximity to the enemy. That at least was the plan.

The strategic role of the German Fourth and Fifth armies, explained above, made their operational plan necessarily simple. Duke Albrecht's army was to advance into the central Ardennes, keeping in touch on the one hand with Third Army in the north and on the other with Fifth Army in the south. The mission, though simple, was challenging, because the front to be protected grew wider the further west they marched and (as has been explained above) Fourth Army had no strategic cavalry reconnaissance or protective screen on their southern front. Crown Prince William's army was to lock itself onto the *Moselstellung* in the south–east while at the same time clinging to the left of Fourth Army further north–west. Despite the relatively short distances to be covered by Fifth Army, it too had a challenging mission, because Fourth Army was on the move westwards, the front was widening exponentially, and gaps threatened to appear. And the Crown Prince, expecting daily an attack out of Verdun by the strong French forces identified by his intelligence, was keen to improve his defensive position by moving forward onto ground more favourable for his artillery.

On 17 August, OHL issued orders for the main German offensive to start the next day, 18 August. The event went unnoticed by French intelligence. On the morning of 18 August Duke Albrecht released his army corps from their positions behind the Alzette and ordered them to cross the border from Luxembourg into Belgium. The narrowness of the front available to Fourth Army at the border (thirty–five kilometres) and the small number of decent roads led Duke Albrecht to put his three regular corps in front, with his two reserve corps following in a second line.[41] This formation, when reported by French aerial intelligence, played to the French preconception that reserve units would not fight in the front line. And when, soon after, the German formation changed, the French preconception did not.

Map 12

Crown Prince William set his army on a long, looping march around the *Moselstellung* from its concentration areas east and south–east of Metz, with his three regular corps also in front and the two reserve corps following in a second line. On 18 August they arrived just north of Diedenhofen (Thionville).[42]

41   *Weltkrieg 1*, p.225.
42   *Weltkrieg 1*, p.229.

Also on 17 August, General Ruffey issued his secret and personal instruction for Third Army's operations on 18 August.[43] The army was given the mission of establishing a front facing north–east, from Jametz to Étain, ready to debouch in the general direction of Longwy. So on 18 August the troops closed up in preparation for an advance, occupying the right (north) bank of the Othain; but it would be four more days before they were launched into the attack.

Map 13

On 19 August, the German Fifth Army began to swing westwards around the *Moselstellung*. 5 AK headed for Arlon with 13 AK close by on its left, whilst 16 AK stayed closer to the fixed defences of the *Moselstellung*. Reports, which reached the French of a German army entering the Arlon region from this day on, were not unfounded but were dismissed.[44] Preparations were also put in hand by OHL and Fifth Army staff for the siege of the French outlying fortress of Longwy, which now lay in the path of a further German advance. A special detachment was set up under a Fifth Army general of pioneers, General Kaempffer, complete with heavy siege guns.[45]

Map 7

Also on 19 August, Duke Albrecht's Fourth Army columns reached a line between Bastogne and Attert, a thirty–three kilometre front. Attert was only nine kilometres north of Arlon where Fifth Army's right wing lay, so liaison was assured.[46] Their front was still east of the line patrolled by French aircraft, which continued to report that the central Ardennes was empty of enemy troops. De Langle was ready on this day to launch his five corps into the central Ardennes and he wrote to Joffre to that effect.[47] But GQG believed that the north–westerly march of large German columns (actually mainly Third Army and the right wing of Fourth Army) observed by their aerial reconnaissance would send more enemy units into the trap on the Ourthe. So it held de Langle back. From this point on, GQG's ignorance of the imminent arrival of the bulk of the German Fourth Army from the east clouded its judgement. Only Fourth Army's own intelligence and operational staff could – or should – have balanced the local risks to the mission they were being asked to undertake. Ruffey's Third Army remained in its defensive positions and engaged in localised patrolling.[48]

Map 14

On 20 August, Duke Albrecht's army made only short marches, but it was provoked into a major skirmish. In the north, 8 AK marched only sixteen kilometres, sticking closely to the left flank of von Hausen's Third Army and ending up on the upper reaches of the Ourthe river. Had it been the only German corps in the central Ardennes, Joffre's plan would have been realistic. But it was not, and in the south, 6 AK (transferred from Silesia) made a leisurely and uninterrupted march, still undetected by French intelligence, to the region east of Neufchâteau, around Léglise which was to be one of the key objectives of Ruffey's Third Army only two days later.

Map 15

But French intelligence had managed to locate Duke Albrecht's third regular corps in the centre of the line. 18 AK had by lunchtime completed its short march westwards to the region north of Neufchâteau, around Libramont, and was settling into its billets when its outposts came into contact with de Langle de Cary's provisional cavalry corps (4 and 9 DC) which was reconnoitring in force.[49] One of 18 AK's two divisions deployed, the other stood on alert and even sent its artillery

---

43   AFGG I/1, Annex 422: *IIIe armée, Verdun, 17 août, 16.00: Instruction personelle et secrète Nr.5, pour la journée du 18 août.*

44   AFGG I/1, Annex 692: [transcript of an enciphered telegramme], *21 août, 0.10: Préfet Meuse à: 1° guerre, cabinet, Paris; 2° grand quartier général, armées de l'Est.*

45   *Weltkrieg 1*, p.230.

46   *Weltkrieg 1*, p.226.

47   AFGG I/1, Annex 549: [Fourth Army], *Stenay, 19 août, 17.00: Compte rendu du général commandant la IVe armée.*

48   AFGG I/1, Annex 545: *IIIe armée, 19 août, 18.00: Compte rendu de renseignements Nr.31 (bis).*

49   On 18 August, Joffre combined de Langle's two cavalry divisions into a provisional corps under the command of 4 DC's General Abboneau, reinforced by a mixed detachment from 17 CA made up of a regiment of infantry,

south in support.[50] The fighting escalated to involve all of the above and lasted until nightfall.[51] Prisoners taken by the French gave valuable intelligence about their enemy's dispositions.[52]

Both 5 AK and 13 AK of the German Fifth Army made short marches down to the upper reaches of the Semoy river near Étalle; 16 AK stood fast in its positions near the *Moselstellung*. The Crown Prince moved 6 RAK up into the widening gap in the centre of his line. He now had four of his five major units in the front line, with 5 RAK held slightly back around his headquarters' town of Esch.[53] Ruffey's Third Army remained in its defensive positions on the Othain this day, gathering information in preparation for an advance.[54] But in the evening of 20 August, Joffre issued orders to Ruffey to commence his advance 'in the general direction of Arlon' the next day.[55]

Map 16

At 06.00 on 21 August, Ruffey's Third Army moved forward from the Othain towards the line of the Chiers–Crusnes rivers, closing up on its advance guards. The march was reported as having been uneventful.[56] But it is now clear from individual unit JMOs that in the evening the leading elements of Brochin's 5 CA encountered the enemy in trenches on the south–facing slopes west of Longwy.[57] These defences were not part of the besiegers' circumvallations, but were outposts of the main army (13 AK) protecting the besiegers, facing south and on the alert for a possible French advance.[58] Brochin's leading troops entered into a series of skirmishes which lasted most of the night, although these events did not impact upon Ruffey's plans at all; indeed it is not clear whether Brochin and his staff actually reported the contact. The bulk of the Crown Prince's Fifth Army had rested in its billets all day, inadvertently thwarting French aerial reconnaissance and adding to the false sense of security pervading the French high command. The only significant activity on Fifth Army's front was the investiture of Longwy by a brigade of infantry from Kaempffer's detachment, the bringing up of the heavy artillery for the siege, and the placement by 13 AK of protective outposts, referred to above.[59]

Duke Albrecht's troops likewise took advantage of a day of comparative rest. The French cavalry corps, after the lively skirmish on 20 August, seemed to have disappeared from in front of their 18 AK, leaving them in the dark as to French intentions. They had no cavalry corps of their own with which to conduct long-range reconnaissance. 18 AK shifted slightly north–westwards (from Neufchâteau–Libramont to Libramont–Libin), making room for 18 RAK to enter the front line at Neufchâteau.

De Langle used the night of 20–21 August to close his main force up onto their advance guards. But the northerly axis of the impending attack required that de Langle's two right–wing corps –

a squadron of cavalry and an artillery battery. See: AFGG I/1 (1936) p.361; and Annex 426: *Armée de Varennes* [Fourth], *17 août, 20.00: Ordre particulier aux 4e et 9e divisions de cavalerie;* and AFGG X/1, p.940.

50   *Das 2 Grossherzoglich Hessische Feldartillerie Regiment Nr 61 im Weltkrieg 1914/1918* [FAR 61] (Stallung, Oldenburg/ Berlin, 1927), p.11.

51   *Weltkrieg 1*, p.227.

52   AFGG I/1, Annex 641: [Fourth Army, 20 August, 23.59]: *Compterendu de la IV° armée,* received at GQG at 23.59 on 20 August by Lieutenant–Colonel Brécard.

53   Weltkrieg 1, p.230 and Karte (map) 3.

54   AFGG I/1, Annex 630: *message téléphoné, Armée Verdun à GQG, 20 août, 18.45: Compte rendu de renseignements Nr.32.*

55   AFGG I/1, (1936), p.364.

56   AFGG I/1, (1936), pp.365-369 and Annex 739: *IIIe Armée, 21 août, 12.45: Compte rendu de renseignements Nr.35, Armée Verdun à GQG;* and Annex 741: *IIIe Armée, 21 août, 21.30: Compte rendu de renseignements Nr.36.*

57   AAT 26N285/1: JMO of 9 DI; and AAT 26N287/1: JMO of 10 DI.

58   Oberstleutnant U. Schwab, *Das neunte württembergische Infanterie-Regiment Nr.127 im Weltkrieg 1914–1918* (Ehr. Belsersche Verlagsbuchhandlung, Stuttgart, 1920), pp.4–6.

59   *Weltkrieg 1*, pp. 303–304.

2 CA and CAC – surrender part of their zone of operations to Third Army; this necessitated a lot of extra marching to free up roads and villages which they had occupied in the eastern part of their original zones. The movement was not organised at all efficiently and this is the activity described by General Cordonnier as 'order, counter–order, disorder'.[60] The troops of 2 CA seem to have been particularly fatigued by this necessary reorganisation, their march discipline was so poor that units got muddled up on the few crowded roads, and their tiredness and disorder had a significant effect on the action on the following day: the advance guard (7 Brigade) failed to reach its objective of securing the exits north of the forest of Virton and remained on the wrong side of the forest for the night.[61] There was also another significant skirmish at Izel, on the edge of the Florenville clearing, between a regiment from General Roques's 12 CA and strong elements of the German 3 KD which was still providing security in the Étalle corridor, in the gap between Fourth and Fifth Armies.[62]

Map 17

On 21 August Joffre issued his preliminary instructions for Fourth Army's offensive into the Ardennes.[63] At almost the same time, Crown Prince William ordered the advance of his Fifth Army from its positions on a rough line from Étalle to Diedenhofen down to the line of the Chiers–Crusnes rivers, in order to improve his defensive position.[64] Because of the relatively short distance between the two sides, the scene was set for an imminent clash between the German Fifth and French Third Armies, probably on 22 August. Both sides had gathered enough intelligence to establish this fact; the Germans, interpreting their intelligence correctly, were on the alert; the French, ignoring small but crucial pieces of evidence, convinced themselves that Ruffey would not face significant opposition.

In the centre, Duke Albrecht von Württemburg's orders to his Fourth Army on 21 August for execution on 22 August were for a continuation of his leisurely advance westwards through the Ardennes. He had no inkling of de Langle's forthcoming attack, just a general awareness of such a possibility, leading him to order a generally heightened sense of alert.[65] But during the night of 21–22 August came one of those 'Clausewitzian' moments of chance, which alter the course of history. The Crown Prince's orders called for his army to march south, and this particularly affected his right–hand corps (5 AK), requiring it to make a long march down through the forests from its pivotal position around Arlon on the Semoy river into the next open clearing (the valley of the river Vire), from where it could protect the flank of the neighbouring 13 AK in the Longwy region. The movement of 5 AK away from Arlon threatened to open a thirty–kilometre gap between Fourth and Fifth Armies and leave the 'Étalle corridor' unguarded. On receipt of his orders and appreciating the potential significance of the gap, the commanding general of V AK sent one of his staff officers, Hauptmann Wachenfeld, to ask his nearest neighbour (25 Reserve Division of 18 Reserve Korps, Fourth Army, at Anlier) to turn south in support. Driven in a fast motor car and with a spare car travelling behind (even if the spare car lost its way!), Wachenfeld arrived at 25 RID's headquarters at 00.30 on 22 August. But the commander of the reserve division felt unable to comply without orders from his own superiors. On his own initiative, Wachenfeld then drove on to VI AK's headquarters at Léglise, arriving at 02.00. General von Britzelwitz, VI AK's commander, appreciated the seriousness of the situation posed by the gap between the two armies (even though, it should be remembered, the German intelligence had at that stage no inkling of the impending

Map 18

60   General Cordonnier, *Une brigade au Feu (Potins de Guerre)* (Henri Charles–Lavauzelle, Paris, 1921), pp.230 & 232.
61   Ibid., pp.240–245.
62   AFGG I/1 (1936), p.395.
63   AFGG I/1, Annex 706: [GQG, 21 August, 21.30]: *Ordre particulier Nr.17, commandant en chef à commandants IIIe armée (Verdun) et IVe armée (Stenay).*
64   *Weltkrieg 1*, pp.305–307.
65   Ibid., pp.309–312.

French offensive) and phoned Fourth Army commander Duke Albrecht. Woken from sleep and despite the unorthodox request from another army's subordinate unit, Duke Albrecht appreciated the risks in the Crown Prince's new plan, and issued orders for 6 AK to march south and close the gap.[66] So within four hours 12 ID was sent south on the road through the forest via Les Fosses to Rossignol and 11 ID from Léglise to Tintigny.

Map 19

The hectic German staff activity which led to Duke Albrecht ordering 6 AK to march southwards, contrasts with the lethargy and complacency shown by the French units opposite them. The leading division of 2 CA (4 DI) had received orders to traverse the forest in front of it and establish itself on the southern slopes of the Semoy valley before bivouacking for the night of 21–22 August. The orders were clear, and necessary to secure the Étalle corridor and de Langle's right flank. But the commander of 4 DI decided – as a result of the additional marching occasioned by Joffre's change of the axis of attack, described above – that his troops were too tired to execute their orders; he informed his corps commander that he was stopping south of the forest but would make up the time by an earlier start in the morning. This unilateral decision seems not to have been questioned, nor did anyone think to inform General Lefèvre, commanding CAC, whose flank would be uncovered if 4 DI was late arriving on the Semoy. Of course, in the morning, that was exactly what happened. When the main body of the French 4 DI eventually occupied the southern slopes of the Semoy valley, they found the German 6 AK in possession of the valley, the river crossings at Tintigny and, crucially, the high ground of the northern slopes, which afforded excellent observation for artillery down the whole of the valley. The consequences of this poor discipline and ineffective command and control were catastrophic for the French, as will be explained in the narrative of the individual encounter at Rossignol. But nothing could better contrast the general state of the French and German command structures and attitudes than the behaviour described above.

Thus it was, through a combination of chance and a markedly different approach to conducting war, that Ruffey's left–hand corps (4 CA) met the German 5 AK at Virton and Ethe, rather than achieving an unopposed march north; and thus also de Langle's two right–wing corps (CAC and 2 CA) encountered their enemy (6 AK) in the Semoy valley rather than in the north around Neufchâteau. The sequence of events which drove the German units south and which precipitated the four encounter battles in the centre of the battlefield show clearly that the French perception – carried forward even today into several respected histories[67] – that the Germans were lying in wait for them in ambush positions is pure myth; and shows instead that the Germans were not actively seeking battle, merely seeking to close gaps in their line and improve their defensive positions. De Langle himself contributed to obscuring the true course of events by seeking in his memoires to pass all responsibility onto Joffre. In these he wrongly claims that on 20 August the Germans opposite him stopped, turned to face south–west, occupied the woods and localities, fortified them and prepared to receive an expected French attack.[68]

The morning of 22 August was hot, humid and foggy. It had rained the day before, causing thick river mist to rise, covering the whole terrain. Air reconnaissance was impossible until the sun burned through the mist, which was at about 08.30 at the earliest. The fog and lack of aerial cover aided the French advance and contributed greatly to the surprise achieved against their opponents.

The French set out early – most units were on the march by 05.00 – but many of them had a long approach march in front of them. On the French left, the main bodies of each column had a

---

66   *Weltkrieg 1*, pp.308–9.
67   For example: Doughty, *Pyrrhic Victory*, pp.66–67; and Herwig, *Marne*, pp.147–8.
68   General de Langle de Cary, *Souvenirs de Commandement, 1914-1916* (N.p., Paris, 1935), p.16.

couple of hours march before they even crossed the river Semoy behind their advance guards, and the prospect of a further twenty kilometres or more to reach their day's objective. The troops would be tired if and when they came into action. The German troops generally had shorter marches in prospect and were consequently likely to be fresher when combat loomed. The longer approach marches of the French units on the left – the most westerly columns – meant that any contact with the enemy, who was approaching at a right–angle from the east, would be during late morning. In the centre and on the French right – mainly on Third Army's front where the Germans were either nearby or closing fast, there was the likelihood of early action.

Map 20

The German Crown Prince's decision to send his army southwards towards more favourable terrain had coincided with Joffre's decision to send Ruffey's army into the attack. So the five corps of Fifth Army were committed to a manoeuvre which would put them directly in the path of the advance of Ruffey's three corps. But, as has been mentioned above, Ruffey had been given the Third Group of reserve divisions as part of his command. These troops, equivalent to an additional one–and–a–half corps and with eighteen batteries of heavy artillery attached, had been ordered by Ruffey on 17 August to extend his refused right flank back to the Meuse Heights; *54 Reserve Infantry Division* (DR) in particular was to hold itself ready to take over flank protection for Third Army from Sarrail's 6 CA.[69] However, for reasons which are not entirely clear, Joffre removed the Third Group of reserve divisions from Ruffey's command on the morning of 21 August, setting up an independent command under General Maunoury which was soon renamed the 'Army of Lorraine'.[70] Since Maunoury was given the Verdun garrison and additional reserve units, as well as responsibility for the defence of Verdun and Toul, this can be seen as a cautious, defensive move on Joffre's part, perhaps influenced by the aftermath of the defeats on 20 August at Morhange and Sarrebourg, and certainly not in the spirit of *offensive à outrance*. Certainly the effect on Ruffey, and on the counter–attack into the Ardennes, was entirely negative. Without the three reserve divisions under his command to counter the German four reserve divisions – and ignoring for the moment the question of the relative quality of each side's reserve units – Ruffey found himself outnumbered. The timing of the removal of the reserve divisions from Ruffey's command highlights the point: at 09.15 on 21 August, Ruffey ordered 54 DR to take over flank guard duties from 40 DI of Sarrail's corps, thus releasing the latter for the main offensive.[71] Joffre issued his Order Nr 14, setting up Maunoury's command, only an hour later, at about 10.30, which was received at Third Army headquarters at 15.00. As a result, only Ruffey's three regular corps met all five of the Crown Prince's regular and reserve corps in battle on 22 August.

In the west, 5 AK met 4 CA at Virton and Ethe, and prevented the French from advancing from their overnight positions.[72] In the centre, 13 AK met and comprehensively defeated 5 CA near the fortress of Longwy, while on the other side of the fortress 6 RAK supported by 5 RAK successfully held off a series of assaults by the elite 6 CA. In the east, advancing from its pivotal position near the *Moselstellung*, 16 AK nearly succeeded in turning Ruffey's flank, forcing the French into a fighting withdrawal.

It is clear from this brief summary of the action between the French Third and German Fifth Armies that from the opening moments of the engagement, Joffre's strategic plan was compromised

69   AFGG I/1, Annex 421: *IIIe armée, QG de Verdun, 17 août 1914, 15.00: Instruction particulière, personnelle et secrète Nr.4 au général commandant la subdivision d'armée.*

70   AFGG I/1, Annex 700: *GQG, 21 août, 15.00:Ordre particulier Nr.14.*

71   AFGG I/1, Annex 745: *IIIe armée, QG de Verdun, 21août 1914,09.15: Le general Ruffey, commandant la IIIe armée, à Monsieur le général commandant le 3e groupe de D.R.*

72   Grasset, *Virton, Ethe*; and Dr E. Bircher, *Die Schlacht bei Ethe-Virton am 22. August 1914* (Verlag R. Eisenschmidt, Berlin, 1930).

and Ruffey's operational plan totally disrupted by the German advance to the line of the Chiers–Crusnes rivers. Instead of marching twenty kilometres or more northwards to protect Fourth Army's vulnerable right flank, Third Army was fighting for its life near its own start line. De Langle de Cary's Fourth Army would be marching north on its own.

And indeed it was to prove worse than that. The two right–hand corps of Fourth Army (CAC and 2 CA) were also stopped well short of their objectives and isolated from the rest of the army by a thick band of forest. This was the result of the serendipitous decision by Duke Albrecht – mentioned above – to send 6 AK south during the night to cover the emerging gap in the German line in the Semoy valley. Instead of traversing the forest north of the Semoy and arriving at Neufchâteau on the flank of the main body of Fourth Army, CAC met the German 6 AK in the Semoy valley and suffered a catastrophic defeat at Rossignol; whilst 2 CA (when its lead division – 4 DI – eventually arrived) was forced to fight a defensive action alongside them at Tintigny. The action in the Semoy valley destroyed de Langle's operational plan. When his right wing was fixed in place so early in the day, fighting the wrong battle in the wrong place, the rest of de Langle's army marched on without it, north through the forests, their right flank exposed now to any German movement from the east. By 10.00 (if not before) de Langle's tenuous command over his operation was already beyond his control.

Only the two corps on the left of de Langle's army (11 and 17 CAs) managed to get close to their objectives for 22 August, which were the occupation of three villages north of the tree–line: namely Maissin, Anloy and Ochamps. But even they met German opposition before they could emerge from the forest and deploy properly. They were, however, together with 12 CA in the centre, the group of French units that through their unforeseen advance caught the Germans completely by surprise and caused them great concern.

For Duke Albrecht did not have it all his own way; he had his own problems. His serendipitous decision to send 6 AK south to the Semoy may have paid off at Rossignol and Tintigny, but he still had nearly sixty kilometres of front to protect with only his four remaining corps. He had allocated the key role of protecting von Hausen's Third Army's flank in the north to 8 AK; it was too far away to be able to intervene in any action on 22 August. He had kept 8 RAK back at his Army Headquarters at Bastogne, as his personal army reserve; it too was too far from the battle zone to play other than a last minute peripheral role. That left two corps, 18 AK and 18 RAK, both situated around Neufchâteau, to meet and resist the advance of de Langle's centre and left. And to make matters worse for Duke Albrecht, the fog concealed the early morning advance of de Langle's centre–left group, which managed to approach into contact without his knowing. Only at midday did reports reach him, revealing the danger he was in, and by that time his two central corps had been in action for over an hour.[73]

It is a long–standing misinterpretation of the Battle of the Ardennes that the Germans were lying in wait for the French and ambushed them in the forests.[74] Nothing could be further from the truth. On the morning of 22 August, both 18 AK and 18 RAK began by implementing Duke Albrecht's orders of the night before for a continuation of their gradual westerly advance. Only short marches were envisaged, because 18 AK had to echelon back from 8 AK in the north and 18 RAK had to keep loosely in touch with 6 AK in the south; together the two were to attempt to hold a broad line of more than fifty kilometres through the central Ardennes. This explains why the rear half of 18 RAK (25 Reserve Infantry Division) did not move at all until the afternoon, and then

73   *Weltkrieg 1*, p.316.
74   See notes 64 and 65, above; also Liddell Hart, *A History of the World War*, p.82.

only to join the fighting which had broken out. It explains why the other half of 18 RAK (21 RID) was engaged in a leisurely route march in column when attacked by the French. And it explains why the southerly half of 18 AK (21 ID), having sent out its advance guard, did not move its main body until noon. Only the northern half of 18 AK (25 ID), with the furthest but still short distance to travel in order to keep in touch with the advancing 8 AK, sent its main body onto the roads during the early morning.[75]

But coincidentally, and unfortunately for the French, the advance guards of these German formations were heading for the same places as the French columns of de Langle's centre–left grouping – the villages of Bertrix, Ochamps, Anloy and Maissin, and the Germans were closer. Thus it came about that the advancing French units, expecting a peaceful day's march through the forests, a deployment the following day and a subsequent advance upon the German 'northern grouping' on the river Ourthe, instead found themselves in contact with German Fourth Army units coming from the east, and engaged in fierce fighting in and on the northern edges of the forests. Thus also it happened that the German Fourth Army advance guard at Ochamps was facing west when a French column came out of the forest from the south;[76] the German advance guard on the road to Maissin had to force–march in order to chase out French cavalry and occupy that village and its commanding high ground before the recently located large French column came up;[77] the German reservists (advance guard of 18 RAK) marching out of Neufchâteau were caught in column by French rifle fire;[78] and the German advance guard which reached Anloy was caught by surprise by French rifle fire coming from the tree–line to the south when it sought to advance further.[79] These were not actions consistent with the suggestions of a well–laid German ambush. This myth (for such it was) had its roots in two factors: the multitude of small German cavalry patrols which had roamed across the central Ardennes over the previous days, giving rise to rumours passed on by civilians of masses of Germans in the forests;[80] and the desire on the part of certain French commanders to explain away their failures at the tactical level. There is even a suggestion that certain German commanders encouraged the propagation of the 'ambush' myth in order to enhance the reputation of German military excellence.[81]

In the central Ardennes zone between Maissin and Neufchâteau, the French, despite faulty intelligence and disrupted operational plans, managed to outnumber their immediate opponents by more than two to one. At one specific point on the thirty–kilometre front, the odds in favour of the French lengthened to more than six to one. Here, ironically and despite mistakes on both sides, was the opportunity for which Joffre had hoped and planned; a clean break in the German centre followed by an envelopment of the 'northern grouping' of German armies. It was not, as has been shown, at all like the plan envisaged, neither in time nor place. Improvisation had become the order of the day, both on a tactical and operational level.

Map 21

On the left, Maissin was first occupied by French cavalry from 11 CA, only to be driven out by the superior firepower of German infantry. Thereafter, three German infantry regiments from 25 ID (18 AK) held off successive attacks by the eight infantry regiments of 11 CA. Only in the evening after more than six hours' fighting did weight of French numbers and superior firepower succeed in

75   *Weltkrieg 1*, p.314.
76   Kaiser, *Bertrix*, p.34.
77   Even French sources confirm this. For example, Colonel Bujac, *Le Général Eydoux et le XIe Corps d'Armée, août – sept 1914* (Nantes, Rue de la Fosse, 1924), p.70.
78   Grasset, *Neufchâteau*, pp.25–26.
79   FAR 61, p.12.
80   Lt-Colonel A.H. Burne, 'The French Guns at Bertrix, 1914' (Vol.LXIII, 1936-37) pp.345–350.
81   Kaiser, op. cit., p.32.

driving the Germans from the field. Maissin was the first of two clear opportunities for de Langle to win an operational victory, not only because of his superiority of force but also because 18 AK's right flank lay open and vulnerable to envelopment without any support or reinforcement on hand. The reasons for the French failure to realise their opportunity will be examined later in the book.

South of Maissin, the remaining regiment of the German 25 ID met and held off the whole of the French 34 DI at Anloy, primarily because of a decision by the French commander to keep his artillery back whilst sending his infantry forward into the forests. German field artillery and machine guns provided the necessary fire power to thwart unsupported French infantry attacks over open ground. Consequently, 34 DI failed to support and protect 11 CA's right flank and thus contributed to the missed opportunity. Without artillery, the French infantry failed to get forward and suffered heavily in turn from German shelling. At nightfall it was the French who retreated, after heavy casualties on both sides.

The right–hand column of 17 CA, 33 DI, suffered the greatest disaster of the day because of a series of catastrophic but avoidable blunders by the French commanders. This encounter is described in detail later, but in short, the French division marched without adequate security into the forest north of Bertrix and there was taken in the flank by 21 ID, coming down from Libramont where it had been based. The result was disaster for the French; 33 DI's artillery was wiped out before it could disentagle itself from the forest, the infantry fought stoutly, incurred huge losses and finally broke; in its chaotic retreat, nay rout, the panic of 33 DI's troops infected those of 34 DI whom they met. 17 CA was effectively destroyed and retreated in considerable disorder.

In the three encounters described above, at Maissin, Anloy and Ochamps–Bertrix, Duke Albrecht's 18 AK acquitted itself well, holding off three times its numbers and inflicting a bloody reverse on 17 CA. But further south, around Neufchâteau, 18 RAK had an even more difficult challenge. One of the corps's two divisions was resting in reserve, holding a position some five kilometres east of the town, from where it could move south in support of 6 AK if needed. This left only one reserve division to face the might of the approaching 12 CA, which also had the reinforced 5 Colonial Brigade in support. So at Neufchâteau the odds against the Germans were initially more than two–and–a–half to one. Once the fighting had intensified and the situation clarified, the commander of 18 RAK ordered his reserve division (25 RID) to force–march to the rescue of its embattled sister unit. The reinforcements arrived successively during the afternoon, just in time to stop the elite French colonial infantry from capturing Neufchâteau town, which would have been a serious reverse for the Germans. But the real opportunity lay west of the town, where the twenty–four battalions and one–hundred–and–twenty guns of General Roques's 12 CA encountered six reserve battalions and eighteen guns from 18 RAK's leading column.

The encounter between Roques's corps and the German reservists west of Neufchâteau is central to the dominant theme of this book: that the French were afforded but failed to capitalise upon an opportunity to break through the centre of Duke Albrecht's front into open and undefended territory beyond. This encounter is described and analysed in its own chapter later. But in summary, the engagement went like this: fighting between the two advance guards started at about 10.00 and each side successively deployed more troops into their respective firing lines. Within two or three hours, Roques's troops had driven their weak opponents back, inflicting severe losses and pushing the German reservists to the limits of their endurance. But with victory within their grasp, the French failed to deliver the *coup de grace*; indeed Roques's right wing actually retreated rather than advanced, a movement ordered to conform to the position of the Colonial brigade on their right. At nightfall, 12 CA was able to bivouac comfortably on the battlefield whilst the Germans licked their wounds and counted their blessings.

To summarise de Langle de Cary's Fourth Army operation: as with Ruffey's plan, de Langle's operational plan went wrong from the very beginning when his right wing was intercepted and held on the Semoy. The left and centre, however, continued to implement their part and achieved surprise against an inferior enemy. However despite two clear opportunities to inflict a significant defeat on their opponent, these French units failed to dominate and indeed, in the case of 17 CA at Bertrix, suffered themselves a devastating reversal.

During the night of 22–23 August, all four army commanders were able to receive the latest reports and take stock of what had happened and decide what to do next. Initially de Langle de Cary felt that he could renew his attacks on his left with 11, 17 and 12 CAs, bringing up fresh troops (9 CA and 60 DR) in support; all the while holding a defensive line 'at all costs' with CAC (supported now by his heavy artillery) and 2 CA on the left bank of the Semoy. He issued orders to that effect at 23.45 on 22 August.[82] But by 05.00 he had received sufficient information to reveal the stark reality: 17 CA had fled back to the Semoy in total disarray, leaving a sixteen-mile gap in the line for the Germans to exploit; the two flanking corps - 11 CA & 12 CA - were seriously exposed to flanking manoeuvres. Furthermore, casualties in all units had been high, there was more confusion than command and control, and time was needed to regroup. De Langle issued new, defensive orders reflecting that reality, ordering the exposed 11 & 12 Corps to withdraw.[83] But Joffre and GQG did not agree with this assessment, still clinging to the belief that Fourth Army's six corps were faced by no more than two or three German corps, and that a further attack would break the enemy. De Langle was ordered to renew the attack as soon as possible.[84] He dutifully obliged, issuing at 10.00 fresh orders for an attack which he knew his troops were incapable of executing.[85]

But Duke Albrecht was in no position to follow up his defensive victories; the cost on 22 August had been too high. Men were tired, supplies were low, units disorganised, casualties severe. Even the victorious 18 AK took a morning of rest before moving out at noon on 23 August.[86] The losses suffered by the units which had fought at Maissin and Anloy were such that they had to be intermingled with fresh units from 8 RAK (which had force–marched to the battlefield arriving at dusk on 22 August). Impromptu divisional–sized detachments were formed under senior commanders in order to effect the follow–up.[87] In short, the Germans were in no position to exploit the gap left by the retreat of French 17 Corps; de Langle was to be granted the time he needed to reorganise and (literally) retrench.

Ruffey's Third Army was in better shape, despite the debacle of 5 CA's baptism of fire. A strong defensive line was formed on the Tellancourt plateau south of Longwy, linking north–west up to 2 CA of Fourth Army on the Semoy. On the right flank, Sarrail's corps was even able to launch a fresh attack on the morning of 23 August, this time making full use of heavy artillery to prepare the way.[88] And the three reserve divisions of what had been the Third Group but which was now renamed the Army of Lorraine, were now brought into the front line, to form a strong defensive

82   AFGG I/1, Annex 866: *IVe armée, Stenay, 22 août, 23.45: Ordres du commandant de l'armée pour le 23 août.*
83   AFGG I/1, Annex 1102: [Fourth Army] *Armée de Stenay, 23 août, 05.00: Ordre général Nr.22.*
84   AFGG I/1, Annex 1048: [GQG], *23 août, 08.30: communication téléphonique, general en chef à commandant armée Stenay.*
85   AFGG I/1, Annex 1107: [Third Army] *Armée de Stenay,23 août, 10.00: Ordre* [sic]; and Annex 1108: [Third Army], *23 août, 10.00: Armée Stenay à généralen chef, telephone general Maistre à lieutenant–colonel Paquette.*
86   *Weltkrieg 1*, pp.336–339.
87   *Weltkrieg 1*, pp.333–336.
88   AFGG I/1, Annex 913: [6 CA] *Arrancy, 22 août, 21.20: Général commandant 6e C.A. à général commandant la 12e division*; and Annex 1080: *IIIe armée QG de Verdun, 23 août, 0.30: Ordre general d'opérations Nr.18 pour la journée du 23 août.*

front linking with Third Army's refused right wing and covering Verdun, the Meuse Heights and southwards towards the fortress at Toul.[89]

Crown Prince William, despite his proclaimed success on 22 August, was only released from OHL's stricture not to cross the Chiers–Crusnes line at 07.00 on 23 August, and therefore had had no immediate opportunity for pursuit on 22nd, only the prospect of preparing a series of fresh attacks to drive the French back.

Joffre's strategy to drive his reinforced Fourth Army north through the difficult terrain of the Ardennes, rather than use a more traditional axis north–eastwards using the river valleys, main roads and the 'grain' of the terrain, was not, as has been previously claimed, completely stupid. But it was complex to execute, and fraught with risk. The virtue of the strategy is demonstrated by the fact that, even with its faulty execution, it still managed to achieve the element of surprise and deliver strong, superior forces at the weakest point of the German defence. Success or failure then depended upon operational and tactical issues.

The German strategy, to defend the hundred–kilometre gap between the *Moselstellung* and their attacking *Schwenkungsflügel* with the bare minimum of forces, was arguably more of a calculated risk. In particular, the lack of a strong cavalry protective screen on the southern flank opposite Sedan, based as it was upon an assumption that the French would not march north, gave Joffre his opportunity to achieve surprise.

Ruffey's part of the French plan seems with hindsight to have been wildly over–optimistic, requiring as it did that 5 CA break through known enemy field fortifications of unknown strength and still achieve a challenging march northwards, in step with its neighbours, in order to reach a position from where it could help protect Fourth Army's right flank. And the execution of the plan, especially by 4 CA on the left, whereby the northern exits from the forests were not secured before the main columns set out, seems foolhardy in the extreme.

Crown Prince William and his Chief of Staff, having decided to turn southwards on the night of 21–22 August, deployed Fifth Army well, and the execution of their part of the German strategy was without major faults. The attempt to outflank Ruffey's extended right flank was the catalyst for the withdrawal of the whole Third Army. They were aided by the absence from the battlefield of the French Third Group of reserve divisions, which put pressure on Sarrail's 6 CA and allowed the Crown Prince to try to turn the French right flank. No wonder that Ruffey raised a strong post–war protest against Joffre's decision to take those troops away from his command.[90]

It has been shown above how de Langle de Cary's army was split in two by German action and how his part of Joffre's plan was consequently fatally compromised. There are questions about Fourth Army's use of intelligence, indeed many questions underlying the army's performance, which will be examined in detail in later chapters. Then there is the crucial issue, introduced above, of the two opportunities for units of de Langle's army to break the German line. These two encounter-battles lie at a crossroads in history, where small events determined which path would be taken to the future; and for that reason will receive detailed analysis in later chapters.

Duke Albrecht's army fought an excellent battle, especially considering the initial shock of finding the bulk of de Langle's army aimed directly at its weakest point. The decisions which appear on the surface to be driven by luck (such as the serendipitous despatch of 6 AK south to the Semoy) were also driven by professional training and sound military principles – in this case the OHL directive to keep the inside flanks of Fourth and Fifth Armies in close liaison. But, as will be shown in more

89   AFGG I/1, Annex 1051: *GQG, 23 août, 15.20: Télégramme chiffré. Général commandant en chef à general Maunoury, Verdun.*
90   Tuchman, *The Guns of August*, pp. 285–286.

detailed analysis later, it was German tactical competence which was tested, and passed the test. Overall, despite flaws in the strategic and operational planning, each side achieved a partial operational success: de Langle delivered the bulk of his army at the weakest point in the whole German front, and Crown Prince William stopped Ruffey's army before it could advance to assist de Langle. Thereafter, the answers to success and failure in the Ardennes 1914 campaign seem to lie at the tactical (battlefield) level. So it is there that the following chapters will start to unravel the detail of events.

2

Army Operations

This chapter examines the way in which each of the four army commanders involved in the Battle of the Ardennes planned to execute his part in his commander's strategic plan and how he then conducted his operation. It examines the comparative effectiveness of the four generals' command, control and communication skills, and analyses the extent to which the army commanders contributed to the outcome of events on 22 August. Although the key role was arguably given to General de Langle de Cary, who was to lead France's striking force into the attack on the enemy's weakest point, this chapter commences with an examination of his opponent, Duke Albrecht of Württemburg, whose Fourth Army was to receive the main French attack. An understanding of Duke Albrecht's role in thwarting French ambitions will illuminate the subsequent analysis of de Langle's own performance.

The operational overview (Chapter 1) has described at army level and above how Duke Albrecht's Fourth Army advanced from the Alzette position on 18 August into the central Ardennes. It has shown how some excellent staff work and a good operational decision by Duke Albrecht on the night of 21–22 August brought 6 AK down into the Semoy valley to fill the gap left by Crown Prince William's advance to the south. The overview has made clear the extent to which the fog and the timing and direction of the French attack caught Duke Albrecht and his army by surprise. And it has described at high level how, in four separate encounter battles– Maissin–Anloy, Bertrix, Neufchâteau and Rossignol –three of Duke Albrecht's five corps held (and in two cases defeated) de Langle de Cary's five corps, frustrating the French operational plan and forcing them to retreat. It now remains to examine the performance of the German Fourth Army in order to identify the critical factors behind its success, and possible weaknesses.

When news of the advance of the French Fourth army reached Duke Albrecht at about noon on 22 August, he was visiting 6 AK's headquarters at Rulles on his left flank. He had arrived at 09.00, almost certainly to see for himself why he had been woken in the night and asked to send 6 AK south.[1] Unlike his French counterpart, who preferred to remain at his headquarters, Duke Albrecht had not only established a forward command–post (CP) at Libramont, twenty kilometres in advance of his main headquarters at Bastogne, but he also preferred to travel and visit his corps commanders in the field. Such a command style differentiates him from his opponent and also pays tribute to the quality of his army's communications systems which allowed him such freedom whilst preserving his ability to control his wide–spread army.

Duke Albrecht was following the development of the fighting in the Semoy valley between his 6 AK and the enemy's CAC and 2 CA. The scale of the fighting, the fog and the lack of reconnaissance and intelligence had already raised in his mind the possibility that the French might

---

1   *Weltkrieg 1*, p.316.

have launched a major attack, and at 10.30 - over an hour before the report of the French advance reached him - he decided to take precautionary measures. He issued orders (transmitted from 6 AK's communications centre via his CP at Libramont to his staff at Bastogne) for the army to swing south and close up on 6 AK; 18 RAK at Neufchâteau was ordered to move down towards the Semoy in order to join 6 AK's battle; 18 AK was to move from Libin–Libramont down to Bertrix–Orgéo; and (crucially as it turned out) 8 RAK was ordered to march from its position in reserve at Bastogne down through St Hubert towards Villance.[2] We now know that two of those units – 18 AK and 18 RAK – were already in action against French forces, so their orders were impossible to execute. But the speed and decisiveness of Duke Albrecht's reaction to his early (and correct) appreciation of the scenario is nevertheless impressive; and the decision to bring 8 RAK down from reserve at Bastogne was to pay dividends at the end of the day.

Having given these orders at 10.30, Duke Albrecht went even closer to the action, driving to the Semoy valley and the heights at Marbehan with 6 AK's commander General von Pritzelwitz, from where 11 ID's artillery was bombarding the French and from where he could personally see the scale of the action, the fog having lifted. It was while he was there that reports from the first aerial reconnaissance of the day caught up with him at 12.00. As he had feared, major French forces had come up hidden by the fog and were threatening his right and centre. The German reconnaissance aeroplanes had taken off at about 09.00 as the fog was lifting, and the information they brought back was already several hours old, so the situation could already have deteriorated.[3] Duke Albrecht's surprise was total but his reaction was fast and positive. His immediate appreciation of the seriousness of his situation led him to return to his CP at Libramont at once. But he still made time to stop in Neufchâteau to give a personal briefing to General von Steuben, commander of 18 RAK.[4] At the time that Duke Albrecht arrived in Neufchâteau 21 RID had been fighting desperately for more than three hours against two–and–a–half French divisions, and there was considerable doubt whether they could hold. One can legitimately speculate that the steadfast and desperate resistance of that division, and the absolute refusal of both divisional and corps commanders to countenance retreat, was bolstered through Duke Albrecht's personal appearance.

Back at his CP at Libramont, Duke Albrecht took stock. At 14.00 he held a face–to–face meeting with 18 AK's commander, General von Schenk, whose headquarters was conveniently adjacent. The movement of that corps previously ordered at 10.30 had been made unworkable by enemy action. 25 ID was totally embroiled in the fighting at Maissin and Anloy; 21 ID was waiting around Libramont, although its advance guard had gone west to Ochamps. There followed a typically Prussian command situation: Albrecht wanted von Schenk to send some support to von Steuben's hard–pressed reservists at Neufchâteau; von Schenk demurred; Albrecht insisted; he personally ordered at least part of 18 AK to go to help 18 RAK by moving on a line Orgéo–Bertrix.[5] This would have taken part of 21 ID towards the French 12 CA at Saint Médard; French historian Pierre Rocolle later mistakenly believed that this had occurred, and wrote an incorrect and misleading account of the ensuing battle.[6] Such a move would have considerably weakened the advance of 21 ID on Bertrix, with incalculable consequences for the ensuing action with the French 33 DI. But in the end, von Schenk's appreciation of his situation was that it was too deeply locked in its own combat for him to be able to comply with the order from Albrecht; a new report to that

2   Ibid.
3   Ibid.
4   Ibid., p.326.
5   *Weltkrieg 1*, p.327.
6   Rocolle, *Hécatombe*, p.143 & note (46); also sketch p.13.

effect received Albrecht's retrospective concurrence.[7] Thanks to the pusillanimous performance of General Roques's 12 CA, von Schenk's decision to ignore his superior's wishes bore fruit; but it was a close call, one of those small events that occurred at that crossroads in history.

At 15.00 Albrecht issued a consolidated general order to all his corps commanders, which confirmed the individual instructions previously given to each and which gave fresh instructions to 8 AK and 8 RAK. The latter was to push forward to Villance, a village just behind Anloy from where it could support the hard-pressed 25 ID, where it would deploy for battle, whilst the former would prepare to send its left–hand division south in the morning, provided that there was no threat from the west (where the French Fifth Army stood on the Meuse).[8] One can deduce from these orders that Duke Albrecht was still taking knife-edge decisions, full of risk, with his wide-spread forces. From 15.00 onwards, there was little for Duke Albrecht and his staff to do, except await the outcome of the day's fighting, and plan for the morrow. A crucial decision made earlier, when calling the rest of his army to swing southwards to meet the threat, had been to keep 8 AK in the north on Third Army's flank. This was a measure both of the importance given to guarding the progress of the main advance on the right wing and of the risks Duke Albrecht was prepared to take in order to fulfil that part of his mission. In then planning for one division of 8 AK to turn south on 23 August – and indeed later adding one brigade of the remaining division to that move, leaving only one brigade to protect Third Army's flank – Albrecht was implicitly acknowledging the seriousness of the French Fourth Army's threat to his army.[9] Who knows what might have developed had the French realized their lost opportunity at Maissin? The appearance of 9 CA and de Langle's provisional Cavalry Corps on the line of the river Lesse to the north–west would have constituted a considerable threat to the security of Third Army's flank. As it was, Albrecht's decision taken at 10.30 to call 8 RAK up from reserve to support 25 ID at Maissin and at Villance was to prove of critical importance: any later and that unit could not have reached Villance before nightfall and the retreating 50 Brigade would have been without the vital support which bolstered the crumbling German line.

The performance of Duke Albrecht and his staff was impressive; in full and immediate command and control of his five corps, he directed the action from his forward CP, only returning to his headquarters at Bastogne in the late evening, when the crisis was known to have passed.[10] It should be noted, however, that even with this timely and hands–on approach, the speed of events still outstripped the army commander's ability to react; orders to his two centre corps could not be implemented because of enemy action. But at least Duke Albrecht was informed and able to take sensible command decisions, several of which proved effective. This was due in no small part to the effectiveness of the German Fourth Army communications.

It is perhaps surprising to find such good and timely communications in Fourth Army, particularly given the apparent poor quality of those of First and Second Armies. Professor Herwig, in his book on the Marne campaign, has written of 'the German army's prewar neglect of communications and control', stating that during the Battle of the Marne: 'There were no electronic ties between First and Second Armies, or between them and their army corps and cavalry corps.'[11] There is, however, contrary evidence that the German army overall did not neglect its communications infrastructure before the war; surviving standing orders for cavalry divisions include detailed regulations for setting up Field Signal detachments,[12] and a 1912 report on an exercise involving 13 AK and 18 AK offers constructive criticism of the performance of the telephone detachments.[13] Herwig's example from First and Second Armies seems to be an extreme case in which the long distances involved stretched the limits of contemporary technology. In the case of Fourth Army, Duke Albrecht's communications network went way beyond just a link back to OHL; he was directly and constantly in touch with all of his corps commanders, whenever he wanted to communicate with them. How so?

Amongst the few remaining records of August 1914 in the archives at Freiburg there is, fortuitously, the war diary of *Fernsprech. Abtlg. VIII AK*, the telecommunications group of Duke Albrecht's 8 AK.[14] It provides a detailed daily record of how this unit laid the telegraph and telephone connections which not only linked 8 AK headquarters with Duke Albrecht's headquarters and thence to OHL, but also providing either telegraph or telephone service to both of the divisions of the corps, to ancillary outposts and to neighbouring units. This group of telephone engineers laid between twenty and fifty kilometres of wire every day from the start of the advance on 18 August until well after the battle on 22 August. On 19 August, for example, when 8 AK was centred upon Bastogne, they ran twenty–two kilometres of wire, setting up a star network with Bastogne as the hub and spokes going out (labelled on an accompanying diagram) to 15 ID and 16 ID. There were four ancillary spokes, one labelled as a *Feldpost* going south–eastwards and another, interestingly, linked to a second network stretching all the way to Libramont. It seems that 8 AK had a direct telephone link to Duke Albrecht's CP as well as to his main headquarters at Bastogne. The unit's target was to have the day's network up and running by 12.00 each day, and judging by the performance on 22 August, when Albrecht was using 6 AK's network at 10.30 to communicate with his CP, some units were able to exceed that target for shorter routes. Such superb communications were a critical success factor for Duke Albrecht and Fourth Army.

Map 24

Map 25

De Langle de Cary's command of the French Fourth Army provides a complete contrast at every level. He remained at his main headquarters at Stenay, sixty kilometres behind the line, for the whole day. Yet despite being constantly at the centre of his whole army's communications network, he was singularly ill–informed. At 16.45 he was still under the mistaken impression that his left and centre were progressing well.[15] And even before the operation had started at dawn on 22 August, there were some questionable decisions and some glaring lack of decisions by Fourth Army's commander and his staff. Unlike Duke Albrecht, whose operational role merely required him to be alert and reactive, de Langle had a difficult offensive to plan and conduct. He had to meet Joffre's strict requirement for secrecy and timing whilst at the same time getting his five corps safely across two bands of inhospitable forest and unforgiving terrain. Security – a concept central to French doctrine – and liaison between columns were prerequisites for success in the first phase of his operation.

And yet, despite the importance and complexity of the proposed operation, there seems to have been very little specific and detailed planning to meet those two crucial criteria. De Langle simply sent his army north in multiple columns on 22 August, with orders to occupy a number of specific features – towns, villages, high ground – on the northern side of the forests. Instructions were given to his cavalry corps to reconnoitre ahead of the army towards Recogne, Libin and Beauraing, which, had they been executed, might have been of inestimable value, given that Recogne and Libin were in the concentration area of 18 AK; but they were not implemented, for reasons which

12   BA–MA PH3/641/: Standing Orders for Cavalry Divisions.
13   BA–MA PH6/I/200: *Die Aufklarungs Uebung zwischen dem XIII und XVIII Armeekorps am 1, 2, 3 August 1912*.
14   BA/MA PH16 -/17: *Fernsbruch Abtlg. VIII (1914–15)*.
15   AFGG I/1 (1936), p.414.

will be explored below along with a brief analysis of the operational role of Fourth Army's cavalry. His operational order was factual, mechanical and lacked context.[16] For example it says: 'Colonial Corps's objective is Neufchâteau. Its zone of movement [will be] between the road from Orval farm via Pin, Jamoigne and Suxy to Neufchâteau and the road from Saint–Vincent via Rossignol, Les Fossés, Offaing'. There was no mention of the previous fighting near Neufchâteau on 20 August or at Izel on 21 August and no sense of impending action. Surely this – or the commander's personal and secret briefing examined below – was the place in which to remind the army of the close proximity of enemy forces, to reinforce instructions for security and to lay down contingency plans in the event of contact? De Langle's personal briefing was not only issued on 20 August, two days before the start of the operation, and not (as far as can be determined from surviving records) subsequently updated, but it also gave a falsely optimistic impression whilst failing to mention any of the risks inherent in the operation. On the contrary, it strongly emphasised the need for secrecy,

Map 26

whilst giving the impression that the advanced detachments which had been, or would be, sent forward would be adequate to secure the army's advance:

> The enemy seems at the moment to be making a flank march across our front which would result in him moving the central mass of his forces towards the north–north–west, without making any important movements south of a general line Longwy–Neufchâteau–Givet. The more the region between Arlon, Audun–le–Roman and Luxembourg is emptied [of enemy troops] when we launch our offensive, the better it will be for Fourth Army's advance, supported on our right by Third Army.
>
> It is therefore of the utmost importance that we let the enemy flow past our front, towards the north–west, without attacking him prematurely. We must ensure that we do not fall into a trap which he may have laid in order to provoke us into launching our offensive too early by directing detachments towards our front.
>
> Consequently I formally command that the advanced detachments, whose advance to secure the Semoy river crossings and the Florenville clearing were laid down in general order Nr.17, fulfil their mission by concealing themselves in the most effective manner. Precise and imperative instructions will be given to them this evening by their corps commanders emphasising that the most advanced outposts must even refrain from firing on groups of enemy soldiers slipping past their front towards the north–west. Under no circumstances whatsoever will the advanced detachments go onto the offensive.[17]

This personal instruction goes on to specify what the advanced detachments should do if attacked before the offensive was launched, which was, in summary, to hold the Semoy river crossings and the Florenville clearing at all costs until reinforced; none of this was relevant to the situation two days later, by which time the presence of at least two German corps in the vicinity had been identified, making the absence of a second secret and personal instruction to cover the planned advance on 22 August all the more surprising. Such a follow–up instruction could and should have referred to the identification of 18 AK at Neufchâteau, an important event which was taking place even as his original secret instruction was being written; it could and should have put the whole army onto a state of high alert, and it could and should have specified what steps were to be taken in the event of contact in the forest, while on the march.

---

16   AFGG I/1, Annex 757: [Fourth Army] *Armée de Stenay, 21 août, 18.00, Ordre général nr.20 concernant les opérations du 22 août.*

17   AFGG I/1, Annex 640: [Fourth Army] *Armée de Stenay,20 août 1914: Instruction personnelle et secrète aux commandants de corps d'armée de l'armée de Stenay.*

The extremely adverse effect of these deficiencies is demonstrated by the fact that within the lower echelons of the Colonial Corps (divisional level and below) there was a widespread belief that 22 August was to be a day of uninterrupted peaceful marching, culminating in a warm billet at Neufchâteau: 'Towards two o'clock in the morning we were woken. A preparatory movement order had arrived from corps. The division was to billet (*cantonner*) at Neufchâteau. Our advance guard would cross the bridge at Breuvannes at 06.30. No new intelligence about the enemy.'[18] Whilst nothing can absolve lower echelon commanders from blame for failing to take basic local security measures as laid down in regulations, the lack of planning and leadership from de Langle and his staff is very apparent.

The other notable absence from the operational order is the failure to co–ordinate the timing between columns. There were in any case many instances of delay and inefficiency in organising units to march, as will be amply demonstrated in the following chapters when individual battles are analysed. But Fourth Army staff set no timings for columns to achieve, no liaison points, no instructions to ensure a coordinated approach. Admittedly there were a few general requirements for liaison included in individual unit instructions: in a specific order issued at 13.00 on 21 August, Gérard's 2 CA was ordered to establish liaison with 4 CA (Third Army) on its right, and was informed that Boëlle's headquarters was at Velosnes.[19] So poorly executed was this order that units of the former, attacking at Virton the next day, ran into units of the latter, also attacking but from a different direction, when each breasted a particular hill crest.[20] In the same instruction, CAC was ordered to ensure that its advance guard set up liaison with 12 CA at Florenville and 2 CA at Bellefontaine. But as will be shown, 2 CA failed to get to Bellefontaine on time. And in any case, CAC's liaison officer arrived there at least an hour after the head of *3e division d'infanterie colonial* (3 DIC)'s column had crossed the Semoy and marched off into the forests.[21] If Fourth Army believed that its corps would automatically follow both instructions and regulations in a professional and timely manner, they were to be sadly disabused by the reality of the execution. The absence of a unifying central control, and the failure to inject any sense of urgency or criticality into an otherwise mundane set of manoeuvre instructions were major weaknesses on the part of Fourth Army's staff.

It was not the case that de Langle and his chief of staff simply underestimated the threat posed by the enemy; on the contrary, they had been engaged in some very worried and worrying correspondence with GQG and with their cavalry corps over the previous two days. The dichotomy is difficult to understand and impossible to explain. At 13.00 on 20 August, even as 9 DC was about to clash with German outposts of 18 AK between Neufchâteau and Libramont, de Langle wrote to General Abbonneau, commander of the provisional cavalry corps: 'There is no change in your mission of exploration towards Bastogne and Saint–Hubert. The enemy appears to be slipping across our front in a flank–march; if he turns towards my army, it is your task to find the right wing of the forces oriented towards me'.[22] Fifteen minutes later (at 13.15), chief of staff General Maistre telephoned Joffre's staff at GQG:

Map 27

You will have received reports indicating that several significant enemy columns are marching west–north–west and that their vanguards reached a line Neufchâteau–Bastogne and further

18   J. Moreau, *22 août 1914, Journal du commandant Jean Moreau, chef d'état-major de la 3e Division Coloniale*, (retranscribed and with commentary by Éric Labayle et Jean-Louis Philippart, Anvoi, Parçay-sur-Vienne, 2002) [Rossignol], p.54.

19   AAT 22N816/29/1: Papers of 1 Bureau, 12 CA: a copy of *Ordre particulier au 2e Corps, Corps Colonial et 12e Corps, de IV armée, 21 août, 13.00*.

20   Grasset, *Virton*, p.125; and Burne, *The Battle of Virton*, pp.47-49.

21   Cordonnier, *Une brigade au Feu (Potins de Guerre)* (Henri Charles-Lavauzelle, Paris, 1921), p.252.

22   AFGG I/1, Annex 636: [Fourth Army] *Stenay, 20 août, 13.00: au général commandant la 4e division de cavalerie*.

north at about 10.00. I cannot predict whether these masses will continue their flank–march tomorrow [21 August] or turn in whole or in part towards me. I must, in any case, envisage the possibility of this latter hypothesis. In the case that the enemy presents himself tomorrow on the front Bertrix, Saint-Médard, Rossignol, Étalle and even in the direction of Arlon and Virton, I must ask what are the Commander–in–Chief's intentions with regard to the steps to be taken by my army? Should I await the arrival of the enemy on my existing front of Montmédy, Sedan? Or should I seek battle in the clearings of Florenville and Neufchâteau?[23]

Thus the argument that de Langle and his Fourth Army were unaware of the threat posed to them by the German forces known to be in the Ardennes, and the very real possibility that those forces would turn and march through the forest towards the Semoy river, is erroneous. This raises the almost unanswerable question as to how de Langle and Maistre subsequently thought that they could reach Neufchâteau unopposed and meet the enemy on the other side of the forest. Perhaps they convinced themselves that the German forces had marched away to the north–west, leaving them free passage, but that is hardly tenable. Even as Maistre was on the telephone to GQG, the cavalry corps was engaged in a sharp four–hour skirmish with large elements of 18 AK just north of Neufchâteau.[24] And reconnaissance reports from 4 DC received at Fourth Army headquarters early on 22 August showed de Langle that those Germans were still in place.[25] This highlights the delinquent behaviour of Fourth Army staff in not sharing their concerns with their corps commanders and not putting in place contingency plans in the event that Maistre's fears were realised. And indeed history shows that the German masses identified by Maistre did indeed turn to confront de Langle's army, on the very line which Maistre had predicted, just twenty–four hours later than he feared. In the meantime, de Langle sent his army north, allowing his troops to believe that the orders of the day where 'for no more than a simple march to get through the forested zone.'[26]

After the war, de Langle tried to blame Joffre for the lack of security, claiming that Joffre had prohibited proper reconnaissance for reasons of secrecy.[27] On the contrary, Joffre's response to Maistre's call for guidance was to authorise de Langle to send strong, mixed–arms advance guards from that evening [20 August] onwards up to 'a general line Bièvre, Paliseul, Bertrix, Straimont, Tintigny in order to secure the advance of your army beyond the Semoy.'[28] In fact, despite this authority to secure his advance, de Langle never secured Tintigny or the Étalle corridor, leading in part to the defeat at Rossignol; and although, as will be shown, he set up a very strong security screen at Saint-Médard between Bertrix and Straimont, he only did this at 05.00 on the morning of 22 August, about thirty–six hours after he was encouraged by Joffre to do so.[29] And, most interesting of all, each of the French Fourth Army columns which engaged the Germans on 22 August did so after they had reached and then marched beyond the cover of such protective detachments as were in place. This needs further analysis in search of an explanation.

---

23   AFGG I/1, Annex 637: [Fourth Army] *20 août, 13.15: communication téléphonique. Général Maistre et commandant de la Fontaine avec GQG (commandant Bel).*

24   AFGG I/1, Annex 641: [Fourth Army, 20 August] *Compte rendu de la IVe armée* [received at GQG by Lieutenant–Colonel Brécard from Captain Godinot at 23.59].

25   AFGG I/1, Annex 808: *Poste de Stenay. Reçu de Baalon, le 22 à 4.50, par téléphone: Général commandant 4e division cavalerie télégraphique suit.* [Telegram relayed to Fourth Army from 4 DC, sent at 20.20 on 21 August, received at 04.50 on 22 August].

26   General J. Paloque, 1914, *Bertrix,* (Charles-Lavauzelle & Cie., Paris, 1932), p.33.

27   De Langle de Cary, *Souvenirs de Commandement, 1914-1916* (Paris, 1935), pp.11–16.

28   AFGG I/1, Annex 593: [GQG] *20 août, 20.50:Ordre au commandant de la IVe armée* à *Stenay.*

29   Paloque, *Bertrix*, p.12.

Many historians have noted the peculiar formation adopted by de Langle's army for its advance, sometimes called the 'stepped–echelon' or 'staircase' formation in which each corps was to march to the right of and a little behind its neighbour, starting with 11 CA on the extreme left.[30] This complex manoeuvre, which in itself reinforced both the need for and the absence of control at army level over timings and coordination, was dictated by the terrain. Firstly, the river Semoy winds significantly to the north–west from Tintigny to the Meuse, so de Langle's left flank started at least twenty–five kilometres further north than his right wing; secondly, the lie of the land and the main road network had a broad north–east to south–west orientation, so an advance due north cut across the grain. The protective detachments were in positions at the head of zones which had been allocated on a north–east facing front, before the axis of advance changed to due north. Thus the protective detachment of 17 CA at Saint–Médard was on 22 August in 12 CA's new zone of operations, that of 11 CA in 17 CA's new zone – and 11 CA had no protective detachment at all, only the advance guard which marched at the head of its main column.[31] These advance detachments were effectively fixed in place, with orders to join the rear of their own column when relieved by the head of the column whose zone they were now in.[32] Ironically achieving the reverse of what has been assumed (that the unit on the right protected the flank of the unit on the left), these fixed flank guards from the unit on the left protected the advance of the unit on the right, at least until they were overtaken. The tactical problems experienced by the French came from poor individual column security after the strong but static mixed–arms screens had been left behind.

Map 28

Apart from specifying those protective detachments, de Langle de Cary allowed his corps commanders to make their own arrangements for the security of their own individual columns, neither adopting the new doctrine nor taking any steps of his own under the old doctrine to secure the passage of his army through that difficult terrain.[33] The best that can be assumed of him and his staff is that they believed Fourth Army to be sufficiently well trained that all could be relied upon at least to protect themselves according to the principles of the 1895 regulations. The reality was to prove them either naively over–optimistic or professionally negligent, or both. The proof, in retrospect, of the need for de Langle to have taken a firmer hand in guiding his army across the forest is shown in particular by the lack of basic march precautions taken by 17 CA and CAC, whose travails are examined in later chapters. But judging Fourth Army's march discipline against the 1895 Regulations, it was not uniformly bad: General Roques's 12 CA marched with a battalion–strength flank guard on its vulnerable right flank;[34] on the far–left, General Eydoux's 11 CA pushed two battalions of infantry, a battery of field artillery and a half–squadron of cavalry up to Porcheresse on its north–western flank, to guard against a German thrust from beyond the river Lesse.[35] Yet 33 DI advanced into the forest north of Bertrix without any flank guard at all. One is struck by the inconsistency that permeates French performance, and reasons for this must be sought.

There remains the question of the role of the army's provisional CC. It has been shown above that de Langle had expressed considerable concern about the danger of a sizeable German force turning south to confront him, and so had ordered General Abbonneau's cavalry to scout ahead of the army. In his general order for operations on 22 August, de Langle ordered the cavalry to reconnoitre the enemy's movements south of the Recogne–Libin–Beauraing road. It was to determine how far

Map 29

30   See for example: Strachan, *To Arms*, p.218; Goya, *La chair et l'acier*, p.17; Stevenson, *1914-1918*, p.53.
31   Bujac, *Le Général Eydoux*, pp.42, 49 and 64.
32   For example: AFGG I/1, Annex 780: *12e corps d'armée, poste de commandement des Deux–Villes, 21 août 1914, 23.00: Ordre général nr13 pour les opérations du 23 août*: paragraph IV.
33   See the discussion of 'Doctrine' in Chapter 7, below.
34   AAT 26N136/1: JMO of 12 CA.
35   AFGG I/1 (1936), p.409.

west had come the enemy columns which might potentially head south, delay the advance of such enemy forces if they threatened the left of the army and, if battle commenced, operate on the left wing of 11 CA.[36] It is a matter of history that the cavalry corps did not do what de Langle had asked them to do, the question is why not?

As usual, there is no one single reason for this failure, but multiple aspects. One of the two cavalry divisions – 9 DC – had been battered in the three–hour skirmish with 25 ID's infantry and artillery on 20 August and now declared itself too tired to continue to operate.[37] It remained virtually inactive in and around Bièvre on the left flank on both 21 and 22 August. This "democratic" tendency, bordering on insubordination, for senior French officers to decide whether they could or would implement their orders can be noticed elsewhere;[38] but in this case it meant that half de Langle's strategic cavalry screen declared itself unable to take part in the most crucial part of the operation – and the decision was not queried or countermanded.

That left the other division – 4 DC – to discharge the scouting mission. On 21 August it was in the right place to do so. General D'Urbal's brigade of dragoons was deployed in front of the army, at the crossroads north of Bertrix, coincidentally at the spot where 33 DI was to be ambushed by 21 ID the next day. D'Urbal sent out squadron–strength patrols (250 horsemen), to watch the Germans at Libramont and at Libin. His reports to de Langle made it clear that significant German forces were still in place, in front of the army and on the eve of the offensive. But despite the obvious requirement to keep track of those enemy forces, the patrols were withdrawn at 15.00 and the brigade packed up at 16.00 – as if on manoeuvres – so they could ride to their billets twenty–five kilometres away at Graide on the left flank.[39] They left the vital crossroads unguarded and according to d'Urbal they regarded their security mission as over.[40] It is worth noting two points: that despite this inauspicious beginning, General d'Urbal rose rapidly in the following months to division, corps and eventually army command; he evidently had qualities of energetic resilience and, perhaps, an ability to learn rapidly from experience. Secondly General Abonneau chose to reinterpret his orders in a way that deprived the army of its reconnaissance screen: 'The cavalry corps's mission (in addition to its scouting mission already defined) is to operate on the left wing of 11 CA and to delay the advance of enemy forces which will threaten the left of the army.'[41] From the left wing, the cavalry could not reconnoitre around Recogne, from where 18 AK would set out to defeat the French at Bertrix, nor could it delay, for example, the German columns which won the race into Maissin village. It was an important difference in interpretation and one which left the advancing columns of Fourth Army far more vulnerable than de Langle had intended.

To compound his delinquent behavior, Abonneau then failed to discharge even the mission he had chosen. On 22 August, d'Urbal records that his brigade covered the concentration of the division into columns preparatory to advancing north towards Vonêche. This town was at the northern edge of the zone allocated by Fourth Army for scouting, so it looks as if Abonneau intended to commence his mission. Had he done so, his cavalry would have been behind 18 AK's right flank, between it and 8 AK. Conditions would inadvertently have been set up to reveal the operational opportunity to turn 18 AK's right flank in coordination with the tactical opportunity at

36   AFGG I/1, Annex 757, op. cit.; de Langle's operational order for 22 August.
37   AFGG I/1, Annex 807: [Provisional cavalry corps] *1k. ouest de Bertrix, 21 août, midi: Général commandant 4e DC* à *général commandant armée de Stenay* à *Stenay.*
38   For example: the unilateral decision of General Rabier to keep his 4 DI south of the forests on the night of 21–22 August; see AFGG I/1 Annex 767: *Compte rendu du général Gérard apporté par agent liaison, 22 heures, 21 août.*
39   General V. D'Urbal, *Souvenirs et Anecdotes de Guerre 1914-1916* (Berger-Levrault, Paris, 1939), p.25.
40   Ibid.
41   AFGG I/1, Annex 982: Corps provisoire de cavalerie. Bièvre, 22 août 1914. 06.00: Ordre nr.3 Opérations du 22 août.

Maissin described in Chapter 4. But Abonneau seems to have been put off by the activity of small columns of German infantry filtering through the woods, and instead withdrew to the south.[42] D'Urbal says that shortly afterwards Abonneau was diagnosed with stress and became unable to command;[43] he was replaced by General de Buyer on 13 October 1914.[44] Ironically, there was no serious German threat in that area, as testified by 8 [German] Cuirassiers, the divisional cavalry of 15 ID (8 AK). On 22 August that regiment stood for hours in the hot sun near the village of Sohier, just six kilometres west of Abonneau's intended target, Vonêche. They watched, they took shelter from enemy artillery and they deduced that they were faced by an enemy cavalry division; but they were not attacked, nor did they themselves advance. In the evening they received orders along with the rest of 15 ID to march south on 23 August, which they did, reaching Porcheresse unopposed.[45] Porcheresse was where the flank guard of the French 22 DI had stood idle for the whole of 22 August, and from where it had been subsequently withdrawn.

The unwillingness of these large bodies of French cavalry to take on and force the German protective screen prevented them from performing a valid reconnaissance role. The right questions were asked by Fourth Army staff, but the execution was neither performed nor supervised properly. As a result, de Langle's powerful cavalry corps failed in its mission to scout in front of Fourth Army during the advance through the forest and in particular failed in the specific task of finding and reporting on the approaching German columns.

On the day of the battle the inherent weaknesses within the whole of Fourth Army revealed themselves. Without good communications there can be no command or control, and Fourth Army's communications proved to be appalling. There was a technical aspect and there was a human aspect. Taking the latter first, it is clear that all units within Fourth Army had extremely poor discipline when it came to reporting up to headquarters to keep them informed. On the far left, General Eydoux reported at about 10.00 that his troops had occupied Maissin and that he was consolidating his position.[46] He failed to report again until after 16.45, by which time he had lost Maissin and was coming to the end of a five–hour battle to retake it. In the centre, General Roques was reporting good progress by 12 CA (as well he might, given the weak opposition he was facing) but in his ignorance of both his tactical and operational opportunities, he failed to give his army commander any useful intelligence about the weakness of the enemy or the gap in the enemy defence between Saint Médard and Bertrix. On the right, General Lefèvre also was unaware of the true situation of his CAC at Rossignol. There was no chance for de Langle to take command or control since he did not know what was going on:

> At this moment [16.45] General de Langle had the impression that the centre and left of his army were continuing their march without incident. 12 CA had just reached Saint–Médard where the enemy was giving way, and the three columns of 17 CA had debouched at 11.00 north of Bertrix, Acremont and Offagne. The commander of Fourth Army could furthermore still have the impression that the German columns were continuing their march to the north–west, because he had received reports that two brigades, having left Neufchâteau that morning were heading via Recogne towards Libin.[47]

42   D'Urbal, op. cit., p.27.
43   Ibid., p.6.
44   Ibid., p.3; and AFGG X/2, p.1023.
45   *History of the 8th Cuirassier Cavalry Regiment*, (1929), IWM Collection.
46   AFGG I/1, Annex 927: [11 CA] *De Paliseul, déposé le 22/8 à 10.10: Général commandant 11e corps* à commandant *armée Stenay.* [Received at Stenay at 10.55].
47   AFGG I/1, (1936), p.414.

The events described above were more than five hours old; 11 CA had failed to report, the others were slow, out–of–date and ill–informed. All of this was primarily due to the senior French commanders simply failing to report properly. But they were not helped by the technical side of French communications systems.

In preparation for the offensive, de Langle set up two new forward telegraph offices, one at Bouillon and one at Florenville.[48] From there, it seems to have been a case of using couriers or the Belgian public telephone network from local Post Offices in order to communicate with the front. The crucial order from de Langle to Lefèvre, authorising the release of 2 DIC from reserve, was sent to Florenville for onward transmission – apparently by courier –to CAC headquarters at Jamoigne: 'let the colonial corps Jamoigne [sic] know that he can, if necessary, use his second division'.[49] This was not an isolated instance; it has already been shown that General Abonneau's last vital message took eight–and–a–half hours to get through to de Langle's headquarters.

The one area where de Langle did attempt to assert some control over the conduct of the day's fighting was on his extreme right, where his 2 CA was supposedly in liaison with Boelle's 4 CA of Third Army in the vicinity of Virton. Following the very early reversal suffered by 5 CA west of Longwy, General Ruffey asked de Langle for the support from Gérard's 2 CA to help him regroup. De Langle responded positively, ordering Gérard to use his 3 DI to help Boelle at Virton, instead of supporting the fighting in the Semoy valley. Communications between the two army headquarters were clearly better than between Fourth Army and its own corps. Because of his ignorance of his own state of affairs, de Langle was influenced to help Ruffey rather than himself.

De Langle's failures in command, control and communication during the fighting on 22 August had been preceded by failures in the communication of relevant intelligence. The data was available, he and Maistre had a clear appreciation of the operational situation, but they did not prepare their subordinates in anything like a proper professional manner. The result was to place the individual corps of Fourth Army in a variety of tactical situations which ranged from fortuitously good (12 CA at Neufchâteau) to the unexpectedly bad (CAC at Rossignol), with shades of difficulty in between. During the tactical encounters, small–unit training within Fourth Army would be tested to breaking point.

The operational overview has shown how the concentration and deployment of the German Fifth Army went smoothly according to OHL's strategic plan. Mobilising and concentrating between 2 and 16 August at various railheads behind the powerful protection of the *Moselstellung*, and with the additional security afforded by the permanent frontier force of 16 AK in front of the fortress zone, the two remaining regular and two additional reserve corps then waited patiently for the order from OHL for the offensive to begin. That order having been given on 17 August for implementation on 18 August, it was actually on the morning of 19 August that Fifth Army began to move out from the protection of the *Moselstellung*.[50] They had the shortest distance to go in order to discharge their mission and had to give time for the other armies to get ahead.

The strategic overview showed how the early invasion of Luxembourg established a south–facing defensive line using units from the *Grenzschutztruppen*, with Arlon as a *point d'appui* on the right flank at the head of the Étalle corridor. On 19 August, Crown Prince William moved the main body of his army to occupy that line in strength. This entailed a long, westerly loop around the *Moselstellung*, a movement that contributed greatly to French intelligence's mistaken assessment

Map 7

---

48   AFGG I/1, Annex 636, op. cit.
49   AFGG I/1, Annex 861: [Fourth Army] *Stenay, 22 août, 16.45: Commandant armée à commandant 12e corps, Florenville.*
50   *Weltkrieg 1*, p.229.

that the primary German manoeuvre in the Ardennes was towards the north-west. Fifth Army was also required to keep closely in touch with Fourth Army on its right.

Once Luxembourg had been secured, and Arlon occupied, William's plan envisaged the capture, if possible, of the ancient French fortress of Longwy. It was important to get the earliest assessment of French intentions, so the German cavalry screen would advance into contact and establish the positions of the French screen and their main defensive line. Then a special siege detachment, complete with the heavy guns necessary for the reduction of fixed fortifications, would be brought into position. William's initial advance was protected by 4 Cavalry Corps (HKK), which had been operating in front of the *Moselstellung*, under the direct control of OHL, since the start of the war.

By 10 August, following a strong probe and major skirmish at Mangiennes, 4 HKK had established beyond doubt that the French had set up their main defence behind the line of the river Othain, twenty–eight kilometres south of Longwy. 3 KD was therefore sent west to determine the extent of the French defences, and if possible find an open flank. It reached Arlon on 11 August and Étalle on 14 August, where it encountered French outposts. In the following days it skirmished with the French 4 Cavalry Division in the Étalle corridor, pushing that unit back down the Semoy valley to the vicinity of Tintigny.[51] Meanwhile 6 KD remained as a security screen in front of Fifth Army in anticipation of a French attack out of Verdun.

Map 30

There was a period of eight days (from 10 to 18 August) during which Fifth Army watched and waited for signs of that attack. On 19 August, as outlined above, 5 AK and 13 AK marched into Luxembourg to occupy the terrain around Arlon in strength. Then on 20 August, the siege of Longwy was initiated. A special detachment was formed under the command of one of Fifth Army's specialist staff officers, Lieutenant-General Kaempffer. It consisted of 52 Infantry Brigade, taken from 13 AK; 23 Reserve Infantry Brigade from 6 RAK; one 210mm mortar regiment, two 155mm heavy field–howitzer battalions and 20 Pioneer Regiment.[52] On 20 August, the Detachment's heavy artillery was hauled to and took up positions around Differdange, some five or six kilometres from Longwy, while the infantry took up investing positions on the heights at Rodingen [Rodange]. The Longwy fortress which Kaempffer was to attack had been built by Louis XIV's famous military engineer Sébastien Vauban in the seventeenth century, and had hardly changed since that time. Star–shaped bastions, ditch and escarpment, low, deep earthen walls buttressed with stone testified to the then state–of–the–art military architecture which had been Vauban's signature; but it was hardly a match for early–twentieth century high explosive. Furthermore, German General Staff efficiency had ensured that, through a long term programme of spying and intelligence gathering, up–to–date records of every single detail of the fortifications and garrison had been gathered by intelligence for decades, updated regularly and held for the moment when they might be needed.[53] Nevertheless, even an obsolete fortress like Longwy was to prove a hard nut to crack, as will be shown below, begging the question whether Joffre might have made better use of its defensive capabilities.

The decision to start the siege of Longwy must be seen in a wider operational context. The likelihood was that it would provoke a French response, and until Crown Prince William moved his main force forwards, Kaempffer's detachment would be in an exposed position. Although nowhere explicitly stated, there is an implication that the siege was part of Fifth Army's overall intent to move down into the line of the Chiers–Crusnes rivers, as they were to do two days later.

51 *Weltkrieg 1*, p.124.
52 *Weltkrieg 1*, p.230.
53 BA/MA PH3/629: Longwy, a file belonging to Pioneer Battalion 20.

The strategic role of Fifth Army may have been one of absolute defence, but that did not mean that Crown Prince William could not exercise the freedom traditionally claimed by Prussian army commanders to choose independently his operational and tactical plans. William's power and independent authority were of course bolstered by his position as heir to the throne. Of the two major operational decisions taken by Fifth Army during the campaign and battle, the first – the operational plan to send the army south on the morning of 22 August – was central to the ensuing action.

After several days of waiting impatiently for signs of the expected French offensive, William decided to act. Intelligence had shown the build–up of major French forces on his front; the French would undoubtedly attack in the very near future. William decided to attack first.[54] In order to persuade OHL to allow him 'off the leash', he and his Chief of Staff, Lieutenant–General von Knobelsdorf, developed the argument that Fifth Army needed to find better defensive positions than those currently occupied.[55] The line from Arlon east to Luxembourg was studded with woods and forests, hills and gorges, small villages and streams, terrain which was unfavourable to defensive artillery, whereas only ten kilometres south, on the plateaux stretching either side of Longwy and (particularly on the eastern side) overlooking the plains stretching down to Verdun, the line of the Crusnes and Chiers rivers offered the perfect battlefield, especially for the Crown Prince's artillery. On the morning of 21 August, just as the French were making final preparations for their attack, the Crown Prince and his staff obtained grudging permission from OHL to advance, but with strict caveats not to go beyond the Crusnes–Chiers river line.[56]

The plans drawn up on the evening of 21 August to implement the advance required 5 AK, on the right wing of Fifth Army, to march due south from around Arlon and achieve defensive positions on the southern edge of the forested belt above Ethe and Virton. This effectively left the Semoy valley and the route up the 'Étalle corridor' into Arlon devoid of protection (an issue which will be dealt with elsewhere) and moved the right flank of Fifth Army down to the next river valley, that of the Vire. There the village of Roblemont, only two kilometres or so north and west of Virton, was situated on a narrow promontory jutting out into the valleys; forests to the north gave the promontory the shape and status of an observation platform, an ideal defensive node upon which to anchor the right wing of the army. Its occupation and defence was part of the mission of 10 ID of 5 AK.

But Fifth Army's change of direction from south–west to due south was taken without consultation with its neighbouring Fourth Army, thus creating a twenty–kilometre gap between the two armies. This was a drawback of the German tendency for OHL to allow its senior commanders a degree of latitude in determining the extent of their operational freedom. It was a consultative process which allowed the strongest will (in this case the Crown Prince) to override and 'persuade' the weaker (in this case von Moltke and his staff). The result was the twenty–kilometre gap which, as has been shown in the examination of the neighbouring German Fourth Army, Duke Albrecht's nearest corps had to fill. However, the command decisions arising from Fifth Army's swing south and the resultant gap became a defining moment in the Battle of the Ardennes, coincidently working very much in Germany's favour. Duke Albrecht's impromptu response to the reports of the gap between him and his neighbour resulted in his left wing (6 AK) arriving at Tintigny, Bellefontaine and Rossignol, in the right place and at the right time to stymie the advance of de Langle's right wing (2 CA). This was not a considered battle–decision based on Duke Albrecht's operational plan, nor was it based on any sound intelligence aimed at thwarting a specific French attack; on the contrary, at this stage Duke Albrecht was largely ignorant of French intentions. But whatever the

54   Herwig, op. cit., p.147.
55   Bircher, *Die Schlacht bei Ethe-Virton*, pp.7–9; and *Weltkrieg 1*, p.305.
56   *Weltkrieg 1*, pp.305–307.

intention, the outcome was the same, a series of encounter battles in which the German forces were placed in better positions than perhaps they had a right to expect and in which tactical superiority would decide victor and vanquished.

Once Fifth Army had committed 5 AK and 13 AK to the move southwards on the right wing, and once contact had been made by those two corps with significant enemy forces, there was little that Crown Prince William and his staff could do except await the outcome of the fighting. Similarly, in the centre, 5 RAK and 6 RAK were committed to march southwards past Longwy towards the Crusnes valley and, once confronted by Sarrail's 6 CA, simply had to fight their own tactical battles. The clashes with the French had commenced while the fog still lay thick over the ground, and several hours passed before a clear picture of the developing action could be gained. But the Crown Prince had one more card to play. He had held back 16 AK (the permanent frontier force) in front of the *Moselstellung* in case the French launched a direct attack out of Verdun. There were five French reserve divisions on the Meuse Heights and in German military understanding there was no reason for the French not to use them in an offensive role. However, reconnaissance and intelligence on the morning of 22 August showed that those French forces were too far away to intervene before nightfall, so eventually William felt secure enough to release 16 AK and order it to execute an enveloping move around Sarrail's right flank. During the course of the afternoon, this operational decision proved its effectiveness, and Sarrail was forced to order his right-hand division to withdraw to avoid being outflanked. The rest of 6 CA had to conform to this move.

Finally in terms of Fifth Army's operational command and control, there was the confident, timely and firm way in which the Crown Prince's staff handled the Kaempffer Detachment. This small but powerful force of infantry and artillery had been drawn largely from operational divisions (mainly from 13 AK) and had consequently weakened them. During 22 August, Fifth Army temporarily returned both infantry and artillery to their original commands in order to confront the French attack. At the end of the day, they were returned to General Kaempfer to continue the siege. So too, the heavy artillery allocated to the siege detachment was used on 22 August to counter the French assault, and was particularly effective with its long-range fire in pursuing the routed infantry of 9 DI over the Tellancourt plateau.[57] Such instant decision-making, and such immediate execution points to a command and control system within Fifth Army that was very much fit for purpose.

Opposite Crown Prince William's front lay Ruffey's Third Army. Ruffey was the first army commander to be relieved of his command by Joffre in the cull of senior officers during August 1914. He lost his job on 30 August, just a week after the battle described in this chapter.[58] One might think that he was therefore the worst of the five initial army generals and that the performance of his Third Army and his staff was so poor that it demanded his removal. But Barbara Tuchman has put forward a suggestion that it was Ruffey's own criticisms of Joffre and GQG which led to his dismissal.[59] It will be argued below that Ruffey's performance stands up well compared to that of his colleague de Langle de Cary, who went on to command a group of armies. After the war, Ruffey certainly felt himself to have been made a scapegoat for the endemic failures during the Battles of the Frontiers.[60]

Joffre's strategic plan required that Third Army protect the right flank of Fourth Army's advance, and to do that it was to orientate itself in the general direction of Arlon. This town, it will be

57   *Weltkrieg 1*, pp.320–321.
58   AFGG X/1, p.157.
59   Tuchman, *The Guns of August*, p.286.
60   Ibid., pp.460–461.

recalled, was situated at the top (north–eastern) end of the Semoy river valley, a classic invasion route into and out of France. Units of the German *Grenzschutzentruppen* had occupied Arlon as early as 12 August as part of their defensive line. But Joffre's plan called for Ruffey to approach it from due south, not the south–west. This in turn would open Ruffey's own right flank to a sally from the *Moselstellung,* which had to be guarded against. It was to be a long approach march into enemy territory; from the start line behind the Othain to the river Chiers was approximately twenty–seven kilometres (nearly seven hours' standard march, planned for 21 August) and from the Chiers to Arlon another twenty–six kilometers (planned for 22 August). To accomplish his task, Ruffey had three corps, but one (6 CA) contained three well–trained divisions of the *couverture,* with six battalions of élite *chasseurs à pied* (BCP) and five groups of heavy artillery attached.[61] Ruffey was also given the Third Group of reserve divisions, initially three divisions, to be used for the defence of Verdun, the Meuse Heights and, potentially, Ruffey's extending flank.

Ruffey's plan seems to have been similar in structure and process to that of de Langle: a set of daily operational orders of a logistical nature (destination and route for each unit) issued to execute GQG's instruction in stages. And as with de Langle, there seems to have been an inexplicable gap between the sum of the intelligence gathered and the analysis and briefing which emanated from Third Army headquarters. Aerial reconnaissance was used extensively but was actually quite misleading: a report sent to GQG at 11.10 on 20 August said that the region Virton, Arlon, Longwy was absolutely empty of enemy forces.[62] It was incorporated into the evening *compte rendu nr. 32:* 'nothing to report up to 15.00. Agents report a battalion of Landwehr still at Joeuf…the general impression from the inhabitants of frontier villages is that the Germans are retiring to the north to reinforce their troops in Belgium.'[63] The report paints an overall picture of security and lack of concern. Yet within hours the German heavy artillery would start to bombard Longwy, and Kaempffer's detached infantry would advance to commence investing the fortress. German sources show that infantry of their 23 Brigade was actually assembling at Rodange, seven kilometers away from Longwy at the time of the French aerial reconnaissance.[64] It would seem then even at this stage of the war, infantry were already in the habit of dispersing into houses, woods and other cover as soon as an aero engine was heard. So Ruffey's staff received, accepted and passed down an inaccurate and over–optimistic picture of what was in front of them.

But unlike de Langle, Ruffey's secret and personal briefing to his corps commanders was issued alongside the order to attack and was both timely and relevant. It laid out in clear terms the mission of the army, and that of each corps, and thus complemented the more formal instructions for the advance and gave his commanders an understanding of the 'why' as well as the 'what'. This was the sixth personal briefing note which Ruffey had sent out, whereas de Langle's (unnumbered) personal briefing to Fourth army on 20 August seems to have been the only one he issued during the planning of the campaign. It is noteworthy that Ruffey made clear to his senior commanders that the heavy artillery accompanying 6 CA was to be used to help mask the German heavy artillery position at Differdange.[65]

In order to plan properly for the successful outcome of his mission, Ruffey and his staff had three operational issues to address. On his left, his troops had to cross a thick band of forest extending

61   AFGG X/1, pp.158–9 and X/2, pp. 96–7, 322–323, 340–341.
62   AFGG I/1, Annex 629: [Third Army] *Verdun, 20 août, 11.10:* Colonel Lebouc [Deputy chief-of-staff of Third Army] à *Général Berthelot* [GQG].
63   AFGG I/1, Annex 630: [Third Army] *20 août, 18.45: Armée Verdun* à *GQG – Compte rendu de renseignements Nr.32.*
64   *Weltkrieg 1,* p.230.
65   AFGG I/1, Annex 747: *IIIe armée, Verdun, 21 août: Instruction personelle et secrète nr.6 pour la journée du 22 août.*

from the valley of the river Vire at Virton up to the valley of the river Semoy at Étalle; in the centre there was the problem of the German forces beginning the investment of Longwy; and on the right there was the risk of a German thrust out of the *Moselstellung*.

On the left, Boelle's 4 CA had the first problem – one of securing an uncontested march through an extensive thick forest in order to occupy the head of the Semoy river valley near Étalle. The plan was to concentrate on 21 August in the valley of the small twin rivers, the Vire and the Ton, around the rivers' confluence at Virton (8 DI) and two kilometres east at Ethe (7 DI) and then march north. A different main road ran through each of the two villages – one for each divisional column – and then through the forests. Boelle's two divisions, having safely navigated the forests, would then be in a position to fortify the upper reaches of the Semoy, capture Étalle, mask the German forces known to be at Arlon, and prepare to continue an aggressive defence in liaison with de Langle's right wing at Neufchâteau.

In the centre, Brochin's 5 CA was deployed west of the upper Chiers valley on the Tellancourt plateau, with Longwy at its head and Longuyon lower down at the confluence of the Chiers and the Crusnes. Its mission was to march past Longwy on the western side and head north to link up with the flank of Boelle's corps near the little village of Bleid, some two kilometres east of, and on a line with 7 DI at Ethe. It would then go on to hold the centre of the long defensive line planned to stretch down from Arlon to Verdun. But there was a problem at Longwy, a bottleneck on the route north. At 06.00 on 21 August the heavy German siege guns of Kaempffler's detachment had started to bombard the fortress,[66] and supporting infantry had marched up to and west around the walls, some to commence the investiture, some to provide protection against a possible French move from the south.[67] The French outposts could see, and reported to 5 CA headquarters, the trenches of the protection force on the slopes opposite the Tellancourt plateau, blocking their route.[68] 5 CA would have to attack and break through known German defences of unknown strength in order to continue their march north. Brochin's main force would have an approach march of more than ten kilometres, followed by an attack across a three–kilometre valley and up the slopes beyond. Only then could his troops begin the final seven–kilometre march to achieve their assigned objective. It was a tall order; in fact it is difficult with hindsight to see how 5 CA could ever have been expected to keep up with 4 CA, given that the latter had planned for an uninterrupted march, whereas the former was planning an attack on those trenches.

The problem on the right flank, of a potential German counter–attack out of the *Moselstellung* towards Verdun, was the one which preoccupied Third Army's staff and GQG the most. As Third Army moved northwards across the face of the powerful German defences, it opened up an ever– widening gap between itself and Verdun. Admittedly it had cavalry (7 DC) to warn of any German movement, and Verdun had its own resident garrison division (72 DR), but the gap needed to be held by a field–infantry force. Ruffey planned to use the Third Group of reserve divisions (54, 55 and 56 DRs) for this purpose.[69] He also planned to echelon his three regular divisions back from left to right, with the extreme right–hand division of 6 CA (40 DI) acting as the immediate flank guard on the march. The ground which 40 DI was to occupy was amongst the most favourable defensive terrain in the region. The high ground at Mercy–le–Haut overlooked the Crusnes valley and provided good observation for artillery. Ruffey had planned well for the protection of his flank.

But the same cannot be said of the other two operational issues. On the left, Boelle's 4 CA closed

Map 32

66   AFGG I/1 (1923), p.374; and *Weltkrieg 1*, p.230.
67   *Weltkrieg 1*, p.230 & p.304.
68   AFGG 1 (1923), p.374.
69   AFGG I/1, Annex 743: *IIIe Armée, Q.G. Verdun, 21 août 1914, 02.00: Ordre général d'opérations nr.16 pour la journée du 21 août*, [section v, para. 6].

up on the southern entrance to the forests and spent the night of 21–22 August firmly ensconced in the village of Virton, with a vanguard out in front and outposts on the forest edge.[70] But Ruffey did not order any operational security – a strong mixed–arms detachment was required by regulations to traverse the forest and secure in advance the exits from the northern side–nor did Boelle think of using his initiative. The consequence was that, on the morning of 22 August, when the first French patrol rode past their outposts into the thick fog, it came into contact almost at once with the advance guard of the German 9 ID which Crown Prince William had sent south during the night from the Étalle region. The Germans had stolen a march from the French through their early departure and were able to stop Boelle's left–hand division in its tracks. The battle was fought at Virton, south of the forest, and not at Étalle in the north on the Semoy as Ruffey had planned. It was a serious blunder by the French commanders, one that would cost them dear, and one that completely upset Joffre's plan.

Maps
33 & 33a

In the centre, the lack of operational planning was more than just a failure to secure the advance through an inhospitable forest. Brochin's 5 CA received no special instructions from Ruffey for dealing with the entrenched German forces in his path. Indeed in the absence of specific evidence, it is not clear whether Third Army headquarters had been informed of their existence by the staff of 5 CA. But the general problem posed by the German siege of Longwy was acknowledged in Ruffey's planning; two divisions of 6 CA were tasked with advancing and masking the German heavy artillery position known to be at Differdange. But the German infantry force (Kaempffer's detachment) on the west side of the fortress received no attention from Third Army's planners.[71]

It was left to General Brochin to plan for what seems with hindsight to have been a formidable task. He set his two divisions in line, side–by–side, with 9 DI on the left and 10 DI on the right.[72] The troops had had two days of rest on 19 and 20 August in their positions south of Longuyon. On 21 August the columns set out at 05.00 for a long march up over the Tellancourt plateau to close with their outposts. At the end of that march the leading reconnaissance units of 9 DI encountered the enemy and launched into an immediate and apparently unplanned and unauthorised assault which continued as darkness fell. After a forty–kilometre march and an impromptu skirmish, the division apparently missed the chance to get its rations.[73] It was not the best start to the operation.

Maps
34 & 34a

9 DI's divisional orders and preparations leave no doubt that a formal attack was planned and with artillery support too.[74] This makes it all the more inexplicable that the high–level operation called for a seven–kilometre march beyond the point of the assault. It is irrelevant that in the event the fog made the artillery impotent – that applied to both sides; from an operational perspective it is clear that 5 CA's advance would at best be delayed for several hours whilst German resistance was crushed, or at worst might not break through. That this was not reflected in the planning by Third Army is inexplicable. To make matters worse, General Ruffey had the reputation of being a proponent of artillery firepower.[75] He had put under Brochin's command his best group of heavy artillery, three batteries of Rimailho 155mm howitzers. These guns were arguably better than the German 150mm of which so much is written, and they were just ten kilometres behind the front.[76]

70   Grasset, *Virton*, pp.18–36.
71   *Weltkrieg 1*, pp.230–231 describes the undisturbed build-up of Kaempffer's detachment from 20 August onwards.
72   AFGG I/1 (1923), p.375.
73   AAT 26N285/1: JMO of 9 DI, entry for 21 August.
74   AAT 25N123/1/1: miscellaneous papers of 131 RI, including a copy of 9 DI's General Order nr.12 for 22 August.
75   Rocolle, op. cit., p.49; and Tuchman, op. cit., p.282; and AAT 7N50/4: a secret note written by Ruffey in August 1913 for the War Ministry on heavy artillery in the field.
76   AFGG I/1, Annex 773: *IIIe Armée, 5e corps d'armée, au Q.G. de Longuyon, 21 août: Ordre général d'opérations nr.17 pour la journée du 22 août,* [section VI]; see also Chapter 8 for a detailed discussion of heavy artillery.

But there were no plans for their use, and on the day of the battle they were left ten kilometres behind the front – just out of range. There is a doctrinal issue here; mainstream French military thinkers did not see a role for slow heavy guns in fast manoeuvre warfare. But Ruffey was supposed to be a proponent of heavy artillery;[77] he if not Brochin could have insisted on a methodical attack using those heavy guns on the Germans known to be west of Longwy, and he alone could have coordinated the movements of the other two corps to fit in to 5 CA's progress. It is possible that Third Army headquarters did not know what 5 CA knew about the German trenches – the archives at Vincennes are silent on the point – in which case Ruffey is absolved of a command error but Third Army's control of its communications was then at fault. So too, only Ruffey could have postponed the start when it was clear that the fog ruled out artillery support. Such staff liaison and activity would become second nature to the French army before the year was out; that it did not happen in August 1914 reflects poorly on French pre–war training and preparation. Looked at from an overall Third Army perspective, Ruffey's planning and preparation were seriously flawed. Only the possibility of a counter–strike out of the *Moselstellung* was catered for, and the failure to anticipate the problems faced by 5 CA was reprehensible. What then of Ruffey's command and control during the battle?

Communications were all–important, as the analyses of de Langle de Cary's and Duke Albrecht's armies have shown, in differing ways. The limitations of technology in August 1914 meant that even the best commander with the best communications (arguably Duke Albrecht) could not keep pace with the development of the action. Nevertheless Ruffey made several good and timely command decisions, which argue in favour of his communication and control capability. He also managed to work from a forward command–post at Marville, forty kilometres closer to the front, leaving his deputy chief–of–staff to manage the main army headquarters at Verdun.[78] This suggests a relatively competent communications system within Third Army. And the surviving record of Ruffey's communications during the battle shows a real–time grasp of the action and an active participation in guiding his units.

During the approach march on the morning of 22 August, 10 DI, the right–hand column of 5 CA, encountered the enemy west of Longwy at about 09.00 and deployed from column to line. This inhibited the forward march of 12 DI on the left flank of 6 CA, and there was for a while a danger that units would get entangled and chaos might ensue. Ruffey's staff made a timely intervention and smoothed the situation out.[79] When it became clear at about 14.45 that 5 CA's attacks had failed, Ruffey asked Sarrail's 6 CA to support 5 CA with its artillery in order to stop the retreat turning into a rout.[80] This event has been recorded by Barbara Tuchman in graphic terms, although she incorrectly attributes it to the battle at Virton, more than twenty–six kilometres away:

At Virton the French VIth Corps under General Sarrail took a German corps in the flank with fire from its 75s. "The battlefield afterwards was an unbelievable spectacle," reported a French officer dazed with horror, "thousands of dead were still standing, supported as if by a flying buttress made of bodies lying in rows on top of each other in an ascending arc from the horizontal to an angle of 60°".[81]

77   Herwig, op. cit., p.146; and Tuchman, op. cit., p.282.
78   AFGG I/1, Annex 850: [Third Army] *Marville, Général commandant IIIe armée à sous–chef d'état–major. Message telephone, 15 heures reçu par le Lt–Colonel Boucher.*
79   AFGG I/1, Annex 845: [Third Army] *Poste de Longuyon, reçu de Marville, 22 août, 09.07: Armée à 6e corps.*
80   AFGG I/1, Annex 849: [Third Army] 14.45: *Armée à 6e corps.*
81   Tuchman, op. cit.,p.284, quoting: Fernand Engerand, *La Bataille de la frontier, aôut 1914* (Brossard, Paris, 1920), pp.499–504. Tuchman's cameo (and error) has been repeated by other authors. See for example: Anthony Clayton,

Ruffey also informed de Langle de Cary of the reverse at Longwy and called for support from Fourth Army's 2 CA to take some pressure off his left wing.[82] He informed Boelle (4 CA) at the same time, and ordered him to support Brochin (5 CA).[83] These are the actions of a general fully in command of his army, adjusting to adverse circumstances and laying alternative plans. Furthermore, as the outcome of 5 CA's defeat appeared ever more disastrous and troops were streaming back in disarray across the Tellancourt plateau, Ruffey sent his chief–of–staff to the spot, where he was able to take charge and set up a fresh line of resistance.[84]

On the left, where Boelle's 4 CA and especially 7 DI at Ethe were in a precarious position, Ruffey had in place his own liaison officer, Captain Pellegrin, who from 09.10 onwards gave lengthy, timely and accurate situation reports back to Third Army headquarters, including at least one telephone call to Ruffey's forward CP at Marville.[85]

On the right wing, a strange command situation had arisen. On the eve of the offensive, at about 10.30 on 21 August, Joffre took Ruffey's three reserve divisions away from him and gave them to General Maunoury, commanding the newly–formed Army of Lorraine.[86] Ruffey had had General Paul Durand's Third Group of reserve divisions under his command from the outset. This group, with support from much of the heavy artillery allocated to Third Army, had been allocated the task in the base documentation of Plan XVII of protecting the Meuse heights, which released the regular forces of Third Army for offensive action.[87] Having been given his orders by Joffre to advance on 21 August, Ruffey's own orders that day included instructions to Durand for 54 DR to relieve 40 DI of flankguard duties around Conflans and Briey.[88] Joffre's major alteration of command arrangements at such a time seems with hindsight bizarre and likely to cause confusion. One might speculate that GQG was hedging its bets by ensuring that, whatever the outcome of the forthcoming offensive, there would be a strong defensive force at Verdun and on the Meuse Heights. If so, the decision demonstrates a cautious, defensive mentality that does not fit in with the generally accepted picture of Joffre throwing everything recklessly into the attack. The change certainly ensured that Ruffey would not put the needs of his offensive ahead of the need for the defence of the gap between Second and Third Armies, but at what cost to the chances of a successful attack?

Ruffey nevertheless worked to make the best of the circumstances. His order to 54 DR to relieve 40 DI (at 02.00 on 21 August)[89] and another at 08.00 for 72 DR to advance and occupy 'centres of resistance' around Hennemont and Pintheville,[90] became at 06.45 on 22 August a request to General Maunoury to move a mixed–arms detachment as soon as possible up to Spincourt.[91] In the event, an outflanking move by the German 16 AK forced Sarrail's 6 CA to retreat to defensive positions, and 54 DR was late in arriving on their flank. But this seems more to do with the sloth of the divisional

(Map 35 note in margin)

Paths of Glory (Cassell, London, 2003), p.28.

82   AFGG I/1, Annex 851: [Third Army] *Télégramme pour Montmédy, Stenay, de Marville, dépôt le 22 août à 15.00: Général commandant armée Verdun à commandant armée Stenay et à général commandant corps Montmédy.*
83   AFGG I/1, Annex 852: [Third Army] *Marville, 22 août, 15.00: Général commandant IIIe armée à général commandant 4e corps.*
84   AFGG I/1 (1936), p.376; and Rocolle, op. cit., pp.120–121.
85   AFGG I/1, Annexes 897 and 898, op. cit.
86   AFGG I/1, Annex 700: *GQG, 21 août, 10.00: Ordre particulier Nr.14.*
87   AFGG I/1 (1936), p.80 & p.351.
88   AFGG I/1, Annex 743: *IIIe Armée, QG Verdun, 21 août, 02.00: Ordre général d'opérations nr16 pour la journée du 21 août.*
89   AFGG I/1, Annex 743, op. cit.
90   AFGG I/1, Annex 744: [Third Army] *21 août, 08.00: Ordre verbal donné par le 3e B.* [Operations Bureau] *de la IIIe armée au Capitaine Corda* [staff officer of 3 group of reserve divisions].
91   AFGG I/1, Annex 844: [Third Army] *au GQ de Verdun, 22 août 1914: Général commandant IIIe armée au general commandant armée de Lorraine, à Verdun.*

general than the change of command. Contrary to what Rocolle has written – that Ruffey's orders were countermanded[92] – Maunoury's first order, at 13.30, confirmed the dispositions which Ruffey had previously made, for 54 DR to advance the five kilometres from Spincourt to a position at Ollières–Domprix, to stop all attacks on the right flank of 6 CA.[93] There was a potential problem of delay inherent in the new command structure, but General Durand, still in command of Third Group under Maunoury, had attempted to minimize this by directly ordering the commander of 54 DR at 08.15 on 22 August to close up his left onto the edge of the Ollières plateau, given Third Army's advance to the north–east.[94] So the onus rested firmly on the commander of 54 DR himself. It should be noted in passing that Durand responded relatively swiftly to Ruffey's request despite the change of command structure – probably because they were both headquartered at Verdun – and that Zuber's pejorative claim that 'they didn't talk to each other…It would be hard to find a worse example of high–level staff work' is simply incorrect.[95] At 16.25, Ruffey's staff was enquiring about the whereabouts of the 54 DR;[96] at 18.30, Durand replied that the division reported that it could only reach Spincourt – not the allocated defensive plateau – by nightfall and then with only one brigade.[97] Given the evidence, the failure of Maunoury's reserve divisions to support Ruffey would have happened without the change of command, because of the poor quality of the lower echelon commanders. Nevertheless, the failure of the reserve divisions, particularly 54 DR, to support Sarrail's (6 CA) right–rear gave the Germans an opportunity which they ruthlessly exploited.

The analysis above finds weaknesses in Third Army's operational planning process with regard to 4 and 5 CAs, although the planning to secure its right flank was sound and only failed in the execution. Ruffey's command and control performance was positive and hands–on during 22 August and his contribution as army commander to the events of the day was considerable. This therefore raises the question whether he deserved to be relieved of his post or was the victim of some internal French military politics, an issue which is outside the scope of this study but deserves further investigation. But in the final analysis, as this operational overview has shown, the initiative was entirely taken from Ruffey by the actions of the German Crown Prince opposite him, something which could have been predicted but which poor French intelligence failed to analyse correctly.

This chapter has examined the performance of the four army commanders and their respective staff organizations, analyzing each individual contribution to the outcome of events in terms of command, control and communications. It has found that French operational planning, as we know it today, was almost non–existent in both Third and Fourth Armies and that specific problems, such as overcoming the German defences west of Longwy and the need to secure the northern side of the forested belt through which many columns had to pass, were inadequately thought through and prepared for. There can be no comparison with the two German commanders on this issue, because their operational role was essentially defensive and reactive.

On the issue of communications, both German commanders were well served by an efficient telephone and telegraph organization, whereas the French Fourth Army's communications were

92   Rocolle, op. cit.,p.113, note 9.
93   AFGG I/1, Annex 880: *Armée de Lorraine, QG Verdun, 22 août 1914, 13.30: Ordre particulier nr.1 à général commandant le 3e gr. De DR., général commandant 67e division.*
94   AFGG I/1, Annex 976: *Télégramme, QG 3e groupe de divisions de reserve à général commandant la 54e Division, reçu à Étain à 08.15.*
95   Zuber, *Ardennes*, p.230.
96   AFGG I/1, Annex 912: *6e CA à armée, Compte rendu, Beuville, 22 août,16.25.*
97   AFGG I/1, Annex 977: *Armée de Lorraine, au GQ à Verdun, 22 août, 18.30: Le général P.Durand, commandant le 3e groupe de divisions de reserve, à M. Le général commandant la IIIe armée. Compte rendu.*

very poor, and contributed significantly to the uncoordinated and ineffective tactical performance of de Langle's units. Ruffey's Third Army seems to have had at least adequate communications infrastructure, which further emphasises the weakness within the Fourth Army, which Joffre had chosen as his strike force.

The quality of communications influenced the quality of command and control; without frequent and timely reports from the fighting line, no army commander could hope to control his battle, and so it proved in the case of de Langle. Both Ruffey and Crown Prince William were, by dint of better information, able to exert some influence over the outcome of their battles, albeit within the constraints of the technology of the period. But Duke Albrecht has been shown to have been the best commander of the four, with a proactive, personal style and strong leadership. His firm handling of his Fourth Army compares most favourably to that of his opponent, and can be seen to have made a significant contribution to the German avoidance of defeat in the Ardennes on 22 August.

Following this operational analysis, it is now appropriate to examine at a tactical level the key individual encounter–battles between de Langle's attacking columns and Duke Albrecht's defensive formations. In the next chapter, the question of the French lost opportunities during those encounters will be explored in full.

General Boelle (with map) of French 4 Corps.

General de Langle de Cary, commander of French 4th Army.

General Eydoux of French 11 CA.

General Joffre.

General Roques of French 4 CA.

General Ruffey, commander of French 3rd Army.

De Langle de Cary (facing camera) with
Joffre on left & unknown general on right.

General Trentinian of French 7 DI.

Generalmajor Crown Prince Wilhelm of Prussia.

Duke Albrecht von Württemberg, command of the German Fourth Army.

The German Chief of General Staff, von Moltke.

French infantry.

French Model 1907 MGs.

French Dragoons operating dismounted.

French 75mm gun.

German infantry.

German Model 1908 MG.

German Cavalry.

German 77 mm gun.

German Howitzer.

General Boelle (4th Corps) watching the fighting at Virton. A good example of a primitive French Corps HQ in action.

Part Two

The French Lost Opportunities

3

Neufchâteau

The operational overview in Chapter 2 has shown that a great opportunity was afforded to Roques's 12 CA to achieve an unexpected victory over its opponents; that the overall odds in favour of the French were more than two–to–one, and higher in specific places on the front; and that only the timidity of Roques's troops prevented the forcing and exploitation of a significant German retreat. Detail now needs to be added to that overview, to examine the extent of the missed opportunity, and to explain why it was missed.

In the twenty–square–kilometre zone between Libramont and Neufchâteau, Duke Albrecht had two army corps, 18 AK and 18 RAK. French intelligence had positively identified the position of the former on 20 August when it fought the French cavalry corps, but lost track of its movements on the evening of 21 August.[1] Evidence of the presence of the reserve army corps at Neufchâteau had been gathered but had been overlooked by staff analysts and operations planners alike.[2] But with the benefit of hindsight, it becomes clear that 18 RAK at Neufchâteau would find itself in the eye of the approaching storm.

Map 36

Several historians, particularly from France as one might expect, have identified that there was some sort of opportunity for the French at Neufchâteau on 22 August, but none have so far come close to explaining how great that opportunity was. One – Pierre Rocolle – has even managed to blur the truth through a significant factual mistake in his account.

Rocolle wrote that Roques's corps was faced by a brigade from the German 21 ID, reinforcing his assertion with a sketch.[3] The individual regimental histories of 21 ID, however, show that that division fought in its entirety on 22 August against the French 33 DI at Bertrix.[4] It only turned southwards, on the course delineated by Rocolle, on the following day, 23 August.[5]

Henry Contamine has produced a reasonably accurate but very short account of the lost opportunity but still without any supporting detail.[6] In 1970 he wrote: 'Finding itself opposite a hole in the enemy line, it [12 CA] hardly engaged at all on 22 August. If it had thrown one of its divisions to the right and one to the left, it might have achieved two notable successes, at Neufchâteau and at Bertrix'.

1   AFGG I/1, Annex 694:*GQG, 21 août, 17.00: Compte rendu de renseignements nr.52.*
2   AFGG I/1, Annex 748: [Fourth Army] *Stenay, 21 août,10.15: Commandant A. Stenay à commandant armée Vitry* [telegramme from Fourth Army to GQG]; and Grasset, *Neufchâteau*, p.3.
3   Rocolle, *Hécatombe*, p.143 and Rocolle's Note 46. See also sketch on p.136.
4   (i) *Das Königlich Preussische Füsilier Regt, Nr 80 im Weltkriege 1914-18, Teil 1* [IR 80] (Oldenburg, Berlin, 1925), pp. 27–35; (ii) *Das Königlich Preussische Infanterie Regt., Nr 81 im Weltkriege 1914-8* [IR 81] (Oldenburg, Berlin, 1932), pp. 26–32; (iii) Walter Rogge *Das Königlich Preussische 2 Nassauische Infanterie Regt., Nr 88 im Weltkriege 1914-18* [IR 88] (Bernard und Graefe, Berlin, 1936), pp. 69–74.
5   *Weltkrieg 1*, pp.338–339.
6   Contamine, *La Victoire de la Marne*, p.122.

English–speaking historians, who in the main have lacked access to un–translated French and German primary sources and rely on translations of mainly secondary sources or the official history, are only now beginning to assess the impact of the lost opportunities. In *Pyrrhic Victory* Doughty merely states: 'XII Corps was, as reported by Fourth Army, in a "good" situation at the end of the day.'[7] Terence Zuber, who purports to have made a tactical study of the whole Battle of the Ardennes, devotes only six short paragraphs to the French perspective, summing up 12 CA's performance thus: 'In spite of the fact that the corps was at most opposed by two German reserve regiments, one of which had no machine–guns or artillery support, the corps stopped 5km short of its objectives. Sixteen of the corps's twenty–four battalions had been engaged. One of the principal reasons for the French defeat in the Ardennes was the inertia of the XII CA'.[8] Zuber adds some detail about the German side but his is still not a balanced assessment, lacking as it does detail on the French side.

None of the above examined the action at Neufchâteau in sufficient detail to prove how overwhelming was Roques's superiority and how great the opportunity afforded him, or most importantly why he failed to grasp it. The two central issues are the relative size of the forces engaged and the use that was made of them. The first key issue, then, is to establish exactly how much resource, in men and firepower, was available to each side.

Map 36a The two divisions of the German 18 RAK opposed two–and–a–half French divisions – two from 12 CA plus the independent 5 Colonial Brigade. But the way in which the two forces collided – the French coming from the south, the Germans from the east – meant that there was an uneven distribution of forces across the battlefield. The Germans were weakest in the west, where their advance guard was out in front, whilst the French were weakest in the east where the 5 Colonial Brigade appeared on its own in front of Neufchâteau. The distribution of weakness versus strength made a significant contribution to the opportunity for French victory.

The French advanced in three columns from the south.[9] Each column fought more or less independently from the others and the action thus divides conveniently into three segments for descriptive purposes. On the French right was 5 Colonial Brigade; in the centre was 23 DI and on the left was 24 DI, both of 12 CA. The corps troops (artillery and reserve infantry) marched behind the left–hand column, which was led by the corps commander, making the French left by far the strongest against the weakest German component. In front of 12 CA rode the 1,000 cavalrymen of the Corps cavalry regiment, providing a strong immediate reconnaissance screen.

The two German divisions were roughly ten kilometres apart, a two–and–a–half hour march at normal road speed. 21 RID spent the night of 21–22 August camped in and around Neufchâteau. 25 RID was further east, under orders to await further instructions near Léglise, still ten kilometres from Neufchâteau. The German high command was undecided whether to send 25 RID south to support its 6 AK in the Semoy valley, or to let it carry on west behind 21 RID; so it stayed where it was on the morning of 22 August, awaiting events.[10]

21 RID was under orders to continue marching westwards, towards Bertrix, on 22 August. In the morning the advance guard marched westwards out of Neufchâteau on the main road towards Bertrix, fifteen kilometres away. It had reached the village of Petitvoir, some five kilometres out of town, when it encountered the advance guard of 24 DI. The three kilometres of ground immediately west of Petitvoir, in which 21 ID's advance guard engaged 24 DI, constitutes the first

7   Doughty, *Pyrrhic Victory*, p.67.
8   Zuber, *Ardennes*, p.141.
9   AFGG I/1 (1923), pp.391–394.
10   *Weltkrieg 1*, pp.311–312.

segment of the battlefield. In the five kilometres between Petitvoir and Neufchâteau, 23 DI engaged the head of the main German column of 21 RID, whilst in Neufchâteau itself, the remainder of 21 RID fought against 5 Colonial Brigade.

In Neufchâteau, the German 41 Reserve Brigade (6000 riflemen), was assembled waiting for the road to clear in front of it before moving out. Three batteries of artillery (18 guns) were with this group. The town was directly in the path of 5 Colonial Brigade – two regiments of infantry (about 6000 riflemen), 12 machine guns, 12 field guns and 25 young reservist cavalrymen. The odds here were about even at the start of the battle.

In the centre, between Neufchâteau and Petitvoir, following the advance guard and leading the main body of the German 21 RID's column was 88 RIR, some 3000 riflemen with two batteries of artillery (12 guns). Their opponents on 22 August were to be 23 DI, approximately 12,000 riflemen, 24 machine guns, 36 field guns and 250 cavalry.[11] The odds in favour of the French were four–to–one in men and three–to–one in guns.

On the western segment of the battlefield, the opposing forces were as follows: the German advance guard consisted of 81 RIR, supported by a squadron of 7 Dragoons, a battery from 21 Reserve Artillery Regiment (21 RAR) and a company of pioneers. There were no machine–guns; the German programme for equipping all units had not yet covered all reserve regiments, and 81 RIR was one that was still waiting for its machine–guns when war broke out.[12] The total complement was some 3000 riflemen, 250 pioneers and 250 cavalrymen with six 77mm field guns. Opposing them would be the whole of the French 24 DI which, when fully deployed, had a complement of about 12,000 riflemen, 24 machine–guns, 36 75mm field guns and 250 cavalry.[13] The divisional column was accompanied by the corps cavalry regiment (1000 horsemen), the corps artillery (48 guns) and the corps's two regiments of reserve infantry (about 6200 riflemen).[14] The odds in favour of the French on this segment were five–to–one in infantry and six–to–one in guns. And the corps cavalry regiment – 21ᵉChasseurs à cheval– was deployed forward and available for scouting and reconnaissance work, where the Germans had but a squadron of reserve horsemen.

It is central to an understanding of the French lost opportunity to appreciate that the fighting west of Petitvoir was limited to three kilometres between Petitvoir itself and the village of Nevraumont; beyond lay a seven–kilometre gap between Nevraumont and Bertrix. Between dawn and 14.00 on 22 August there were no other German troops within twenty kilometres of the gap. The nearest other unit was the small flank guard of two companies from 21 ID which was fighting at Bertrix. This is what Contamine meant when he wrote that if it had thrown one of its divisions to the left, it might have achieved notable success at Bertrix.[15] It is impossible to speculate on what might have happened if Roques had thrown his over-abundant cavalry out to the left into the gap, but it is fair to highlight the military potential arising from a French advance into the seven–kilometre gap onto the flank of 21 ID, and to seek to establish why the French failed to realise that potential. The odds in favour of the French in that area were five–to–one in men and six–to–one in guns, more than enough to fix the enemy in front of them and seek an open flank. Furthermore, the corps cavalry regiment, 21 Chasseurs, was deployed to the left once the main action had started and was perfectly

11   AFGG X/2, pp.185–7.
12   Generalmajor a D von Jordon, *Das Reserve Infanterie Regiment Nr 81 im Weltkrieg* [RIR 81] (Hans Druner, Osnabrück, 1933), p.7.
13   AFGG X/2, pp.193–5.
14   AFGG X/1, pp.723–5.
15   See Note 8, above: Contamine, *Marne*, p.122.

positioned to push out strong patrols to discover the gap. French doctrine clearly states that the role of the cavalry in battle was to do just that: push forward, discover weaknesses, report back. But the commander of *21 Chasseurs* did not do so of his own initiative, nor was he ordered to do so by Roques, his immediate superior.

The second opportunity suggested by Contamine was for 12 CA to throw one of its divisions to the right and 'achieve a notable success' at Neufchâteau. Following the exposition of forces, terrain and orientation above, it becomes clear that Contamine was referring to the opportunity for the central French column (23 DI) to break the fragile German defence between the town and Petitvoir and encircle the town from the open west side while the remaining German forces (the eastern segment) were fixed in place by the frontal attack of 5 Colonial Brigade.

It is time to look at the fighting, starting with the units on the French right flank, with the encounter between the French 5 Colonial Brigade and the German 41 Reserve Brigade reinforced later by 25 RID. 5 Colonial Brigade was an ad–hoc, independent mixed–arms formation attached to CAC and under the command of General Goullet. It was made up of un-brigaded units left over after CAC had taken its official complement: two surplus regiments of colonial infantry, supported by one surplus field artillery group (three 4–gun batteries) and a platoon of reserve cavalry.[16] Apart from the cavalry, it was, like all the colonials, made up of experienced officers and soldiers – white colonials not non–European troops such as the famous Moroccan Division – many of whom had seen action abroad. It was considered an elite formation. When the main column of CAC, led by 3 DIC, was brought to action in the Rossignol forest, 12 kilometres south of Neufchâteau, 5 Colonial Brigade, marching on a parallel track through the forest, reached Neufchâteau unopposed and proceeded to assault the town. While never under the control of Roques's 12 CA, it nevertheless fought alongside them.

On the German side, the main body of 21 RID, 41 Reserve Brigade, was initially spread out across the town in column, waiting for the road ahead to clear so they could march westwards behind their advance guard. When the action began, the brigade deployed onto the slopes facing south towards the oncoming enemy. The German corps commander, General von Steuben, had placed his second division, 25 RID, about ten kilometres away to the south–east. Given the general movement of the whole army to the west, it meant that this division was coincidentally in a good position to intervene on the flank of the French attack. It was scattered in its overnight positions in Léglise and the surrounding villages. The nearest battalion was at Assenois, seven kilometres by road to Neufchâteau but only two kilometres away from the battlefield if approaching directly from the right rear via the village of Le Sart; the main body at Léglise was ten kilometres south–east of Neufchâteau. When called upon, the division could and would deploy piecemeal, depending on each unit's starting distance from the battlefield.

5 Colonial Brigade set out at 07.00, marching through the dense fog down a narrow forest track. The four-and-a-half hour march up to Neufchâteau was disturbed only by irritating but small German cavalry patrols, as daring young Uhlan troopers took great delight in galloping out of the fog across the road in front of the French column. The 25 French reservists, on their plodding requisitioned horses, were thoroughly discommoded by this aggressive behaviour, but the experienced Colonial infantrymen soon drove the enemy off. Finally, after the fog had lifted,

16   In fact, the brigade was initially loaned half a squadron of the elite *Chasseurs d'Afrique*, part of the cavalry regiment supporting CAC. But on the day before the offensive, the *Chasseurs* were reunited with their regiment and replaced by a third–rate unit, a troop (25 men) from 6 (Reserve) Squadron of 6 Dragoons... See AAT 24N3009/34/4b: miscellaneous papers of 5 Colonial Brigade.

Map 37

the advance guard – two battalions of 23 RIC – came into action at 11.30.[17] The opening of the engagement between the colonials and the German reservists gives the strongest evidence of how great was the element of surprise achieved by the French in the Ardennes that day. The French 'point' unit, a company from 23 RIC, reaching the final crest before Neufchâteau, were surprised to see on the other side a German supply column (wagons escorted by cavalry) resting on the road leading westwards out of Neufchâteau, directly in front of them; the experienced riflemen quickly opened fire at such an inviting target, at a range of 800 metres.[18] It was the combat train of the German 42 Brigade guarded by a squadron of 4 Dragoons; the cavalry was decimated, the supply train disabled, and the surprised German infantry in front of and behind the wagons hastened to deploy into makeshift firing–lines.

After an hour's hard fighting, the colonial infantry had advanced up to the western outskirts of Neufchâteau while their flank guard on their vulnerable right fought for the tactically important woods called *Bois d'Ospot*. During the next three hours, they continued their aggressive assault on the town, taking casualties but making progress. This was the time of greatest danger for the Germans:

> The 41st Reserve Brigade, fighting on the left wing, had to put in its last few men in order to hold the heights south west of Neufchâteau. The batteries west of that place [the town] came to dire straits because of enemy fire which had stalked them in the many hollows and depressions of that terrain.[19]
>
> Towards 16.00 the crisis peaked; two batteries of 21st Reserve Division, positioned on the slopes west of Neufchâteau, called for immediate infantry support. They were on the point of being captured by the assaults of the French colonial infantry. But 21st Reserve Division had not a single infantryman to spare. [Corps commander] von Steuben sent one of his staff officers in haste to find the last regiment of 25th Reserve Division with orders to bring it immediately to Neufchâteau to support the centre... General Rampacher [21 RID commander] remained stoically just a few hundred metres from the nearest French skirmishers under a hail of fire which mowed down his liaison officers.[20]

But the Colonial Brigade was simply not strong enough on its own to deliver the final decisive blow and force its way up and into the town. This is where de Langle's operational plan demonstrably broke down as a result of German action: the main Colonial column, 3 DIC, which was supposed to occupy Neufchâteau, had been stopped at Rossignol by 6 AK and was sixteen kilometres short of 5 Colonial Brigade, whose right flank was now hanging in the air. The growing threat on its right flank was draining resources, and casualties had been heavy. It had however fixed and held a force equal to its own, denying the German divisional commander the ability to reinforce his centre. Despite there not being a coordinated plan between 12 CA and 5 Colonial Brigade – for lack of a unified chain of command – the colonials had serendipitously bought time for 12 CA to act decisively against the weak forces opposed to it. But the tide gradually turned against the colonials. As soon as he realised the enormity of the threat faced by 21 RID, von Steuben had sent orders to 25 RID, received at 13.00, to march to its support.[21] The nearest battalion had only a

---

17   AAT 24N3009/34/4b: Miscellaneous notes of 5 Colonial Brigade, a handwritten ink note *Rapport sommaire sur le combat de la 5° Brigade devant Neufchâteau*, dated 22 August 1914; and Grasset, *Neufchâteau*, p.16.
18   Grasset, *Neufchâteau*, p.16.
19   *Weltkrieg 1*, p.337.
20   Pugens, *Neufchâteau*, pp.367–369.
21   Ibid.

two–kilometre march and at 13.30 the first troops arrived at the village of Le Sart, more than one kilometre south of the *Bois d'Ospot*, advancing from a south–easterly direction into the right rear of the French colonial position. Although well–sited French machine–guns and artillery held off this threat, it certainly put paid to any chance of the Colonial Brigade itself capturing Neufchâteau. Further German attacks developed towards the *Bois d'Ospot* from Hamipré as the more distant units of 25 RID arrived on the battlefield. These battalions and guns had been directed further north, a longer march but one which placed them in direct support of the failing German line in the town. Gradually from 15.30 onwards, the leading brigade of 25 RID deployed its battalions and its artillery consecutively in front and on the flank of the Colonial firing–line, which was forced back step–by–step in a fighting withdrawal.[22]

It is impossible to say what might have developed on the French side had 5 Colonial Brigade been under direct command of 12 CA. General Goullet, the Colonial Brigade commander, had asked for assistance from 23 DI on his left, and as a result three battalions were approaching from the west to strengthen the colonials' line. The overwhelmingly powerful corps artillery of 12 CA was also moving into positions of support.[23] A withdrawal in a westerly direction towards the supporting strength of 23 DI was the obvious military solution. But 5 Colonial Brigade was part of CAC whose headquarters was to the south, even if their corps commander had not communicated with them at all since their orders arrived at 06.30 that morning.[24] So at 17.00 a staff officer was sent back south to find General Lefèvre, Colonial Corps commander, supposedly at Les Bulles on the Semoy. In the meantime, General Goullet started organising a fall–back position to the south around his command post at Montplainchamps from 15.50 onwards, complete with shallow trenches dug by the engineers. Unable to hold and wait for a reply, Goullet gave the order to retreat to the fall-back line at about 17.00. At 18.00 the first retreating company of infantry moved into the trenches, and immediately the German pressure eased. Stragglers continued to find their way back until about 19.00. At 20.00, having still not heard from Corps command, Goullet decided to withdraw upon Suxy, about seven kilometres back on his original route, southwards towards his corps commander rather than westwards towards the strength of Roques's 12 CA.

Map 37a

It was the end of a day of very hard fighting, and General Goullet had learned that 23 DI on his left was itself retreating: 'The General judged that his decision to retreat could not be put off even for a minute, once he had been informed of the retreat of 12 CA which up until then had been covering his left'.[25] At 21.00 'in the most profound silence, the column set out. It arrived at Suxy at 22.00'.[26] There had been no pursuit by the Germans when the colonials disengaged.[27] It is clear that the reason why they were able to disengage and withdraw without interference was because the resistance of the elite colonial troops had left 25 RID in no position to pose any further threat to anyone that day:

> Towards 19.00 the retreat of all isolated troops seemed over. Held back by their respect of our guns, whose fire never ceased, and by the fire from Montpleinchamps, the enemy did not intervene. The German regiments, exhausted, gathered near the bridge where they still suffered from our artillery fire.[28]

22   Ibid., and Grasset, *Neufchâteau*, pp.57–69.
23   AAT 26N136/1: JMO of 12 CA, Entries for 22 August; and AFGG I/1 (1936), p. 404.
24   Grasset, *Neufchâteau*, p.72.
25   Ibid.
26   Ibid.
27   AAT 24N3009/34/4b: Miscellaneous notes of 5 Colonial Brigade, op. cit., a handwritten ink note: *Rapport sommaire sur le combat de la 5e brigade devant Neufchâteau*, dated 22 August.
28   Grasset, *Neufchâteau*, p.71.

Casualties in 5 Colonial Brigade were high – at roll–call on 24 August, only 2156 officers and men of an original complement of over 6500 were fit for duty, a 67% casualty rate.[29] But their opponents had suffered badly too. According to French Medical Orderly Tramini, who remained behind to tend the wounded and who remained on the battlefield for four days before going into captivity, the Germans lost 1300 dead and 3000 wounded in front of Neufchâteau. He claimed to have seen eleven 77mm German guns destroyed, together with caissons and horses.[30]

The important contribution of 5 Colonial Brigade on 22 August was that, despite being isolated from the rest of its corps and despite being gradually outnumbered during the course of the day, it had through its fierce fighting and its stubborn resistance created the conditions whereby 12 CA was faced by a mere brigade of reserve infantry and thus given the opportunity to obtain a victory. This narrative now moves on to examine how 12 CA made use of that advantage.

On the central sector of the battlefield, the German 42 Brigade, with 88 RIR in the main column, was marching west out of Neufchâteau towards Bertrix. On the French side, the mission of General Leblond's 23 DI was to advance and occupy the important railway town of Libramont. Its route, as the right–hand column of 12 CA, would take it north between Neufchâteau and Petitvoir. Unknown to the French, the German 88 RIR lay right in their path. But the Germans were equally ignorant of the whereabouts of the French and were initially spread out along five kilometres of road in their marching column. 23 DI marched north in a single column to Straimont, where the column divided.[31] The advance guard continued due north on the Harfontaine road which would then bisect the main Neufchâteau–Petitvoir road some two kilometres outside the town. Behind the advance guard, 138 RI was sent off on the right flank towards Grapfontaine and the colonials. But divisional commander Leblond was clearly not coordinating his march with Garreau's 24 DI on his left or with that of 5 Colonial Brigade on his right, because his advance guard only came into action at about 13.30, by which time the units either side had already been fighting for two hours; precious time had been wasted. Nevertheless, in its own time, Leblond's advance guard – 107 RI, astride the Harfontaine road – struck at the very thin extended German firing–line. Within an hour [circa 14.30] the Germans were forced back and Leblond informed Roques that he would push forward and cross the Petitvoir–Neufchâteau road.[32] This was the moment of opportunity: such an advance would cut the fragile German line in two, virtually guarantee the annihilation of the forces west of Petitvoir and allow the encirclement of Neufchâteau town.

It was a moment for élan, for the much vaunted *offensive à outrance*; a swift and vigorous follow-up of a retreating enemy was clearly what the situation demanded. Instead there was caution, prudence, delay. Rather than simply follow up the retreating Germans, Leblond organised a formal set-piece attack, bringing up 63 RI on the left of 107 RI and setting up all three groups of divisional artillery – 36 guns *en batterie* – on the high ground behind the infantry.[33] But organising this took time and an hour or more elapsed before Leblond actually issued his order to advance, at 15.50, adding that the enemy seemed to be giving way and the French artillery seemed to have a marked superiority, both of which assessments we now know to be true.[34] Despite the delay, it still looked as if the fate of the Germans at Neufchâteau was about to be sealed. With hindsight, and full knowledge of what 5 Colonial Brigade was achieving alongside them during this time frame, it

Map 38

Map 38a

Map 38b

Map 38c

29   AAT 24N3009/34/4b: miscellaneous papers of 5 Colonial brigade, *compte rendu, 24 août.*
30   Grasset, *Neufchâteau*, p.101: Annex 9, Report of Medical Orderly Tramini of 23 RIC, returned from captivity in July 1915.
31   AFGG I/1 (1923), p.394.
32   Ibid., and AAT 22N817/30/3: orders and notes of 12 CA.
33   AAT 26N307/1: JMO of 23 DI, entry for 22 August.
34   AAT 22N817/30/3: miscellaneous orders and notes of 12 CA, *ordre général nr.14.*

is now clear that even then a timely and vigorous drive by Leblond's battalions, supported by his massed artillery, would have fractured the Germans' thin line and broken its resistance. Indeed General von Steuben had decided to pull back and concentrate the meagre forces of his 21 RID on the heights west and south–west of Neufchâteau but east of the Neufchâteau–Straimont road, falling back towards the strength of the corps' other division in the east .[35] This was the movement noticed by the French at about 15.30, and Leblond gave the order to advance north across the main road after the retreating Germans.[36] The German retirement to the north and east of the Straimont road would leave the more westerly route – the Harfontaine road astride which Leblond's attacking force was assembling – clear for the French to advance virtually unopposed.

But something occurred during those inactive hours before the French advance was ready to be implemented that caused General Leblond to order a retreat instead of a victorious advance. The official contemporary record suggests that Leblond ordered a withdrawal because of the retreat of 5 Colonial Brigade which uncovered his right flank.[37] Given what we know today, how close to the truth was that official account of events? Leblond seems to have first been made aware of the difficulties encountered by the colonials on his flank at about the time he was reporting his initial success to Roques, around 14.30. At 14.45 he sent a note to General Goullet that he was sending a battalion to help him via Grapfontaine.[38] So Leblond's attention and concern was directed to the possible vulnerability of his flank almost from the outset of his battle. This was reinforced just as he was giving the order to cross the Neufchâteau road. His divisional JMO stated that just as he gave the order to advance across the main road, CAC [ie 5 Colonial Brigade] reported that strong forces were opposing it. So he sent two battalions of 78 RI and one of 138 RI under Colonel Arbalasse to its support.[39] The time was about 16.00 and the battle hung in the balance, with the colonial attack on the town threatening to shatter the fragile German defence but with their defensive flank under increasing threat from the east. The lack of a unified command structure across the front meant that 23 DI's support for the colonials was difficult to coordinate and control. Meanwhile another issue was arguably starting to influence the conduct of 23 DI's own battle – that of the state of mind of its divisional commander. His JMO records that 23 DI had only three battalions left in reserve, two of which were reservists. One battalion of reservists from 300 RI had even been put in the firing line.[40] One senses a touch of anxiety in the use of the word 'only'. Having to divert most of his remaining reserve to prop up the colonials and protect his own right flank must have increased Leblond's growing anxiety. But there was more to it than that. Sometime between 14.00 and 17.00, some of the troops in Leblond's attack force panicked and gave way under a German artillery bombardment. A pencilled battlefield note has recently come to light, written at 18.20 to Leblond by the colonel of 46 Brigade and stating that 'the moment of panic', caused by the abandonment of a battery, lasted only five minutes, but that then several companies of infantry in the front line became 'demoralised' and had to be rallied by their officers. The colonel himself had to take matters in hand, leading a charge, flags flying, music playing, which 'recaptured' the original positions.[41] The divisional JMO confirms but underplays the incident, stating only that under an accurate, rapid and violent bombardment by German artillery, some troops gave way for a moment but, under the energetic leadership of their officers, all calmed down; the infantry went forward *bäionette au canon* and a few gunners, who had momentarily abandoned their posts, returned to

35   *Weltkrieg 1*, p.335.
36   JMO of 23 DI, op. cit.
37   JMO of 12 CA, op. cit.
38   Miscellaneous notes of 5 Colonial Brigade, op. cit., *Rapport sommaire.*
39   JMO of 23 DI, op. cit.
40   Ibid.
41   Miscellaneous orders and notes of 12 CA, op. cit.

their guns.[42] However, the fact that a brigade commander was required to restore discipline and morale points to the seriousness of the incident. Furthermore it would have taken a considerable time to rally the disrupted troops, organise them and re–launch the assault referred to. The records do not give the time at which the incident commenced, only that the brigadier felt able to take the time to write a note at 18.20 after it was over. But there is one further note on file which illuminates the timing of the incident as well as Leblond's possible reaction to it. Leblond scribbled a note to General Goullet at 14.45 to inform him that 23 DI was occupying the heights 500m north of Menguette (2km south west of Grapfontaine) and asking to be kept informed of the Colonial Brigade's situation. That note then contains a semi–illegible phrase which seems to refer to a group of artillery and several infantry units fleeing, which suggests that Leblond had heard of the panic within his 46 Brigade as early as 14.45 and was already considering the possibility that he might have to fall back.[43] The delay between informing Roques that he planned to cross the main road and issuing the order for the advance coincides with the time slot in which Leblond was made aware of the panic in the ranks of his troops. It is certainly credible that as his fear and uncertainty increased, compounded by anxiety over his right flank, Leblond would seize upon an excuse to stop and consolidate his line, even withdraw. That excuse was provided by the situation in which 5 Colonial Brigade found itself. Leblond sent a note to 12 CA headquarters that he was withdrawing about 1000m because the 5 Colonial brigade's retreat had uncovered his right flank. He called for reinforcements.[44] Once again, the note does not indicate the time it was sent, but Roques's reply ('Received your news of today on the subject of [your] 1000m withdrawal and your general order nr.15. Remain where you are.') was timed at 19.30, far too late to reverse the action, but suggesting, given average times for messages to move up and down the chain of command, that Leblond finally gave way to his inner fears at about 17.30, roughly when news of Goullet's retreat to his fall–back position might have reached him but before he had heard from the colonel of his 46 Brigade that the panic of his men had been stopped. It is as well to be reminded at this stage that before ordering the retreat and calling for reinforcements, Leblond had placed six battalions astride the Harfontaine road, supported by twenty–four of the thirty–six divisional guns, and that he had sent a further five battalions towards Grapfontaine on his right. The three German battalions opposed to him had been ordered to retreat away from the Harfontaine road and indeed had been observed withdrawing to the north. To put Leblond's cautious approach into further perspective, one only has to look at his division's casualties. According to the corps's casualty return, 107 RI lost 11 men killed (no officers) and 66 men wounded (2%); 63 RI seems to have suffered no casualties at all; 78 RI lost 1 man killed and 18 wounded (0.6%); 138 DI lost 1 officer killed, another wounded, with 3 men killed and 25 wounded (0.1%). The artillery regiment, whose gunners fled under the German shelling, recorded only four wounded men.[45] These trivial numbers speak for themselves and evidence the total lack of élan, leadership and drive, which in turn explain the failure of 23 DI to break its weaker opponent. Before midnight Roques removed Leblond from command, with no official reason recorded. He became one of the many *limogés*[46] and was replaced on the spot by one

42   JMO of 23 DI, op. cit.
43   AAT 24N3009/34/4b: Miscellaneous notes of 5 Colonial Brigade. The relevant portion of the note seems to read 'J'eut mettre pouce de disposer dans la fuite d'un Gr [groupe] d'Artie [artillerie] et de quelques éléments d'infanterie.' The French phrase *mettre les pouces* is old–fashioned slang for 'giving way after resistance' (see: *Nouvelle Petit Larousse*, (Librarie Larousse, Paris, 1970), p.808): and the final phrase clearly refers to a group of artillery and several infantry units 'fleeing'.
44   Miscellaneous notes of 12 CA, op. cit.
45   AAT 22N795/8/1: *État des Pertes, 12 CA*.
46   Throughout August and September, General Joffre removed over 150 senior generals from their posts for perceived incompetence. Rather than go through the formal procedure of sacking them, Joffre simply reassigned every one to

of his subordinates, Colonel Bapst.[47]

The failure of 23 DI to press forward at 14.30 across the Neufchâteau–Petitvoir road was a pivotal moment in the battle. With the panic and dislocation of some of his troops, the opportunity for Leblond to force his way through the centre of the German line faded away. And the decision, at around 17.30, actually to retreat ended any possibility of capturing Neufchâteau.

Turning to the action between 24 DI and 81 RIR on the French left, the role which one single German reserve regiment played in denying France her best opportunity for a victory in the Battle of the Frontiers was so important that its precise composition, location and movement need to established beyond all doubt. The commander of 81 RIR wrote that his regiment of three battalions was supported in the advance guard by a squadron of cavalry from Dragoon Regiment 7, a battery of Artillery Regiment 21 and a company of pioneers.[48] The regiment marched five kilometres down the Bertrix road out of Neufchâteau until it reached the high ground at Petitvoir, and the village of that name nestling in the valley below. There von Jordon received orders to occupy the heights

Map 39   north–east of Rossart up to the heights north–east of Nevraumont and to halt there. One company, 6/81 RIR, was sent to the heights north–west of Grandvoir as protection for the right flank. The regiment was to set up a strong defence. Shortly after this, the first French prisoner, a *chasseur* whose horse had been shot, was brought in.[49]

Map 39   Two important points emerge from this narrative. Firstly, the defensive line that 81 RIR was ordered to occupy faced west, not south. The German command was even at that late stage unaware of the true axis of the French advance. The proposed defence line straddled the main road from Neufchâteau to Bertrix some two kilometres further forward from Petitvoir. The main road was in a valley and on either side the ground sloped up to the Nevraumont plateau, extending both north and south, on which were situated the two villages which became central to the fighting, Rossart in the north and Nevraumont in the south. It is not clear from the regimental history how far the deployment to the defensive line had progressed when the fighting started. However the possibility exists that some elements of the leading battalion (I/81 RIR) had reached the vicinity of Rossart, in response to their orders, when the first shots were fired. Secondly, it is important to track the approximate location of the twelve companies of infantry that made up the German regiment. It will be shown that French sources claim at various points to have been confronted with strong German forces coming down from the north, from the direction of Rossart. Already it is clear that few, if any, of the troops of 81 RIR were likely to have progressed west of the designated defensive line. It must also be noted that one company (6/81 RIR) was ordered off to the north–east at Grandvoir, away from the impending encounter. The four companies of III/81 RIR and the pioneer company were retained at Petitvoir as regimental reserve.[50] The seven remaining companies formed the initial German firing–line which confronted the French; one of those seven companies might have reached Rossart before the fighting started.

The French advance guard had arrived at Saint–Médard at about 10.00, from where, once the fog had cleared, it had a clear view of Nevraumont on the ridge in front, two–and–a–half kilometres away across a valley. The leading infantry unit was the first battalion, 108 RI (I/108), supported by a group of artillery (12 guns) and a company of engineers.[51]   In front of them,

a desk job in the remote provincial military post at Limoges.
47   AFGG X/ 2, p.185.
48   Jordon, RIR 81, p.7.
49   Ibid.
50   Jordon, op. cit., p.7 & p.9.
51   AAT 26N509/1: JMO of 47 Brigade.

during the scouting and skirmishing phase, Nevraumont had been occupied by 3 squadron of *21 Chasseurs*, who reported at 10.30 that a group of German infantry was approaching from the east.[52] The first skirmishing shots were fired at about 10.20.[53]

The leading companies of the German I/81 RIR on the right advanced over open fields towards Nevraumont, despite receiving fire from its open right flank. On its left II/81 RIR went forward through the woods known as the *Bois du Ban*. The first casualties were taken; thick swarms of troops strengthened the thinning forward line...[the infantry] advanced slowly but surely, springing forward in groups'[54] – an informative comment on contemporary German infantry tactics. The skirmishing had developed into a full fire–fight by about 11.30.[55]

The six German field guns of their supporting battery deployed on the Petitvoir promontory and were able to observe and use direct fire west towards Nevraumont, but not due south, where higher ground obscured their line of sight.[56] The fire–fight developed over the next two hours, by which time, about 13.30, the firing–lines were only 300–400 metres apart. French machine–guns were much in evidence, causing the German infantry some difficulty. The lack of machine–guns on the German side was keenly felt.[57]

On the French side, the cavalry occupying Nevraumont seems to have retreated in the face of the advancing German skirmishers because at 11.15, I/108 formed up and advanced to take the village, to be met by a few shots.[58] This initial attack was made without artillery support, but nevertheless in the absence of German machine-guns and artillery made rapid progress. Behind it, III/108 formed up in a double column and, as enemy fire grew brisker, deployed into line on the right. The last battalion, II/108, then moved up to the far right, and by 12.00, about the time when the field guns that were with the French advance guard opened fire, all three battalions (twelve companies) faced the increasing rifle–fire coming from the German infantry (seven companies) approaching from the north–east.[59] The French infantry, now supported by the artillery of the advance guard, still only made slow progress, using the guns to bombard the edges of the little coppices that served as enemy strong–points.[60]

The second regiment of 47 Brigade (50 RI) marched up and deployed, one battalion to the east of Nevraumont, another to the west of the village and the third in reserve.[61] It would have been difficult for the regimental commander to retain command and control over his three widely dispersed battalions. But the commander of 47 Brigade, Colonel Descoings, seems to have taken direct control at around this time, leading from the front. The two remaining groups of the divisional artillery regiment (34 RAC) came up and positioned themselves in support of Descoings' brigade.[62] Around this time also, a battalion of 126 RI was brought up to strengthen the French line, and after a heavy bombardment of the woods the Germans who had occupied them fell back.[63] The French now had twenty companies in their first line, eight more in a support line, and thirty–six guns in action; the Germans still only seven companies in one thin line, with six guns.

52   Ibid.
53   AAT 26N309/1: JMO of 24 DI.
54   Jordon, op. cit., pp.7–8.
55   JMO of 24 DI, op. cit.
56   Jordan, op. cit., sketch (*Stitze*) 1.
57   Jordon, op. cit., p.8.
58   JMO of 47 Brigade, op. cit.
59   AAT 26N678: JMO of 108 RI.
60   *34° Régiment d'artillerie, Historique du Régiment* [34 RAC] (Henri Charles-Lavauzelle, Paris, 1920), p.7.
61   AAT 26N640/1: JMO of 50 RI.
62   34 RAC, op. cit., p.7.
63   JMO of 24 DI, op. cit.

It was at this time, according to the French official history, that major German forces debouched from the woods to the north and disputed possession of the village.[64] The diarist of 47 Brigade also recorded that the woods west of Nevraumont seemed to be very strongly occupied.[65] But it is beyond doubt that no German units other than those of 81 RIR were in that area, so that the only German troops likely to have been in the north at that time, coming from the general direction of Rossart, were those elements of I/R81 which had been ordered to the northern ridge around Rossart as part of the original westerly deployment onto the defensive line ordered for R81. The exact number is unlikely ever to be established; however arguably the smallest German tactical unit to be ordered to march to defend a regimental flank, would have been a company. The natural conclusion is that the major German forces debouching from the woods north of Nevraumont observed by the French were no more than a flanking company of I/81 RIR hastening to the sound of gunfire. Whatever the number, the few German riflemen west of Nevraumont appear to have been sufficiently aggressive to have convinced many French officers that they were faced by much stronger forces. The Germans also seem to have made sufficient use of the cover afforded by the many copses and small woods that only artillery could dislodge them. But there seems to have been a lack of urgency and an almost drill–like approach by the French gunners. Their JMO recorded that the batteries took up their positions just like on the practice ground, with the battery captain's observation post alongside each battery; each battery had been given a specific mission and 'in a short time' regular fire was laid down. The guns crushed the copses under their salvos, after which the infantry was able to advance.[66]

By 14.00, casualties, enemy numbers and weight of fire were beginning to tell on the weak German line. Von Jordon decided to bring forward his third battalion and the attached company of engineers to strengthen his line. But his orders were overruled by his brigade commander, who ordered the whole brigade to pull back and defend the heights east of Petitvoir.[67] The higher German command was by now particularly aware of the possibility that 23 DI might cut the German advance guard off from their main body, and that Neufchâteau was in danger of capture. But the operational significance for the French, and for General Roques in particular, was that a retreat by von Jordon's men at 14.00 would have opened up in front of Garreau's 24 DI a free passage through Rossart to the north, with five or six hours of daylight left. Fortunately for the Germans, not only did 23 DI fail to follow up on its initial threat to cut their line in two, but von Jordon felt confident enough about his local situation to be reluctant to withdraw and twice sent messengers to Brigade HQ to query his orders:

> Oberst von Jordon, who clearly appreciated the situation of his two leading battalions, recalled the lessons learned in training, that "Retreat leads to Annihilation", and refused to carry out the order, sending first the Regimental Adjutant then the Adjutant of II/R81, (Oberleutentant d. l. kav. Röhrig), to brigade commander Lieutenant–General v Diotmann to ask again for the support of III/R81. In vain![68]

This was the time when the French perceived their enemy to be defending the ground foot–by–foot.[69] Nevertheless the French command had noticed the slackening of German resistance. Colonel

64   AFGG I/1 (1923), pp.394–395; note however that the 1936 revision is more circumspect, omitting this detail: AFGG I/1 (1936), pp.403–404.
65   JMO of 47 Brigade, op. cit.
66   34 RAC, op. cit., p.8.
67   Jordon, op.cit., p.9.
68   Ibid.
69   JMO 47 Brigade, op. cit., entry for 13.00 on 22 August.

Descoings scribbled a note for his divisional commander at 13.50 at his position at a crossroads north of the woods situated north of Nevraumont; he reported that after a series of bayonet attacks by 108 RI and I/50 RI, the enemy was retreating, pursued by 50 RI. He had ordered the pursuit to continue towards Rossart and the woods between Rossart and Petitvoir.[70]

Map 39b

It would seem at this stage, with von Jordon ordered to retreat and Descoings ordering a pursuit, that a French breakthrough was not only possible but highly likely. But shortly after 14.00 Descoings's 'pursuit' became a formal assault on the village of Rossart, culminating at 19.00 with a bayonet charge in which all the regiments of the division took part.[71] Five hours elapsed, during which the opportunity for 24 DI to turn its initial success into comprehensive victory before nightfall drained away. Part of the reason lies in von Jordon's reluctance to withdraw and his troops' continued resistance, but this in turn was only made possible by French caution and reluctance to use their massive superiority in men and guns to advance *à outrance*.

In addition, two events are recorded on the French side, which most probably contributed to Descoings's 'pursuit' becoming a formal assault. At some time during the afternoon (the exact time is not recorded) Colonel Descoings was wounded, shot through the right arm.[72] And at 15.50 corps commander Roques sent a note to General Leblond to tell him that 24 DI was on the point of reaching Grandvoir, well in advance of 23 DI. Roques tersely requested that Leblond should avoid firing on his own side, 'as had already happened while 24 DI was at Hill 403', 1500 metres east of Nevraumont.[73] The French unit on the right flank at Hill 403 was 108 RI; this regiment suffered 1292 casualties on 22 August, a 40% loss rate, which was nearly ten times higher than any other regiment of 24 DI that day.[74]

It is probable that Descoings had to leave the field to have his wound dressed, and at roughly the same time, the leading regiment, 108 RI, was hit by friendly fire from their neighbouring division, which caused significant casualties including up to twelve officers, amongst whom were four company commanders.[75] This latter event would not be one that Roques would want to see written into the official accounts of his battle. The two events together would have been enough to drain the impetus from the French attack. Descoings was a relatively young, competent brigade commander with potential: in five months' time, on 5 January 1915, he would be appointed to command 12 CA in place of Roques, having been given command of 24 DI immediately after this battle.[76] He was an important and charismatic figure, and critical to 24 DI's success thus far, having led the assault from the front. His departure from the front for the dressing station just after ordering the pursuit would have left command and control of the battle in the hands of the two remaining senior officers, Generals Garreau and Sorin, commanders respectively of 24 DI and 48 Brigade. It is an interesting fact that not a single message from either of them, up or down the chain of command, remains in the archives.

The formal attack on Rossart was undoubtedly organised by Garreau and Sorin, and involved

70   AAT 24N468/3/1: papers of 3 Bureau of 24 DI, 8–24 August 1914.

71   JMO of 24 DI, op. cit.

72   *12 CA État des pertes*, op. cit.; Col. Descoings was wounded 22/8 in right arm by a bullet and again on 23/8 in combat at Orgéo by a shrapnel wound in the neck.

73   AAT 22N816/29/3: papers of 3 Bureau of 12 CA: a handwritten note from the general commanding 12 CA to the General commanding 23 DI, from St Médard, at 15.50 on 22 August.

74   *12 CA État des pertes*, op. cit., the regimental record within the corps's file shows that on 22 August, 108 RI lost 7 officers, 25 NCOs and 218 men killed and 6 officers, 75 NCOs and 961 men wounded. None were missing on that day.

75   Ibid., the record shows that on 22 August, 108 RI lost 3 captains (company commanders) and 4 lieutenants killed and 1 captain, five lieutenants wounded, with at least 100 NCOs put out of action.

76   AFGG X/1, p.723 and X/2, p.193.

Map 39c all the regiments of the division.[77] The divisional artillery (34 RAC) also moved forward to take up a new position north of the village of Nevraumont. Led by Descoings's 47 Brigade, this formal assault on the village inevitably succeeded. Following a crushing artillery bombardment, the French infantry entered the village with fixed bayonets and flags flying.[78] But the assault on Rossart helps to explain the delays and lack of action during the missing hours. The move of five fresh battalions and eight batteries of field guns about three kilometres forward would normally take well over an hour.[79] The change of command, the re–establishment of control and the preparation for a formal assault would also take time. The apparent inactivity on the French side between 14.00 and 17.00 is finally explained by this hypothesis. Confirmation is provided by the JMO of the final regiment to deploy, 100 RI, which reported that it was ordered to assemble at 15.00 and to march in combat formation, starting at 17.30, the four kilometres to join the 'capture' of Rossart. It suffered from German artillery fire as it crossed the plateau.[80] The march would take about an hour at regulation speed, indicating that there was little or no resistance to the 'capture' of Rossart at bayonet point at 18.00. Furthermore, the regimental casualty return shows that this regiment suffered not a single fatality on 22 August, just 57 wounded, probably from the shell–fire mentioned in its diary.[81]

At 16.00 German time (15.00 according to our chronology) von Jordon had finally given his own order to retire in the general direction of Grandvoir and Tournay, deploying all his reserves (which were units of 7/R81) to protect the retirement.[82] That he was able to remain so long in the field against such superior numbers indicates that the German line was not under particular pressure from the French; furthermore, during the retirement (which produced additional casualties from French fire) the enemy did not follow up and merely sent out patrols into the area around Petitvoir.[83]

Roques had reported to Fourth Army headquarters at 16.20 (in a formal *compte rendu*) that '24 DI, having taken Nevraumont, has pushed up to a crest one kilometre north, with two regiments and five batteries engaged. It is bringing up its last two regiments from reserve.'[84] Given that this is precisely the position from which Descoings had ordered the pursuit more than two hours earlier, it would seem that Roques and his staff had only a poor appreciation of what 24 DI was doing, and that Garreau's and Sorin's regrouping and preparation for an assault on Rossart had halted Descoings' brigade on the ridge.

It is difficult to find evidence of any German defence of Rossart. As has been shown above, von Jordon had ordered his regiment to withdraw towards Petitvoir, away from Rossart and east instead of north. Undoubtedly some stragglers from the few German companies which had attacked the western side of Nevraumont earlier in the day might have found their way back to Rossart, but without artillery or machine–guns; there might also have been a few German cavalrymen from von Jordon's scouting squadron; but there were no other German units in the vicinity. Confirmation of this fact comes from the regimental histories of the nearest German division, 21 ID some five or six kilometres away at Bertrix, which did however send out some scouting and security forces from its integral cavalry (6 Uhlans):

77   AFGG I/ 1 (1923), p.395.
78   JMO of 47 Brigade, op. cit.
79   *Handbook of the French Army 1914* (War Office, 1914, The Imperial War Museum Department of Printed Books, 1912).
80   AAT 26N673/15: JMO of 100 RI, entry for 22 August.
81   AAT 25N83; miscellaneous papers of 100 RI.
82   Jordon, op. cit., p.10.
83   Ibid., p.9.
84   *AFGG I/1*, Annex 934: [12 CA] *Compte rendu à l'armée, 22 août, 16.20.*

From the left at Rossart came reports from Assistant Guard Commander (*Vizewachtmeister*) Busse of the approach of very strong enemy cavalry.[85] It was very unlikely that in the current tactical situation the enemy cavalry would breakthrough. In any case they could hardly be considered a serious threat given that the terrain beyond the road was unsuitable for horses.[86]

Nevertheless the German cavalry commander took no chances:

> Sergeant Glenneberg of the 1st Squadron would be deployed with a strong patrol towards Rossart for security and defence with their firearms ... but Sergeant Glenneberg encountered no French riders. Instead there were scattered enemy infantry everywhere, who to some extent and completely irresponsibly let off their bullets whilst running. He took seventeen prisoners. Sergeant Welz even managed to capture a Frenchman and his horse and brought him back with him to the squadron.[87]

There was one final mission for 6 Uhlans; General von Schenk, commander of 21 ID, wanted to make contact with his neighbour (21 RID) at Neufchâteau, and at midday ordered a patrol. Oberleutenant Buek of 3rd Squadron, 6 Uhlans, set out with six troopers. He wrote in his daybook:

> Through beautiful deciduous forest our path took us to Rossart. There were enemy infantry in the town and I sent one rider back to report. Shots were fired at us. We rode further on. We saw enemy riflemen crawl forward on the heights. From a wooded crest I made a sketch of the whole situation. Here the enemy even fired at our small patrol with their artillery. We disappeared into the woods. A messenger took our report back. It was sunset and the shelling slackened off. We rode back.[88]

These reports from 6 Uhlans demonstrate conclusively that Rossart was not heavily defended and did not merit a full–scale assault by two brigades supported by thirty-six guns. It suggests a degree of French disorganisation, with infantry running around firing their rifles or crawling over empty hills and with artillery firing at a handful of cavalrymen. And it supports the hypothesis that a vigorous 'pursuit', started at 14.00 as ordered by Colonel Descoings, would have brushed aside the final German resistance and gained Rossart, and the open ground between that village and Grandvoir in the east, with several hours of daylight left.

General Garreau must be criticised for the excessive caution with which he directed his division, or by default allowed his division to proceed, against minimal opposition. Through his inadequate leadership he allowed a significant opportunity for French tactical success to slip away. The casualties sustained during the battle support the case. Apart from 108 RI which, as has been shown above, sustained 40% losses, including those from friendly fire, the other regiments of 24 DI had relatively small numbers of casualties. 50 RI suffered no more than 150 killed, wounded and missing out of about 3200 over a three day period from 22 to 24 August, which is roughly 5%. Even if all the casualties had been incurred on 22 August, it seems hardly *offensive à outrance*,

85   This would most likely have been the French 12 CA cavalry regiment, *21 Chasseurs*, operating on the left (open) flank of Roques's corps.
86   Herman Freiherr Hillier von Gaertringen, *Geschichte des Thüringischen Ulanen-Regiments Nr 6 von 1813 bis 1919* [6 Uhlans] (Wilhelm Rolf, Berlin, 1930), p.51.
87   Ibid.
88   Ibid., p.53.

by any standard.[89] 100 RI suffered 57 men wounded and 14 missing on 22–23 August (2%);[90] 126 RI suffered 15 killed and 48 wounded in front of Nevraumont on 22 August, out of 3393, less than 2%.[91] These statistics do not support the 48 Brigade JMO's assertion of 'considerable casualties' within the brigade as a whole. Nor do they give evidence of any truly aggressive action by the infantry of 24 DI.

By comparison, German leadership was much more positive. Early in the day Major Seeleman, commanding one of von Jordan's two battalions in the firing line, called out to the regimental commander: 'We are giving the enemy too much honour. It is doubtless only dismounted cavalry!'[92] Major Seeleman commanded I/81 RIR, opposite the 50 and 108 RIs, and that day his battalion lost 244 men dead or missing (wounded are not mentioned but would considerably increase the total) out of a total of approximately 1000, in other words a mortality rate of nearly 25%. Projected to include an average number of wounded for such a number of dead, the overall losses of this one battalion would most likely have exceeded 60%. Judging from the evidence from the French side, the majority of those casualties would have come from French artillery fire. The morale of these German reserve soldiers is exemplified by the words of one wounded corporal: 'Today things did not go at all well, Herr Oberst, but when we come back from hospital, we will give it to those Frenchmen properly'.[93] Corporal Fröhlich of 5/81 RIR actually buried the regimental colours rather than let them fall into French hands, and was able to retrieve them the next day.[94]

The contrast between the performance of the officers and men of the German 81 RIR and those of the French 24 DI could not be more starkly illustrated at every level. German morale was very high, as was their ability to take severe casualties and still stay on the field; French morale was low, particularly when they lost their officers, and they showed little appetite for attack until their artillery had completely destroyed all opposition. Even then, their progress was very slow. This was not *offensive à outrance,* indeed the degree of caution went beyond even the dictates of the 1895 doctrine, an issue which will be discussed later. German regimental and battalion command was resolute and professional, demonstrating an aggressive unwillingness to concede ground; the French command (other than Colonel Descoings) was cautious, even hesitant, with a total inability to assess the fighting correctly, appreciate the opportunity before them, and drive their men forward. One exception was Lieutenant Hérier of 10/108 who was wounded by a bullet in the face and who nevertheless insisted on reporting to his brigade commander, calling out *en avant, pour La France* ['forward, for France']. His behaviour is cited in the regimental JMO as one of supreme courage and heroic conduct when it might equally have been an impassioned call for leadership based on an appreciation of the opportunity unfolding at the front.[95] Apart from Colonel Descoings, the French senior commanders were at best laborious, at worst weak; the German brigade and divisional commanders showed an astute and accurate assessment of the battle as it developed around them. The German reserve regiment continued to function as a coherent fighting unit despite losing fourteen of its officers killed, including two company commanders, and an unknown number wounded. On the French side, officer casualties in the regiments of 24 DI were almost as high, but the resulting inertia caused by lack of leadership was out of proportion. 108 RI lost 3 captains killed, 1 wounded and 4 lieutenants killed, five wounded; 100 NCOs were killed or wounded. 50 RI lost 21 officers (42%) over three days, starting on 22 August. These two regiments

89   *État des pertes du 12e CA*, op. cit.
90   AAT 25N83: miscellaneous papers of 100 RI, including *État des pertes 21/8–21/10/1914.*
91   AAT 25N118: miscellaneous papers of 126 RI: *État des pertes.*
92   Jordon, op. cit., p.7.
93   Jordon, op. cit., p.10.
94   Ibid.
95   JMO of 108 RI, op. cit.

bore the brunt of the early fighting at Nevraumont, and were the force Descoings expected to pursue the retreating enemy. In those days, officers believed it right to expose themselves to fire in order to encourage their men, but it seems that the French officer corps often took this to an absurd degree: sub–Lieutenant Fayolle of 50 RI graduated from Saint Cyr during the mobilisation period, put on his plumed St Cyrian cap and his white gloves before the assault. He was mortally wounded by a bullet through the forehead.[96] The "white gloves" stereotype was made popular by Tuchman in the 1960s: 'Officers from St. Cyr went into battle wearing white–plumed shakos and white gloves; it was considered "chic" to die in white gloves.'[97] But it is clear from the case of sub–Lieutenant Fayolle, and other instances, that it was founded on a real attitude of naive pride, ignorant of the reality of modern war, prevalent in the French army at the time.

After the action had finished, there was no overt criticism of the performance of 24 DI, by Roques or anyone else in the French army, then or since. Nevertheless General Garreau (like Leblond of 23 DI) was quietly removed from command of 24 DI that same night, without any record of explanation.[98] If proof were needed that Roques was aware of some sort of missed opportunity, despite the absence of written records, it lies in his removal of both his divisional generals immediately after the battle. The JMOs of both division and corps are not overtly untruthful, except arguably for the hyperbole of 'major German forces' west of Neuvramont to describe the opposition from at most the remnants of a few companies of German reserve infantry and some dismounted cavalry patrols. But the JMOs simply fail to record events during the pivotal period of the battle between 14.00 and 19.00, and so a detailed explanation of what happened and why has had to be constructed from disparate lower–level source material.

The inference drawn from this is that the action of 24 DI was written up in the divisional and corps JMOs to present an inadequate performance in the best possible light. Given that General Roques quietly removed General Garreau from his post within hours, and given that the inactivity of *21 Chasseurs* on the open left flank, and the deployment of the powerful corps artillery and reserve infantry, was the responsibility of the corps operational staff, the inference is that an attempt was made to conceal the extent of this lost opportunity in order to preserve the reputation of General Pierre Roques. As will be shown later, Roques was a political general, more familiar with activity in the Ministry of War than in the front line. And he was an old comrade of General Joffre, whose own early career in the colonial army his had closely mirrored.[99] His operational control of his corps must be called into question. It is abundantly clear that 24 DI and *21 Chasseurs* between them had a significant opportunity to brush aside the weak if energetic opposition of von Jordon's regiment within three hours of the start of the fight. Had they done so, then reaching a line from Rossart to Grandvoir was within their grasp during the afternoon, with hours of daylight left. And there was a road or track from Rossart which leads directly north which would have placed them, after an hour's march, on the left rear flank of the German 21 ID fighting in the Forest of Luchy north–east of Bertrix. A second open road, from Grandvoir northwards to Libramont, led directly to Duke Albrecht von Württemburg's forward Command Post – a prime target for a regiment of aggressively–led French light cavalry.

But neither Roques nor his staff seem to have had the slightest appreciation of what lay before them. In the firing–line, companies and company commanders were intent on what was immediately

96   JMO of 50 RI, op. cit.
97   Tuchman, *The Guns of August*, pp.284–5.
98   AFGG X/2,p.193: Garreau was removed from command on 22 August, replaced temporarily by Colonel Deffontaines and four days later by Colonel Descoings, who presumably was by then recovered from the wounds he received on 22 and 23 August.
99   Rocolle, op.cit., p.143.

in front of them and not on the task of finding their enemy's flank. Little information seems to have found its way back to corps headquarters; the absence of any evidence other than Descoings's messages in the files supports this point, as does the fact that 24 DI spent hours organising a formal assault, using the techniques set out in the 1895 regulations, on a position at Rossart defended by less than a battalion of exhausted German reservists. On the flank, *21 Chasseurs* were content with a passive role, not even sending out aggressive scouting patrols. Again, the absence of positive evidence, together with the testimony from the German 6 Uhlans opposite them, supports the point. Over and above the lost opportunity for tactical battlefield victory, an appreciation of the prospects for exploitation (even if Roques and his staff were incapable of appreciating them) following a vigorous tactical success at Rossart and Grandvoir, leads one to conclude that the opportunity lost by 24 DI had potential operational and strategic significance.

Each individual action, incident and event described above about the battle at Neufchâteau contributes to a composite picture of the overall behaviour and performance of the two combatants, and illuminates a generic conclusion as to the contributing factors to success, and failure.

On the French side, it is clear that there was a marked difference between the performance of the colonial and metropolitan troops. The Colonials, like their German opponents, showed a level of tactical proficiency, discipline and morale which was lacking in the metropolitan soldiers. They showed a willingness to take heavy casualties and still remain in the firing–line, absorbing pressure and continuing to fight against increasing odds. The metropolitan troops on the other hand demonstrated a tendency to panic under fire, especially under artillery bombardment, losing cohesion, discipline and morale. This was particularly the case with the infantry and artillerymen in the firing–line of 48 Brigade of 23 DI, but was also evident (perhaps more understandably) within 108 RI of 24 DI. The lack of impetus shown by virtually every regiment of 12 CA in this action signals a tendency to 'go to ground' when deprived of clear leadership. In all cases, it required senior officers to rally and regroup their units into battalion and regimental formations, using traditional methods of dense formations, music, flags and drums to re–establish command and control. These factors point to issues of training within the metropolitan army which require further analysis.

The German soldiers demonstrated much the same characteristics of high morale and ability to absorb casualties whilst remaining in the firing line as the French colonials. This is the more surprising in that they were all reservists of the older classes. The youngest, most recently trained reservists went to regular units to bring them up to war strength; reserve formations like 21 RID and 25 RID took the next tranche of conscripts.[100] There is clearly an issue regarding the relative quality of French and German reserve soldiers, which once again points towards pre–war training.

Junior French officers (of the rank of captain and below) demonstrated an almost foolhardy courage and old–fashioned belief in leading from the front. Too many officer casualties reinforced any tendency for leaderless troops to 'go to ground'. A real–life (and death) example of the "white gloves" stereotype has been quoted from amongst the officer fatalities of 50 RI; it is not the only instance to be found in archive material pertaining to the Battle of the Frontiers. The French learned the hard way and at the cost of a large part of their pre–war officer cadre that such behaviour could not survive the test of modern firepower. And German officer casualties were equally heavy, as has been shown above. The difference was that French junior–officer casualties seem to have made a major contribution to failures in unit cohesion, morale and discipline, whereas on the German side their strong NCO cadre and the inherent self–discipline and self–motivation of individual soldiers

100 *Weltkrieg 1*, p.675 and Herman Cron, *Imperial German Army 1914–18* (transl. C.F. Colton, Helion & Company, Solihull, 2001), pp.313–4.

seems to have held units together and kept them in action longer.[101]

Perhaps surprisingly, the tactics used by both 23 and 24 DI showed nothing of the élan or *furia francese* which one might expect of an army supposedly indoctrinated by the cult of *offensive à outrance*. On the contrary, insofar as any doctrine can be seen to have been put into practice within 12 CA, it was that of the old 1895 Regulations, in which artillery prepared the way for the infantry attack.[102] But if what happened within 12 CA was a deliberate application of the 1895 doctrine, it seems to have been taken to excess, in that the French infantry demonstrably failed to move forward until the enemy was blasted out of their improvised strong–points or (in the case of 24 DI) until the enemy himself withdrew. Finally, one cannot but help being struck by the similarity between the final attack on Rossart by all the regiments of infantry and artillery of 24 DI and the traditional massed charge with which the French ended their annual autumn manoeuvres, suggesting that the lack of realism of the latter had ill-prepared many senior French officers for the reality of war.

German doctrine as applied by 81 RIR adheres closely to the 1906 field regulations, with swarms of skirmishers reinforced into thickening lines which went forward bound–by–bound. Use of copses and other natural features shows an attention to field–craft which must have compensated for the lack of firepower due to weak numbers of guns and the absence of machine–guns. Strong individual and small–unit self–discipline was demonstrated in the execution of a fighting withdrawal. Again one has to draw a parallel conclusion about the French colonial infantry.

French artillery had overwhelming superiority in numbers, and the French 75mm field piece was superior to the German 77mm gun; so it is unsurprising that they eventually gained fire–superiority. But there is evidence of a slow, methodical, almost text–book application of deployment and fire movements. Time, according to Napoleon, was the most precious commodity on the battlefield: a French artillery unit in column could accelerate its advance to at least six or seven kilometres an hour at a trot or even gallop over short distances when needed;[103] but there is no evidence that the urgency existed on the French side during this battle to bring their artillery into action earlier than the prescribed routine walking speed of march and deployment. On the contrary, the first attack on Nevraumont by I/108 went ahead without waiting for artillery support, although this may also be evidence of the unofficial 'cult of the offensive' which drove ill-disciplined junior officers to impetuous early attacks. When it did come into action, the tenor of 34 RAC's JMO for 22 August hints at pride in a routine performance. The French organisational system provided for a very strong corps artillery unit – four groups compared to the three groups allocated to each division. In theory this allowed the corps commander to have under his hand a powerful reserve to apply to the decisive point. In practice, the battle at Neufchâteau highlighted the flaw in the theoretical logic; Roques positioned his corps artillery in its entirety behind his left–hand column, only to find that it was needed to support his extreme right flank. It took several wasted hours to move the guns to where they were needed, and that was after the time taken for requests and orders to pass up and down the chain of command across a confused and chaotic battlefield. More than one–third of the total firepower of 12 CA remained unused whilst these movements took place. On the positive side, the French guns seemed to have been very effective once they were deployed, as judged by the witness statements describing batteries of German field guns destroyed. There is also a slight suggestion (one of only two which can be found in archive material regarding the Battle of the Ardennes) that the French did perhaps use the capability of their 75mm field guns

---

101　See: M. Kitchen, *The German Officer Corps 1890–1914* (Clarendon Press, Oxford, 1968), pp.49–63, pp.115–142 and pp.222–227 passim; and D. Stone, *Fighting for the Fatherland* (Conway, London, 2006), p.231; and Zuber, *Ardennes*, pp.12–79 passim.
102　See Chapter 7 for a discussion of doctrine.
103　*Handbook of the French Army 1914*, p.403.

to fire shells in a howitzer–like trajectory[104]: 'The batteries west of that place [Neufchâteau] came to dire straits because of enemy fire which had stalked them in the many hollows and depressions of that terrain'.[105] But the overriding impression left by the French artillery supporting 12 CA was the 'friendly fire' incident when 23 DI's guns fired upon 24 DI's infantry. Not even the supposed high visibility of the red-trousered *poilu* stopped an elementary error in identification, and the ramifications upon the outcome of the battle were significant.

The Germans of 18 RAK were weak in artillery. Reserve divisions in the German army had one regiment of field artillery instead of two. This meant that (since the light field–howitzer group was invariably in the second regiment of a regular division) it was most unlikely that 18 RAK possessed howitzers. There is certainly no mention of their use. Nor did 18 RAK have any heavy artillery.[106] But what they lacked in numbers, the German guns seem to have made up for in effectiveness. The sudden, accurate counter–bombardment by one battery onto 23 DI's collected batteries had a disproportionate effect on the outcome of the battle, temporarily dislocating several artillery and infantry units, causing panic and, arguably, influencing General Leblond to call off their potentially decisive attack into the weak German centre.

The French also had an overwhelming superiority in cavalry, and a golden opportunity to use that strength opposite the seven–kilometre gap on the German right flank. Admittedly, one German assessment at the time judged the terrain to be unsuitable for mounted action and consequently dismissed the threat. But French cavalry doctrine was here found wanting. Firstly they did not use the twelve– or six–man patrol system practiced by the Germans to scout forward and provide accurate battlefield intelligence. Secondly, they did not engage in dismounted fighting, despite the adverse terrain. *21 Chasseurs* seem to have adopted a purely defensive, protection and security role on the flank of a major French offensive operation. Apart from the doctrine which was arguably proven not to be fit for purpose, the performance of *21 Chasseurs* also shows signs of passive caution rather than aggressive intent. Their presence on the left flank of 24 DI is recorded by both French and German sources, but there is no record of any activity on their part.[107] Whether this was due to failures in corps command, to lack of regimental officer initiative or to lack of training in combined–arms manoeuvres is difficult to judge. Whatever the reason, the failure of such a powerful force of cavalry to find and report upon, let alone exploit the magnificent opportunity to turn the flank of the German 21 RID was a key factor in this French lost opportunity.

Whether it be regarding infantry, artillery or cavalry or – viewed from a different perspective – at rank and file, NCO, junior officer or senior officer level, it is impossible to avoid concentrating on major French weaknesses and comparing their performance unfavourably to that of the Germans. All of the issues specific to the battle at Neufchâteau can be found in other encounter battles across the Ardennes operation. Together they will be examined in the analysis section of this book in order to draw generic conclusions as to the relative significance of the factors which contributed to German success and French failure in the Ardennes.

The reasonable conclusion from a detailed examination of the battle at Neufchâteau is that the French 12 CA could and should have broken the German 21 RID in two places. Moreover they could have done so sufficiently early in the day to have sufficient time for follow–up manoeuvre and exploitation. Better feedback from the firing–line would have given Garreau and Roques

---

104   See Chapter 8, 'Equipment', for a discussion of the use of the *plaquette Malandrin* device to give the 75mm field gun a higher trajectory.
105   *Weltkrieg 1*, p.331.
106   Cron, *Imperial German Army 1914-18*, pp.313–4.
107   AAT 25N593: JMO of 21 Chasseurs: no papers whatsoever for 22 August 1914.

information to plan from, as would reports from scouts of *21 Chasseurs*, had they been posted. A more positive (and in the event more realistic) assessment by Leblond and Roques of the ability of 5 Colonial Brigade to hold firm long enough for 12 CA to complete its attacks would have led to greater success; but such an assessment would have required better battlefield intelligence and better communication between the command structures of two different corps. And, in truth, it would have required a more aggressive and confident leadership from the three senior French commanders – Generals Roques, Garreau and Leblond – than they proved capable of delivering.

On the left General Garreau's caution and inertia, together with his lack of tactical appreciation of the battle in front of him, prevented 24 DI from pursuing a beaten enemy (albeit one who, Foch–like, did not know he was beaten), driving through to a line between Rossart and Grandvoir and thereafter breaking through into open country. Garreau thereby missed the opportunity to place a strong force on the vulnerable flank of the German 21 ID at a time when that unit was locked in battle with the French 33 DI in the Forest of Luchy. Had he done so, the whole outcome of de Langle de Cary's operation would have arguably swung in favour of France. As well as his own caution, inertia and lack of professional insight, Garreau's failure turned on the misuse of the French cavalry, the loss of key officers (particularly Colonel Descoings) at critical times, and the impact of a friendly–fire incident upon troops whose morale and training were insufficient to stand the test of their first live combat. Garreau applied the tactics of laborious formal assault, using massed artillery and massed battalions of infantry to a situation which required – dare one say it? –élan and *offensive à outrance*.

The evidence from 23 DI's action provides a compelling argument that General Leblond lost his nerve when on the point of victory. It was not necessarily his fault that some of his front–line troops panicked and ran under German artillery fire, yet a more dynamic leader with more dynamic subordinates might have pressed on despite such a set–back and used his superiority in both men and guns to force his way through the weak German line in front of him. Leblond's fixation on the potential (or merely possible) threat to his own right flank rather than on his own ability to threaten the German defence demonstrates the very traits which Colonel Grandmaison had identified in his two speeches in 1911 as generic French command weaknesses: deploying on a wide (and therefore thin) front in order to avoid being outflanked by an enemy whose whereabouts were uncertain; displaying a negative and defensive mentality fostered by a preoccupation with protection and security; adopting a mentally reactive mode, seeking to find out (or guess) what the enemy was about to do and working to protect against that move. Grandmaison argued that this mindset was atrophying French performance;[108] Leblond's performance certainly fits that description. In allowing himself to be dominated by the fear of being outflanked, Leblond missed the opportunity to break the German 21 RID in two, isolating the German advance guard and leaving it at the mercy of 24 DI west of Petitvoir. Leblond also missed the opportunity to drive his troops north across the Neufchâteau–Petitvoir road, swinging east around and into Neufchâteau itself and rolling up the rest of 21 RID. It can be legitimately argued that such a manoeuvre would have taken the pressure off 5 Colonial Brigade more successfully than simply sending it reinforcements. There is also a case to be made that this might have altered the German commanders' actions. It has been shown that the situation in Neufchâteau was so critical that the final regiment of 25 RID was diverted from the flank attack against the French colonials in order to march to the defence of that town.[109] Had Leblond actually started to roll up the German flank in the town, there exists the possibility that

108   Colonel de Grandmaison, *Deux Conférences faites aux officiers de l' État-Major de l'Armée (février 1911)* (Berger-Levrault, Paris, 1911), p.22: *Une conséquence beaucoup plus grave de nos idées sur le combat de sûreté est une atrophie presque complète de la notion d'offensive.*
109   See page 125, above.

more German units would have been diverted to oppose him, changing the whole dynamic of the action. But Leblond's negative and reactive behaviour allowed the German corps and divisional commanders to grasp and retain the initiative.

General Roques failed to impose any central command or control over the action of his corps. The cavalry regiment was under his direct control, therefore responsibility for the failure to find and turn the German western flank falls ultimately upon him. So too, the decisions which led to the powerful corps artillery being so ineffective lie at his door. His decisions appear with hindsight to be reactive and defensive, like those of his two divisional commanders. There is no sign that he possessed the vision to identify the opportunity in front of him or the leadership to drive his subordinates forward in an energetic and positive manner. But he was a good political general, as his career up to the moment he led 12 CA into battle shows.

Pierre Roques was a career soldier, an engineer whose appointments before the war had eerily mirrored those of Joffre himself.[110] Roques had spent half of his service as an engineer in the French colonies, half in the bureaucratic environment of the Engineering Directorate in the War Ministry, where he rose to the position of Director. Whilst he was at the Ministry, he took a particular interest in the growth of the fledgling French air force, managing to win the internal political battle against the Artillery Branch for control and ownership.[111] His management of the unit which built the French air arm was the crowning achievement of his pre–war career. During this period in the War Ministry, he rose from Lieutenant–Colonel to General, a senior rank warranting a senior field post, hence his appointment as commander of 12 CA. During Roques's time in the War Ministry he walked the corridors of power and he undoubtedly made influential friends and allies. His success in that environment, especially his winning the control of the air force for the Engineering branch, is testament to his political skill and his understanding of the internal politics of that vast bureaucracy, the French army. And his reward when he left the Ministry on 9 April 1912 was a field command, 7 DI, followed rapidly by command of 12 CA;[112] prior to that, his largest field command had been twenty–five engineers in Madagascar in 1900. He had no true command experience, he had not attended the *École supérieure de guerre,* he had no experience of handling infantry and artillery in combined–arms operations, nor handling large bodies of troops. Contamine wrote of him: 'This engineer with little presence, short, with a goatee beard and strawberry birthmark, was a friend of his old comrade in arms Joffre, as well as a man of valour who would rise to great heights', [113] while Rocolle, quoting Pichot-Duclos, wrote that: 'his ability to command fell far short of his unfettered intelligence'.[114] His was an unfortunately typical appointment of the French pre–war army; in part patronage, in part reward for long service, facilitated by political not military skills and an ability to fit in with the social and bureaucratic manners of the day. His prompt action in dismissing both his divisional commanders on the very night after the battle shows astute political judgement, as does the way in which the high–level accounts of the action (corps and divisional JMOs) manage

110 Roques's and Joffre's careers have been extrapolated from: *Annuaire Officiel de l'armée de France pour l'année,* (Berger-Levrault, Paris). The years 1886 to 1911 were available at AAT for examination. In 1886–8, Joffre and Roques worked together as captains in Tonkin. In 1893 when Joffre was in Sudan, Roques was in Dahomey, French West Africa; from 1897 to 1906, Roques was in Madagascar whilst Joffre established himself in the Engineering Directorate at the War Ministry. In 1906 Roques succeeded Joffre as Director of Engineers at the War Ministry when Joffre went to take his field posting at 6 DI in Paris.

111 *Annuaire Officiel de l'armée de France pour l'année 1911,* op.cit. For details of the political infighting over ownership of the French air arm, see: Claude Carlier, *Sera maître du monde, qui sera maître de l'air; la création de l'aviation militaire Française* (Economica, Paris, 2004), pp.24–192 passim; and especially p.136 and pp.171–175.

112 Carlier, *Sera maître de l'air,* p.231.

113 Contamine, *La Victoire de la Marne,* p.122.

114 Rocolle, op.cit., p.144, quoting General Pichot-Duclos, *Au GQG de Joffre: Réflexions sur ma vie militaire* (Arthaud, Grenoble, 1947), pp.253–4.

to omit the unsavoury whilst accentuating small positives. One outcome from Roques's ability to present himself in the best possible light was the positive way in which his personal performance was eventually recorded in the official history:

> On first receipt of the news of combat on the left at Nevraumont, the GOC 12 CA moved to Saint-Médard. From there, he hastened the entry of the artillery into the line and when after the enemy's retreat, his left–hand column resumed its march and was close to taking Grandvoir, he pushed for movement by his right–hand column which was still very much lagging behind…When at the end of the day he learned that the left–hand column of CAC had been forced to retreat as well as the right–hand column of 17 CA, he ordered into place fighting outposts, holding the front Nevraumont–Warmifontaine.[115]

Preserving his reputation after his poor combat debut, Roques also furthered his career, rising to army command in January 1915 and to be Minister of War in 1916.

The opportunity given to General Roques's 12 CA to achieve a significant success over a weak and over–stretched enemy has been outlined. The reasons for the French failure to grasp that opportunity, and win a battlefield victory which might have developed into operational, even strategic success, have been explored. Many generic deficiencies of the French metropolitan army have been shown to have contributed to this French failure. At Neufchâteau, the French conceded operational initiative to the Germans, and were not to regain it until September on the Marne.

---

115 AFGG *I/1* (1923), p.396. Note, however that the second edition (1936) is less generous, merely stating (p.404): 'After discussion with the corps commander… the corps artillery, which was part of the left–hand column, was also directed to go from Saint-Médard towards Martilly, at about 17.00.'

4

Maissin–Anloy
The Second Lost Opportunity

The operational study demonstrated that at Maissin, 11 CA (General Eydoux) encountered three regiments of 25 ID in a battle for the extreme north–western corner of the Ardennes front. Outnumbering his opponent by more than three–to–one, Eydoux also had the opportunity to turn the right flank of the whole German Fourth Army, but failed to achieve anything more than the occupation of Maissin village at nightfall. Alongside him, 34 DI (17 CA), which was supposed to protect his flank, failed to do so and additionally failed to make any progress at Anloy with its four infantry regiments against a single German infantry regiment. This chapter examines the conjoined encounters at Maissin and Anloy in order to establish why this second French opportunity was missed.

Map 40

On the morning of 22 August, starting at about 05.00, General Eydoux's 11 CA set out from the Semoy river bridgeheads in two columns: on the right 22 DI and on the left, 21 DI with the corps artillery. Eydoux marched with 21 DI.[1] On his right, and echeloned slightly behind him, General Poline had organised his 17 CA into three brigade–columns.[2] Each corps was preceded by its own reconnaissance cavalry regiment. As was the case all across the Ardennes that morning, thick fog lay across the land, prohibiting aerial reconnaissance until the sun burned through at about 08.30–09.00. The French columns all had long approach marches in front of them; the heads of each column were expected to march at least twenty kilometres (five hours at regulation speed) in the heat of an August day before reaching their planned destinations; those at the rear even further and longer. They would be tired and there was the prospect of delay. Because of the overall failure of French intelligence, they were not necessarily expecting to fight at the end of it.

North of Neufchâteau on the night of 21–22 August, Duke Albrecht's 18 AK was camped around the towns of Libramont (21 ID) and Libin (25 ID). French intelligence had lost track of the movements of these two divisions after the skirmish near Longlier on 20 August, but believed them to have marched north–westwards. In fact, 25 ID had marched the ten kilometres from Libramont to Libin, which was indeed to the north–west, even if the short distance still left it within striking distance of the advancing French. The other division, 21 ID, remained in the vicinity of Libramont, from where its activity on 22 August would have a profound effect on the overall French operation, although that is beyond the scope of this chapter. French cavalry patrols had, until the afternoon of 21 August when they were withdrawn, monitored the position of these German units, but that intelligence had not been properly used.

---

1   Bujac, *Eydoux*, p.64.
2   AFGG I/1 (1936), pp.405–408.

Duke Albrecht's orders for 18 AK on 22 August were for a continuation of its cautious westerly advance on the flank of Third Army. It was planned to be a relatively easy day, with marches of no more than five to ten kilometres for each division. For 25 ID this specifically meant a leisurely march through the forests and over the hills to the region around Jehonville, coincidentally right into the path of the oncoming French columns.[3] Major–General Rühne, commanding 25 ID, organised his division into two brigade–columns, each with a supporting artillery regiment. 50 Brigade on the right was sent towards Jehonville via Maissin and 49 Brigade on the left was to go via Anloy. After breakfast the two columns set out from their billets around Libin at 07.00. Although at this stage the German commanders at all levels from Fourth Army headquarters down to individual regiments had no idea that the French had launched their offensive, the shorter marches planned for 25 ID gave them an opportunistic advantage. At Anloy, 49 Brigade's column arrived in good time to rest, to set up its artillery and to reconnoitre its position – this was standard doctrine not a response to an impending attack – before the French arrived. 50 Brigade, with a slightly longer approach march, took a rest break at about 08.30, during which its commanders received and absorbed the latest cavalry reconnaissance reports, before setting off again towards Maissin.[4]

Maissin was also the objective of Eydoux's 11 CA, and Anloy that of 34 DI (General Alby), part of 17 CA. Alby's left–hand column, (68 Brigade) was supposed to cover 11 CA's right flank.[5] In the context of de Langle's operational plan, the occupation of these two villages was a very important preliminary step towards fulfilling Joffre's strategic intention, because of their location and the terrain. They both lie north and west of the great forested belt through which de Langle's army had to pass in order to gain the open region of the central Ardennes, the region north of Neufchâteau. They both also lie on the river Lesse behind which, as has been shown, French intelligence had identified a strong German defensive screen.[6] Maissin anchored the north–west corner of the impending battle zone, there being only ten kilometres of impassible forest between it and the river Meuse; the heights around Anloy gave excellent observation and fire–positions over the open land to the east. On the right, the rest of Poline's 17 CA was supposed to come out of the woods between Anloy and Ochamps (north of Bertrix), while in the distance, Roques's 12 CA would (in theory) push past Neufchâteau onto the open land near Libramont, forming the end of a huge arc of troops from the latter place back to Maissin.

The village of Maissin lies on the north–eastern edge of the narrow band of hilly, forested terrain north of the river Semoy and east of the river Meuse; a region which justly typifies the classic description of the impassable Ardennes. At Maissin, although the village itself lies in a clearing on some south–facing slopes, the land to the south and west – through which the French were to advance – is covered with bands of forest. A pastoral valley lay between the village on its south-facing slopes and the plateau on which the French infantry were to appear. The plateau, heavily forested but with scattered clearings, and stretching back almost to Paliseul, fell away sharply on its eastern side. The main column of 22 DI would march up onto the plateau; on its left, down in the valley of the river Our, was 21 DI; and on the right 68 Brigade of 34 DI was supposed to be below in the valley of the Lesse, protecting their flank. The river Lesse flows north–westwards around Anloy and Maissin from its source five kilometres away at Ochamps on its way to the Meuse at Dinant.

Map 41

---

3   *Grossherzogliches Artilleriekorps, 1 Grossherzoglich Hessisches Feldartillerie-Regiment Nr 25 im Weltkrieg 1914–1918* [FAR 25] (Verlag Rolf & Co., Berlin, 1935), p.22.
4   FAR 25, op. cit., p.22.
5   AFGG I/1 (1936), pp.390–392.
6   Ibid., Annex512: *GQG, 19 août, 06.00: Compte rendu de renseignements nr.47*; and Annex 749 : [Fourth Army] *Armée de Stenay, 21 août*, [c.13.45] : *Bulletin de renseignements nr.7.*

It was important for the French to secure Maissin and Anloy, to anchor their platform for attack. But it was equally important to the Germans. As has been shown, Duke Albrecht's expanding front was too large for the forces allocated to him. There were necessarily huge gaps in his line and he was balancing one risk against another. Having decided to keep 8 AK in the north in touch with Third Army's left wing, and having retained 8 RAK as his army reserve near Bastogne, there was no other major unit near enough to support 18 AK if it got into trouble. Once the importance of the major French offensive was realised on 22 August, the German Fourth Army command knew that it was facing just such a crisis situation. 18 RAK at Neufchâteau had significant problems of its own. What was needed was a strong defensive position, and the high ground around Anloy and Maissin, combined with the unfavourable terrain further west, was the ideal place to make a stand. But even so, there were so few German troops available that, were the Maissin position to be turned and outflanked, there was nothing to plug the gap.

The German attempt to seize and hold the Maissin–Anloy position fell to Major–General Rühne's two brigade–columns, each supported by one of his two artillery regiments. The corps heavy artillery was not available to him, having been allocated in its entirety to 21 ID further south. The right–hand column (50 Brigade) was made up of 117 and 118 IR supported by 25 FAR. Its destination was Maissin, coming in from the north road. The left–hand column (49 Brigade) contained 115 and 116 IR supported by 61 FAR. It marched on Anloy, from the north–east. Together the two columns had an approximate strength of 12000 rifles, 72 guns (18 of them light howitzers) and 24 machine guns.

Opposing them were three French divisions with a total strength of approximately 39,000 rifles, 156 guns and 72 machine guns, an overall superiority of at least three to one. But as elsewhere on the overall front, notably at Neufchâteau, the distribution of forces was uneven: three German regiments (50 Brigade plus 115 IR of 49 Brigade) would fight two divisions (eight regiments) of 11 CA for possession of Maissin, while one regiment (116 IR of 49 Brigade) was faced with the whole of 34 DI (four regiments) at Anloy.

The failures of intelligence on both sides meant that neither was expecting a major battle. At the beginning of the day, the French were only vaguely aware of the German dispositions ('digging in behind the Lesse'[7]), and were at divisional level and below very much focused simply on a march through the forests. The Germans of 25 ID were similarly barely aware of any possibility of combat when they started out on the morning of 22 August.[8] The combination of secrecy and fog had shrouded the French advance, and it was only when local cavalry patrols revealed the imminent arrival of significant French infantry units that a true idea of what was unfolding formed in the minds of the German commanders. The original daily orders on each side had to be significantly modified as and when intelligence was received.

At 07.00 French and German cavalry patrols encountered each other about 3 kilometres south of Maissin. The 2nd squadron of *2 Chasseurs à cheval*, the corps cavalry of 11 CA, met a German cavalry patrol from 6 Dragoons, 25 ID's integral divisional cavalry, on the plateau about three kilometres south of Maissin, at a place called Bellevue farm. The fog was thick, the Germans were outnumbered and they retreated into Maissin, pursued by the French. By 09.30, as the fog was lifting, they had evacuated Maissin, and the French cavalry regiment started to organise its defence, setting up two squadrons and a machine gun detachment at the northern exits of the village, as well as sending out patrols in all directions. To the north, towards the heights at Transinne (on the right bank of river

7   AFGGI/ 1, Annex 580: *GQG 2e Bureau, Compte rendu de renseignements, nr.49, du 20 août, 06.00.*
8   A. Hiss, *Infanterie-Regiment Kaiser Wilhelm (2 Grossherzoglich Hessisches) nr.116* [FAR 61] (Oldenburg, Stalling, 1924), Chapter 2.

Lesse), it seemed that the Germans were gathering in force.[9] Had they but known it, the French cavalry patrols were observing the approach of the main columns of the 50 Brigade of 25 ID.

It would seem at this stage that the French had seized the initiative, with their corps cavalry regiment fortifying their objective (Maissin), the advance guard of 22 DI coming up behind followed by the main column, and with the whole day in which to consolidate and develop their operation. Indeed, Eydoux informed de Langle's Fourth Army headquarters at 10.10 (from his command post at the northern end of the village of Paliseul), that his cavalry had taken Maissin and that he intended to occupy it and then march east onto the heights at Anloy to link up with 17 CA.[10] But already small but important things had started to go wrong.

The advance guard of 22 DI, (19 RI of 44 Brigade) had started out at 04.50 but almost immediately got entangled with the wagons and supporting infantry of the corps artillery at Les Hayons, an important crossroads just two kilometres north of the start line on the river Semoy. They lost an hour untangling the chaos and, despite speeding up their march, only reached Paliseul by 09.30. That lost hour would be crucial later in the morning when the possession of Maissin was disputed. Next in line in the column, the divisional artillery regiment (35 RAC) took the wrong road out of Les Hayons and then instead of cutting across on a minor road to rejoin the column, chose to retrace its steps to its correct starting position, thus losing more valuable time and separating the advance guard infantry from its artillery support. Third in line, 118 RI was also late; Colonel François decided to delay his regiment's departure because their night's rest had been disturbed by a German aircraft. This in turn held up the entire 43 Brigade which only reached Paliseul (still 8 kilometres short of Maissin) at 14.30.[11]

Map 41a

The consequences of this poor French staff work, slack discipline and weak command were devastating for their chances of achieving an operational victory. Firstly the lost hour cost 19 RI the race to the village. They arrived on the southern slopes above Maissin at 11.30, just as their cavalry was withdrawing and German infantry (the leading battalion of 118 IR) entering the village from the other side. So they had to mount an assault to recapture the village. Secondly, because their artillery had lost its way, 19 RI delivered its initial assault on the village without artillery support.[12] Thirdly, 118 RI and the rest of the column came up so late that the tactical situation had changed, the initiative had passed to the (outnumbered) Germans, and 22 DI was forced to fight a defensive battle, leaving its advance guard isolated in Maissin village. To cap a very poor staff performance, General Eydoux failed to report this dramatic reversal of fortune to his army commander until 16.45, leaving de Langle completely in the dark as to what was happening on his left wing.[13]

The French failure to consolidate their early hold on Maissin was the first element of this lost opportunity, because the fighting, which then lasted all day, centred thereafter around a bitter struggle to occupy the houses, which formed natural strong points. The narrowness of the margin by which I/118 IR beat 19 RI in the race to occupy the village suggests that a stout defence by the 1000 French cavalrymen – if dismounted and supported by their machine–gun company – might have held the Germans up long enough for 19 RI to reinforce them. It also highlights the crucial absence of French artillery, which could have halted the German advance by bombarding the road as they approached the village. But the artillery was late and *2 Chasseurs*, like their sister regiment at nearby Nevraumont, did not take on the German infantry.[14] The German regimental history of the

9   Bujac, op. cit., p.65.
10 AFGG I/1, Annex 927: [11 CA, 22 August, 10.10]: *Général commandant 11e corps à commandant armée Stenay.*
11 Bujac, op.cit., p.69.
12 Ibid.
13 AFGG I/1, Annex 929: [11 CA] *Poste de Stenay, reçu de Paliseul le 22/8/14 à 16.45 par telephone: Général commandant 11e corps à commandant armée Stenay*; and Annex 930: *11e corps d'armée*, écrit à *17.30.*
14 Bujac, op. cit., p.70; and FAR 25, op.cit., p.23.

leading regiment describes how easy was the capture of the village: 'At 12.00 I/118 took fire from Maissin...Initially the French fire was ineffective. The battalion advanced in long bounds, crossed the "rather wide and deep" Lesse stream and by 12.30 had reached the east side of Maissin. I/118 entered Maissin without encountering significant resistance.'[15] At this very time, Colonel Chapès, commanding 19 RI, having lost the race into Maissin by a whisker, was already deploying his three battalions for an assault on the village.[16]

The time taken for 19 RI's deployment was time used by the Germans on the other side to pour into the village. At 12.15 German artillery opened fire on the advancing French infantry; by this time the machine–gun company of 118 IR was hastening to the front of the main column to support the action.[17] The Germans were rapidly consolidating their hold on the village, but the attacking French firing–line was deployed at ever shortening range and advancing in short rushes up the slopes south–east of the village, supported by their own machine guns on the flanks of their advancing riflemen.[18] By about 13.30, the French infantry were in the centre of the village, disputing possession house–by–house, but impeded by German machine guns firing down the streets and enfilading the crossroads.[19]

In theory, 19 RI should have been reinforced by the next regiment in the column as well as by the artillery. The French firing–line should have thickened and widened so that their superior numbers could envelop the thin German line. But the late arrival of 118 RI left a gap in both time and space, and allowed the Germans to seize the tactical initiative. German troops from 115 IR (part of the left-hand column, 49 Brigade) advanced from Anloy onto the French flank and managed to intersperse themselves between the French advance guard and the main column. As a result, the fight for the village became an equal struggle between one French and one German regiment, despite the large numbers of French infantry in column stretching back to Paliseul. Furthermore, the main battle then developed on the plateau, some two or three kilometres short of the village, for reasons which will be given below.

Because of the delayed arrival of the French 118 RI, the second and third battalions of the German 118 IR were given the time and opportunity to deploy to the right of the village and, using fire–and–movement tactics, infiltrate around the flank of the shorter French line, forcing the fighting back up onto the plateau:

> The whole region north of Maissin was swarming with German troops infiltrating through the woods...in the west came a vigorous push; elements of this group reached a large copse southwards between Maissin and Bellevue Farm. The group of 35ᵉ Artillery, against which the German guns had ground away, received severe losses in a very short time.[20]

This German attacking movement was made that much easier by the late arrival of General Eydoux's other division (21 DI) which was supposed to appear on the Germans' right flank – delays which will be examined in detail below. So when the second regiment of the German 50 Brigade (117 IR) arrived in its turn, it had time and space in which to manoeuvre. Two battalions deployed on the left and linked up with 49 Brigade; the other, for the time being, remained in reserve.[21] The

15   Zuber, *Ardennes 1914*, p.153, quoting: H. Freund, *Geschichte des Infanterie-Regiments Prinz Karl (4.Grossh. Hess) Nr 118 im Weltkrieg* [IR 118] (Gross-Gerau, 1930), pp.29–28.
16   Bujac, op. cit., p.71.
17   Hiss, IR 116, p.29 and Zuber, op.cit., pp.152–153, quoting: Freud,IR 118, pp.29–38.
18   Bujac, op. cit., p.72.
19   Ibid., p.73.
20   Bujac, op. cit., p.74.
21   Zuber, op.cit., pp.153–154, quoting: K. Offenbacher, *Die Geschichte des Infanterie-Leibregiments Grossherzogin (3.*

brigade's artillery (25 FAR) occupied commanding positions on the heights east of Maissin and, as will be shown below, was very proactive in its support. While 50 Brigade came down from the north and occupied Maissin, 49 Brigade came in from the east. The axis of its advance took it up the slopes of the plateau towards the open right flank of 22 DI's column. Its two regiments were in line, with 115 IR on the right and 116 IR on the left, both deploying out of Anloy. Because of the delay to the French artillery, 115 IR was able to cross the three or four kilometres of open pasture between Anloy and Maissin unimpeded by enemy shellfire and scale the steep wooded slopes (in places a near–vertical incline) up to the plateau without opposition from enemy rifle fire. There, in the vicinity of Bellevue farm, they were able to attack 118 RI in the flank, disrupt the French artillery, and force the remainder of 22 DI to fight a defensive battle rather than reinforce 19 RI in Maissin: 'Elements of 5 and 8 Companies [of 116 IR] supported 4 and 6 Companies of 115 IR in storming an enemy battery which they captured after a hard struggle and held despite several ferocious counter–attacks.'[22] The effectiveness of the German attack was evident:

> Parmentier's battery risked being captured by skirmishers arriving within rifle range on the nearby crest. Lieutenant Granchi ran towards some infantry passing nearby calling for help since his own support (I/118) was too far to the left. The leader of this troop (a battalion from 17 CA which was separated from its main body) replied that his men were exhausted, that he had lost nearly half his men and that they could not continue in action. He marched off, abandoning the artillery.[23]

The attitude of that junior French officer, citing exhaustion and casualties as an excuse to stop fighting, points to serious morale problems within the unit. And that errant battalion from 17 CA, turning up during the afternoon amongst the battalions and batteries on the right flank of 22 DI, points to another aspect of French failure. As stated above, the left–hand column of 17 CA (68 Brigade of 34 DI) was supposed to be protecting the right flank of 11 CA from just such an attack as has been described above. But its advance had not been coordinated with that of the unit it was supposed to be protecting, and it arrived too late. Although the need for each French corps to protect the open right flank of the one in front and to its left was an operational imperative, there is no evidence in the JMOs of 34 DI and its subordinate units that there were any tactical instructions designed to implement such action or any intent on the part of their commanders to fulfil such a mission. On the contrary, one regiment of General Alby's 34 DI (83 RI) recorded that at 12.00, after a prolonged halt at Jehonville, the regiment received orders at 13.50 to march from Jehonville in the direction of Anloy.[24] Nearly two hours were wasted, during which a march on the Anloy heights might have been accomplished, to greater operational effect. This diary entry, like many others, hints at a total lack of urgency on the French side, even though the fighting at Maissin was already entering its third hour. General Alby's left–hand column (68 Brigade) was powerful; two regiments, two groups of divisional artillery and two groups of corps artillery, led by Alby himself.[25] But the leading regiment (59 RI) was at 12.00 still marching from Jehonville to Sart, six kilometres short of a proper screening position on 11 CA's open flank.[26] To compound the problems arising within 34 DI, General Alby left all his artillery at Sart, on the 400m–high knoll north–east of

Grossherzoglich Hessisches) Nr. 117 [IR 117] (Oldenburg i.O.1931), pp.29–40.
22 IR 116, op. cit., p.26.
23 Bujac, op. cit., p.75.
24 AAT 26N665: JMO of 83 RI, entry for 22 August 1914.
25 AAT 26N326/1: JMO of 34 DI, entry for 22 August 1914.
26 AAT 16N889/1: JMO of *9 Chasseurs à cheval* [9 Chasseurs], entry for 22 August 1914.

that village.[27] Although technically just within range of Anloy which was about five kilometres away, the thick screen of woods prevented it from firing in support of its infantry.[28] The French artillery, it seems, did not as a rule use indirect fire, preferring line-of-sight; hence an obstacle such as a deep belt of forest rendered them ineffective. At the same time the gunners seemed to have difficulty finding adequate firing positions further forward. So the infantry of 59 RI went forward unsupported. This decision to separate infantry from its supporting artillery was so far outside French doctrine as to be inexplicable, particularly when the divisional commander (Alby) had received information which suggested imminent contact. The orders added that if Jehonville and Sart were held by the enemy, the advance guard was to attack immediately.[29] 17 CA's intelligence staff had learned that a German infantry company previously at Jehonville had withdrawn, and 17 CA's corps cavalry patrols were reporting multiple contacts. But the French cavalry failed to provide any useful intelligence: a squadron of 9 Chasseurs had encountered German cavalry south of Anloy at Sart but had found it impossible to determine their strength.[30]

A noticeable feature of the French Ardennes campaign was the frequency with which their cavalry reported that it could not penetrate a German defensive screen to establish the strength of what lay behind. In part this seems to have been due to the French habit of using squadron–sized patrol units (250 mounted men), or even (as above) marching a whole cavalry regiment from one location to another. These tactical units were too large to slip through gaps like the small German 6– and 12–man patrols, but too small to force through opposition. And the French reluctance to fight dismounted seems to have encouraged an even greater tendency not to try to force a screen.

The significance of the late start of the French 118 RI with the consequent delay to 22 DI's main column, combined with the separate slow arrival of 68 Brigade on its right flank, becomes fully apparent. The fight for Maissin village became an independent action by the French advance guard (19 RI), while the main column led now by 118 RI fought a second action on the plateau. This second action was shaped by the aggressive initiative of two battalions of 118 IR in the north and west, by the equally aggressive attacks by 115 IR from the east and by the strong defensive action of 116 IR, facing south and holding back the bulk of 34 DI. The inferior German forces had seized the tactical initiative and 22 DI, despite its numbers, was fighting a defensive action. Of the flanking movement by 21 DI on the left there was still no sign at this stage. But the German brigade simply did not have the numbers nor the fire power to convert its initial tactical advantage into outright victory. Meanwhile the eventual arrival of 34 DI on the right of 11 CA (where, it will be remembered, it was supposed to be protecting a flank) initiated the fighting around Anloy.

Map 41b
When at about 15.00 the advance guard of 17 CA's left-hand column, 59 RI, came out of the woods opposite Anloy they encountered and were stopped by 116 IR. The German 49 Brigade artillery (61 FAR) had excellent fire–support positions on the heights east of Anloy; the French artillery back at Sart was powerless to intervene. The French infantry were thus pinned to the forest edge despite repeated gallant attempts to get forward without artillery support, in which they suffered heavy casualties. 59 RI lost its colonel and two of three battalion commanders, with about 60% officer casualties and 30% casualties in other ranks.[31] The remnants of the regiment merged

27   JMO of 34 DI, op. cit.
28   Ibid.
29   Ibid.
30   JMO of 9 Chasseurs, op. cit.
31   AAT 26N650/1: JMO of 59 RI, *2 août–21 décembre 1914*.

with 88 RI when it came up and retreated with it at about 18.00 in response to orders from 68 Brigade headquarters.[32]

Alongside, on their right, marched the column of 67 Brigade (83 RI and 14 RI). 14 RI, which was heading directly for Anloy village, was leading. At about 14.00 when it debouched from the northern edge of the woods and occupied the crest of Hill 453, about one kilometre south of Anloy, it surprised a German battalion in march formation coming from the east via Hill 416 and stretching back to the slopes south of Anloy. The leading company and the machine–guns opened fire and inflicted heavy losses, forcing the German battalion, supported by its company of machine–guns, to defend the slopes south of the village. The French regimental JMO records that the German position was solidly fortified by trenches and by wire 30–40 metres in depth; bearing in mind that the German battalion had been caught by surprise whilst on the march, these German field fortifications must have been temporary, constructed for that specific fire–fight.[33] This is not the first occasion that historians have been confused by French after-battle reports of German trenches. The truth is that, unlike the Germans, the French were neither instructed nor expected to dig in during a fire–fight, and so they tended to assume that German field fortifications were pre-prepared rather than dug during the action. Within half–an–hour, two more French companies were fed into the line, but were subjected to heavy fire from a German artillery battery and two machine–guns set up on the north edge of the woods about 900 metres north-east of Hill 453. The French now started to take heavy casualties, and their commander reported that he could not advance without artillery preparation.[34] The importance of combined arms cooperation to achieve fire superiority was being dramatically illustrated, and the French, despite far superior numbers, could not get forward, having left their artillery behind. The French version of events here at Anloy is confirmed by their opponents:

> Hardly had the first waves of II & III/116 reached the heights south–west of Anloy at about 14.00 when they were hit at a range of barely 400 metres by brisk infantry and machine–gun fire. And yet the enemy could not be seen. In the cornfields and on the edge of the woods they found themselves pressed by superior forces so that no reliable fire could be returned. But the enemy showed no sign of that furious impulse to press forward which had become second nature to our infantrymen. Despite the strong fire and despite being hampered by the wire fencing in the fields, they [the German infantry] after repeated assaults began to clear the cornfields completely of the enemy and to reach the nearest coppices.[35]

What is interesting in comparing the two sides' versions of this event is not only the corroboration of the main facts but also the contradictions shown in interpretation. Both agree that the Germans were ambushed by French infantry, reinforcing the point that Joffre's strategic and operational surprise was also occasionally achieved at the tactical level. But despite this, the Germans see fence wire bordering the cultivated fields where the French see wire set up as part of field fortifications. The French also give the impression (which is explicitly stated elsewhere[36]) that the German trenches were part of a pre–prepared defensive system, which was not at all the case. The German observation about the lack of French élan compared to their own aggressive behaviour resonates with the speculation over French morale raised earlier, and with evidence cited in the discussion

32   Ibid.
33   For a discussion of comparative use of, and attitudes to field fortification, see Chapter 10.
34   AAT 26N586/2: JMO of 14 RI, *2 août 1914–31 janvier 1915* (microfiche).
35   116 IR, op. cit., pp. 25–26.
36   Bujac, op. cit., p.72.

of the battle at Neufchâteau. But the absence of French artillery support can be cited in defence of the performance of their infantry; in trying to get forward 14 RI suffered 25% casualties in officers and 12% casualties in men.[37] The German infantry of 116 IR at least had the backing of the guns of 61 FAR, which set up in a semi–open position offering the batteries a dominating view south–westwards from the crest of the hill. Although observation was hindered by hedges and forests, there could be seen, half–exposed above the hedges, the red–blue figures of French infantry, so the regiment opened fire at a range of 1600 metres.[38]

The upshot of the fighting at Anloy was that, despite a superiority in infantry of more than four–to–one, 33 DI was unable to get forward for lack of artillery support. If they were adhering to their doctrine, they should not have attempted to go forward without it. But go forward they did, attempting many times to gain ground; the outnumbered Germans were able to hold their position thanks mainly to their artillery support, and inflict heavy casualties on their opponent. It should be recognised that this was not an issue of reckless French élan, nor an issue of a faulty doctrine of *offensive à outrance* being used on an open, planned battlefield. It was a matter of deficient command – sending columns of infantry to march unprotected through thick forest without their field guns. It was an issue of lack of combined–arms expertise and of lack of reconnaissance for suitable artillery positions before committing the infantry. It was also an issue of inadequate scouting ahead of the main column. Despite these failings, one French column managed to surprise their German opponents but could not capitalise upon this without their artillery. The failure of 34 DI to get forward at Anloy early enough to secure the high ground for their artillery was a major contributing factor to the overall missed opportunity at Maissin–Anloy.

Meanwhile on the plateau, all three of 22 DI's artillery groups had set up, two groups to the right of the road and the other to the left, some 300–400m forward in a slight fold in the ground. They received considerable counter–battery fire almost immediately, whose effectiveness can be judged by the fact that Captain Gallate's battery was very soon virtually wiped out and Gallate killed.[39] The French guns were also at risk from German infantry infiltrating from the flanks. The leading battalion of 118 RI had halted in response to the German initiative and was at this time protecting the guns around Bellevue Farm; the other two battalions were deployed as impromptu flank guards, defending against the German infantry working forward on both flanks.[40] At this time – it was about 14.00 – 43 Brigade (22 DI) with 116 RI and 62 RI in column, was still back at Paliseul.[41] The achievement of numerical superiority by 22 DI was a slow and painful process.

If 22 DI was making slow progress, then 21 DI was arguably worse. Earlier in the day, this division, commanded by General Radiguet, was actually half–an–hour in front of General Pambert's 22 DI, reaching Paliseul first (on a parallel road) at 09.00. General Eydoux had just reported to Fourth Army that his cavalry held Maissin. Based on this news and the developing tactical situation, he decided to commit 22 DI to a frontal attack whilst sending 21 DI onto the western flank of the enemy.[42] This plan was of the classic 'fix and hold' type, often attributed to German doctrine but equally lauded by French military teachers like Foch and Grandmaison. Had it been executed with speed and skill, 21 DI would have found itself in a position to outflank the German 50

37   JMO of 14 RI, op. cit.
38   FAR 61, op. cit., p.12.
39   Bujac, op. cit., pp.73–75.
40   Ibid. p.73.
41   Ibid. p.74.
42   Ibid. p.66.

Brigade north of Maissin, and with plenty of time to execute further operational manoeuvres. Behind 50 Brigade was nothing but empty space for eighteen kilometres to the north (where 8 AK stood) and eighteen kilometres or more to the east (where 8 RAK was force–marching towards the danger zone). The opportunity was there for General Radiguet (21 DI) to force the German 25 ID back from the dominating high ground north of Maissin using an outflanking movement, thereby delivering one of Fourth Army's key operational objectives. But it did not happen.

The distance from Paliseul to Maissin via the western route – the valley of the river Our – was just over twelve kilometres, which should take a column about three hours at French army regulation speed, or less if a forced–march was initiated. In theory, Radiguet's advance guard could or should have been threatening the German flank a little after 12.00, with the main body about half–an–hour behind it. In fact, the head of the column (93 RI) only reached the village of Our at about 13.00, still four kilometres (one hour) short of Maissin and with an extremely tough final climb in front of it out of the valley up to the plateau on which Maissin stood. Even General Eydoux himself realised that the slow arrival of 21 DI was stripping his planned flanking movement of its effectiveness.[43] He ordered General Radiguet to intensify his attack, no longer to flank the enemy but to relieve pressure against the left of 22 DI which he considered to be threatened by the German infiltration.[44] And when this flank attack did go in, just after 14.00, 93 RI attacked in consecutive battalion waves without waiting for artillery support and from a distance of well over 1000m. The regiment suffered heavy casualties and was driven to ground.[45] Yet this was not the stuff of official French doctrine or *offensive à outrance,* but rather the product of the unofficial cult, described later in the chapter on Doctrine, which infected all too many of the young French junior officer class: 'Colonel Hétet placed in the front line his 2nd Battalion, under Commandant Lafouge who, without waiting for the support of the artillery and without liaison with 22 DI on his right, launched his attack. It was nailed to the spot.'[46]

Apart from the undisciplined *furia francese* of the French junior officers and men, one of the reasons why the flank attack failed was that the German command was given plenty of time to reorganise to face the new front. The two remaining battalions of 117 IR, so far held back in reserve, were deployed to face west, just inside the tree line; their rifle–fire, together with their machine–guns and with artillery support from I/25 FAR, was sufficiently powerful to stop the injudicious French assault. A second assault, organised this time with full artillery support and with regiments of both 41 and 42 Brigades in line, was launched at about 16.00 and was progressively more successful: 'From the moment our batteries opened fire they surprised and disrupted the enemy. Until dusk they [the German guns] directed their fire upon those batteries which they had been able to locate, but with little effect.'[47] The relentless pressure on the Germans west and north of Maissin took its toll. At 17.00, 50 Brigade was formally ordered to retire,[48] which it did in good order to start with, using a battery of field guns right in the front line to break up the threatening French infantry attacks and even launching three limited counter–attacks of its own.[49] To the north, 117 IR melted away into the woods. In the village 118 IR finally gave up its resistance. 50 Brigade retreated behind the river Lesse, towards Villance.[50] The exhausted troops were close to breaking and only the energetic efforts of their senior officers managed to stop the backward movement at Villance and

Map 41c

43   Bujac, op.cit., p.77.
44   AFGG I/1, Annex 928: [11 CA, 22 August, 14.00]: *A Monsieur le général commandant la 21e division.*
45   AFGG I/1, pp.399–401; and Bujac, op.cit., pp.78–80.
46   Bujac, op. cit., p.79.
47   Bujac, op. cit., pp. 79–80.
48   *Weltkrieg 1,* op.cit., p.329.
49   See Bujac, op.cit., p.81; and FAR 25, op.cit., p.28.
50   *Weltkrieg 1,* p.329

form an impromptu firing–line to protect the guns.[51] But its strong defence over six or seven hours had left General Eydoux no time to exploit this even limited success before nightfall.

The retreat of 50 Brigade had a knock–on effect on 49 Brigade and the fighting at Anloy. But the position of 49 Brigade was stronger, and the artillery–less French situation weaker, so it was able to hold until nightfall. Here, it was the French who retreated, albeit in a somewhat haphazard fashion. The retreat of 34 DI has been described as something of a rout brought on by the debacle suffered by 33 DI in the Forest of Luchy:

> But due to the destruction of 33 DI in the *Forêt de Luchy*, 34 DI was ordered to retreat, front to the east towards the German 21 ID, which was pushing into its rear area. This, on top of the pounding that the division had taken from 25 ID, caused a panic. The division collapsed, with only two battalions and two groups of artillery turning to face 21 ID. The rest traversed the woods and retreated as far as Florenville.[52]

In fact, the overriding characteristic of the retreat of 34 DI was command chaos rather than panic. Certain units did not receive the order to fall back and remained in position all through the night and into the next morning, thus confirming that the Germans were in no position to exploit the situation. III/59 RI received the order to retreat at about 18.00, and it was then passed slowly to the rest of the regiment. But many units remained on the battlefield all night, including 6 and 8 Companies of II/59, 11 Company and some elements of 9 Company of III/59; there remained also a battalion of 88 RI.[53] Others withdrew in good order to their designated fall–back position only to find no staff officer to direct them, so they continued to march to the rear. 83 RI's JMO reported that the retreat was conducted in an orderly manner protected by two companies of 59 RI. It left its third battalion at Jehonville to cover any threat from Ochamps, and that unit remained undisturbed until about 19.00. But, having received no further instructions and feeling increasingly isolated, it withdrew spontaneously via Acremont–Assenois where it joined the rest of the regiment. At 21.00 the regiment, more or less regrouped, escorted three groups of artillery back via Offagne, Fays and Dohan and Muno, to Hessincourt, which it reached on 23 August.[54]

Similarly, the JMO of 14 RI reported that it was ordered to withdraw at 21.00. Having arrived [at Jehonville] at 22.00 it left again at 23.00 to march through the night to Dohun. But at Dohun they found the village virtually abandoned and the barns and granaries locked. Because the troops were excessively cold and could not sleep they soon continued their march to Muno, which they reached at 15.30 on 23 August. The troops were exhausted, having marched seventy kilometres in thirty–eight hours and fought a six–hour combat. But they were in no way demoralised and they set up camp in very good order.[55]

The threat of an intervention from Ochamps, mentioned in 83 RI's JMO, refers to von der Esch's detachment of 21 ID, which was fighting nearby in the Bertrix encounter battle.[56] But the threat did not materialise, judging by these accounts of 34 DI's withdrawal. Moreover the German 49 Brigade at Anloy was in no position to exploit the French withdrawal at all, hence its failure to

---

51   Ibid.
52   Zuber, op. cit., p.157, paraphrasing AFGG I/1 (1936), p.408, but omitting a key point; that the Germans failed to pursue the retreating French, so that one unit of 68 Brigade, which did not receive the order to retreat, remained unmolested on the edge of the *Bois Piret* all night.
53   JMO of 59 RI, op. cit.
54   AAT 26N665, JMO of 83 RI, entry for 22 August 1914.
55   JMO of 14 RI, op. cit.
56   'AGM', *Bertrix 1914, seen from the German side* (*Journal of the Royal Artillery*, Vol. LXIV 1937–8), pp.245–252.

locate and destroy the small French detachments left behind in the firing–line. The German troops went back into night quarters and regrouped and consolidated their defensive position:

> At last nightfall brought the fighting to an end. Completely exhausted, the battalions gathered on the heights near Anloy. Through the lack of security for the whole position – the right wing of the division had had to evacuate Maissin at 17.00 because of the threat of encirclement – the heights and the outskirts of the town were ordered to be fortified...the troops remained near Anloy until the afternoon of 23 August.[57]

By nightfall the German situation had markedly improved. Reinforcements in the shape of both divisions of 8 RAK had arrived, 15 RID at Maissin and 16 RID at Anloy. Most importantly, additional artillery had arrived with these columns, the presence of which particularly helped to bolster the deteriorating morale of 50 Brigade, whose heavy casualties and long exposure to superior fire–power had weakened them almost to breaking point:

> During this perilous moment of the flood of retreating men of 50 Brigade, the forward elements of 8 RAK arrived on the battlefield behind 18 AK, after an average forty–five kilometre forced march, accomplished through the difficult hilly country of the Ardennes and under the burning rays of an August sun without regard for those who fell out...15 RID was directed to continue its march through Libin towards Villance. A group (*Abteilung*) of field artillery and half a group of heavy field howitzers were brought into position at 18.45 east of Villance. The whole artillery was soon brought into operation. If this help came too late to turn around the outcome of the battle at Maissin, the protective fire of 8 RAK did stop the enemy's exploitation of his partial success.[58]

The German perspective of 50 Brigade's low combat capability at the end of the day simply underlines how much the French delays and slow deployment cost them. The wasted hours were hours during which the French window of opportunity closed, hours in which Duke Albrecht managed to shore up this particular gap in his line. 8 RAK, the designated Fourth Army reserve, had started the day around Bastogne. As early as 10.30, Duke Albrecht had decided to call his reserve south as a precautionary measure. By the time the situation had clarified, and 8 RAK was ordered to go to Villance to support 25 ID, it was already marching to the front. The soldiers of 8 RAK, reservists of the older categories, force–marched doggedly in the intense heat for hour after hour, covering about forty-five kilometres before arriving at the Villance, just five kilometres short of both Maissin and Anloy, at about 18.00. There the staff of 25 ID was busy rallying the remains of 50 Brigade. The reinforcements, exhausted as they were, improved morale and re–established a strong defensive line. The artillery was especially welcome. At this stage and at this local level, the Germans had every reason to expect a fresh French assault in the morning; the events elsewhere which caused the French Fourth Army to retreat would only become clear during the evening as reports came in and a consolidated picture was communicated to them.

So ended the encounter battle at Maissin–Anloy. Despite their early occupation of Maissin village, the French forfeited that advantage and failed to capitalise upon their superiority in numbers and fire–power. The open right flank of the German 25 ID and the large empty space behind them was

57   IR 116, op. cit., p.27 and p.28.
58   *Weltkrieg 1*, pp. 329–330.

not even sought, let alone found, by the French commanders. And yet General Eydoux believed that he had won a notable victory, while the retreat of 34 DI was blamed on the disaster of 33 DI at Bertrix. But in fact Maissin–Anloy was, if a tactical stalemate, a German operational victory; they only had to avoid losing until their reinforcements arrived, and in that they achieved total success.

There are several prominent features of the battle which explain why it ended in a favourable outcome for Germany. At the operational level, General Eydoux's failure to keep de Langle informed of the significant change in the situation when Maissin village was lost – there was a six–and–a–half hour gap between his reports – meant that Fourth Army staff had no opportunity to influence events or make revised plans – even if they had wanted to. De Langle had the extra resources to make an operational manoeuvre: as the operational study has shown, there were two French cavalry divisions (4 and 9 DCs), one infantry corps (9 CA) and one reserve infantry division (52 DIR) all within striking distance of Maissin on that open westerly flank. This not inconsiderable force would have been more than sufficient to turn a tactical envelopment of 25 ID's right flank into an operational manoeuvre of some significance. But even if the vital intelligence had been passed to Fourth Army headquarters, de Langle would have to have reacted faster and got his units to move faster than had hitherto been the case.

On the German side, communications between 18 AK and Duke Albrecht's headquarters were much more efficient and effective, even though the Duke was at his forward battle command–post rather than his main headquarters at Bastogne. By 15.00 Duke Albrecht and General von Schenk had discussed and agreed what to do to counter the French attack. Part of that was the order to rush 8 RAK to the right part of the front. Of course the reality of war was such that the fighting at Maissin had already been underway for three hours or more when the senior commanders debated the issue.

In order to exploit the opportunity to turn the German right flank, the French would first of all have had to scout and find the open end of the German firing–line. Here one looks first for what use Eydoux made of 11 CA's integral cavalry regiment, *2 Chasseurs à cheval*. Just as with 12 CA's *21 Chasseurs* and the missed opportunity at Neufchâteau, this powerful reconnaissance unit, having fulfilled its first mission of scouting ahead of the corps and occupying Maissin, disappears off the tactical scene; despite being deployed on the left of the corps, it played no further part in the battle. Had it been ordered or had it used its initiative to probe round the north side of the battlefield, beyond the short firing line of 117 IR, the gap would have been found. This did not happen.

A second more local opportunity to turn the flank of 117 IR was ignored by General Radiguet (21 DI). Even though the cumbersome execution of his flank march allowed 50 Brigade time to turn and face him, he still had numbers enough to extend his firing–line and infiltrate round the northern–end of his opponents' shorter line. French doctrine had long established that frontal attacks against unbroken defence were costly and most likely to fail and that an attack against a flank was to be preferred. Foch wrote that 'one can no longer...come to grips with an unbroken opponent';[59] Grandmaison wrote that 'normally in open terrain a frontal attack by infantry under fire is impossible';[60] and the new October 1913 Regulations stated that the commander–in–chief should 'combine direct attacks, pushed straight out in front of armies, with wide enveloping movements directed against the enemy's lines of communications'.[61] But Radiguet made no attempt

59   Commandant A. Grasset, *Précepts et Jugements du Maréchal Foch* (Berger–Levrault, Paris, 1919), p.79, citing *De la Conduite de la Guerre*, pp.482–483.
60   Colonel de Grandmaison, *Dressage de l'Infanterie en vue du Combat Offensif* (Berger–Levrault, Paris, 1912), p.8.
61   *The Operations of Large Formations (conduit des grandes unite):* (translated from the *Field Service Regulations of the French Army*, dated 28 October, 1913, HMSO, London, 1914), hereafter 'Operations of Large Formations, 1913'

to overlap his enemy's flanks, opting instead for a frontal attack on an unbroken enemy. So the manner of Radiguet's execution of Eydoux's plan for 21 DI was not a doctrinal issue but one of his and Eydoux's poor command and control of their units in the field.

At the tactical level, the analysis of this battle has shown stark disparities between French and German performance in all arms. The use (or otherwise) of cavalry has already been examined in the analysis of the battle at Neufchâteau. But there is an additional point which comes from a regimental history which highlights the close cooperation of cavalry and artillery in the German army and the level of alert and preparedness they routinely undertook. The diarist of 61 Field Artillery Regiment described how his commander sent out numerous patrols as soon as there was any possibility of going into action, scouting the whole wide–ranging forested terrain in order to find the best routes in the direction of the advance. He also pushed forward artillery officer patrols alongside the divisional cavalry.[62] No instance has yet been uncovered of French artillery officers scouting daily for positions ahead of the advance alongside normal cavalry reconnaissance, as a precaution against only the possibility of contact.

As for the infantry, key points are clear. One battalion of 17 CA wandering, disorientated and demoralised, into the zone of 11 CA's action was asked to help defend some guns, and declined to intervene. Albert Hiss's contemporary account of the action at Anloy opines that the French lacked the élan typical of the German soldier.[63] German infiltration tactics exercised by 117, 118 and 115 IRs proved most effective whereas in contrast the French 93 RI resorted to an unauthorised massed frontal attack without waiting for the readily available artillery support.

Regarding the use of artillery, it has been shown how General Alby (34 DI) actually decided to leave his guns behind, and how 22 DI deployed all 36 guns in battery in open spaces on the plateau and suffered heavy counter–battery fire as well as rifle–fire from infiltrating infantry. In both cases, French handling of their artillery was inept. On the other hand the role of the German field artillery was crucial to German success at Maissin and Anloy.

Of 25 ID's two field artillery regiments, 61 FAR was with 49 Brigade at Anloy, and 25 FAR marched in the 50 Brigade column towards Maissin. When the first cavalry patrols came in and reported the presence of the enemy, 25 FAR immediately deployed to the nearest high ground, so that it was in good firing positions even before the first enemy was sighted.[64] When 118 RI was ordered to seize Maissin, the artillery immediately supported the attack, only receiving French counter-battery fire after two hours. Observing two French batteries standing very close to each other in a clearing near Bellevue, they were able to suppress their fire. And when called upon to support the infantry more closely, they sent a group (*abteilung*) forward to closer positions, firing at a range of 600m–800m and causing the French infantry to retreat.[65] Such a performance sits in direct contrast with that of its opponent, 35 RAC which, quite apart from getting lost and causing 1½ hours delay, seems to have marched at regulation speed in column until it reached the plateau and the clearing at Bellevue where, as recorded by the Germans, two of their batteries were spotted, bunched together. The much–vaunted manoeuvrability of the 75mm field gun seems not to have been matched by a similar agility of mind when the French commanders put doctrine into practice. But there is one element of similarity: the guns of 5/25 FAR opened fire forty–five minutes after the infantry went forward. They were clearly supporting not preparing the attack,

   p.32, Article 64.
62   FAR 61, op. cit., p.11.
63   IR 116,op. cit., p.24.
64   FAR 25, op. cit., pp.23–28.
65   Ibid.

throwing an interesting light on the debate about similar French doctrine enshrined in their new 1913 Regulations.

There was a further instance of the German tactic of using their guns proactively to meet the needs of the moment. A single battery (1/25 FAR) was ordered by divisional staff to support 117 IR in its resistance against 21 DI. It actually entered the firing line and engaged the French infantry at a range of 700m. There was no French counter–battery fire as the guns broke up the French attacks.[66]

The 61 FAR performed equally valuable work with 49 Brigade at Anloy. *I Abteilung* deployed south–east of Anloy in a semi–open position on a crest offering the batteries a dominating view to the south–west, from which it observed the red–blue figures of French infantry, half-exposed above the hedges. The guns opened fire at a range of 1600m on the French infantry before switching to a new target – French artillery coming into range in an exposed position.[67] The second group of 61 FAR (*II Abteilung*) II had the division's 105mm light howitzers, but from the dominating heights above Anloy, their high–trajectory fire was hardly distinguishable from that of the 77mm field guns. There was however at least one instance where a combination of German adaptability and a high–trajectory weapon made a difference. 116 IR was faced with the consecutive arrival of the four French regiments of 34 DI, and found itself in danger of being outflanked on its left. At the moment of crisis, three junior infantry officers commandeered a howitzer and had it dragged into the firing line, from where it bombarded the tree line from which the French were about to assault. Its fire enabled the German infantry to push forward again.[68] It is noteworthy that here, as in many other places in the Ardennes on 22 August, the German infantry were attacking at the tactical level even though their strategic and operational stance was defensive. Nor was the ad–hoc use of individual artillery pieces the only recorded instance at Anloy that day. At a second crisis point within 116 IR, two guns were brought forward to beat back a French assault. The absence of any French artillery to prevent such moves was crucial. The two guns tore huge holes in the overlapping enemy ranks.[69]

It is instructive that in both of the instances above, junior German infantry officers used their initiative to get the guns forward in order to save the situation and, conversely, junior artillery officers used their initiative to allow it to happen. It is difficult to conceive of a similar circumstance in the French army.

One last lesson can be drawn from the analysis of the battle at Maissin. General Eydoux, like several of his peers in other battles in the Ardennes, genuinely believed that the Germans had been waiting for the French in ambush positions from pre–prepared trenches with wire and machine guns:

> 19 RI progressed slowly. To the south–west, trenches stopped the left of the attack. These defences revealed the ingenuity of the enemy. Prepared over the previous few days, they consisted of barbed wire entanglements, shelters (*abatis*), false trenches adorned with cabbage–heads, stalks in the air to simulate a line of helmets, and flanking machine–guns.[70]

It has been made clear in the operational study that, apart from cavalry patrols, no German forces had reached as far west as Maissin before 22 August. This fact is corroborated by all the regimental histories of the German units involved. These sources show in fact that the Germans were as

66   Ibid., p.28.
67   FAR 61, pp.12–13.
68   IR 116, op. cit., p.26.
69   Ibid., pp.27–28.
70   Bujac, op. cit., p.72.

surprised by the French advance as the French were to find opposition. Furthermore, even given the very unlikely possibility that German cavalry had prepared the trenches earlier, they were facing in the wrong direction: it has been shown that the German high command expected any future threat to come from the west across the Meuse, and not from the south through the forests.

However, there is one excellent example elsewhere in the history of the Battles of the Frontiers that shows exactly how quickly and efficiently German infantry built field fortifications, even for the briefest encounter. At Landrecies, as is well known, the British Guards under General Haig's command were surprised at night by a violent skirmish with a German advance guard following them in pursuit during the retreat from Mons. There Captain O'Rorke, Chaplain to the 4th Field Ambulance Unit attached to the British 2nd Division, volunteered to stay behind to look after the wounded. In the morning he walked up the road from the village to view the scene of the previous night's fighting. He found German trenches lining the sides of the roads and a garden wall with firing embrasures knocked through it. It was impossible for those trenches to have been pre-prepared:

> Just beyond the houses was a pile of German field-gun cartridges [sic], and some German spades very long and narrow in the blade. The German trenches were littered with bottles; apparently the German soldier had had a couple of bottles of wine to keep up his spirits in the trench. The red brick wall about 100 yards from the top of the road had been loop-holed, and they had even put in rough seats behind. The work obviously took some time, and the Germans must have been at it all the time of the false alarm of the day before.[71]

There is very good evidence that German infantry were trained to dig temporary field entrenchments during a fire–fight and even when they were going forwards. Their pre–war doctrine on the subject shows both how relatively sophisticated such works could be and how quickly they could be dug.[72] So contrary was this to French practice that they could not believe any other explanation than that the trenches had been prepared in advance. Until now and for lack of comparative evidence from the German side, the French explanation has passed as fact.

To sum up the twin battles of Maissin and Anloy, it has been shown that the French were tactically inferior to the Germans in all arms. The reasons for that inferiority will be examined in detail in the analysis section of this book, but the evidence above points to superior German artillery tactics, superior combined–arms cooperation and superior speed and efficiency in execution. The French inferiority in these respects cost Joffre and the French army its second opportunity to inflict a significant defeat upon the Germans in the Battle of the Ardennes.

Operationally, the French weaknesses in command, control and communication, and their inability to conceive of an effective reconnaissance role for their cavalry, robbed them of the chance even to find and recognise the opportunity to turn the German flank, let alone attempt to pull it off. In the analysis section of this study, an examination of French doctrine and officer training will seek to establish the reasons why the French didn't even know what an opportunity they had missed.

---

71   B.G.O'Rorke, Chaplain to the Forces, *In the Hands of the Enemy* (Longman, Green & Co, London, 1916), p.25.
72   See Chapter 9 'Equipment', for detail of German doctrine with regard to digging temporary field fortifications.

5

The Other Battles

Despite the inefficiencies, delays and poor tactical performance that denied the French their two opportunities to achieve a decisive result on 22 August, they nevertheless were in relatively strong positions at both Neufchâteau and at Maissin from which to launch further offensive action on 23 August.

At Neufchâteau, 12 CA had encamped on its battlefield and, with relatively low casualties, was in good shape to continue on the morrow. At Maissin, 11 CA similarly ended the day in possession of the ground and the village. Despite heavier casualties, they had the advantage of potential strong reinforcement from 9 CA, the provisional cavalry corps and 52 DIR in the immediate vicinity. At first sight, Fourth Army was well positioned to continue the attack on 23 August, and de Langle initially issued orders to develop his attack on his left.[1] But an hour later, at about 19.00, news started to reach Fourth Army headquarters of the disasters at the other encounters, at Bertrix and Rossignol. By 05.00 on 23 August, de Langle had accepted the reality of the overall adverse situation across his front. He ordered a general withdrawal of his left and centre, hinged on the continued defence by CAC of the south bank of the Semoy.[2]

Joffre and GQG thought otherwise. When de Langle signaled that he intended to retreat and regroup, Joffre replied: 'All our Intelligence shows that you have only about three enemy corps in front of you. Therefore you must return to the offensive as soon as possible.'[3] Joffre and his 2ᵉ Bureau were technically correct: Fourth Army had fought against 18, 18 Reserve and 6 AKs. But GQG had not yet picked up on the late arrival of 8 RAK in the Maissin–Anloy area and was not yet fully aware of the general state of Fourth Army's troops. De Langle sought to comply with Joffre's command – it would have been career–limiting to do otherwise – although reading between the lines he was less than convinced, merely repeating Joffre's words almost verbatim as his rationale for continuing the offensive. He ordered his left wing (11 and 12 CAs but including this time 9 CA, 52 DIR and 60 DIR and excluding 17 CA) to attack northwards again.[4] But, as the official history succinctly put it: 'Whilst de Langle attempted despite everything to order a renewal of the offensive, his troops were forced by enemy pressure to accelerate their rearward movement.'[5] It was not enemy pressure, however, that caused the French withdrawal; it was the internal disintegration of command, control and communication arising from the earlier fighting. On 23 August, the French Fourth Army was not under the control of de Langle or his staff; it had its own momentum

---

1   AFGG I/1 (1936), pp.415–6; and Annex 862: [Fourth Army] *Armée de Stenay, 22 août, porté* à *18.40 par l'officier de liaison: Ordre particulier au 9e corps*; and Annex 863: *Armée de Stenay, 22 août, 18.00, Ordre particulier au 9e corps faisant suite* à *l'ordre particulier nr257/3.*
2   AFGG I/1, Annex 1102: *Armée de Stenay, 23 août, 05.00: Ordre général nr.22.*
3   AFGG I/1, Annex 1048: *communcation téléphonique, 23 août, 08.30: général en chef* à *commandant armée Stenay* [Fourth Army].
4   AFGG I/1, Annex 1107: *Armée de Stenay, 23 août, 10.00: Ordre.*
5   AFGG I/1 (1936), pp.423–424.

of retreat, driven by events, and it took de Langle a day to regain control.[6]

Of all the other encounter battles which took place on 22 August, two in particular stand out. At Bertrix and at Rossignol the French were comprehensively beaten.[7] By nightfall, Duke Albrecht's and de Langle's units had each won two tactical victories: de Langle at Maissin and Neufchâteau, Duke Albrecht at Bertrix and Rossignol. But Duke Albrecht's were both decisive, de Langle's marginal. The delays and inefficiencies on the French side meant that they had failed to achieve the sort of decisive battlefield advantage which could have been theirs; by simply holding on until nightfall, the Germans diminished the significance of the two French successes, which could and should have been much greater. That was the first measure of their lost opportunity. But in terms of the operation as a whole, a second measure of loss must be taken into account. When news of the magnitude of defeat at Bertrix and Rossignol reached de Langle, it was clear that he could not stand overnight and in the morning attempt to capitalize upon his advantage at Maissin–Anloy and Neufchâteau. Operational advantage passed to the Germans, without de Langle or anyone else truly realizing what they had missed. This was the real significance of Bertrix and Rossignol, and one should therefore ask whether those defeats might have been prevented and why they were not. Because they were not, the events at Bertrix and Rossignol became the defining encounters of the day.

The battle at Bertrix has been relatively well covered by historians over the years.[8] Most recently, Bruce Gudmundsson has written a comprehensive account from the French perspective, whilst Terence Zuber devoted a chapter to it from the German perspective in his book on the Ardennes battle.[9] In essence, 33 DI marched into the Forest of Luchy, north of Bertrix, was stopped by a detachment of 21 ID at Ochamps on the northern edge of the forest and was then hit by the rest of that German division in its right flank whilst still in column in the trees. The whole of the French divisional artillery was wiped out as well as their 66 Brigade, and they retreated in considerable disorder to the west.

Maps 42, 42a & 42b

However, none of the studies have sought to place the events at Bertrix into the context of the whole operation. Consequently there are three key elements of the disaster at Bertrix which have not yet been adequately explained: the strange role of the French divisional flank guard; the complex command situation which led to the French artillery being trapped and annihilated in the forest; and the impromptu but once again highly effective role played by the German artillery.

General Poline (17 CA) organised the strongest flank guard of the whole Fourth Army, a complete brigade (65 Brigade) supported by a group of artillery (12 guns) and the corps cavalry regiment. In accordance with the 'stepped-echelon' formation adopted by de Langle de Cary, this flank guard from 17 CA actually protected the march of 12 CA on its right. Early on the morning of 22 August at about 05.00, it set itself up in the fog in a strong defensive position on the heights just a short distance south-east of Bertrix, between Orgéo and Saint–Médard. That latter place was to become the command post of General Roques (12 CA) when he came up later in the day; Poline's 65 Brigade had to remain in place until relieved by the vanguard of 12 CA.[10] Not only was 65 Brigade a particularly powerful flank guard in a particularly strong defensive position, but it was commanded by 33 DI's commander, General Villeméjane, accompanied by his divisional

Map 42

6   AFGG I/1 (1936), pp.423–427.
7   AFGG I/1, pp.397–409 and *Weltkrieg 1*, pp.326–339.
8   In particular see: Palat, *Grande Guerre: Batailles des Ardennes & de La Sambre III* (Librairie Chapelot, Paris, 1918), pp. 142-151; Lieutenant–Colonel A.H. Burne, *The French Guns at Bertrix 1914*, Journal of Military History, LXIII, 1936–37; and 'A.G.M', *Bertrix*; and Kaiser, *Bertrix*.
9   Gudmundsson, *Bertrix*, pp.25–36; and Zuber, *Ardennes 1914*, pp.144–151.
10   AFGGI/1 (1936), p. 405.

staff, including the divisional artillery commander, Colonel Paloque.[11] Facing north–east towards Neufchâteau and Libramont – the very area where the major skirmish between the provisional cavalry corps and 18 AK had taken place on 20 August – it was ideally placed to guard the advance of 17 CA and 12 CA from any German foray from that direction.

All this suggests that the French command was, after all, alert to the possibility of the German units swinging south towards them and was taking steps to guard against a German attack. So it is all the more surprising that, having gone to such lengths to secure his most vulnerable flank during the first part of the march, General Poline (or his subordinates) then let his right–hand column (66 Brigade and the remaining two groups of artillery from 33 DI but no scouting cavalry) march past the static flank guard, up into Bertrix, down into the Forest of Luchy and on towards Ochamps without further precautions. That column, commanded by a brigadier (General Fraisse), was neither preceded by scouts nor protected on its right by any security.[12] This behaviour was directly contrary to French doctrine – both the 1895 FSR and the newly published December 1913 FSR – and can only be explained by individual or collective incompetence among the senior officers of 17 CA. The lack of security set up by the officers of 33 DI after they had passed through Bertrix into the hinterland beyond was a serious tactical mistake. But the stark contrast between the setting up of the strong static flank guard and the subsequent slack attention to basic march procedure points to a randomly inconsistent level of competence within the French officer corps.

The destruction of the French artillery in the forest has been ascribed by Gudmundsson to a disagreement between the divisional general and his brigade commander, the latter having ordered the guns into the forest whilst the former countermanded him and ordered them to turn and go back;[13] Rocolle, on the other hand, writes that the entry of the artillery into the forest was simply as a result of a mistaken order.[14] The issue is central to the scale of the disaster and requires further clarification. It has already been mentioned that both the divisional commander, General Villeméjane, and his divisional artillery commander, Colonel Paloque, were with the static flank guard. The main column was therefore under the command of 66 Brigade's commanding officer, General Fraisse, who was supported by the commander of 18 RAC, Lieutenant–Colonel Picheral. These four senior officers were the key players in the drama which was to unfold.

Paloque in particular is an interesting character: former professor at the École supérieure de guerre and author of a 1912 book on artillery tactics, he was also former commander of 18 RAC – 33 DI's artillery regiment – before his promotion to divisional artillery commander. After the war Paloque, by then a general, felt it necessary to publish his own version of events at Bertrix in order to explain the destruction of his beloved regiment.[15]

According to Paloque, there were in the Regulations (which he had helped to write) two distinct commands for calling forward the artillery: one called for officers to go forward without the guns in order to assess the situation, the other called both officers and guns immediately forward. Paloque claims that General Fraisse issued an imprecise order direct to the commanders of the two groups of artillery via a junior artillery officer (Sub–lieutenant Legueu), by–passing Lieutenant–Colonel Picheral, which had the effect of inadvertently calling the guns as well as officers forward into the forest. According to Paloque, Legueu called the officers for a reconnaissance, which according to artillery regulations (Fraisse was an infantryman) had a specific and immutable meaning:

11   Paloque, *Bertrix*, p.12 .
12   Goya, *La chair et l'Acier*, p.177.
13   Gudmundsson, op. cit.,p.32.
14   Rocolle, *Hécatombe*, p.138.
15   Paloque, *Bertrix*, p.10, 'It is not for me to pass judgement on those whose mistakes led to the destruction of my superb regiment, whose officers, non–commissioned officers and gunners were ready to follow me to the ends of the earth, except that an event has provoked a corps commander to expose all those responsible.'

'According to the rules, which are still [in 1932] in place, when the command "reconnaissance" is not accompanied by an indication as to where the guns should wait (*l'indication d'une position d'attente*), the group commanders must organise their batteries to follow them.'[16] This seems today to be a narrow distinction, and with hindsight points to a tendency towards blind obedience to rules as against common sense – the guns were about to plunge into a vast forest along a narrow forest track. Lest this judgement seem somewhat harsh, it must be pointed out that, prior to Legueu's unfortunate contribution to the confusion, the two artillery–group commanders had been clearly ordered to remain outside the forest: at about 14.00, Picheral had sent an officer with an earlier set of orders, whom Paloque had also met and interrogated: 'I am charged (said reserve Sub–lieutenant Portrait) by Lieutenant–Colonel Picheral to tell the artillery to come forward to the southern entrance to the Forest of Luchy.'[17] In this case, combined–arms protocol had been followed. General Fraisse (the general officer) had given a written order to Picheral (the artillery commander) at 13.30 that specifically included the phrase: 'Do not commit your artillery to enter the woods until such a move is possible'.[18] It is an interesting observation on core French military ethos – orders are to be obeyed and not necessarily understood – compared to that of the Germans – the mission is to be understood – that Picheral did not deem it necessary to pass on to his two subordinates the rationale for remaining outside the forest: that the vanguard was in action against the enemy and firing positions were being sought. When the third order came direct from Fraisse via Sub–lieutenant Legueu and by–passing Picherel, it apparently overrode the earlier ones. Paloque was undoubtedly arguing the finer points of the law (or rather regulations) to excuse himself and his beloved regiment from blame and there is undoubtedly logic in his argument. In the confusion of war, such mistakes are common, and a scapegoat has retrospectively to be found. But the case illuminates many small points: General Fraisse clearly intended to keep the guns out of the forest and call the officers alone up for reconnaissance, but the use of junior officers to relay messages (*à la* Captain Nolan, perhaps) distorted the outcome. Combined–arms co–operation was not good enough to bridge the technical language gap between two arms. The two artillery–group commanders obeyed the last order to be received despite the evident caution implicit in their previous instructions and despite the sound of heavy firing coming from the east; nor did they uncover their pieces until specifically ordered to. The two most senior divisional officers (Villeméjane and Paloque) were absent – taking hot drinks from the townsfolk of Bertrix at the time[19] – and Fraisse and Picheral were of a rank less experienced in combined–arms co–operation when called on to deal with such a complex command situation.

Paloque himself comes across as a stickler for the rules, and undoubtedly trained his beloved regiment according to his own standards. His 1912 book on artillery tactics contains some illuminating passages. Chapter 2 ('How the artillery marches to battle') contains forty–five pages – forty–six individual Articles – on the minutiae of marching; the professor in Paloque shines through.[20] On the subject of the afore–mentioned rules which caused the disaster at Bertrix, Paloque the writer and professor had laid out his guidance:

Article 166 – What orders should the commander of the artillery send to his group commanders, whom we envisage being on the march at the tail of the advance guard? The orders are extremely simple in the artillery; they are generally verbal; each level of authority entitled to receive orders receives communication from superior authority entitled to give

16 Ibid., p.15, note (1).
17 Ibid., p.14.
18 Ibid., p.17.
19 Ibid., p.14.
20 Colonel J. Paloque, *L'Artillerie dans la Bataille* (O. Doin et Fils, Paris, 1912), pp.169–171.

him orders through the agency of a *Liaison Officer*. The commander of the artillery, addressing one of his Liaison Officers, tells him: 'Order to the group commanders: "Reconnaissance!"' This order will be often completed by: 'Batteries to go at such and such a speed, according to such itinerary, to take such formation at such position'.

Article 168 – reconnaissance by group commanders: ... such reconnaissance should never take place until the group commander has called his battery commanders up for reconnaissance according to the same principles and with the group *in waiting position (en position d'attente)* [italics from Paloque's text] behind the spot chosen by the commander of artillery.[21]

Paloque adds in a footnote that the phrase '*en position d'attente*' was 'a useful phrase which deserves being included in the Rules, so familiar is it to gunners; its clarity and neatness of phrase is such that it will lead to less confusion.'[22] It looks as if Paloque himself was the initiator, if not the author, of the rules that he regarded as so simple as to avoid confusion, and yet which ironically led to the destruction of his very own regiment. And, to rub salt into Paloque's wounded pride, it would seem that his two group commanders were technically in breach of Paloque's Article 168!

Whatever the explanation, the bare facts are that two groups of 75mm field guns (24 pieces) were ordered forward, limbered and with caissons, horses and harness, onto a narrow forest track in which they did not have the space to turn or even deploy. To compound the insouciant lack of security evident in the column, evidenced through the absence of flank guards and scouts, the artillery were equally unconcerned and unprepared:

These reports [that the woods north of Bertrix were full of Germans who had organised and concealed positions over several days] were taken to be so exaggerated that the leading group (2ᵉ) had removed neither tampions nor breech covers, and the colonel [Paloque] had to admonish the commander of this group as he passed, saying: 'Are you going to wait until you are under fire before you prepare for combat?' There was even as he spoke the sound of firing from the north–east [Neufchâteau].[23]

It is difficult to reconcile this behaviour by 18 RAC with Paloque's claim that they were a superb regiment, unless one accepts that peace–time attributes like smartness and obedience to orders were more of a requirement than military awareness and readiness for real war. The poor state of French pre–war preparation and in particular combined arms liaison is once again brought into focus.

The performance of the German artillery of 21 ID, which made the major contribution to the destruction of 33 DI, actually demonstrates most of the qualities that the French lacked. Marching in the middle of the divisional column (but with the corps heavy artillery at the back), the two regiments of field artillery entered a terrain which was characterised by tall gorse (or broom) on either side of the paved road, obscuring vision and hindering deployment. Admittedly the road (a section of the old Roman road from Sedan towards the Rhine) was better and wider than that which the French were using, and the gorse was slightly less constrictive than the trees, but there are similarities of circumstance. The German divisional commander, General von Oven, professed himself to have been as much surprised by the time and place of the contact as his opponents were;[24] and the artillery was limbered, with caissons and horses and harness, on the road when the firing started. The guns

21   Ibid., pp.170–171.
22   Ibid., p.171, footnote 1.
23   Paloque, *Bertrix*, p.14.
24   Kaiser, op. cit., p.33.

Anloy, seen from German firing line. The French infantry were in the trees. Today the French cemetery is 200m into the trees, down a slight hill on the left.

Rossignol: Memorial at the crossroads in the forest north of the town. The French took the right-hand fork and encountered the Germans approximately one mile up the road.

French cemetery at Anloy, an unknown soldier.

Anloy, from the German starting position, the French were in the trees in the distance - a classic fire and movement German infantry action.

Anloy, showing a slight uphill advance for the German infantry.

German cemetery at Anloy.

French graves at Anloy; a double row, with the shadow forming a Cross of Lorraine.

Open fields at Anloy.

Maissin – The French attacked from the treeline in the distance over 2km of open ground, without waiting for artillery support and were "nailed to the spot": the only true example of 'attaque á outrance' in the Ardennes.

The village of Maissin seen from the French firing line. The French 19th Regiment advanced across the valley into the village in classic fire and movement.

The village of Maissin looking along the front line, where the French 19th Regiment assembled ready for its charge.

The village of Maissin from the left flank of the 19th Regiment.

The village of Maissin from the right flank of French 19th Regiment.

The road to Rossignol from the River Semoy to the bridge at Breuvanne. Note the hill in top centre that dominates the road, which the French left undefended.

The forest north of Bertix, and a typical forest track, similar to the one in which the French artillery was ambushed whilst still limbered up.

were on low ground, overlooked by the high ground north of Bertrix; it was fortunate for them that the French artillery had not remained on those commanding heights where they had halted only an hour earlier and from where they might have annihilated the German artillery.

When contact was made and the German infantry of the advance guard deployed and moved forward either side of the road, the artillery was left in column. But the divisional artillery commander, General Scherbening, was in the column and was able to gallop up and take control. Despite the absence of proper firing positions, he ordered the guns to deploy and set up as best they could, to left and right of the road, in the gaps in the gorse.[25] Even the heavy howitzers were then brought up and similarly deployed in order to increase the weight of firepower. The guns opened fire in the general direction of the enemy, using the principle of weight of fire rather than accuracy. Furthermore, in a fashion similar to the Germans' behaviour at Anloy, a battery was taken forward by the infantry and deployed right in the front line, from where it destroyed much of the French 1st group of artillery at the rear of the column, blocking the French retreat back to Bertrix.[26]

The German artillerymen proved adept at improvisation both in the swift ad–hoc deployment of large numbers of guns onto unfavourable terrain, and in the non–standard use of individual batteries or guns to meet infantry requests in support of a local tactical situation. The swift establishment of fire superiority, by weight of shell and by whatever means, was the priority of the German command.

The three events described above help our growing understanding of the French disaster at Bertrix. While the immediate cause of the French failure was the lack of security on their open right flank in the Forest of Luchy and the failure to scout ahead and to the sides of a vulnerable marching column, the conundrum of the use of the strong static flank guard for the first half of the march indicates an inconsistent approach to war within the French units and a lack of consistent operational planning by the French command. The rigidity of the French artillery command and control system compares unfavourably with the flexibility and willingness to innovate shown by their opponents. It all points to serious underlying inconsistencies in French preparation. And yet the individual French soldiers, infantry and gunners alike, fought bravely and with great self–sacrifice. The performance of 33 DI was not wholly bad, it was randomly bad and good. This leads on to the need to explore how French pre–war arrangements were organised, which is the subject of a later chapter. From the German perspective, one sees again their ability to react swiftly to unforeseen circumstances and to improvise, especially in their use of artillery. The massed fire from ninety guns, most of which could not see a specific target and all of which were deployed on low–lying flat and gorse–covered terrain, bears witness to the less–than–scientific German approach to achieving fire superiority. In the German case at Bertrix, it may not have been strictly according to doctrine, but it worked.

Rossignol was an encounter battle of an entirely different character. For a start, the French force involved was the elite 3 Colonial Infantry Division (DIC) whose professional officers and experienced soldiers had for the most part engaged in combat in France's overseas colonies. They were in many respects similar to the British regular battalions that policed the Empire. That they were comprehensively defeated by their German opponents and suffered crippling casualties as a result of their refusal (and inability) to retreat was a severe blow to overall French morale.

The operational study has shown how Duke Albrecht sent his 6 AK south at extremely short notice on the night of 21–22 August in order to plug the gap between Fourth and Fifth German

---

25   Kaiser, *Bertrix*, p.10.
26   A.G.M., op. cit., pp.245–247.

Map 43

Armies. From the German point of view it was a serendipitous decision entirely unconnected to French movements, of which the Germans were wholly ignorant at the time; but it reaped tremendous dividends. Two divisional columns, 12 ID on the right and 11 ID on the left, plunged into the Forest of Neufchâteau on parallel roads. By 07.00 on 22 August both columns were close to the southern edge of the forest and the valley of the Semoy river, the whole terrain wreathed in fog. The right–hand column met the French colonial vanguard in the forest between one and two kilometres north of Rossignol, and commenced the action which will be described below. If all had gone according to plan on the French side, the left–hand German column (11 ID) would have debouched from the forest into the valley to be met by the infantry of 4 DI occupying Tintigny and the bridge over the river, with its artillery dominating the scene from the heights at Bellefontaine. But once again French delays and inefficiencies conspired to give the tactical advantage to their opponents.

Map 43a

General Rabier of 4 DI (2 CA, on the right flank of the Colonials) had been ordered to establish his advance guard at Bellefontaine, on the southern heights overlooking the Semoy valley, on the evening of 21 August.[27] It will be recalled that the river valley – dubbed the *Étalle corridor* in most histories – was a key tactical location which had been fought over by cavalry divisions since the beginning of hostilities; indeed the German 3 KD was still operating in that area.[28] It was imperative for French security that they should prevent any German incursion down the valley. Had General Rabier fulfilled his orders, his artillery (at least the group accompanying the vanguard) would have been fortuitously in the perfect position to shell 11 ID's columns as they debouched from the woods opposite, as the fog lifted during the morning of 22 August. But Rabier had decided that his men were too tired and his units too disorganised to reach the Semoy on the night of 21 August, so he informed his corps commander, Gérard (2 CA), who in turn informed de Langle de Cary, that 4 DI would camp south of the forest lying between them and the Semoy.[29] Rabier undertook to make an early start and catch up with the timetable in the morning of 22 August, promising to be ready to debouch from Bellefontaine at 06.00 as ordered and occupy the bridge over the Semoy at Tintigny. He specifically ordered, firstly, his cavalry to occupy Tintigny and then scout ahead into the forest, and secondly 87 Brigade with a group of artillery to dominate the valley from the heights at Bellefontaine.[30] Had his troops even then managed to catch up with the overall timetable, had they executed their own commander's orders, they would have been, if unintentionally, in ideal positions to thwart 11 ID. The reconnaissance squadron of divisional cavalry (19 *Chasseurs*) would undoubtedly have met the German advance guard in the forest on the road to Rulles. But almost inevitably further inefficiencies on the part of 4 DI meant that they failed to redeem their promise. When the advance guard of 11 ID debouched from the forest at 08.30 into the Semoy valley, there was only a single French regiment (without artillery) in Bellefontaine; and that regiment was not even the AG of 4 DI but part of the main body under General Cordonnier who had taken the initiative to push ahead.[31]

So the infantry of the German 10 Grenadier Regiment marched unopposed through the village of Tintigny and across the Semoy by the town bridge.[32] During the rest of the day, the whole of 11 ID was deployed and was able not only to attack and contain 4 DI in Bellefontaine but to spread westwards down the south bank of the river, completing the encirclement of the French 3

27   AFGG I/1, Annex 756: *Armée de Stenay, 21 août, 13.00: Ordre particulier au 2e corps, corps colonial et 12e corps*; and Annex 766: *2e corps d'armée, Montmédy, 21 août, 20.00: Ordre préparatoire pour la 4e DI, Villers–la–Loue.*
28   *Weltkrieg 1*, p.317.
29   AFGG I/1, Annex 767: [2 CA] *Compte rendu du général Gérard apporté par agent liaison, 22.00, 21 août.*
30   AFGG I/1, Annex 802: *Corps G., Division Rabier, 21 août, 23.30: Ordre général d'opérations nr.13.*
31   General Cordonnier, *Une Brigade au feu, (Potins de Guerre)* (Henri Charles-Lavauzelle, Paris, 1921) pp.239–249.
32   *Weltkrieg 1*, p.315.

DIC at Rossignol. Zuber fulsomely describes this as 'the last in VI AK's series of brilliant tactical decisions'[33]; in fact it was the only and obvious thing to do and it was only made possible by the late arrival of 4 DI and the dire inefficiency of the French deployment.

More important to the tactical situation, and equally simple to implement given the lack of French opposition, the artillery of 11 ID was able to set up openly and unopposed on the high ground north of Tintigny. From those excellent positions it was able to dominate not only Bellefontaine but also the whole river valley downstream to Rossignol, limited only by the range of the guns. Starting at 09.15, when I/6 FAR set up 500m southwest of Harinsart and opened fire on the stationary main column of 3 DIC, the fire from these guns intensified until the bridge across the Semoy at Breuvanne was first made impassable then destroyed, preventing reinforcements reaching 3 DIC's beleaguered advance guard.[34] The free passage of 11 ID into the Semoy valley on the right flank of the CAC was the defining operational feature of the battle at Rossignol. What happened at Rossignol itself was a second and consequential action, primarily tactical but nevertheless important because of the devastating outcome.

Map 43b

When the infantry of the German 12 ID deployed to meet the colonials in the woods north of Rossignol, a separate battle broke out, one which, initially, either side might win. The two artillery regiments of 12 ID were stuck in column on a narrow forest track, just like the French guns at Bertrix, and were vulnerable to a successful infantry attack. The advance guards of each side were initially evenly matched. That battle became a matter of infantry tactics, doctrine and training. Doughty has described it thus:

> After French cavalry discovered enemy soldiers in a forest north of the small village, 3rd Division sent six battalions, one after the other, on a narrow front against solidly entrenched German troops and suffered more than 5,000 casualties. The Germans responded by going around 3rd Division's flank and destroying all its cannon, caissons, and vehicles.[35]

There are some errors of detail in Doughty's description – five French battalions were committed, not six and the Germans were not solidly entrenched.[36] It is clear that this was a genuine encounter battle, and any German entrenchments were dug during the fighting; 12 ID's advance guard marched into contact with 3 DIC at about 08.30.[37]

The fight in the forest north of Rossignol was not the classic example of French *offensive à outrance*, which is its popular image.[38] As Zuber has pointed out, 'it is difficult to envisage an offensive *à outrance* in the thick undergrowth of this forest: bayonet charges would have been physically impossible.'[39] Furthermore German accounts of the battle describe a close–range and very costly firefight in which the Germans themselves used fire and movement to drive themselves forward and the Frenchmen back.[40] Casualty figures support this view; the French 1 RIC suffered

33   Zuber, *Ardennes 1914*, p.115.
34   Palat, *La Grande Guerre III*, p.143.
35   Doughty, *Pyrrhic Victory*, p.67.
36   Doughty's source is given as Commandant Grasset's *Rossignol*, op. cit., and his error is understandable. Divisional commander General Raffenel did indeed order two regiments (six battalions) forward. But when the personal diary of 3 DIC's Chief of Staff, Commandant Moreau, was rediscovered and republished in 2002, Moreau revealed that brigade commander General Rondonay held back the third battalion of the second regiment from the slaughter in the forest.
37   *Weltkrieg 1*, pp.314–315.
38   Liddell Hart, *History of the First World War*, p.82; and A. Clayton, *Paths of Glory*, (Cassell, London, 2003) pp.28–29.
39   Zuber, op. cit., p.113.
40   *Weltkrieg 1*, p.315; and Zuber, op. cit., pp.111–112 & 119.

2,800 casualties (killed, wounded, missing and captured) out of about 3,200 (88%) compared to the German 157 IR which lost 931 (29%) killed, wounded and missing.[41] But it must be taken into account that the French were eventually surrounded and in the end had a simple choice between death and captivity; there is no clear evidence as to how many of the French soldiers listed as casualties fell during the initial fire-fight and how many were in fact made prisoners of war after they had been encircled. The German casualty rate of 29% is itself very high, and would be notable if it were not for the awesome extent of the colonial soldiers' sacrifice.

Two doctrinal issues stand out as having given the Germans victory in the forest: firstly they began to dig themselves in as soon as the firing started and sought fire superiority from behind temporary field emplacements before attempting to get forward; whereas the French – whose doctrine neither precluded digging nor required it and who had not been trained to dig whilst on the attack – sought to gain ground by fire and movement only, against an unbroken enemy. Secondly, the tactical error by General Raffenel, which sent two extra battalions into a narrow and already crowded firing line simply multiplied the number of targets available to German fire. And yet the myth of *offensive à outrance* persists. Michel Goya writes of the French 'charging furiously' at an enemy 'going immediately onto the defensive and taking advantage of the favourable terrain.'[42] And Professor Herwig, in his recent book on the Marne 1914, describes Rossignol with almost Churchillian rhetoric:

> In short order it [3DIC] sent five battalions of *pantalon rouges* in waves against the Germans on a front roughly six hundred meters wide. One furious frontal bayonet charge after another, accompanied by lusty cries of "*En avant*", was mowed down by murderous artillery and machine gun fire.[43]

Herwig is wrong on several points: colonial troops did not wear red trousers, they had their own distinct blue uniform;[44] there was no German artillery fire in the opening attacks because the guns could not deploy off the road into the dense mass of trees; and it was more a question of fire and movement than bayonet charge. Since it has been shown that the long–standing cliché is invalid, why then did the French 3 DIC – considered an elite unit – commit itself to an attritional firefight on a narrow front while allowing itself to be outflanked on each side? Recently an important source has resurfaced which illuminates the inner working of 3 DIC on 22 August – the journal of its chief of staff, Commandant Moreau, written whilst he was dying of tuberculosis in captivity in Switzerland and including testimony from many fellow prisoners. It provides a fascinating insight into the command, control and communication status of one of France's avowedly elite formations, and raises questions about the fitness of General Raffenel for divisional command.[45]

In the first phase of the encounter, each side committed its lead regiment (three battalions) to the firing–line. The Germans then sent their second regiment (with a battery of field guns) out on an outflanking movement to their right, marching through the forest to the southern edge and out into the open, eventually reaching the village of Termes on the river and the high ground nearby.[46] This manoeuvre meant that the French were in danger of being cut off from the west. Meanwhile General Raffenel also had his second regiment (2 RIC) to hand and had to decide how to use it. Up–to–date

---

41   Moreau, *Rossignol*, p.26.
42   Goya, op. cit.,p.176.
43   Herwig, *Marne*, p.150.
44   Rocolle, *Hécatombe*, p.131.
45   Moreau, op. cit. passim.
46   *Weltkrieg 1*, p.315; Zuber op. cit., pp.112 & 114.

information was available to him from the firing–line; Lieutenant–Colonel Vitart, of 1 RIC, had been wounded in both hands and was coming back for treatment when he met chief of staff Moreau. He said: 'This won't do. We are enmeshed in a trap and we have fallen under well prepared infantry and machine–gun fire from enemy positions prepared in advance in the woods.'[47] Vitart was not the only officer who mistook the German infantryman's ability to dig temporary field fortifications for more permanent ambush positions.[48] Vitart compared the situation to an ambush experienced in Tonkin and he and Moreau concluded that the tactical situation required a withdrawal from the trap and a fresh manoeuvre. As chief of staff, Moreau recommended to Raffenel that 2 RIC should not be sent forward to reinforce the firing–line; their front was too narrow and the exact position of the enemy's front uncertain. But Raffenel insisted on committing three more battalions to the existing firing–line, using language which betrays a somewhat cavalier approach:

> The general replied in a humorous way 'you bore me (*baillez*) with your talk of fronts.' Then, turning to the group of officers, said 'Let's go! Take the order to 2 RIC to engage; one battalion on the track parallel to and three hundred metres west of the road, one on the east of the road and the third battalion on the road itself.'[49]

In the event, this order was not fully obeyed. Worried that there was no sign of the main Colonial column appearing behind the advance guard, the brigade commander, General Rondony, took it upon himself to hold back the third battalion in the village, thereby saving it from the slaughter, at least for a while.[50]

The kindest interpretation of Raffenel's decision is that he still believed he could force his way through weak opposition and continue his march on Neufchâteau, despite the evidence of an experienced senior regimental commander who had seen the action developing first–hand, and against the advice of his chief of staff. But, taken with other evidence from Moreau, it now seems more likely that Raffenel had reached the point where, under the strain of combat, he was proving to have been over–promoted and incapable of handling the situation.

General Raffenel was still ranked as a brigade general, having only been promoted to command of 3 DIC in June 1914 and not yet confirmed at the higher rank. He had been a brigadier for less than four years and a regimental colonel before that for only four years.[51] With such rapid promotions compared to many, he was considered a rising star. But Moreau's early impression was of an officer lacking the command attributes required at divisional level; one who interfered with detailed staff work rather than devolving responsibility:

> Furthermore, what was his concept of a divisional general staff? Everything pointed to a belief that we were a sort of honour guard provided to trot behind the chief. As to his role and his activity, as to his effectiveness as part of the command structure, he had no idea. He was the leader of a very big battalion; he more or less thought that he had at his disposal several adjutants of whom I was the oldest. It was perhaps because of his consideration for my age and with a benevolent intent that he avoided giving me anything to do. Indeed, the very idea of what I could and should be doing was of no importance to him.[52]

47 Moreau, op. cit., p.61.
48 For example at Maissin: see Bujac, *Eydoux*, pp.72–73.
49 Ibid., p.62.
50 Ibid., p.63.
51 Ibid., pp.9–12.
52 Ibid., p.46.

There is in Moreau's journal a catalogue of minor events from mobilisation to the eve of battle which build up to and give evidence in support of this conclusion.[53] With the onset of battle, Raffenel's weaknesses (in Moreau's eyes) were tested beyond breaking point. The decision to send his second regiment up into the confines of the forest was a serious tactical mistake, ignoring expert advice. There were other instances which will be enumerated below. He took to walking about, his staff trailing after him, as a substitute for getting to grips with the situation. Finally, he seems to have mentally fallen apart:

> At one stage the general looked me in the eye for a long time without speaking. His face was convulsed. Is this an illusion [sic] or indeed did my own nervous tension give me the ability to understand his silence? But I believe I could read in his eyes what he was thinking. The unfortunate man had had revealed to him his incapacity [for command] and at the same time the irredeemable disaster [facing his division]. He looked questioningly at me, waiting for me to make another suggestion, but I too thought that all was lost.[54]

The quotation above refers to the situation at 12.30; a long and bloody afternoon and evening lay before them. General Montignault (1 Colonial Brigade) had also reached the limit of his physical and moral strength in the fighting in the forest. His brigade was shattered, decimated; he had 'abandoned the contest while General Rondony took his place, and remained hidden in the woods, stretched out in a ditch totally incapable of moving.'[55] He was later captured by the advancing Germans. General Rondony (3 Colonial Brigade) took command of the defence of the village and died fighting, towards the end of the day. Raffenel continued to walk about, without purpose. Finally at about 15.30, Raffenel wandered off again. Moreau followed but, struck in the right thigh by shrapnel, had to stop: with the words 'well then, sit down here, I'll just go and have a look in this direction [west] and I will pick you up when I return', Raffenel disappeared for the last time.[56] His body was later found just a few metres south of the river Semoy; he had managed to cross the river, alone, for reasons unknown. Rocolle writes that it was believed that he may have committed suicide.[57]

The situation of 3 DIC's advance guard north of the river Semoy became critical. On its right, the German 11 ID had crossed to the south bank of the river via the undefended bridge at Tintigny and was threatening envelopment. The direct route for the main column of the division, over the Semoy river by the bridge at Breuvanne, was interdicted by intense German artillery fire. Only on the left could 3 DIC's commanders have set up an improvised withdrawal plan. There was one obvious *point d'appui* (strongpoint), which dominated the terrain. Between Rossignol and Termes, the next village downstream, the river Semoy forms a large ox-bow loop, in the centre of which lies Hill 363; whoever controlled that hill controlled the last available route to safety for the trapped colonial troops. It was to become central to the fighting later in the day and crucial to 3 DIC's communications both with corps headquarters and with 2 DIC at Jamoigne once German artillery fire interdicted the bridge at Breuvanne.

Yet Raffenel had made no proper attempt to secure it. The actions which he did initiate to secure his left were half–hearted and not followed through properly. At 08.00, just as the first shots from the vanguard were heard by the main body, Raffenel ordered the cavalrymen of his

53   Ibid., pp.41–44, pp.46–47.
54   Ibid., pp.70–71.
55   Ibid., p.74.
56   Ibid., p.73.
57   Rocolle, op. cit.,p.131.

Chasseurs d'Afrique (Colonel Costet) to reconnoitre firing positions for the artillery both east and west of the road.[58] At 09.30 the artillery was ordered to take up the positions which were to have been found by the cavalry.[59] In between, at 8.45, staff captain Laurans had delivered a second order to Colonel Costet, ordering him to act as support for the guns. Raffenel had decided to commit all his available infantry to his frontal attack and had none to spare for security duties. But Costet on his own initiative abandoned the west flank, and Hill 363, even though he had seen the commander of 1 group of artillery seeking a position there for his batteries.[60] Costet apparently told General Rondony (3 Brigade) what he was doing, but never thought to report formally to divisional headquarters; the information never got through. As a result, the artillery in the west could not sustain an unsupported position on Hill 363 once German infantry arrived at the forest edge, and the regimental commander, Colonel Montguers, ordered it to withdraw to a less exposed position. He too failed to inform divisional headquarters until, meeting up with General Raffenel at 10.10, he was asked the direct question 'have you placed a battery in position west of the village?' to which he perforce answered that it was withdrawn. Raffenel angrily ordered it back into position, without infantry or cavalry protection.[61] But they were too late. The infantry of the German 63 IR, supported by a group of artillery – II/57 FAR – which had been sent out on the German right to find and turn the French left, arrived at the edge of the woods opposite Termes at about 11.00 and was able to move a battery of guns unopposed onto Hill 363.[62] The German guns were subsequently driven off from what was an exposed position by French artillery fire, but that is not the point. The hill was held by German infantry with indirect fire support from their guns. Raffenel had failed to secure this vital position with his own infantry and consequently contributed to the eventual encirclement of his division.

To cap an already very poor performance, Raffenel and his officers also failed in the area of communications. Those failures within 3 DIC and between that unit and its corps headquarters compounded the problems with which it found itself confronted. Starting with the outcome: at 10.45 CAC headquarters reported to Fourth Army regarding the 08.00 situation (fighting had started over three–and–a–half hours before this report was sent), saying that no enemy had been encountered that morning; at 11.45 it reported that enemy artillery, firing from the east, had been suppressed, when in fact by that time 3 DIC was unable to cross the Semoy (in either direction) via the bridge at Breuvanne because of the overwhelming intensity of German shelling. At 12.15, CAC headquarters ordered 3 DIC to turn to face east in order to support 4 DI which was being attacked at Bellefontaine, as if that not Rossignol was the danger point; the degree to which corps headquarters was out of touch is dramatically highlighted by the contemporaneous entry in Moreau's journal; this was the very time of which he subsequently wrote: 'I also thought that all was lost; all we could do was put on a brave face in order to show the image and illusion of command to all those brave men who observed us and who would soon die.'[63]

It is clear that, despite being less than five kilometres away from 3 DIC's headquarters, CAC's staff were singularly ill–informed. Partly this was because there seem to have been no corps liaison officers up front with the division, partly because 3 DIC was not sending any reports. Commandant Moreau's journal confirms that the first (and last) attempt by 3 DIC's staff to update CAC took

58 Ibid., p.59.
59 Ibid., p.62.
60 Ibid., p.63.
61 Ibid.,pp. 65 & 66.
62 Zuber, *Ardennes 1914*, p.112 & p.114.
63 Moreau, op. cit., p.71.

place at 11.30 – after four–and–a–half hours' fighting, and it was Moreau, not his commanding officer, who decided to send the report. But Captain Scheidhauser, who was charged with delivering the message, was unable to get across the river and finally destroyed the message shortly before he was captured that evening.[64] So it would seem likely that not a single report from 3 DIC reached CAC headqurters to inform them on one of the most critical engagements of 22 August. Certainly there are none remaining on file in the annexes of the official history, and research has failed to uncover any in the archives at Vincennes, so Moreau's testimony seems to be corroborated.

Communications within the division were equally poor. General Montignault, leading the vanguard, wrote a report at 08.30 for his divisional commander which stated that they were powerless to advance. Bizarrely, Montignault's staff officer, Captain Javouhey, who had just joined his commander, decided that the report was too pessimistically premature and went to see for himself. He was killed in the firing line, the message still stuffed in his pocket.[65] Consequently a further hour passed, during which the vanguard continued to lose men, before (as we have seen above) Colonel Vitart arrived at the divisional headquarters with the same assessment. It is not clear why Montignault allowed this to happen.

The picture painted by Commandant Moreau of a dysfunctional staff led by an incompetent general provides a credible explanation for the frontal attacks which decimated 3 DIC's vanguard. Given that (like the regular British battalions brought back from overseas to form 27 and 28 Divisions and which initially performed badly when committed in France in January 1915) the French colonial regiments were not permanently encadred before the war, but were formed into brigades and divisions for use at pre–war manoeuvres and then for the opening battles, the apparent dichotomy between elite regiments and a dysfunctional division is partially explained; inherent generic weaknesses in the French general officer and staff establishment would seem to be evident in the performance of Raffenel and his subordinates.

The final chapter of this sorry French saga concerns the attempt by the corps commander, General Lefèvre, to mount a rescue of his beleaguered 3rd Division. His headquarters and that of 2 DIC (General Leblois) were at Jamoignes, less than seven kilometres from Rossignol, but the route via the village of Termes was dominated by Hill 363. If Raffenel had occupied that position, keeping open a route westwards, and if 2 DIC could have reached the hill, there might have been some hope of relieving the troops trapped in Rossignol.

But on the one hand Raffenel did not have it in him to take command decisions of that magnitude, and on the other there were more command and communication difficulties at CAC level. De Langle had taken 2 DIC as his strategic army reserve and it could only be released on his personal authority. General Lefèvre had first asked for it at 11.35 but without any sense of urgency. Indeed, his report includes the phrase 'the Colonial Corps continues its attack'.[66] This is now explained by 3 DIC's failure to report what was happening. Vital hours passed before Fourth Army received a second message from Lefèvre, sent at 14.00 but arriving at 15.30, which laid out in more graphic terms the increasingly difficult situation of 3 DIC: '3rd Division marching on Rossignol has been violently attacked on its right flank and from the northern edges of the forest since 07.00.'[67] De Langle finally agreed to this second request at 16.45 but, in a further adverse

64   Ibid., pp.68–70.
65   Ibid., p.60: testimony of Captain Nicholas, 1 RIC.
66   AFGG I/1, Annex 967: [CAC] *Général commandant le C.A.C.*[Lefèvre] à général commandant l'armée de Stenay, 22 août, 11.35, 500 mètres N. de Bellefontaine.
67   AFGG I/1, Annex 969: *Stenay de Breux à 15.30; official extreme urgence operations priorité; Corps L.* [Lefèvre] à *armée*

commentary on the state of Fourth Army communications, seems to have sent his reply via 12 CA at the telegraph station at Florenville: 'Let the colonial corps at Jamoigne know that it can if necessary make use of its second division.'[68] This was too late to have been of any use but, surprisingly, the division was already on the march, its commander, Leblois, having taken the initiative to march to the sound of the guns – a rare enough instance in the French army on that day.[69]

As a result, the first two battalions of the Colonial 6 Brigade (2 DIC) counter–attacked the German 63 IR on Hill 363 and its accompanying artillery during the early afternoon in a bid to break through to Rossignol and link up with 3 DIC. They captured Termes which was only four kilometres away, and only two battalions of Germans on Hill 363 stood between them and the remnants of Raffenel's division;[70] but it was too late to change the outcome of the battle. Moreover, for reasons which are not entirely clear, the attempt was called off at 17.00 and 2 DIC ordered onto the defensive.[71] The official history states that it was an appreciation of the overall situation, at Rossignol and Saint–Vincent, compounded by the retreat of 5 Colonial Brigade from Neufchâteau, which caused General Lefèvre to take up a defensive posture.[72] One might speculate that it was caution, fear of the unknown and lack of offensive spirit on the part of corps commander Lefèvre that stopped the counter–attack. Rocolle quotes an assessment of both Lefèvre and Leblois by de Langle de Cary, made in January 1915. Lefèvre the corps commander was apparently brave, vigorous, possessing sound judgement, but lacking authority and very much influenced by his subordinate Leblois's more dominant personality; Leblois was however lacking in offensive spirit, sowing discouragement amongst the men. He was 'defensive, in the worst sense of the word.'[73] A continuation of the counter–attack by Leblois would not have saved Raffenel's division, but certainly hindsight and information from German sources suggests that it might have broken through before nightfall, and saved the remnants of 3 DIC from captivity.[74] That this was not attempted provides further evidence of the poor senior command performance of the supposedly elite CAC.

The magnitude of the disaster at Rossignol is encapsulated in 3 DIC's casualty figures: 10,520 officers and men lost out of a total of little more than 12,000 (87.7%). The two events which might have prevented the disaster, or at least mitigated the situation to manageable proportions, were (firstly and obviously) if 4 DI had carried out its orders and been where it was supposed to be at the right time. Secondly, if communications within CAC had been better, then 2 DIC could arguably have been released by de Langle earlier and linked up with Raffenel via the western route (the bridge at Termes from Jamoigne). That neither of these two events happened, and that ultimately 3 DIC suffered a defeat of such magnitude that it has come to symbolise overall French performance in Joffre's offensive, has been shown to have been less about doctrinal weaknesses and more about training and efficiency in staff and general command.

The four encounter battles analysed in detail, in this and the two previous chapters, support the argument that France's Lost Opportunity in the Ardennes on 22 August 1914 was of a magnitude never yet realized by historians. A large part of the reason for this lies in the fact that the French

   de Stenay. Poste de Jamoigne, 14 heures.
68   AFGG I/1, Annex 861: [Fourth Army] *Stenay, 22 août, 16.45: Commandant armée à commandant 12e corps, Florenville.*
69   AFGG I/1 (1923), p. 401.
70   *Weltkrieg 1*, p.315; and Zuber, op. cit.,p.117; and Rocolle, op. cit., p.133.
71   AFGG I/1, pp.401–2.
72   AFGG I/1, p.402.
73   Rocolle, op. cit., p.133.
74   *Weltkrieg 1*, p.315.

did not realize it at the time, so poor was their Command, Control and Communication. French records at the time paint a one-sided, distorted picture that is only today balanced by records from German sources.

De Langle had two opportunities to break through Duke Albrecht's weak and extended front, at Maissin and at Neufchâteau. Because of the extremely poor communications within Fourth Army de Langle was never aware of the magnitude of the operational opportunities which might have arisen from better tactical competence on those battlefields. His battlefield commanders not only failed to keep him properly informed but also failed to use their superior strength and their superior tactical situation – including the advantage afforded them by the achievement of operational surprise – to press home their attacks in a way that might have delivered to de Langle two swift and decisive tactical victories which he might then have attempted to convert into successful operational manoeuvre.

Duke Albrecht's commanders on the other hand delivered two crushing tactical defeats to their opponents at Bertrix and Rossignol, aided in no small part by French errors. In the heat of battle, the two French defeats, and the urgent necessity for the French Command to react to them, drove all thought of what was happening elsewhere on the battlefield from the minds of the French staff. Whereas Duke Albrecht had been kept fully informed throughout the day's fighting, de Langle had been kept largely in the dark. Lacking information (except at Rossignol), de Langle did not intervene in the individual encounter battles, nor attempt to use his reserves to impose a coherent operational plan out of evolving events. Left to their own devices, French corps and divisional commanders showed various levels of weakness, tactical deficiencies and lack of aggressive intent. In total contrast the German corps and divisional commanders generally showed a competent, decisive and professional approach to the conduct of their individual encounters. With the clear exception of the French colonial soldiers, a glaring gap was revealed in the levels of training, discipline and morale between the two sides.

The differences in performance revealed in this examination of the four key encounters demonstrate that the Germans possessed an overall superiority at both operational and tactical levels. We will now go on to examine the underlying reasons for this evident German superiority.

Part Three

Analysis

6

Preparation for War

The general reader of the history of the opening battles on the Frontiers, that involved predominantly French and German conscript armies, will have most likely absorbed in the first place the writings of Winston Churchill and Basil Liddell Hart. Those two authors have, when taken together, painted a picture of a pre-war French army imbued with a crazy doctrine of 'all-out offensive' (*offensive à outrance*) which irrationally promoted the idea that superior morale could overcome superior material, as measured in numbers of machine guns and artillery pieces. In a combined Liddell Hart-Churchillian scenario, the French armies throw themselves at Joffre's command recklessly across the frontier, disregarding German activity, disregarding all sensible precautions, and attacking the enemy wherever they were to be found. Today, one hundred years after the event, similar perceptions of the French Army's performance are to be found in many histories; one has only to look at Anthony Clayton's book on the French Army, 'Paths of Glory', written in 2003, to realise how little has changed: 'Wave after wave of French infantrymen rushed forward regardless and with no thought of envelopment on their flanks, only to be cut down by German machine-gunners in the absence of any French artillery support to protect them'.[1]

The narrative of the Battle of the Ardennes laid out in Part One of this book presents an alternative scenario for one of the three major frontier confrontations, a scenario that is greatly at odds with the received wisdom of the past. That alone demands explanation, and requires detailed substantiation of the alternative scenario that is being presented. The purpose of the Second Part of this book is to provide that explanation and detailed substantiation of this new narrative of the Ardennes Campaign.

The key areas to be explored lie in the areas of Doctrine and Training. Other areas, such as the type and use of certain types of weapon or equipment, need also to be explored because they will have been used in the past to justify incorrect conclusions as to why the French lost and the Germans won the battle of the Ardennes. Undoubtedly however the big issue is the question of whether it was a faulty French doctrine of *offensive à outrance* (properly executed) that lay at the heart of French failure, or whether, as I shall suggest, it was more a question of inadequate preparation on the part of France. The word 'inadequate' is used here in a comparative sense. In war it is sufficient to be better than the opposition in order to gain victory, rather than to measure performance against some pre-set standard. Although this is not the place to engage in a full discussion of such a complex subject, it seems to this author that one can, and indeed must, separate the relative merits of a military doctrine from the issue of how well such a doctrine is executed in practice. Doctrine is the starting-point for an army preparing for war; for a nation to prepare for war, however, it is essentially a question of how far the government is prepared to go in terms of committing resources – time, money, manpower, material - for long-term development of the means to wage a future

---

1   Anthony Clayton, *Paths of Glory: The French Army 1914-1918*, p.28.

conflict. So that is where this Second Part of the book begins, in the relative willingness of two national governments to engage in long-term preparation, with all that that entails.

The best and most effective armies benefit from clear and unitary line of command. In an era of universal conscription and mass citizen armies, this applies to the whole organisation of the nation-in-arms: 'The decision-making latitude of each command...derived from the political apparatus of the state.'[2] In this respect Germany in the decades preceding the war had a distinct advantage, in that all political and military power led inexorably to the Supreme warlord, Kaiser William. The autocratic Wilhemine regime facilitated swift decision-making and – given the Kaiser's personal preference for things martial – military focus.[3] In democratic France, every proposal, every decision was the subject of extensive debate. The President was head of the armed forces, delegating his powers to the Minister of War, both answerable to a watchful and volatile parliament. The fractured state of French politics and society only exacerbated this propensity towards dialogue and delay rather than diktat and decision. Extreme tensions between church and state, between Monarchist, Bonapartist and Republican, simply made the French social and political dialogue more complicated.[4]

This utter contrast between two political systems was reflected in the next level down, the machinery of military management. In Germany there were three separate organisations reporting direct to the Kaiser, the War Cabinet, the War Ministry and the Great General Staff. Responsibilities were spread between them with the Kaiser as the ultimate arbiter of disputes. All three were essential components of the German war machine, intent on creating and maintaining an effective fighting force. There were tensions and rivalries, but these were merely frictions that sub-optimised the performance of an essentially good and stable organisation. In France on the other hand, it seems that the politicians deliberately set out to reduce the efficiency of their armed forces in the greater interest of internal political stability:

> The issue of republicanising the Bonapartist French army had arisen with the formation of the Third Republic and had become more acute when the elections of 1876 closed the door on any possible return to the monarchy. During the Boulanger Affair in the late 1880s, the risk of subversion of the Republic and dictatorship by a popular general demonstrated the need for greater civilian control. The French political-military structure set up as a result was designed to assure ministerial control and to prevent the concentration of too much power in the hands of one military leader.[5]

Thus France's most senior generals were gathered in a powerless purely advisory body, the *Conseil supérieur de guerre (CSG)*, of which their designated commander-in-chief was merely the vice-president, with no executive power over how the army which he was designated to lead was built and trained. That power lay with the War Minister and with the technical Directorates in his War Ministry; and the War Minister in turn was responsible to parliament, where even minutia were often up for debate. Until 1911 when Joffre was appointed, the Chief-of-Staff reported not to a commander-in-chief designate but to the War Minister. The gap between the senior generals in the CSG and the more junior decision-makers in the War Ministry was palpable.

Germany had gained another significant advantage over France, that of the relative stability, longevity and consistency of their military institutions and processes. From the Prussian military

2   R.A. Prete, *Strategy and Command: the Anglo-French Coalition on the Western Front, 1914* (McGill-Queen's University Press, Canada, 2009), p.xv.
3   Martin Kitchen, *The German Officer Corps 1890-1914*, in particular, pp.1-21; Brose op. cit., pp.112-137.
4   David B. Ralston, *The Army of the Republic* (The M.I.T. Press, Cambridge MA, 1967).
5   Prete, op. cit., p.28.

reforms of Scharnhorst in 1816, through the testing ground of the Danish and Austrian wars of the 1860s, the golden era of von Moltke the Elder and the war of 1870, the Prussians and then the German Empire developed an organisation with systems and processes very much fit for purpose.[6] When, after their comprehensive defeat in 1870, France decided to set up similar institutions in imitation of the German model, Germany already had over fifty years of development behind them, and the French institutions were pale imitations with built-in flaws demanded by their political fear of a military coup.

In the key German military role – Chief of the General Staff – there were only four men in post during the fourteen years between 1870 and 1914: von Moltke the Elder, Waldersee, Schlieffen and von Moltke the Younger. In stark contrast, in France in only the three years between 1911 and the outbreak of war, Joffre had to work with no less than eight ministers of war. His analysis was succinct: 'They fell from power without having had the time to familiarise themselves with the complicated way in which their department functioned.'[7] In the absence of continuity and authority at the top, the deficiencies in the French system lower down were not only exposed but were released to cause maximum damage to French progress. There was also a strange status issue, with French generals preferring a comfortable seat on the advisory CSG to the perceived career-threatening hot seat of War Minister, leading to junior and inexperienced generals – often political generals like André – taking the top executive job: 'André, a poor soldier, is a mason, sectarian, a Dreyfusard and a Brissonist'.[8]

An American business consultant named W. Edwards Deming introduced a management concept called 'Total Quality Management (TQM)' in the 1950s. Its fundamental objective was to reduce errors in business processes, including an intent to 'aim for modernization of equipment and ensure workers have the highest level of training.'[9] Many managers have regarded this as a brilliant application of common sense, based on the principle of 'getting things right first time, every time.' TQM was essentially a structure of systems and processes, with feedback loops and correction mechanisms, which gave form to an organisation's desire to achieve continuous improvement. It has evolved and has been adopted by most of the world's largest and best corporations. Quality management processes can now be inspected and examined against demanding international standards (ISO 9000). Its guiding principles seem to have been presaged within the German military machine.

The relevance of TQM to war preparation lies in acknowledgement that the French and German military machines in 1900-1914 were merely giant corporations. Key elements of TQM, for example fit-for-purpose processes, continuous improvement, inspection, a concentration on modernizing equipment and delivering high class training, can be identified in the German military 'corporation', something which has been examined in detail and dubbed 'Prussian military excellence' by Colonel Dupuy.[10] This is not to say that the German war machine was perfect, no organisation run by human beings has yet achieved that; it can be noted, for example, that there were ongoing frictions and internal political manoeuvring between the Kaiser's three key offices, War Cabinet, War Ministry, and General Staff, and that senior German generals had developed

6   Colonel T.N. Dupuy, *A Genius for War, The German Army and General Staff 1807-1945* (Macdonald and Jane's, London, 1977), pp.17-147.
7   Joffre, op. cit., p.59: *Ils tombaient sans avoir eu le temps de se mettre au courant du fonctionnement compliqué de leur département.*
8   Porch, *Marne*, p.76, quoting General Galliffet, André's predecessor; and for general background, Ibid., pp.76-77, 102 and 170.
9   Wikipedia, 'Total Quality Management', accessed 3 July 2010.
10   Dupuy, op.cit., p.5.

a disturbing tradition of independence of command;[11] but these were frictions in an otherwise relatively smooth operation, relative to the French anyway. French historians have acknowledged this. Contamine quoted contemporary historian Georges Michon as saying 'it is not a question of numbers but of quality' going on to remark that:

> [I]f one notes that, even without mentioning heavy artillery, the German army has many more training camps, twice as much firing practice as us, that their rifle, their equipment, their uniforms are more modern and less visible, one must admit that the effort we will have to make [to catch up] will be enormous.[12]

The French had made an effort; despite their relatively late start and the political impediments described above, the French army did improve markedly between 1874 and 1894, such that by the turn of the century it was regarded as a formidable force.[13] Then there was the infamous Dreyfus Affair, which split the nation and weakened the army to an immeasurable degree.[14] Dreyfus was a Jewish officer who was falsely accused and convicted of passing military secrets to the Germans. When the true culprit was discovered, the institutional bonds that held the army together led to an attempt at cover-up. The innocent Dreyfus remained in prison for several more years before a press campaign orchestrated by the famous author Émile Zola galvanized public opinion and ensured that the miscarriage of justice was corrected. It was the attempt at a cover-up, rather than the original mistake, which brought the French officer corps most into disrepute. And worse was to follow, as the Dreyfus Affair led directly to an attempt to 'republicanise' the army under War Minister General André. From 1900 to about 1909, the focus within the French parliament and therefore the War Ministry was on turning French conscripts and French officers into model citizens rather than better soldiers. This period in French military development – although stagnation might be a better description – has been well researched by historians, Douglas Porch and Leonard V. Smith in particular.[15] The ways in which the 'republicanisation' programme weakened the French army are manifold, from attempts to discriminate against catholic officers (uncovered in the *Affaire des Fiches*) to the lowering of officers' social status and pay whilst at the same time asking them to educate their conscript troops to make them better republicans.[16]

But of all General André's changes, the most pernicious was, arguably, the decision to abolish the inspection regime; after which members of CSG were no longer responsible for monitoring the quality of corps commanders' training, and corps commanders were stopped from inspecting the units that they would command in time of war. Although reinstated by Joffre in 1911, it took time to re-establish standards and in any case ten classes of reservists had already received training of poor quality and variable consistency dependent upon the personal qualities of their officers. A key component of an essential quality management control system had been removed for a long and important period. There were indirect consequences as well. For example: Director of Artillery General Deloge, a dynamic, competent leader who between 1897 and 1905 oversaw the roll-out of the 75mm field gun programme and who equipped the army with the Rimailho 155mm heavy howitzer as well as the 120mm mobile field howitzer, was removed for political reasons and replaced

11 Kitchen, op. cit., pp.64-95; Brose, op.cit., pp.40-42 & 154.
12 Contamine, *Marne*, p.30.
13 Brose, op. cit., pp.108-111.
14 Porch, op. cit., pp.54-72; Ralston, op. cit., pp. 203-251.
15 Porch, op. cit., and: Leonard V. Smith, *Between Mutiny and Obedience: The Case of the French 5th Infantry Division during World War I* (Princeton, 1994).
16 Ralston, op. cit., pp.252-315; Porch, op. cit., pp.73-103.

by a series of 'safe' political appointees.[17] Production of heavy artillery and indeed any gun except the famous '75 was stopped almost at once. One wonders how and when the Rimailho factory production line was closed and dismantled, when it could have been producing the heavy artillery that France then lacked in August 1914.

All of the evidence above leads to the conclusion that in the key period from 1900 to 1911, the French lacked the political will to prepare their armed forces as effectively as the Germans. The first Moroccan crisis came and went in 1905 without any perceptible change in French military policy, and it was only the second (Agadir) crisis in 1911 which catalysed change; whereas in Germany the year 1905 signalled an ongoing increase in the tempo of their own preparations. These were the years, for example, in which Germany gave each regiment a machine gun company and introduced a second regiment of field artillery - including a group of mobile field howitzers – into each regular division. These were the years in which Germany equipped all its units with field kitchens and all its regular troops with field grey uniforms.[18]

It has been asserted above that France lacked the political will to prepare properly for war in the key decade before 1911, whereas Germany actually accelerated its already constant rate of progress from 1905 onwards. Further evidence to support this conclusion lies in an analysis of financial commitment. Money is a key indicator of a nation's willingness and ability to commit to effective preparation for war. Absence of adequate funding places an unbreakable constraint upon what can be reasonably achieved by those responsible for building and maintaining their country's armed forces. But the raising of funds through taxation is itself a political and social issue and one not only of will but of demography as well.

Between 1871 and 1914, Germany's population grew from 41 million to 65 million, outstripping France, whose total population was still only 40 million in 1914.[19] And Germany's demographic growth was accompanied by similar industrial and economic expansion; this was the period of Germany's Industrial Revolution. As well as allowing the Germans to be increasingly more selective in their choice of conscripts, an issue which will be explored at greater length elsewhere, their advantage in numbers and in wealth generated more taxable income.

One German historian, General Hofacker, writing in the immediate post-war period, went to some length to try to disprove the widely held belief that Germany's militaristic aggression was responsible for the war. He quoted statistics: over the period 1909 to 1913, he said, France's military spending grew from 17.6 marks to 33 marks per head compared with Germany's growth from 12.2 marks to 20 marks per head.[20] If these figures are correct, then he could claim that France increased her military commitment in the build-up to war by a factor of 1.9 compared to Germany's 1.6. But given the disparity in populations, these per capita figures merely show the extra effort France had to make just to try to gain equality with Germany in terms of absolute military expenditure. France was spending 36% of her national budget on the military as against only 20% by Germany and yet, according to General Langlois, that amounted to only 914 francs per soldier compared to Germany's 1770 francs per soldier.[21]

Marshal Joffre makes it clear in his memoirs what political and bureaucratic difficulties he faced in his attempts to close the gap in terms of absolute levels of funding with France's principle

17   General Baquet, *Souvenirs d'un Directeur de l'Artillerie* (Henri Charles-Lavauzelle, Paris, 1921), p.41 and pp.33-34.
18   Brose, op. cit., pp.174-177.
19   D.B. Nash, *Imperial German Army Handbook 1914-1918* (Ian Allen Ltd, London, 1980), p.14.
20   Generalleutnant z D. Von Hofacker, *Der Weltkrieg* (Verlag von W. Kohlhammer, Stuttgart, 1928), p.9.
21   Porch, *Marne*, p. 227 and quoting: *Le Temps*, 15 November 1908 with regard to General Langlois.

prospective enemy.[22] Between 1901 and 1909, on average a little over a half (57%) of the funding requested by the armed services was finally voted into law. As a result programmes had to be curtailed, or their delivery delayed (or both); constraints were placed on budgets for exercises and annual manoeuvres and on railway costs for transporting troops to training grounds.[23] And yet Joffre himself concedes that the French legislature never refused to vote the funds demanded of them by the different ministries; the bulk of the problems and issues which hampered the French efforts to fund its armed forces lay in the bureaucratic and administrative web – particularly between the bureaucrats of the Ministries of War and Finance - which linked and yet diluted professional assessment of need with political ownership and authority. The outcome shows clearly that in time of peace, the Finance Ministry dominated the War Ministry; and the quality of long-term preparation of the army for war suffered as a result.

Joffre too asserts that there were major disparities between levels of French and German funding. Between 1901 and 1905, he says, average German military expenditure was about 115 million francs a year, compared to 47 million by the French. The figures are broadly corroborated by Klotz, the president of the French parliamentary budget committee, who put the 1904 French defence budget at 38 million francs to Germany's 99 million francs.[24] Joffre goes on to say that between 1906 and 1910, these figures increased to 95 million and 190 million respectively.[25] Joffre ascribes this large disparity to a general belief in France during the first decade of the 20th Century in 'the mirage of universal peace'[26]. It was only the Moroccan political crises of 1905-6 (Tangier) and 1911 (Agadir) that woke the French people to the reality of prospective war and to the need to apply their will to confronting their enemy. General Hofacker's quoted statistics on the relative growth of French per capita spending from 1909 to 1913 fit nicely with Joffre's thesis of a gradual increase in the French people's political and social will to prepare for war. But despite their late awakening to the need for increased military spending, the French still had less money available to allocate to the military and still spent significantly less than the Germans in absolute terms.

What is more, Germany continued actively to increase its own military spending over this period, making the French task of catching up virtually impossible. In October 1911, in reaction to the Agadir crisis and the German perception that they were not militarily strong enough to face up to a combination of the other Imperial powers, Chancellor Bethmann Hollweg, introduced an Army Bill, calling for two new corps commands, two new infantry divisions, four new field and four new foot (heavy) artillery regiments as well as a number of administrative improvements (for example, mobilisation support). This was a huge one-off increase in expenditure and commitment, equivalent to the sum of all the annual increases since 1893.[27] When, during 1912, discussions took place regarding the financing of another Army Bill in 1913, it is clear that it took considerable political and social will on the part of the German Government, politicians and people to swallow the economic and fiscal consequences of raising the extra money: 'the government was therefore once more forced to issue short-term treasury bills at a time when money was already tight because of the Balkan wars, thereby making the already difficult economic situation even worse.'[28] The German 1913 Army Bill went ahead, at an estimated cost of between 200 and 300 million marks. It provided for an extra 14,900 NCOs and 117,000 men in the peacetime army – the equivalent of

22   Joffre, op. cit., pp 41 – 59: *Les budgets de la Guerre.*
23   Ibid., p. 46.
24   Porch, *op. cit.*, p.227 quoting: L. Klotz, *L'Armée en 1906* (Paris 1906), p.101.
25   Joffre, *op. cit.*, p.47.
26   Joffre's actual words were: 'la chimère de la paix universelle'.
27   Fritz Fischer, *War of Illusions: German Policies from 1911 to 1914* (translated by Marian Jackson, Chatto & Windus, London, 1975) pp.116-121.
28   Ibid. p.137.

about eight extra divisions, although in this instance the resource went towards the increase in the peacetime permanent strength of existing units. The German Chief of General Staff, von Moltke, had actually asked for three more completely new army corps (six divisions) as well, but this was a fiscal step too far, and the Kaiser deferred that request for another occasion.[29] Nevertheless by March 1913, Germany had committed about 2½ % of its gross national product to its armed forces[30], a significantly high figure that the French would have had to exceed in order to achieve parity of absolute expenditure; France did not have deep enough pockets to do that.

The importance of these fiscal issues in the analysis of the comparative state of the French and German armies on the eve of war cannot be overestimated. Major programmes of capital expenditure take years to prepare and complete. Accumulated investment over a long period gives far greater return than larger sums committed at the last moment. In the end no amount of extra money can compensate for irretrievably lost time. Continuous long-term investment allows for considered decision-making and a higher quality of output (all other things – such as the standard of decision-maker – being equal). One example – training camps – illustrates the point.

In 1911 Germany was on the point of completing its long-term programme for providing one training ground for each of its 26 army corps, and each one was large enough to accommodate a full division in training.[31] France, on the other hand, had at that time only 8 partially completed camps and only two of those (Châlons and Mailly) were of comparable size to the German standard. French building programmes, announced in 1897 and again in 1908, were not pushed through with vigour nor with remotely adequate funding and it was only after Joffre was appointed commander-in-chief in 1911 that the issue of building an adequate number of adequately sized training camps was properly addressed.[32] The 1911 programme called for an increase in the number of division-sized training camps from 2 to 14, starting with the upgrading of existing smaller camps. But work had hardly started (there were further bureaucratic delays) when war broke out.[33] The impact upon French effectiveness in 1914 as a result of the lack of adequate training facilities will be examined in more detail elsewhere in this book. But the difference between German and French commitment to funding is starkly laid bare.

The German system was designed to provide continuity of military funding. As a result of Bismark's iron hold on the reins of power, and his and the Kaiser's insistence that the army report directly to the monarch without political intermediaries, the new German constitution in 1871 enshrined the principle of an army grant based upon a fixed annual amount per soldier that the Reichstag could review only every seventh year - hence the term 'Septennate' for the grant.[34] Even when, as in 1887, the Reichstag sought to extend its influence by trading its agreement to substantial increases for a reduction of the review period to three years, Bismark was powerful enough to dissolve them and (manipulating popular fears of 'a revanchist France under General Boulanger') obtained an election result which granted him his increased funding without condition.[35] His successor, Caprivi, was not so successful in keeping army funding away from political interference. In 1892, faced with the prospect of a war on two fronts as a result of deteriorating relations with Russia, Caprivi only obtained the massive increases that he and Schlieffen believed necessary by

29   Ibid. pp.180-181.
30   Ibid. p.184.
31   Porch, *op. cit.*, p. 200.
32   The 1908 programme, for example, was scheduled to be completed in 1930. Joffre, *op. cit.*, p.79.
33   Joffre, *op. cit.*, pp. 79-84.
34   William Carr, *A History of Germany 1815-1990* (Edward Arnold, London, 1969) p.107 & p.139.
35   Ibid.p.139.

conceding to the Reichstag the right to debate the army grant every five years.[36] But even this shorter period guaranteed German military planners and German arms manufacturers a degree of continuity of funding that the French, with their annual parliamentary votes and frequent changes of government, could never dream of achieving. When the significant increases in expenditure called for in the Army Bills of 1911 and 1913 were put before the *Bundesrat*, the German army had already benefited from forty years of uninterrupted, regular underlying base funding.

It has been asserted above that in France junior officials in the Technical Directorates took the spending decisions rather than the potential users (the front line soldiers). A classic example is that of the case for mobile field howitzers. In Germany the need for such a high-trajectory artillery piece in the front line was identified in 1901 and approved almost immediately by the Great General Staff; a piece was commissioned, built, mass-produced and rolled out to front-line units before 1909, when improving modifications were introduced.[37] In France, despite the German example and despite the evidence of the Russo-Japanese War, nothing was done during the 'somnambulant' period between 1905 and 1911. Even the progress made prior to 1894, noted above, through which the de Bange 120mm howitzer was included in the French armoury, had been halted, indeed reversed.

When Joffre came to power in July 1911, he immediately raised the issue of the Army's requirement for a new light mobile howitzer, only to be told by the Director of Artillery that nothing could be done for two or three years.[38] But in March 1912, Schneider offered their 105mm howitzer – produced for export to the Bulgarian army – for field trials. A battery was immediately ordered for the Mailly practice range with the expectation that it would take part in the autumn 1912 manoeuvres. The full saga of the French light howitzer is to be found in the chapter on 'Equipment'. In brief, and to exemplify how the bureaucrats in the War and Finance Ministries conspired to subvert the wishes of the soldiers in funding decisions, the Mailly trials were deemed successful and a credit of 80 million francs allocated by Joffre for the production of the howitzer, only for the technical services to persuade the Government (during parliamentary debate to vote funding) that further trials were required. Then the Artillery Directorate proposed a cheaper alternative, the modification of the 75mm gun so that it fired at the higher trajectory – the 'Malandrin plaquette' – which was finally adopted in March 1913. The French entered the war without a piece comparable to the German 105mm Light Field Howitzer. The disconnect between the demands of the field army and the decisions of the technical directorates introduced confusion, delay and sub-optimised solutions into the process of funding new programmes and contributed significantly to identified French weaknesses in August 1914.

In summary, the following points exemplify the comparative lack of political will in France to prepare for war during peacetime: The Germans with their larger population and stronger, growing, economy had more fiscal resources available to fund their armed forces, and were more than willing to apply them. Over the key period 1901-1910, the Germans spent more than twice as much as the French and were consequently able to invest in long-term programmes which had matured by the time war broke out. When the 'arms race' really increased in pace, with major German spending increases put before the Reichstag in 1912 and 1913, similar French increases were voted. However, bureaucratic delays and conflict between technical directorates and the field army conspired to slow down French programmes so that little progress on key programmes such as training camps and field howitzers had been achieved before time ran out in August 1914.

36 Ibid. p.169.
37 Joffre, *op. cit.*, p.61.
38 Ibid. p.63 .

In every respect on fiscal issues, Germany's political and social will to prepare effectively for war outstripped that of France, from the ability and willingness to commit large long-term sums of money, to the cleaner lines of politically-unencumbered decision-making which allowed them to obtain the best return on their investment in the faster time. For the French, it was very much the case of too little, too late. The results of this huge imbalance in fiscal preparedness can be followed through every programme – training, equipment, exercises and manoeuvres – leading up to the war and can be traced to the French failures in the Ardennes battles of August 1914.

This chapter has set out to demonstrate how at the highest social and political levels, German willingness to commit available resource on a continuous basis to prepare for war outstripped that of France. The following chapters will examine in detail how this comparative level of commitment impacted upon the various elements of each country's military machine, starting with an examination of Doctrine.

7

Doctrine

Even today, some historians continue to describe the military doctrines with which France and Germany entered the war in terms of the Churchillian myth of French *offensive à outrance*, red trousers and bayonets, against German trenches, wire and machine guns. Doctrine is a complex subject, requiring greater analysis than that, and its diverse yet interrelated strands are gradually being identified and subjected to greater scrutiny.

This chapter will examine French and German military doctrines in the light of the performance in battle revealed in our detailed examination of the encounter battles in the Ardennes on 22 August 1914, in order to determine the extent to which they were responsible for the outcomes of the battles. It will start with an overview of what has been written about doctrine in general, and then continue by examining doctrine against performance in the Ardennes at the strategic, operational and tactical levels.

B.R. Posen defines military doctrine as setting, within grand strategy, priorities among various military forces and prescribing how those forces should be structured and employed to achieve the ends in view.[1] He classifies doctrine into offensive, defensive and deterrent categories, examining each against a series of parameters such as 'Political–Military Integration', 'Innovation' and 'Environmental Uncertainty', using Organisation Theory and Balance of Power Theory to test his hypothesis on chosen case studies. Given the way in which terms such as 'offensive strategy', 'strategic offensive/tactical defensive' and *offensive à outrance* are generally discussed in the context of both Joffre's and Moltke's opening moves in August 1914, Posen's research and conclusions provide a useful context within which to examine the doctrines used in the Ardennes campaign.

Azar Gat, in his study of the history of military thought, examines the development of both French and German doctrine as expressed by key and influential people – soldiers, thinkers, teachers, writers – over nearly four hundred years.[2] His research into 'The Cult of the Offensive' is of particular relevance to this study, since the French doctrine of 1914 has been indelibly associated with that term.

There is also the question of which level of a military organisation one is discussing. In his analysis of the theory of war Clausewitz divided the conduct of war into two levels, 'strategy' and 'tactics', defining the former as 'the use of engagements for the object of the war' and the latter as 'the use of armed forces in the engagement'.[3] But it is now common to add an 'operational' level to the conduct of war.

---

1   Barry R. Posen, *The Sources of Military Doctrine*, p.7–13.
2   A. Gat, *A History of Military Thought from the Enlightenment to the Cold*.
3   C. von Clausewitz, *On War* (Edited and translated by Michael Howard and Peter Paret, Everyman's Library, London, 1993) p.146.

The words 'operation' or 'operations' have been used in the context of war as far back as the time of Frederick the Great, perhaps earlier. Sir Michael Howard has described 'operational art' as 'the grey area between strategy and tactics', going on to make the clear distinction that 'strategy is about *thinking* and *planning*. Operations are about *doing*'.[4] Gat, in his detailed examination of Clausewitz's ideas on the purpose and means in war, wrote that: 'he [Clausewitz] now gives an equal status to a variety of war aims and operational objectives, or, to use the terminology of 1804, purposes of war and purposes in war.'[5] Claus Telp, in his work on 'The Evolution of Operational Art: From Frederick the Great to Napoleon' develops a persuasive argument as to how the concept started to evolve in the late 18th century to the point where it required a classification of its own. Briefly, Telp identifies as a key evolutionary step the decision by Prince Henry (Frederick the Great's brother) to create mixed–arm divisions of his army. The individual deployment of divisional and later corps columns directly from march into combat blurred the distinction between Clausewitz's 'strategy' and 'tactics', and gave the need for definition of 'operations' that much more prominence. Telp's argument gains more credence when measured against the increasing size and complexity of modern armies and the widening of fronts.[6] Martin van Creveld has called Napoleon's way of war 'the Dawn of Operational Warfare'[7], whilst Dennis Showalter has written persuasively of 'Prussian–German Operational Art, 1740–1943'.[8]

Jehuda Wallach, on the other hand, writes that 'it is widely assumed that Schlieffen was the creator of the level of the operative art between strategy and tactics'.[9] Wallach's assertion arises in the context of a discussion of Schlieffen's preferred method of using his forces: always in offensive mode ('Schlieffen rejected every thought, even in case of tremendous inferiority, of exchanging offense for defense [sic]')[10] and always by envelopment of a flank or flanks ('Schlieffen rejected frontal attacks; time and again he criticised them in his final discussions of exercises, war games, and staff rides by emphasising that, at best, an ordinary victory might be achieved').[11] Wallach's argument might well be challenged on the basis that he is describing 'manoeuvre warfare' rather than 'operational art'. Wallach describes Schlieffen's views on generalship: 'Owing to the concept of attack in front, flanks, and, if possible, in the rear, it is the duty of the higher commanders to make the necessary arrangements for shortening the unavoidable interval between the clash in front and the arrival of the enveloping forces in flanks and rear.'[12] Schlieffen's operational teaching, which as described by Wallach might be termed 'operational science' today, is evident on the battlefields of the Ardennes.

Between them, Howard, Olsen, Creveld (and their contributors), Telp and Wallach provide an appreciation of pre–war operational art, such that a study of the activity by which the French and German commanders in the Ardennes in August 1914 sought to use engagement(s) to further their strategic objectives can be taken as a valid proposition.

Michel Goya has recently written a valuable assessment of the French army's development from its pre-war state through wartime transformation. In his book 'La Chair et l'Acier' (Flesh and Steel)

---

4   M. Howard in his prologue to: *The Evolution of Operational Art, from Napoleon to the Present* (edited by John Andreas Olsen and Martin van Creveld, Oxford University Press, Oxford, 2011) p.ix.

5   Gat, op. cit., p.226.

6   C. Telp, *The Evolution of Operational Art 1740–1813* (Frank Cass, London & New York, 2005), passim.

7   Olsen & Creveld, op. cit., pp.9–34.

8   Ibid., pp.35–63.

9   J. L. Wallach, *The Dogma of the Battle of Annihilation* (Greenwood Press, Westport Connecticut and London, 1986) p.62, Note 18, citing Ferdinand M.v. Senger und Etterlin, *Cannae, Schlieffen und die Abwehr* (Wehrwissenschaftliche Rundschau, Jg.13 (1936)), H.1–2, p.27.

10   Ibid., p.49.

11   Ibid., p.45.

12   Ibid., pp.47–48.

he also divides the art of war into three levels – strategic, operational and tactical – each with its own characteristics and level of doctrine constituting 'the sum of the notions which allow the most effective use of the available means'.[13] He examines just the operational and tactical levels, tracing the development of French doctrines at those levels from about 1870 up to the start of the war. All the major powers produced and published Field Service Regulations (FSR); in France they were known as *règlements de service en campagne* (RSC). For Goya, these were 'operational' documents setting out operational doctrine, although they were not necessarily recognised as such at the time. A reading of the 1895 FSR generally supports Goya's thesis, in that it was primarily concerned with the activity preceding the actual encounter, although it does include a high–level section on 'combat'. Extending Goya's argument, the German FSR of 1900 and 1908 constitute the equivalent German operational doctrine, and again a reading of those two documents confirms their 'operational' intent.[14]

At the tactical level, Goya identifies the various instructions issued to each branch of the armed forces, for example the *règlements de manoeuvre d'infanterie* (RMI), as the instruments which laid down doctrine for each arm during the encounter itself, the tactical level. The German 1906 *Exerzier–Reglement für die Infanterie* (ERI) and similar instructions for the other arms similarly form the corpus of German tactical doctrine.

A key issue raised by Goya is his contention that French doctrine as a whole was, in the key period leading up to the war, full of confusion.[15] This confusion stemmed from two principal causes: firstly the fact that the distinction between operational and tactical doctrine was not properly understood by the French officer corps; secondly the French failure to keep all their different low-level regulations updated regularly and in step with each other, particularly ensuring that a consistent set of ideas flowed down from the 'operational' FSR to the 'tactical' RMI.[16] On Goya's second point, the French conceded at the time their difficulty in keeping the various texts in step with the overall RSC, as noted in the minutes of the 22 March 1905 session of the CSG.[17]

Dimitry Queloz, examining the development of French doctrine from Napoleon's time to the start of the war, concurs with Goya's conclusion that at the heart of the French army in the immediate pre–war period there was doctrinal confusion, emphasising a well–argued point that during the crucial period from 1900 to 1913 the ESG (staff college) lost its key dual role in ensuring unity of doctrine and in disseminating that unified doctrine across the whole officer corps.[18] Central to this argument is the fact that, while tactical regulations were amended and changed regularly, the higher level FSR of 1895 remained unaltered until October 1913. The debate about whether and how to update the 1895 FSR continued during the crucial decade between the Russo–Japanese War of 1904–5 and the outbreak of war; it grew relatively heated and contentious after Colonel de Grandmaison's two lectures of February 1911 and, finally, the

---

13   Goya, op. cit., p.70: 'l'ensemble des notions' qui permettent d'y utiliser les moyens le plus efficacement possible constitue la doctrine.'
14   *Manuel sur le service en campagne de l'infanterie* (Librarie Militaire de Berger–Levrault et cie, Paris, 1899): hereafter referred to as 'French FSR 1895; and *The Field Service Regulations (Feld Dienstordnung 1900) of the German Army 1900:* (translated by Colonel H.S. Brownrigg, Intelligence Dept. at the War Office & published by HMSO, London, 1900), hereafter 'German FSR 1900', and *The Field Service Regulations of the German Army 1908* (translated by the General Staff, War Office and published by HMSO, London, 1908) hereafter 'German FSR 1908'.
15   Goya, op. cit., pp.71–72.
16   Ibid., pp. 71–71.
17   AAT 1N11: Notes and Minutes of the *conseil supérieure de guerre, 1905–1913, session of 22 March 1905*: at that meeting it was noted that the rules for the Staff (État-Major, 20 Feb. 1900), Railways (21 Feb 1900), Rear areas (11 Feb. 1900) and gendarmerie (13 Feb 1900) were all out of step with the 1895 FSR. But no action was recorded to correct the situation.
18   D. Queloz, *De la manoeuvre Napoléonienne* à *l'offensive* à *outrance*, p.364.

changes were officially made when (with hindsight) it was too late for them to be properly absorbed and implemented before the war started.

As if by way of explanation, Posen has written that 'changing doctrines takes time; it disorients a military organisation. A war during such a period of transition can be very dangerous.'[19] His analysis and argument states that 'innovation in military doctrine should be rare. It will only occasionally be sponsored by the military organisation itself.' It is rare because it increases uncertainty: 'While innovation is in progress, the organisation's SOPs (Standard Operating Procedures) and programs [sic] will be in turmoil. Should a war come during the transition, the organisation will find itself between doctrines. Under combat conditions, even a bad doctrine may be better than no doctrine'.[20] Posen has described almost exactly the state of French doctrine in August 1914, with the three new regulations of October and December 1913 and April 1914 in place but not fully implemented nor practiced. No such confusion is evident on the German side, where continuity and gradual evolution of doctrine seems to have prevailed, and where continuous and more or less seamless teaching and practice had been the norm for decades. The powerful link between the *Kriegsakademie* (War Academy) and the Great General Staff, and between the army inspectorates and the trainers on the ground, meant that the confusion and dislocation experienced by the French during the vital pre–war period was largely avoided in the German army.

The argument presented by both Goya and Queloz that French doctrinal confusion extended to a general misunderstanding about doctrine at different levels is exemplified by an incident during the preparation for the Ardennes attack. Joffre sent de Langle an instruction on the eve of the offensive which concluded with the words 'the enemy will be attacked wherever he is found'.[21] It has been used by historians to point to the supposedly flawed nature of the French doctrine of *offensive à outrance*: they (the historians) have interpreted Joffre's intent as one of throwing everybody and everything at the enemy the minute you see him, regardless of terrain or circumstance. On the contrary, it is in fact a clear example of the confusion existing in the minds of French officers at all levels (and many historians who have looked at this afterwards) about the nature of doctrine. A strategic doctrine which requires an army to 'attack the enemy wherever he is found' conveys an entirely different intention from a tactical doctrine of the same wording.[22] Sir John French used similar words in his Operational Order Nr.36 on 15 October 1914, and he has not yet been accused of championing the cult of the offensive within the BEF.[23] The point is that an acceptable strategic imperative can become an unacceptable tactical order; the problem with Joffre's exhortation to take the fight to the enemy was that it was repeated verbatim down the whole French chain of command. De Langle's operational order nr.20 for 22 August started by copying Joffre's words: 'Tomorrow, 22, Fourth Army will commence its offensive movement to the north supported by Third Army in echelon back on our right. The enemy will be attacked wherever he is encountered'.[24] And the lowly *9 régiment de chasseurs à cheval* (9 Chasseurs), corps cavalry for 17 CA, noted that when it received its orders for 22 August the Colonel then told his men '17 Corps must attack the

---

19   Posen, op. cit., p.30.
20   Posen, op. cit., p. 55.
21   *AFGG I/1*, Annex 696: [GQG, 21 August, 07.25]: *Le commandant en chef au commandant de l'armée de Stenay. 'L'ennemi sera attaqué partout où on le rencontrera.'*
22   It is worthy of note that no such confusion seems to have existed in German minds. It has been highlighted elsewhere that the strategic instruction for the German 4th Army was to adopt a defensive posture, yet that did not inhibit almost universal tactical offensive behaviour on the battlefield.
23   Nikolas Gardner, *Trial by Fire* (Praeger, London, 2003), p.125: quoting GHQ Operational Order Nr.36, issued at 23.40 on 15 October 1914; '... attacking the enemy wherever met'.
24   *AFGG I/1*, Annex 757: [Fourth Army]: *Armée de Stenay, 21 août, 18.00: Ordre général nr.20 concernant les operations du 22 août: 'l'ennemi sera attaqué partout où on le rencontrera'.*

enemy wherever he is encountered'.[25] Between commander-in-chief Joffre and the commander of a cavalry regiment, only the two words 'will be' (*sera*) had been changed to 'must be' (*doit*), and that is a tactical change for the worse.

This incident speaks as much to the poor quality of French command as it does to the issue of doctrine, but a lack of understanding of the distinction between levels of doctrine is clearly exemplified. There is also a question of how top-level orders were disseminated down through the military organisation. French regulations stated: 'The intentions and orders received by the various grades of the military hierarchy are put into new instructions and orders, or into new orders only, for the use of immediate subordinates. Every effort must be made to diminish the time taken in the issue of these new orders.'[26] It would seem that in practice, insofar as any French officer understood and sought to execute that instruction, the final exhortation for speed of transmission outweighed any other aspect of the regulation. In contrast, the equivalent German regulation stated: 'Only in very exceptional cases should the orders of a subordinate leader be merely a copy of those of his superior with his own additions tacked on. It will be clearer and serve the purposes of the superior better, if he writes an independent order containing whatever is necessary'.[27] The German staff officers also received specific training in the art of writing orders: 'Once the military technical vocabulary had been mastered, orders were to be clear, precise, complete, and brief... Brevity implied that orders should never contain one word the omission of which would not immediately affect their meaning... Training in the art of issuing orders was one goal of war games'.[28] It is clear that on the French side, none of the officers in the chain of command sought to distinguish between strategic and tactical doctrine, but were more concerned with executing a mindless but swift mechanical process.

Before moving on from this consideration of overall military doctrine, the issue of the French *offensive à outrance* or 'cult of the offensive' must be addressed. Historians in the immediate post–war period wrote of it as if it were an official doctrine that was some sort of aberration, driving the French army to costly defeats in the opening battles, a view which remained common into the 1960s. The myth, for such it is, was first propagated by Winston Churchill in 1923 when he published his history of the Great War, 'The World Crisis 1911-1914'. He wrote of 'an ardent faith' that Joffre's offensive into Alsace and Lorraine would succeed.[29] When in 1931 he wrote an abridged and revised version for more popular consumption, Churchill chose to use more colourful language:

> The doctrine of the offensive raised to the height of a religious frenzy animated all ranks, and in no rank was restricted by the foreknowledge of the modern rifle and machine gun. … Everywhere along the battle front, whenever Germans were seen, the signal was given to charge. 'Vive la France!' 'A la baïonnette,' 'En Avant' - and the brave troops nobly led by their regimental officers, who sacrificed themselves in even greater proportion, responded in all the magnificent fighting fury for which the French nation has been traditionally renowned.[30]

The reader may judge for himself, having absorbed in earlier chapters the detail of the encounter battles in the Ardennes on 22 August 1914, how far from the truth Churchill's florid rhetoric lies.

25   AAT 26N889/1: JMO of 9 Chasseurs, entry for 22 August: '*Le 17 CA doit attaquer l'ennemi partout où on le rencontrera*'.
26   *Operations of Large Formations, 1913*, p.29, Article 47.
27   German FSR 1900, p.15, Article 55.
28   A. Bucholz, *Moltke, Schlieffen and Prussian War Planning* (Berg, Oxford, 1991) pp.192–3.
29   Churchill, *The World Crisis 1911-1914*, p.265.
30   Churchill, *The World Crisis 1911-1914*, p.157.

But the arguably more sober assessment of historian Basil Liddell Hart reinforced the growing but incorrect perception in his 1930 book 'A History of The World War', writing that 'in their enthusiasm for the offensive they had blinded themselves to the defensive power of modern weapons' and that 'the troops attacked blindly with the bayonet and were mown down by machine-guns.'[31]

The myth thus had firm foundations. But three decades later it was revived and if anything made more potent by a new generation of scholars. Professor Cyril Falls, one-time holder of the prestigious Chichele Chair of Military History at Oxford University, extended the Churchillian argument of ardent enthusiasm for a doctrine of the offensive to include greater, and equally colourful, detail:

> A disastrous doctrine had, however, been spread among them. It was a sort of fanaticism, a veritable *mystique* of the offensive. Colonel de Grandmaison, a Peter the Hermit with flaming eyes, preached the new crusade: 'For the attack only two things are necessary: to know where the enemy is and to decide what to do. What the enemy intends to do is of no consequence'. Artillery support was hardly taken into account by this high-minded and selfless but crack-brained seer. It is impossible to calculate how many men were sent to their deaths through his agency, but the roll must have been a long one.[32]

The narrative constructed by Churchill, Liddell Hart and Falls, amongst others, is one of an official French doctrine – a so-called 'doctrine of the offensive' – constructed by one Colonel de Grandmaison and disseminated throughout the army so successfully that soldiers in their tens of thousands charged to their deaths, throwing themselves ardently into a storm of German machine gun fire. An alternative narrative taken from the battle chapters of this book shows how far from the truth is that 'Churchillian' picture.

Further evidence in support of our alternative narrative comes from an examination of the text of the actual doctrinal documents in use by the French Army in August 1914. A certain amount of background knowledge is needed to follow the argument. French doctrine was set by the 1895 Field Service Regulations, underpinned and expanded by various lower-level regulations for each arm of the service. Doctrine was taught at the *École superieur de guerre* (the French War Academy) and practiced in training exercises and field manoeuvres. Formulation of doctrine, teaching and training were loosely overseen by the Operations Bureau of the French General Staff within the Ministry of War. In 1911, Colonel de Grandmaison was the Head of the Operations Bureau, reporting to the Chief of General Staff and through him to the War Minister. Grandmaison was by all accounts an excellent, charismatic, staff officer. Incidentally he proved to be an excellent, charismatic field officer when war broke out, rising from command of a regiment to command of an army corps in seven months before being killed in February 1915 by German fire whilst visiting his front line trenches.

Grandmaison had formed a view from observation of training manoeuvres that the French Army lacked aggression, that divisional and corps commanders were overly cautious and tended to react to 'enemy' moves rather than taking the initiative. This state of affairs, he believed, was in part due to the fact that the 1895 FSR was out of date, and out of tune with more recent low-level regulations. In February 1911 he gave two lectures to the staff officers of the Operations Bureau at the War Ministry, laying out his criticisms and proposing some radical solutions. At the heart of his thesis was the argument that the 1895 FSR needed to be updated, and that a revised FSR should

---

31   B. Liddell Hart, *A History of The World War 1914-1918* (Faber & Faber, London, 1930) p.80 & p.82.
32   Cyril Falls, *The First World War*, p.16.

distinguish for the first time between 'operational' rules for the handling of large formations (army corps and above) and 'tactical' rules for the handling of subordinate units (division and below). At the operational level, argued Grandmaison, there needed to be a much more aggressive ethos that would seize the initiative from the enemy and dictate the battlefield agenda. The present state of reactive, security-conscious, command would in Grandmaison's view lead to 'atrophy' - a paralysis of will that would hand the initiative to the enemy. This in his opinion was what had happened in 1870 and it seemed likely to happen again under present conditions. Change was required if France was to win the next war.

Grandmaison's two lectures were intended for a small select audience of professional staff officers. But they appealed directly to an unsatisfied desire for change across the whole of the younger generation of junior French officers. One might add here in parenthesis that the fact that General Joffre found it necessary to remove more than 150 senior (brigade, divisional, corps and army) generals from their posts during the first eight weeks of the war validates Grandmaison's thesis and justifies the general feeling of discontent within the junior officer class. The message of the two 1911 lectures soon spread outside the confines of the War Ministry, and Grandmaison found it necessary to publish his text in order, he said, that his message might not be distorted. In this objective Grandmaison failed. The core message of aggression, of *offensive à outrance* (all-out attack) and of the triumph of will was picked up and spread - unofficially and out of context - throughout the junior officer class some of whom, as we have seen on a few occasions during the battles in the Ardennes in August 1914, sought to apply the operational 'message' at the tactical level. Sadly there was no such enthusiasm amongst the senior officers to apply the core message where Grandmaison intended it, at the operational level, and this too is evidenced by the actions of many divisional, corps and army commanders during the August battles.

To complete this brief history of the changes to French doctrine between 1911 and 1914: Grandmaison left the Operations Bureau to take up a regimental field posting at the end of 1911. But the seed that he had sown in his two now famous lectures was nurtured and grown by his successors, with Joffre's support. Work was started in the War Ministry to rewrite the 1895 FSR, indeed to split it in two as Grandmaison had suggested, into 'operational' and 'tactical' regulations, and at the same time, to round off the task, a new set of tactical infantry regulations were commissioned to reflect the high-level changes. The three new doctrinal documents were completed and published on the eve of war; the twin high-level FSRs in October and November 1913 and the low-level infantry regulations in January 1914. Therein lies the problem; there was insufficient time between the publication of the new doctrine and the outbreak of war for any teaching, training or practice to take place. Instead there was confusion, and uncertainty, as French historians Goya and Queloz have ably demonstrated.

Returning to our starting point of the 'Churchillian' narrative of a disastrous official French doctrine, it is now clear that in fact Grandmaison's two lectures sparked an unofficial 'cult of the offensive' that was taken up and incorrectly applied at the tactical level by a few ardent junior French officers. As a result of Grandmaison's teaching, revised operational regulations were written and published, but too late to have any effect other than to inadvertently sow confusion. And evidence from the battles in the Ardennes in August 1914 confirms that insofar as any operational doctrine was applied, it was still the 1895 FSR that the senior commanders adhered to.

In conclusion, modern research has demonstrated that there was a finely nuanced difference between an official offensively–minded but basically sound doctrine – that was applied too late – and certain unofficial tenets that seem to have seized the imagination of many in the junior ranks of the French officer corps. The difference can be ascribed in great part to the influence of a group of 'Young Turks' on the French General Staff, and they in turn were especially influenced by Grandmaison's two notorious lectures in February 1911.[33] Grandmaison's name has been indelibly and unfairly associated with the supposed aberrations of French tactical behaviour in August 1914.[34] As a result of the way in which Grandmaison's core message was distorted, one can see a clear if subtle difference between official French doctrine and an unofficial cult of the offensive.

Historian Azar Gat argues for a slightly different interpretation, tracing the evolution of what he calls the 'cult of the offensive' from its roots, and places it firmly on the main line of French doctrinal development:

> When, after 1911, the national revival again changed the political setting, forces and ideas which had matured in the previous half-decade suggested themselves as possible solutions to the army's problems. Young middle-ranking officers in the general staff advanced the notions of superior morale and out-and-out offensive as the answer both to the problems of modern firearms and to German material superiority. In this they were expressing, and in turn were supported by, the quest for moral regeneration and by the vitalistic philosophies engulfing French culture and society. Newly appointed to high command, Joffre perceived the ideas of the 'Young Turks' as an excellent means to revitalize the army, boost its morale, and provide it with a unifying doctrine. The official adoption of the doctrine of the offensive and Plan 17 were the result.[35]

Gat's analysis, with the exception of his use, in places, of the word 'cult' instead of 'doctrine', fits our alternative narrative. But Gat merely describes the theoretical state of French doctrine, ignoring how it was put into practice on the battlefield. There, as we have seen, theory and reality diverged in marked fashion, an issue that must be explored later when we look at training.

Queloz too pays particular attention to the French army's doctrine on the eve of the war.[36] He, like Gat, gives the name *offensive à outrance* specifically to the doctrine enshrined in the totality of the three new French regulations of 1913–1914, rather than to a general ethos within the French army.[37] But he makes a nice (and accurate) distinction between the teachings of Grandmaison and the doctrine codified in the new regulations, arguing that whilst they cannot be disassociated from each other, nor can they be regarded as identical. He points out (as did historian Henry Contamine before him[38]) that many historians (like the soldiers at the time) have had difficulty in identifying whether the concept of *offensive à outrance* concerned the strategic level, the operational level, the tactical level, or all three. But he concludes that the new regulations were much more balanced and intelligent than is generally thought, that while they were characterised by a strong spirit of the offensive, they were nevertheless clear, consistent, less schematic and more realistic, embracing modernity (aircraft and modern communications); and – perhaps most surprising of all to those who have swallowed the 'Churchillian' myth – whilst balancing fire and movement in attack, gave an important place to the defensive at the tactical level.[39]

---

33   Colonel de Grandmaison, *Deux Conférences faites aux officiers de l'État-Major de l'Armée (février 1911)* (Berger-Levrault, Paris, 1911).

34   For example: Falls, op. cit., p.16, Porch, op. cit., p.213, A. Clayton, *Paths of Glory* pp.36–37, I. Ousby, *The Road to Verdun* (Jonathan Cape, London, 2002) p.28, Doughty, op. cit., pp.26, 28.

35   Gat, op. cit., pp.402–440.

36   Queloz, op. cit., pp.367–469.

37   Ibid., p.371.

38   Contamine, *Marne*, p.124.

39   Queloz, op. cit., p.469.

One is drawn to the conclusion that confusion between tactical and operational levels of doctrine seems to lie at the heart of the debate about the nature of *offensive à outrance*. In identifying that fire and movement defined the attack and that the tactical defensive had an important part to play, Queloz has finally demolished the old Churchillian assertion that 'the doctrine of the offensive raised to the height of a religious frenzy animated all ranks, and in no rank was restricted by the foreknowledge of the modern rifle and machine gun.'[40] In fact, the new rules advocated taking sensible security precautions to avoid unnecessary losses before launching the final decisive bayonet attack. The concept of security or protection was central to both French and German operational doctrine throughout the period.

As with the official regulations, Grandmaison's text is permeated both by the offensive spirit and by the advocacy of *sûreté*.[41] Contrary to some impressions, he did not advocate the total abandonment of protection of individual columns in his haste to advance into contact: 'Because ultimately [a brigade column] needs to know exactly where to strike and to guard against a local surprise attack on its flanks, it will attack behind an advance guard and it will reconnoitre its flanks'.[42] Had General Fraisse of 66 Brigade, 33 Division adhered to this principle, the disaster at Bertrix might have been averted. Grandmaison's earlier work on infantry tactics during offensive operations, republished in 1912 and therefore concurrent with his operational treatise, makes it clear that he believed that enemy defensive fire would pin down any attacking force until fire superiority was obtained to allow the assault to go in.[43] Nor did he advocate the abandonment of operational *sûreté* during the offensive. The task of providing protection in front of the army (*mission de couverture*) was given to the first line security screen:

We will take precautions; we will take them in advance bearing in mind our predetermined goals. Having decided to attack as soon as we know where the enemy is, we must not risk making contact prematurely on unfavourable terrain...We will also cover our flanks as required, and send out mixed arms detachments when necessary.[44]

But Grandmaison also believed, and taught, (at the operational level) that a swift and violent advance into contact would seize the initiative, fix the enemy on his front, paralyse the enemy command and render him incapable of counter–manoeuvre.[45] He wrote:

During the offensive, the *sûreté* of a unit should above all be found from within, in its ability to attack, that is to say in the dispositions taken to attack swiftly and violently. An adversary attacked brusquely and at many points at once will try to parry the blows; he will no longer manoeuvre and will rapidly become incapable of all serious offensive action. It is the speed of our engagement which will guarantee us surprise and the violence of our attack which will protect us against a manoeuvre by our enemy.'[46]

Grandmaison put forward a balanced argument between traditional protection of tactical columns and the additional operational security gained from paralysing one's opponent's ability to

40   Churchill, *World Crisis*, p.218.
41   Grandmaison, *Deux Conférences*, p.17: the French word '*sûreté*' translates literally as 'security', but more properly in military parlance refers to the need to guard against surprise attack.
42   Grandmaison, *Deux Conférences*, p.34.
43   Grandmaison, *Dressage de l'infanterie en vue du combat offensif* (Berger–Levrault, Paris, 1912) p.5.
44   Grandmaison, *Deux Conférences*, p.45.
45   Ibid., pp.7,18, 32.
46   Ibid., p.25.

manoeuvre. The arguments laid out in his two speeches are technical and complex as befitted his professional audience, and cannot be covered adequately here.[47] But at the heart of his teaching lies his belief that senior French commanders were demonstrating a total atrophy in offensive thought, which would lead once again to the sort of command paralysis which had led in turn to the loss of the war in 1870-71.[48] For example he observed that in manoeuvres so many large flank guards, advance guards and rear guards were being deployed that there were too few troops to conduct the main attack. And he was not alone in this view; the German Military Attaché at the French 1908 manoeuvres wrote: 'overall this year the high command showed excessive caution and little enterprise.' In 1910, the German report concluded: 'So the manoeuvre took a slow course and went on all day without decision, over the same terrain. The leadership failed to show any appetite for responsibility, the troops showed little interest.'[49] Grandmaison's purpose was to inject some much needed energy and spirit into the French army within the framework of existing if updated doctrine, certainly within the bounds of sensible military technique. But in the end, all that is usually remembered of his closely argued theory is his peroration, with most often only the last sentence being quoted out of context:

Our conclusion will be that we must prepare ourselves and others [for the coming war] by cultivating with passion, with exaggeration and down to minute details of instruction, all that bears the mark, however small, of the offensive spirit. Let us go as far as excess and that will perhaps not be far enough.[50]

Grandmaison's two speeches fall into the category of an unofficial doctrine, a personal set of tenets, albeit delivered from an official platform; on the one hand his influence on Joffre's operational doctrine of 1913–14 is beyond doubt,[51] and on the other hand his unintended influence on the attitudes and actions of junior officers is equally clear. He intended to catalyse change, but not in the way that it occurred. Even a young Charles de Gaulle, who was otherwise a protégé of Pétain, advocate of a doctrine based on firepower, fell under the influence of this desire for change:

One must have the offensive spirit. This means that one must in all places and at all times have one single idea, that of advancing. As soon as the fighting begins everybody in the French army, the commanding general, the chiefs and the soldiers have only one idea left – advancing, advancing to the attack, reaching the Germans so as to spit them or make them run away.'[52]

Grandmaison's unwitting yet pivotal role in spreading an emotionally aggressive ethos amongst the younger French officers has become apparent. But his tenure of high office was short; he was not, as some historians have assumed, Chief of the Operations Bureau during Joffre's period in command:[53]

47   For a longer dissertation on this subject see: Simon J. House, *The Scapegoat: Colonel de Grandmaison: Deux conférences faites aux officiers de l'état-major de l'armée (Février 1911)* presented to the International Conference of First World War Studies, September 2009 and published online at <www.firstworldwarstudies.org/?m=200907>

48   Grandmaison, *Deux Conférences*, p. 22.

49   BA–MA PH 3/655: Reports on French Manoeuvres.

50   Grandmaison, *Deux Conférences*, p.69.

51   For example see: Queloz, op. cit., p.440; Contamine, *Revanche*, p.167; Goya, op. cit., pp.106–109.

52   Jean Lacouture, *De Gaulle: the Rebel, 1890–1944* (trans. Patrick O'Brian, Collins Harvill, London, 1990), p.23: quoting from de Gaulle's personal papers.

53   Porch, op. cit., p.219: 'Colonel de Grandmaison, chief of the 3rd bureau, was responsible for drawing up the controversial 1913 infantry regulations'. And: D. Stevenson, *Cataclysm* (Basic Books, New York, 2004), p.41: 'Probably influenced by advocates of the tactical and strategic offensive such as ... Grandmaison, chief of the

only months after delivering his lectures and immediately after the arrival of Joffre as commander–in–chief designate he was sent to command 153 RI within 20 CA, where he proved himself to be an excellent field officer, rising rapidly to command a group of reserve divisions before being killed in action in January 1915. It is ironic that Joffre himself, who 'admired the young [turks] group for its energy and promise', also 'regarded it as one of his primary missions to rid the army of its confusion and lack of confidence by providing it with a clear, unified, and inspiring doctrine.'[54] But he was not granted enough time to implement his new regulations properly before the war came; the confusion was, if anything, increased. Joffre wrote that his new offensive doctrine was codified into the single new regulation 'on the conduct of large units' (October 1913) and that it was an operational rather than tactical doctrine.[55] Unfortunately for him, and for the French army, the doctrinal confusion within the officer corps and their general failure to distinguish between strategic inspiration and tactical movement meant that, whilst most senior officers remained unmoved – as evidenced by the number of French generals removed from post by 30 August 1914[56]– a small body of junior officers sought to effect change where they could. We must now recognise a clear distinction between the offensive doctrine promulgated by Joffre and that occasionally adopted, unofficially, at the tactical level by frustrated young officers.

This short examination of doctrinal theory and development has set a context for the analysis of the actual performance of both sides in battle at strategic, operational and tactical levels. In particular it has identified on the French side a crucial weakness not present on the German side, namely doctrinal confusion. This confusion originated in a failure to update their 1895 FSR in the light of developments such as the Russo–Japanese War and a consequent lack of alignment between the higher and lower level regulations. Furthermore, the doctrinal debate raged as in Germany but without formal resolution until the autumn of 1913, too late to allow improvement, merely adding to the confusion. Arising from this confusion was not only the conflict between the official doctrine under which all French soldiers had been trained and the new official doctrine only recently promulgated but also a second level of conflict between official and unofficial teachings regarding the cult of the offensive, particularly as to which level – operations or tactics – it might be applied. It remains to be seen whether there is evidence of such confusion on the French side in the engagements in the Ardennes, and whether the Germans demonstrated a more rational application of their own doctrine at each level.

Strategic Doctrine

At the strategic level, military doctrine is an expression of how grand strategy will be implemented through war. Grand strategy – 'that collection of military, economic, and political means and ends with which a state attempts to achieve security'[57]– requires analysis of likely threats and the formulation of political, military or other remedies for those threats.[58] The prioritisation of means and the establishment of a preferred structure and organisation for the employment of military forces to respond to recognised threats and opportunities arguably constitute the basis of a strategic doctrine. According to Posen it 'includes the preferred mode of a group of services, a

operations bureau in the E.M.A., he [Joffre] wanted an immediate attack'.
54   A. Gat, op. cit., pp.432–433.
55   Joffre, op. cit., p.39.
56   AFGG X/1, pp.157, 203, 641–898.
57   Posen, op. cit., p.7.
58   Ibid., p.13.

single service, or a subservice for fighting wars. It reflects the judgements of professional military officers, and to a lesser but important extent civilian leaders, about what is and is not militarily possible and necessary'.[59]

Following Posen's analysis, it is clear that both France and Germany adopted offensive strategies, albeit for different reasons. In his book 'The Ideology of the Offensive', J. Snyder's conclusion is that neither side based its choice on 'a rational strategic calculus', but on many irrational factors such as 'military bias' and perceived change in the military balance of power.[60] One may justifiably add that the French army's rational strategic calculus of military need had led Joffre to advocate an immediate advance into Belgium, only for French politicians to deny him that option for reasons of grand strategy. Conversely it has been argued that the failure on the German army's part to integrate their war planning with foreign policy led to undue military bias in the decision to commit their main attack through Belgium.

Most of the complex arguments put forward by Posen, Wallach, Snyder and others do not bear directly upon the issue of why the Battle of the Ardennes turned out as it did. But it is interesting to note where the Ardennes operation falls in the spectrum of analysis of strategic doctrine. On the one hand, the evidence from the battle chapters shows clearly that the Germans adopted an unusual 'strategic defensive/tactical offensive' doctrine in the Ardennes, although this has not yet been fully recognised by historians. Duke Albrecht's 4 Army's operational mission was to defend the gap between the Metz fortified region and the left flank of the *Schwenkungsflügel;* yet in every tactical engagement his troops advanced into contact and fought aggressive 'fire and movement' actions to gain ground. The Crown Prince's 5 Army was instructed not to advance beyond the defensive potential of the Chiers and Crusnes rivers, but during the advance each of his corps attacked their opponents wherever they encountered them. On the other hand, the French strategy was clearly that of counter–offensive, a direct response to the German manoeuvre into central Belgium, rather than an outright *offensive à outrance*, as some have claimed.[61] What is more, Joffre envisaged an envelopment strategy, not a frontal attack. The operational study has shown that from the first day of the war Joffre was altering the dispositions laid out in Plan XVII in order to put greater focus on his left wing; the timing of the launch of his counter–strike was geared to an appreciation of German movements.

One other issue is often cited as a key flaw in French strategic doctrine: the failure to use reserve units in the front line. Regarding Germany's use of reserve corps, the study of the battles has confirmed what a vital role was played by 18 RAK at Neufchâteau and by 5 RAK and 6 RAK at Longwy. The failure of French intelligence correctly to predict such use, despite evidence to the contrary, was clearly a significant error on the part of the French high command. But Gat correctly argues that the issue of the reserves was not as crucial to the events of 1914 as has been claimed in retrospect. He points out that 'the French high command fed its available reserve–units [sic] into battle very quickly, even before the German practice was fully recognised'.[62] In support of Gat's assertion, this study has noted the attempted use by Ruffey of divisions from 3 Reserve Group to extend his defensive flank on 22 August – an attempt frustrated not by doctrine but by slow deployment. It is evident that French reserve divisions were drawn into the Ardennes campaign on 23 August, the day after the main battle. Furthermore it is often forgotten that each French corps had an integral brigade of reserve troops, and this study has shown that in one encounter at least –

59   Ibid., p.14.
60   J. Snyder, *The Ideology of the Offensive: Military Decision making and the disasters of 1914* (Cornell University Press, London, 1984) pp.9–40.
61   For example: Gat, op. cit., p.436; Tyng, op. cit., p.75.
62   Gat, op. cit., p. 436.

that of 12 CA at Neufchâteau – the two reserve regiments were committed into action on that very first day. On de Langle's left flank, 60 DIR, initially employed to protect the Meuse and Semoy crossings in 4 Army's rear, was instructed on 21 August to cover the left flank of 11 CA during the attack.[63] And orders for 23 August placed both 60 and 52 DIRs in the front line.[64] The evidence shows that the issue of the French reluctance to use reserve formations in the front line is by no means as clear-cut as has hitherto been assumed.

In short, at the level of strategic doctrine, what the two sides had in common was the strategic intent to gain and keep the initiative through offensive action, with the object of bringing about – on their own terms – the big decisive battle that would bring a swift end to the war.[65] In this sense it can be argued that both sides implemented in the broadest sense a strategic doctrine of *offensive à outrance* and, if anything, Germany's was less flexible than that of France.

Operational Doctrine

Turning to the operational level, it is difficult to discern a specific written doctrine for operations as opposed to tactics, on either side, excepting of course the French 1913 publication on the conduct of 'large units', and that as we have seen was published too late to be implemented. In the immediate pre-war period, issues of size and scale and the need for operational manoeuvre melding into combat were being increasingly recognised, and the word 'operation' was being used with increasing frequency in articles and books;[66] but there were not yet any specific operational regulations. There was, and is even today, further doctrinal confusion between definition of higher level 'operational art' and what has been called 'grand tactics'. The debate still has some way to run.

As has been briefly mentioned above, the FSRs on each side are now being called 'operational' regulations but were not necessarily recognised as such at the time. One can appreciate how difficult it is to apply our modern concept of 'operations' to French and German pre–war FSRs, and how the intellectual debate about the difference between 'operational art' and 'grand tactics' has not yet fully played out, by the fact that both French and German FSRs contain articles which clearly overlap into the tactical domain, that is to say the encounter. The French 1895 RSC contains a detailed section on 'combat' and the German 1908 FSR included a new section on 'fire effect'[67], both of which will be examined below as part of the discussion of tactics.

Before the war, only Grandmaison attempted to differentiate between operational rules for large units (armies) and regulations for tactical units (corps and below).[68] Even then, his primary objective was to suggest a way in which Germany might be beaten in the coming war;[69] the differentiation between operational and tactical doctrine was a by–product of his thinking, arising from his belief that it was the conduct of large units by senior commanders that was deficient and needed greater definition and clarity.[70] The result of his influence was the splitting of the 1895 FSR into two new regulations in 1913, one for operational, the other for tactical units. But, notable as

63 AFGG I\1, Annex 755: *Stenay le 21 août 1914, 11.45: Ordre particulier pour les 9e, 11e, 12e, 17e corps d'armée, les 52e et 60e divisions de réserve.*
64 AFGG I/1, Annex 1105: *Stenay 23 août, 08.00: Ordre particulier aux 11e et 9e corps, 52e et 60e D.R. et corps de cavalerie.*
65 Posen, op. cit., pp.22–23; Snyder, op. cit., pp.15–40; Gat, op. cit., pp. 363–369.
66 For example: General Pierron, *La Stratégie et la Tactique Allemande au Début du XXe Siècle* (Henri Charles-Lavauzelle, Paris, c. 1905), chapters 3 & 4; and General H. Langlois, *Conséquences Tactiques des Progrès de l'armement; Étude sur le terrain* (Henri Charles–Lavauzelle, Paris, 1905), passim.
67 German FSR 1908, passim.
68 Grandmaison, *Deux Conférences*, pp.33–69.
69 Ibid., pp.7–13.
70 Ibid., pp.1–7.

that development was in the theory of doctrine, it must not be forgotten that the French army had been trained under the old 1895 regulations. So a comparison of the way in which the French FSR of 1895 and the German FSRs of 1900 and 1908 were put into practice will help determine the influence of doctrine on events at the operational level.

The most striking difference between the two sides' FSRs is one of style; the German conveys a sense of guidance and advice: 'the best reconnaissance is useless if its results become known to the commanding general too late'[71] – whereas the French is somewhat more directive, or prescriptive: 'the purpose of reconnaissance is to give the commander general information'.[72] In this respect they very much reflect the prevailing military ethos of their respective armies.

FSRs laid down rules (articles) covering the management of military units in the field, but they did not generally differentiate between a regiment, division, corps or army. Only occasionally and in a specific context did certain articles start to acknowledge this question of scale, for example the German FSR of 1900 (article 142) makes a point of differentiating between the security of an army as opposed to individual columns.[73] French regulations did not make this difference until 1913. Leaving to one side for the moment the sections on 'combat' and 'fire power', which are arguably tactical issues, the key issues of the FSR concerned intelligence and security during manoeuvre.

The operational study has demonstrated that both sides experienced failings in the gathering and use of intelligence, but that those on the French side led to the greater misfortune. One can point particularly to the lack of urgency with which de Langle's corps commanders reported back to him about what was happening on the battlefields, leaving him powerless to exert any effective operational control. The conduct of General Eydoux at Maissin was a most striking example, allowing de Langle to believe mistakenly for over seven hours that the village was in French hands. On the German side, the failing was one of resource. The long–range cavalry patrols performed by the HKK earlier in the campaign were, in the lead up to the battle, directed west towards Dinant rather than south towards Sedan; as a result Joffre managed to achieve strategic surprise through his timing and axis of attack and only the short–range patrols of the divisional cavalry squadrons prevented tactical as well as operational surprise. On both sides, doctrine regarding intelligence gathering failed to be applied effectively, if for different reasons.

Regarding security, the German failure on the southern flank in the Ardennes, seldom recognised by historians in the past, stemmed from that same lack of resource. In front of von Hausen's 3 Army von Richthofen's cavalry corps with its Jaeger infantry, its horse artillery and its machine gun companies provided, as per doctrine, a strong security screen to good effect in front of Dinant.[74] The absence of a similar force on the southern flank was keenly felt. German march security was somewhat better than the French, overall good with some random weaknesses. On the good side, 25 ID advancing on Maissin and Anloy in two columns, halted when the divisional cavalry patrols reported in whilst their commander took stock. He sent his field artillery routinely to occupy good defensive firing positions on nearby heights without even knowing the full extent of the opposition. Artillery officers accompanied cavalry patrols in order to find fresh firing positions for the artillery to leapfrog into. But despite these precautions, one infantry battalion of that very division marched in column within range of French infantry lining the edge of some woods south of Anloy, and suffered casualties before deploying and going to ground. And at Neufchâteau, French colonial

---

71   German FSR 1900, Article 132, p. 32.
72   French FSR 1895, Article 19, p.46.
73   German FSR 1900, op. cit., Article 142, p. 37.
74   Brose, op. cit., pp.155–156; and BA–MA PH3/641: Standing Orders for Army General Staff Officers, Section B: HKK.

riflemen were able to surprise a supply column of 21 RID with flanking rifle fire, for lack of proper German flanking protection. In contrast, in a proper application of doctrine, at nearby Bertrix the commander of 21 ID sent a classic flank guard of two infantry companies down the railway line that delineated his vulnerable left flank.

The French situation is complex, because of the confusion about doctrines. According to the 1895 FSR, each column was responsible for its own protection, requiring advance, flank and rear guards with corps cavalry out in front to provide longer range security. In practice it was randomly different in every case. Eydoux of 11 CA, who failed the intelligence and communication test, nevertheless applied the old security doctrine well. His cavalry regiment, well out in front of his advance guard, met the enemy patrols early, chased them back, occupied Maissin and reported back – allowing Eydoux to tell de Langle (erroneously as it turned out) that Maissin was in French hands. Eydoux also sent an infantry battalion with a battery of guns and a squadron of cavalry out on his forward left flank at Porcheresse, to guard against any surprise from that direction. But General Boelle, of 4 CA (3 Army), in an example not elaborated in this study, failed to send his corps cavalry north through the forest to reconnoitre or a mixed arms detachment to cover his infantry advance and as a result wrecked Ruffey's operational plan. General Poline (17 CA) operated a strange system, setting a strong fixed flank guard at de Langle's direction but then allowing his infantry columns to advance beyond it into contact without even the flank protection prescribed by the 1895 rules. In short, the French performance regarding operational security varied from clear incompetence to proper execution of the 1895 rules, with variations in between.

Overall there is little evidence of a consistently competent application of the 1895 FSR by the French commanders, whereas the Germans showed much greater consistency in applying their own doctrinal rules of 1908. However, due to the confusion of doctrine evident on the French side, their performance should also be measured against both Grandmaison's teachings and the new rules of October 1913, to see if there is evidence of the application of those doctrines.

The question whether Grandmaison's personal doctrine was applied in August 1914 is easily answered – it was not. Grandmaison's two lectures laid out a clear plan for a new method of defeating Germany in the coming war. It proposed to take advantage of a perceived weakness on the German side; Grandmaison had observed, or thought he had observed at the German manoeuvres he had attended, a tendency for the German commanders to take their time planning and preparing, before they launched their violent and rapid attack.[75]

He proposed to take advantage of that perceived German delay by launching his own pre–emptive strike. Advancing at speed behind a corps–strength advance guard (sûreté de première ligne[76]) that would fix and hold the enemy along his whole front, the French army commander would use intelligence delivered to him on the march to choose the decisive point at which to concentrate his main force and, without stopping or hesitating, deliver the decisive assault.[77] Grandmaison himself admitted at the time that the French army would have to improve considerably before attempting his proposed methods.[78] So it is hardly surprising to note that neither de Langle de Cary nor Ruffey attempted to advance behind a sûreté de première ligne, nor throw their armies precipitously forward.[79]

75   Grandmaison, *Deux Conférences*, pp.20–22.
76   Grandmaison, *Deux Conférences*, pp.16–18.
77   Grandmaison, *Deux Conférences*, passim.
78   Ibid., p.33.
79   And, although outside the scope of this thesis, we can note that neither Castelnau nor Dubail adopted the 'Grandmaison' model; Castelnau's advance in particular was cautious and measured. See: AFGG I/1, pp.176–255; and *Weltkrieg I*, p.263.

Queloz concurs with the conclusion that the new regulation of 28 October 1913 on the operation of large formations is recognisably taken from Grandmaison's teachings, but is not identical. The difference is evident in the preamble written by the committee of the CSC that produced the document for the War Minister's approval, which fails to make a clear choice in favour of the key tenets of Grandmaison's operational theory:

> So far as regards the conception of the plan of battle, the Committee has been confronted by two different theories. The first, which would extend to an army the principles contained in Section XIV [on combat] of the Field Service Regulations (1895), bases the battle on successive actions (preparatory engagements lasting sometimes several days – decisive attack launched when the preparation is considered sufficient). The second theory is based on the synchronization of efforts in the battle (secondary actions holding the enemy on the whole or part of his line – principle action against a wing). After examination, the Committee considered that there was no need to choose between the two systems, each of which has its value, and the application of which is above all a question of circumstances. It has been decided to leave to the commander, who is alone capable of appreciating all the factors which affect his decision, the absolute right of making his choice in complete freedom.[80]

By avoiding a decision between two conflicting operational doctrines, the CSG was in one sense opting out (and increasing confusion) but in another sense leaning towards the German model where individual senior commanders were expected to use their experience and judgement to do the right thing within a loose framework of oral and written teaching. By letting French army commanders in August 1914 choose between two operational doctrines, the French War Minister was to inadvertently highlight the qualitative differences between the one hundred–year–old embedded German system (*Kriegsakademie,* General Staff rides, war games, map exercises, inspections) which gave their generals the skills to exercise sound judgement in the field, and that of France, whose systems and processes, especially in the period of 'republicanisation' between 1900 and 1911, failed to develop the required standard of military proficiency in their future field commanders. The deficiencies in French senior command performance noticed by Grandmaison, Joffre and others during the autumn manoeuvres from at least 1908 onwards were not properly addressed before the war and therefore had to be eradicated as the war progressed. What is beyond doubt is that Grandmaison's theories of <u>operational</u> *offensive à outrance* were not implemented in 1914.

There remains then to see whether any attempts were made to put the new October 1913 regulations into practice in August 1914. With regard to army security, the new rules said:

> The decree of 28 May 1895, concerning the Field Service Regulations, does not touch upon the operations of formations larger than the army corps...The Committee considers that [for the operation of large formations] the cavalry corps is not sufficiently strong to carry out the many tasks which are given it and that the duty of strategical protection, as indicated by the decree of 28 May 1895 leads to a dispersion of force.[81]

Instead, the new regulation advocated 'the employment of detachments of all arms (protective detachments) [which] will permit him to gain the necessary time and space for the development of

---

80   *The Operations of Large Formations, 1913,* op. cit.,p.14.
81   Ibid., pp.7 & 11.

his manoeuvre'.[82] The operational study has shown how Joffre authorised de Langle on 20 August to send mixed–arms detachments forward to protect the advance of his army; this certainly seems to be in line with the new regulation, even if the size of the protective detachment (none was larger than a brigade) was smaller than advocated by Grandmaison. The execution, however, was imperfect on two counts: firstly de Langle did not put the detachments in place until the late evening of 21 and early morning of 22 August, thereby failing to use them to gather useful intelligence for the final stage before contact; secondly due in part to the 'stepped–echelon' formation and in part to poor performance, they failed in their primary mission of protecting the main columns. One concludes that there is no evidence of the application of the 'Grandmaison' model, instead an imperfect application of part–1895, part–1913 doctrine at the operational level.

Turning to the higher operational level, that unregulated grey area called operational art, the battles generally demonstrate on the German side the very conditions described by Wallach as having been taught by Schlieffen. 5 AK at Virton and Ethe (not described in detail in this book) operated in two separate divisional actions, but in each action the divisional commander sought to fix his enemy in front and envelop either one or both flanks.[83] Similarly at Rossignol, the commander of 6 AK achieved a double envelopment of 3 DIC, fixing in place both the colonial advance guard and the neighbouring 4 DI, before moving supports to the flanks. 50 Brigade at Maissin attempted the same despite being seriously outnumbered and eventually forced to retreat.

The essence of this operational system was, according to Gat, intellectual flexibility and an understanding of the chaotic nature of war:

> The fundamental conception of the nature of war and military theory clearly set the framework within which every military question, past or present, was approached and judged. On the one hand, all dogma was rejected, and allowance made for great theoretical flexibility. On the other, a whole cluster of ideas was regarded as embedded in the very nature of the phenomenon of war, which was unaffected by change. 'Lasting nature' and 'changing forms' cohabited. This was not merely the bequest of Clausewitz and Moltke; it expressed the all–pervasive and fundamental tenets of German culture.[84]

In action, this unwritten German system expressed itself in an operational doctrine akin to the 'Grandmaison' model, ironically just as Grandmaison had identified and predicted.[85] Furthermore it is impossible not to be struck by the similarity between what they put into practice in August 1914 and what Goya describes as the Napoleonic system taught by General Bonnal at ESG in the 1890s. The large and powerful German HKK cavalry screens were, in French terminology, sûreté de première ligne. Goya has written of Bonnal's Napoleonic system, which he asserts was the basis of the French 1895 Field Regulations: 'The cavalry, operating several days' march in front of the main body, has the task of scouting and protecting against any surprise by surrounding the infantry columns with a protective zone. It must make contact with the enemy and establish his strength.'[86] The efficacy of this German application of operational doctrine can be shown by the fact that in the one instance where they did not implement it, their Fourth Army fell victim to operational surprise.

82   *The Operations of Large Formations, 1913*, op.cit., p.11.
83   *Weltkrieg I*, pp.317–319.
84   Gat, op. cit.
85   Grandmaison, *Deux Conférences*, p.32.
86   Goya, *La Chair et l'Acier*, p.85.

Both French and German planners had recognised that the technological improvements during the first decade of the twentieth century had undermined the ability of traditional cavalry to provide effective security. The German response to this problem was to strengthen their HKK with mobile *Jaeger* infantry, horse artillery and mobile machine gun detachments, as well as training them to fight dismounted. The French, on the other hand, seem to have developed the concept of strong mixed–arms detachments formed around infantry, arguably stronger but less mobile.

Operational art on the French side seems not to have developed with anything like the same level of skill or confidence. Lacking that intellectual flexibility and understanding of the chaotic nature of war that Gat identifies as German attributes, the 'all–pervasive and fundamental tenets' of French culture seem to have centred around a logical and structured codification of requirement. For example, Article 13 of the October 1913 regulation for the conduct of large units required the commander to arrange a plan of action,[87] to 'consider with an open mind the various alternatives open to his opponent'. It emphasised that 'any disposition prompted by a definite opinion arbitrarily formed concerning the intentions of the enemy would be premature so long as the enemy remains free to move'. It is easier to write such instructions than to absorb them into one's mind set and enact them spontaneously when under pressure. And it is clear that neither de Langle nor Ruffey took these dicta to heart when seeking to implement Joffre's instructions.

Professor Strachan has written that 'Joffre was wrong to conclude that the Germans would not fight in the wooded and broken ground of the Ardennes but would be found on the other side'[88]; true, but his two army commanders must shoulder the responsibility for the operational detail. De Langle's one secret and personal briefing of his corps commanders shows him to have had an unclear and essentially erroneous idea of his opponent's position and intentions, despite intelligence details that might have enlightened him if interpreted correctly. He left his tactical commanders with a false sense of security regarding the enemy's whereabouts that exacerbated their own tactical weaknesses. Ruffey failed to appreciate that his opponent might advance on him, and gave operational orders, especially to 5 CA, which ignored the realities of his opponent's position around Longwy. Articles 32–36 of the October 1913 regulations concerned strategic reconnaissance, in which 'the commanders of armies have at their disposal for this purpose large bodies of cavalry formed into divisions'.[89] Ruffey chose to deploy his one cavalry division on what he perceived his most vulnerable point, his right flank; but his cavalry commander failed him, and he had no *sûreté de première ligne* to his front. De Langle had a provisional cavalry corps of two divisions; he deployed it as a *sûreté de première ligne*, and gave it appropriate orders which were obeyed on 20 and 21 August and which gave him vital intelligence (which he ignored); but on 22 August the cavalry commander failed to provide the required screen in front of the army, and contributed to the flawed execution of Joffre's strategic intent. The reason for this failure points to an endemic weakness in the French military ethos of 1914. In mid-afternoon on 21 August the French cavalry corps commander ordered his troops to pack up for the day, as he would have done during peacetime pre-war manoeuvres, and seek their night-time billets in a village on the left flank of the army. There he stayed for the whole of the next day, the day of battle. He thus deprived de Langle's army of its *sûreté de première ligne* just at the vital moment. The failure to transition from unrealistic peacetime exercise habits to the reality of war points to poor training and low levels of skill and experience.

When it came to the exercise of individual judgement in the execution of operational matters, French commanders were sadly lacking. This study has shown examples of divisional commanders such as Rabier of 4 DI deliberately ignoring operational orders that he thought were unachievable;

---

87   *The Operation of Large Formations, 1913*, op. cit., p.22.
88   Strachan, op. cit., p. 218.
89   *The Operation of Large Formations, 1913*, op. cit., pp.25–26.

and Radiguet of 21 DI at Maissin whose painfully slow advance turned a supposed envelopment of an enemy flank into a frontal attack on a new axis. It has shown how 5 CA's commander (Brochin) asked his infantry to move to assault enemy trenches of unknown strength in a fog without artillery when his orders required him to undertake a twenty kilometre route march. It has demonstrated that at Maissin and at Neufchâteau, Generals Eydoux and Roques failed to use their cavalry regiments in the prescribed manner to threaten their enemy's flank and rear. The full list of French operational failure is longer, leading to the conclusion that, whatever happened at the tactical level, senior French generals were outclassed and outmanoeuvred in the field.

Terrain was difficult, making liaison between columns both necessary and complicated; but it was difficult for both sides, and once again the Germans fared better than the French. The German 49 brigade of 25 ID at Anloy sought and obtained the help of an artillery battery from neighbouring 21 ID at Ochamps,[90] whereas the French 34 DI on the same battlefield failed to protect 21 DI's flank. At Rossignol the German 10 ID's column cooperated with that of 11 ID to complete the encirclement and destruction of 3 DIC, as described above, whereas the French 4 DI was too tired and disorganised to protect the Colonials' flank. At Neufchâteau the German 25 RID successfully marched to the rescue of the beleaguered 21 RID, whereas the French 23 DI only succeeded in firing on its own side.

To sum up the comparison of operational doctrine with actual performance, it is fair to say that one can identify elements of both the 1895 and 1913 regulations being applied in a confused way on the French side; but the overwhelming impression is one of poor execution, of a variety of levels of skill and judgement being applied, from the very poor to the mediocre but nowhere achieving the standard set by their opponents. The evidence on the German side shows clear signs that Schlieffen's teachings, and those of the *Kriegsakademie* and General Staff, had been learned, absorbed and put into practice in a most professional manner.

Tactical Doctrine

In the French FSR of 1895, section XIV is the all–important section on 'Combat'. It is important to remember that the key principles ('general considerations') which it sets out were those under which virtually all the officers and soldiers who fought in August 1914 were trained. They stated, inter alia, that combat can be either offensive or defensive but always its objective is to break by force the enemy's will and impose yours on him, but only the offensive can obtain decisive results; that the principle of engagement is to 'fix' all known enemy forces with the minimum necessary force, to keep part of your force ready for the violent, concentrated effort at the decisive point and to hold a reserve ready to follow up success or limit the effect of failure. Note that, even in 1895, the French called this follow up *la poursuite à outrance*. Finally it was envisaged that a decisive effort against a wing or a flank would require shorter but more energetic preparation, whereas a longer, fuller preparation would be required when two well–prepared adversaries confront each other.[91] One can see that at the level of grand tactics, the rules of 1895 were not too far removed from the 'Grandmaison' model.

The general principles attached to each arm in the tactical section of the 1895 FSR (above) were supplemented by detailed tactical instructions. For the French infantry, their doctrine was encapsulated in the *règlements de manoeuvre d'infanterie* (RMI) of 1904, which remained current until April 1914 and which 'guided the training of French infantry up until the outbreak of war.'[92]

90   Kaiser, *Bertrix*, op. cit., p.6.
91   French FSR 1895, Article 128, pp.196–197.
92   Goya, op. cit., p.92.

It was a doctrine of fire and movement and, acknowledging the effect of smokeless powder, modern rifles and quick–firing artillery, it advocated more open deployment of troops. It was a product of General André's ministry – a time when inspections were abolished and individual (republican) responsibility encouraged – so unsurprisingly it advocated dispersed formations in which the section of fifty men was the basic tactical unit and the section commander's role was all–important.[93] The intention was to 'develop a spirit of initiative at all levels in order to achieve "more flexibility and speed in deployment and greater variety in combat formations"'.[94] Such a sophisticated system required well–trained soldiers and even better trained officers. But unfortunately for the French, training fell far short of the required level; there was a shortage of NCOs, of officers and of trainers throughout the period.[95] And there was a shortage of training facilities, leading to soldiers spending too much time in barracks and doing route marches and drill instead of field exercises.[96] When General Menestrel inspected 11 CA in 1913 his report concluded:

> We must recognise that there are serious failings in the combat training of the infantry stemming in great part from our regulations of 3 December 1904. Under the pretext of developing initiative at all levels and of allowing subordinate commanders the choice of means, we have refrained from issuing rules of even slight precision. Our cadres have been deprived of the directives which they need. They must be given them as soon as possible.[97]

But it was already too late. There was little time for combat training in the spring of 1914, and 11 CA fought at Maissin on 22 August as described in Chapter Four. Indeed it was one of that unit's subordinate commanders, battalion commander Lafouge of II/93 RI, who launched his men across more than a kilometre of open ground without waiting for the artillery in his column to deploy in support.[98] And one can see in several other examples analysed in the battle chapters how much the performance of a unit depended upon the quality of an individual officer; and how, as in the case of 24 DI at Neufchâteau, a senior officer had to take control, only for the attack to grind to a halt when that senior officer was absent. After Colonel Descoings was wounded and once the initial élan had worn off, battalions appear to have waited for the artillery to literally blast the enemy out of small copses before they would advance. So too with 23 DI; it has been shown how panic set in amongst several infantry units and they had to be rallied with flags and bugles by a brigade commander before they would advance against minimal resistance.

On the other hand, Colonel Chapès of 19 RI at Maissin executed a text–book infantry attack, using fire and movement in small rushes over a few hundred metres of open ground supported on the flanks by machine guns for extra fire power, after using the terrain to approach in relative safety. And at Neufchâteau, the experienced infantry of 5 Colonial Brigade conducted an exemplary engagement using fire and movement in both offense and defence against increasingly overwhelming numbers.

Goya's research supports the case outlined above, concluding that the 1904 RMI contained many faults and weaknesses: it broke with the more formal structures of the 1895 RSC, thereby sowing confusion; it placed heavy responsibility on junior officers who would need the very best

---

93   Ibid., pp.92–93 & p. 97.
94   Ibid., p.93: *de développer l'esprit d'initiative à tous les degrés afin d'obtenir <plus de souplesse et de rapidité dans les évolutions, une élasticité et une variété plus grandes dans les formations de combat>*.
95   AAT 7N108: miscellaneous staff papers: a secret note, internal to the Ministry of War, regarding the effects of the new (1911) German military law and the steps France should take to counter it; and AAT 1N13: Inspections, 1888–1906 and 1911–1913; see also Porch op.cit., pp.193, 196–197.
96   Porch op. cit., pp.191–212.
97   AAT 1N13: Inspections 1888–1906 and 1911–1913.
98   Bujac op. cit., pp.77–81.

instruction and practice themselves to implement it; and its abstract style meant that its content and meaning was beyond most officers' comprehension.[99] To compound these weaknesses, there were many technological changes during the ten years leading up to 1914, which arguably required the RMI to be amended. The Germans, for example, issued a revision to their infantry instructions in July 1905 in order to accommodate machine guns into tactical doctrine.[100] Further issues in 1906 and 1908 incorporated the lessons of the Russo–Japanese war. Perhaps the French tactical confusion on the battlefields of August 1914 owed more to their failure to update the 1904 RMI than has hitherto been recognised. In the absence of a new infantry regulation between 1904 and 1914, Grandmaison's less famous work, his *Dressage de l'infanterie en vue du combat offensive*,[101] was one of many unofficial publications which must have contributed to French officers' confusion, especially when the unofficial doctrines allowed for recent innovations and developments where the official doctrine did not.

The role of French field artillery bears detailed examination, especially because of its pre–war reputation and that of its 75mm field gun. In so many cases, this study has identified instances where the artillery was slow to deploy, got lost on the march, failed to find proper firing positions; and there were many cases where the infantry either consequently or independently attacked without artillery support, let alone preparation. These are issues of execution, not doctrine. Articles 129 and 135 of the 1895 RSC laid down clear rules for artillery preparation of the attack. Grandmaison's two lectures, even when applied erroneously to the tactical level, refer to the use of artillery batteries alongside infantry in the advance guard;[102] his tactical doctrine explicitly states that against superior artillery the infantry would not be able to get to within rifle range of the enemy, whereas when supported by a more powerful artillery it would get much closer before opening fire;[103] the 1913 FSR states clearly (Article 125) that 'the primary duty of the artillery is to support the advance of the infantry' and that (Article 99) 'as a general principle the artillery is close to the head of the main body of each column, ready to intervene quickly in the action.'[104] Some historians have argued that relegating artillery from a preparatory to a support role was a grave error within the doctrine of the offensive. But Grandmaison made it clear that in practice the 'preparation' phase had become an exclusive artillery versus artillery competition with no relevance to the infantry's tactical requirements; and that the term 'support' in his view included achieving fire superiority before launching the decisive attack, a subtle but important distinction.[105] One might add in parenthesis that by November 1914, with the end of the war of movement and the onset of siege-warfare in the trenches, the preparation phase by artillery came into its own again. But it is wrong for historians to retrospectively apply trench-warfare requirements to the war of movement.

In describing the cooperation between infantry and artillery, the new regulations specified that:

> The artillery…must in fact profit by the first encounters of the infantry to attempt to gain from the very beginning superiority over the hostile batteries in action…in the preparatory action the infantry must be employed with economy, so that the commander can keep as much of it as possible for the attack.[106]

99   Goya, op. cit., pp.92–94.
100   Brose, op. cit., p.152.
101   Grandmaison, *Dressage*, op. cit.
102   Grandmaison, *Deux Conférences*, p.15.
103   Grandmaison, *Dressage*, p.6.
104   *The Operation of Large Formations, 1913*, op. cit., Article 99.
105   Grandmaison, *Dressage*, pp.24–25.
106   *The Operation of Large Formations, 1913*, op. cit., Article 117.

The performance of the French artillery in the Ardennes encounters bears no resemblance to any of the various doctrines, official or unofficial, current at the time. Given time and superior numbers, as at Virton or Neufchâteau, the French artillery did eventually manage to achieve fire superiority. But it was the German speed and flexibility, born of better combined-arms training, together with a desire to fire first and in quantity rather than waiting for designated targets, which gave the German artillery arm the edge.

As for the cavalry arm, a similar situation can be discerned. The 1895 RSC (Article 133) required the cavalry to scout and provide information to the commander; in combat it was to act against the enemy's flank or rear. Two clear opportunities have been identified by this study – at Maissin and at Neufchâteau – for corps cavalry regiments to work around the enemy flank and operate effectively against his rear; neither was taken and the cavalry remained passive. Scouting and provision of information by de Langle's cavalry was patchy, and definitely deficient during the crucial twelve hours before contact; Ruffey's cavalry division was ineffective.

Overall, the evidence from this study supports the assertion that French tactical doctrine was confused during August 1914. It has been shown that individual engagements evidence a range of tactical behaviours, some recognisable as akin to one or other of the doctrines debated between 1904 and 1914, others simply demonstrating a complete absence of doctrine. Most demonstrate a low level of military competence, pointing towards deficiencies in practice and training.

German tactical doctrine seems to have been more solidly grounded in a set of clear and (compared to the French) unified regulations. The tactical section on fire power included in the 1908 FSR clearly aimed to consolidate the twin doctrinal principles of (i) establishing fire superiority before assault and (ii) using open order tactics in the attack.[107] It laid out some key precepts:

> The fire effect of infantry…will be materially impaired by the effect of the enemy's fire. Enfilade fire is especially effective.[108] Lines of skirmishers on the move in the open will suffer severely from the fire of unshaken infantry at medium and even long ranges. Their losses will increase with the density of the skirmishing lines. Long and uninterrupted advances of dense skirmishing lines are therefore impossible under effective hostile fire at short and medium ranges. A further advance can consequently only be effected by working forward gradually, supported by fire from alternate flanks.[109] The result of a bayonet charge depends upon the losses already inflicted on the enemy by infantry and artillery fire, and upon the vigour of the charge.[110]

As with the French, the tactical element of the German FSR was supplemented by rules for individual arms. The key infantry document was the *Exerzier–Reglement für die Infanterie* (1906), which had been published to include the lessons learned from the Russo–Japanese war. There was a consistency and coherence in what was published and when. But it was not completely straightforward. The debate leading to these revised regulations, conducted over a long period from 1888 onwards, followed a narrow path of compromise between the theories of different military thinkers such as Scherff, Schlichting and Caemmerer, as well as staunch traditionalists such as General von Plessen, seeking to find a balance between open order tactics and delegated command on the one hand and on the other hand the control and cohesion required to make liaison between infantry and artillery

107   German FSR 1908, passim.
108   Ibid., Article 177.
109   Ibid., Article 576.
110   Ibid., Article 580.

work effectively.[111] Noting Gat's argument, quoted above regarding the great theoretical flexibility with which the Germans addressed doctrinal issues, one can better understand what Brose has written about the 1906 Infantry regulations:

> Genuinely impressed by the heroic efforts of Japan, the German infantry rededicated itself to the offensive. Indeed, the aggressive spirit of certain passages almost seemed to contradict the commitment in other parts to dispersed formations; prudent use of terrain, foxholes, and field fortifications; waiting for artillery support; and patiently developing the attack.[112]

Somewhat surprisingly, given the known German tactical imperative for achieving fire superiority, 'charging with the bayonet was still considered the finishing act of the attack.'[113] Only a well-trained cadre leading well-trained troops could implement such a complex tactical double-act. And it is noticeable that during the time that the theoretical debate was working itself out in public, individual divisional and corps commanders could – and did – decide to change tactics from close-order to open-order formations and back again, confidently expecting their disciplined regiments to respond in an effective and professional manner:

> A tactical experiment was held outside Berlin at the Döberitz parade ground in February 1902 ...The purpose was to test the new attacking techniques used in the Boer War and 'to pay more attention than usual to the ravaging effect of modern weapons.' After a second drill and considerable publicity that winter and spring, the division exercised before William II at Templehof in May 1902.[114]

This example was of the elite Prussian 1 Guard Division; and in the spring exercises of May 1903 Guard Corps commander Lieutenant-General von Kessel 'reverted to assaults with massed battalion and company columns.'[115] One might expect the Prussian Guard to be perfectly disciplined, but the example was not confined to the elite. In 1904 Karl von Bülow, commander of 3 AK, trained his units:

> to stay in dispersed skirmish lines as long as possible. Every method of advance was fair in wartime: slithering, crawling, or short sprints to the next available cover...repeated drill and "the fullest possible use of leaders in the ranks" would teach every man what he had to do. The key was close hand–and–eye contact among squad, platoon and company officers and NCOs during the advance, practiced to the point of 'meticulous order'.[116]

The debate between traditionalists who favoured close–packed frontal infantry assaults and modernists who advocated open–order skirmish and 'fire and movement' attacks was settled in favour of the latter by the 1906 regulations.[117] But that did not stop individual corps commanders from ignoring official doctrine and continuing to use their own preferred methods despite General Staff pressure and inspection reports. There were in 1904 and 1907 manoeuvre lapses back into

---

111   A.J. Echevarria, II, *After Clausewitz* (University of Kansas, Lawrence KS, 2000), p.102 & pp.124–125.
112   Brose, op. cit., p.154.
113   Echevarria, op. cit., p.124.
114   Brose, op.cit., p.88.
115   Ibid., p.90.
116   Ibid.
117   Ibid., pp.85–111 and pp.147–153.

linear formations.[118] And there were in August 1914 several examples of close order assault which somewhat tarnished the reputation of the 'institutionalised excellence' of the German army at war: for example 10 AK at Liège,[119] 9 AK at Mons;[120] and in the Ardennes, Prince Oskar's Prussian Grenadiers at Virton.[121] However, the overall standard of adherence to doctrine was very high, as can be seen in the battles of 22 August.

But there was evidence too of practical flexibility and improvisation, when the situation warranted it, especially in combined arms cooperation. At Anloy, 116 IR's junior infantry officers hauled a howitzer into the front line to boost their fire power; their regimental commander chose to deploy his whole machine–gun company, six guns *en masse*, at the critical point on his left flank; the infantry, far from concealing themselves in trenches, went forward in short rushes, gaining ground by fire and movement.[122] They held off the best part of a French division all afternoon and evening, using their artillery support to best advantage. In their regimental historian's opinion, their French opponent 'showed no sign of that furious impulse to press forward which had become second nature to our infantrymen.'[123] Elsewhere, for further example, the company commanders of III/125 IR west of Longwy led their men through thick fog using compasses to find the direction of their designated objective, whereas their opponents, 113 and 191 RIs from the Paris garrison failed to stand under fire and ran.[124] The close cooperation between infantry and artillery was as much doctrine as improvisation. In April 1907 the Field Artillery Regulations had been revised to include instructions that would ensure that 'close co–operation with foot soldiers – eschewed in 1866, achieved in 1870, and glorified thereafter – could not be lost in the next war'.[125] The operational study of the Ardennes encounter battles in earlier chapters has shown how well rehearsed that combined arms doctrine had been, and how well it had been put into practice.

German artillery doctrine differed from the French in one key respect: the new section on 'fire effect' in the German 1908 FSR included specific principles for the incorporation of heavy artillery into field doctrine. It said: 'The heavy field howitzer is especially adapted for engaging standing targets such as batteries, trenches, villages. Its common shell possesses very considerable explosive and splinter effect, and is capable of penetrating the stoutest overhead cover likely to be met in the field. Against moving targets, the effect of heavy howitzers is limited.'[126] The French had no such doctrine and no clear consensus as to how to use the heavy howitzers that they did possess. General Brochin's failure at Longwy to utilise the heavy artillery given to him by Ruffey is the most glaring example of this lack of doctrine.

With regard to regulations on field craft, Zuber has identified the importance of the 1911 *Feld-Pionierdienst aller Waffen*, which gave instruction on 'integrated engineer training, principally digging in'.[127] This, together with the *Feld–Befestigungs Vorschrift* of 1893,[128] makes it clear that battlefield entrenchment by infantry was an essential part of German tactical doctrine during the two decades preceding the war; there seems to be no comparable French instruction. The difference

118   Herrmann, *The Arming of Europe and the Making of the First World War* p.88.
119   Herwig, op. cit., p.111.
120   Ibid., p.154.
121   Burne, *Virton*, p.39.
122   Infanterie–Regiment nr.116, op.cit., pp.1–30.
123   Ibid., pp. 24–25
124   General Stühmke, *Das Infanterie-Regiment 'Kaiser Friedrich König von Preussen' (7 Württ.) Nr 125 im Weltkrieg 1914-1918* (Ehr. Belser AG, Stuttgart, 1923), p.10; and for the French, see: AAT 26N285/1: JMO of 9 DI.
125   Brose, op.cit., p.147.
126   German FSR 1908, p.182.
127   Ibid., pp.58–61; Zuber, op. cit., pp.58-61.
128   *Feld-Befestigungs Vorschrift, 1893,* (translated and published for the Corps of Royal Engineers by The Royal Engineers Institute, Chatham, 1895).

can be seen on the battlefield, and has been noted in the battle chapters as having contributed to German success at Rossignol, at Maissin, at Longwy, to name but three encounters.

This brief overview of comparative doctrines has shown that in broad terms there was remarkably little difference between the two sides, merely differences in detail, some of which admittedly made a difference in battle. But there is considerable evidence of differences in the execution of doctrine. Both sides showed a variety of levels of individual performance across units, but the overall German standard of execution was higher.

At the strategic level, both sides used offensive doctrines, but with the French demonstrating greater strategic flexibility by their decision to switch forces from right to left to mount a strong counter–attack through the Ardennes.

At the operational level, Germany used a doctrine remarkably similar to that proposed by Bonnal, incorporated into the 1895 FSR, and developed theoretically by Grandmaison. One key difference lay in the 'grey area' of operational art, where Schlieffen's teachings in particular seem to have influenced a generation of senior German commanders to perfect the implementation of envelopment manoeuvres and avoid wherever possible frontal attacks. France's new operational doctrine of the offensive was issued too late, in October and December 1913, causing more confusion than clarity; most commanders had learned their art under the auspices of the 1895 FSR; but even that was put into practice with all the weaknesses identified by Grandmaison in his two 1911 lectures – multiple columns, multiple advance guards, slow and reactive approach and poor combined–arms liaison. The generally poor level of skill in command shown by French generals has been made evident in the battle chapters, and supports the rationale for Joffre's wholesale removal of generals during August and September. In dramatic contrast, the German generals involved in the Ardennes battles demonstrated much higher levels of competence.

Tactically, the official French doctrine enshrined in the 1904 RMI seems to have been too sophisticated for the level of competence of the French cadre and for the level of training of the French soldiers. In several instances French tactical units reverted to closer–order deployment, where their few competent officers could exert control; alternatively when their officers were killed, they went to ground. At least two examples have been cited in which poor training of both officers and men led to French units failing to stand under enemy fire. In contrast, German tactical behaviour in the main mirrored their tactical doctrine, demonstrating a high level of competence in open–order deployment and devolved authority. Junior German officers showed initiative, especially in adapting the principles of combined-arms liaison to specific battlefield conditions. German infantrymen, and one should cite particularly the reservists of 21 ID at Neufchâteau, showed the very qualities of élan as well as resilience under fire, which their opponents were supposed to possess. Where French soldiers showed élan, it was all–too–often during their naive baptism of fire and was replaced by fear and inertia once the reality of war had struck home.

Overall, one must conclude that French and German doctrine was remarkably similar in its general characteristics and intent. The differences in detail identified in this analysis do not adequately explain why the Germans managed to push back the French offensive in the Ardennes. Some, such as heavy artillery doctrine (or lack of it), and the German regulations on field fortification, did make a difference; but in general the analysis has revealed differences in the level of execution of doctrine, rather than in doctrinal principles themselves. So the real question is how far each side converted theory into practice through training.

8

Training

The most significant issue which differentiated between the quality of the French and German soldiers engaged on 22 August in the Ardennes was arguably the one which has been least discussed: the impact of the French Three Year Law passed in 1913. As a consequence of that law, nearly two–thirds of the men in the ranks of France's regular divisions had had no more than a few months' basic training when war broke out.

The standard term of conscription for young Frenchmen had been reduced to two years by a law passed in 1905, having been proposed in 1901–3 under War Minister General André's 'republicanisation' programme.[1] The political intent behind the change was to support the drive towards a citizen army, a 'nation–in–arms' made up of multitudes of trained reservists, as opposed to a long–service professional standing army. As a political statement this policy is unexceptionable, but militarily it made the army more dependent upon the quality of refresher training given to those reservists; and it made the standing army smaller.

Debate and action on the issue of the length of conscription was not new: the Germans had reduced their national service period to two years in 1833 in order to be able to train an extra class and thus increase the size of their mobilized army. They reverted to three years in 1860 and, under Colmar von der Goltz's intellectual influence over the *Volkskrieg* school of thought in the 1870s, contemplated returning to two years again, although from the 1890s onwards they maintained three classes in the standing army.[2] A key difference between France and Germany is thus highlighted: when Germany changed to two years it was for military reasons, when France did so it was primarily from political motivation.

After the first Moroccan crisis in 1905–6, Germany started to expand its armed forces, accelerating progress with Army Bills in 1912 and 1913. With its larger population it was able to increase the number of men in the standing army simply by increasing the percentage conscripted out of each year's eligible young men. France was slower to start its military revival, but in 1913 as part of the response to the Agadir crisis and the German Army Bills, both the military (Joffre) and the politicians (variously Poincaré, Briand, Clemenceau, Barthou) agreed that it was necessary to combat the growth of the German army by the reintroduction of three years' military service. The military intention was to increase the size of the standing army in order to match Germany and to ensure the continued viability of France's new offensive strategy. The rationale presented to the public was the need to defend against an *attaque brusquée* by the larger German standing army.[3]

It was the way in which the 1913 law was implemented, because of political expediency, which led to the damaging reduction in the quality of the standing army in August 1914.[4] The original

---

1   Ralston, *Army of the Republic*, pp.260–280 & pp.304–310.
2   Dupuy, *Genius for War*, pp.51 & 63; Bucholz, *Moltke*, p.67.
3   Krumeich, *Armaments and Politics*, pp.44–52.
4   Ibid., p.113.

proposition, and Joffre's obviously preferred option, was to keep the oldest and best–trained class of conscripts on for an extra year. This meant that the Class of 1910, due to go home at the end of September 1913, would remain until September 1914.[5] But political opposition from the Left and unrest among the troops themselves (revolts by several units across the country were called mutinies – *mutineries* – at the time) led to a political compromise in order to get the law through parliament. In the end, it was decided to call up the twenty–year olds of the Class of 1913 a year early, that is to say October 1913 rather than October 1914, immediately after the induction of the Class of 1912.[6] It was a politically effective move and persuaded a majority to vote for the law, but the military consequences were in the short term quite the reverse of what was originally intended.

By August 1914 two of the three classes of conscripts in the regular divisions, those which had enlisted in autumn 1913, had barely completed their basic training, and their experience of combat exercises would have been limited to company, battalion and regimental exercises in the Spring of 1914 with (for the lucky few) the possibility of a short spell at a minor training camp. For example an old soldier of 81 RI recalled after the war that, as a member of the Class of 1913, he took part in an exercise on 1 July 1914 at the small Larzac camp [in the 16th Military District].[7] And Leonard Smith's study of 5 DI confirms this interpretation:

> The regulations anticipated that soldiers would spend their first year becoming 'soldiers of the rank learning only the 'mechanics of movement' under the constant supervision of their immediate commanders'. Only in their second year would they become acquainted with the 'special functions that might fall to a soldier on the field of battle'...3 CA's commander in August 1914, General Henry Sauret, complained in October 1914 that he had been given command of an army corps that 'had not during this year undergone either instruction in shooting or in a sojourn in the instruction camp. Their whole preparation in the application of the new infantry regulations thus had to be inevitably incomplete'.[8]

Note that Sauret refers to a failed attempt at applying the 'new' infantry regulations - presumably those issued in April 1914; this example supports the argument of doctrinal confusion put forward in Chapter 7. Furthermore, because of the increased numbers in the standing army, fewer reservists were needed to bring it up to war strength; and ironically the reservists of the recently released Class of 1910 were better trained than any other class. These men would, presumably, either have joined a reserve division – putting a new slant on the French high command's traditional disdain of those units and on their actual combat effectiveness when after 22 August they entered the front line; or the Class of 1910 would have been used as replacements for casualties in the regular divisions. Either way, it suggests that the quality of the French army would have actually improved after the casualties of August 1914 had been replaced.

Many of the incidents in the Battle of the Ardennes can be put into a fresh perspective as a result

---

5   The French system for identifying conscript classes was based on the year in which the young men reached their twentieth birthday. For example those turning twenty in 1910 became the Class of 1910 and were eligible for conscription to commence in the autumn of their twenty–first year (1911). Under the two years' service law they were due for discharge in the autumn of 1913. See Krumreich, op. cit., p.113 and Jules Maurin, *Armée-Guerre-Société, Soldats Languedociens (1889-1919)* (Publications de la Sorbonne, Paris,1982), p.282.

6   Krumeich, op. cit., pp.110–117 & p.126.

7   J. Maurin, *Armée-Guerre-Société, Soldats Languedociens (1889-1919)* (Publications de la Sorbonne, Paris, 1982), p.570.

8   Leonard V. Smith, *Between Mutiny and Obedience: The Case of the French Fifth Infantry Division* (Princeton University Press, Princeton MJ, 1994), pp.14–15 & p.31, citing Personal Dossier, Henry–Sébastien Sauret, Gx/3, G.D., 550.

of this injurious effect of the Three Year Law. One would expect twenty–year old raw recruits to exhibit certain behavioural patterns: to be exceptionally reliant upon their officers and NCOs for leadership; to tend towards close order ('bunching') for moral support; to show young and naive courage (élan) in their first encounter; but to become demoralised very quickly under fire when their officers were killed and the reality of gruesome death and mutilation impinged upon their young consciousness. One can now better understand the performance of the French 113 RI, (9 DI) at Longwy, which broke and ran after less than an hour under fire but with only eleven men killed and one hundred and thirty–six wounded.[9] Those twenty– and twenty–one year old young men fresh from their Paris barracks were alone and isolated by a fog which reduced visibility to less than twenty metres; they could not see their enemy and live fire was coming at them for the first time. Similarly the men of 130 RI (8 DI) at Virton, who had suffered comparatively heavily in their first action – a skirmish at Izel on 21 August – and who advanced into the fog the next day to encounter the élite Prussian 7 Grenadiers commanded by Prince Oscar the Kaiser's younger son, failed to stand in a close-quarters fire-fight.[10]

On the other hand, when there were defensive positions, or good officers, French performance can be observed to have been better. The men of 103 and 104 RI (7 DI) fighting at Ethe, were able to take cover among the houses of the village and behind the railway embankment, and fought steadfastly until nightfall.[11] And 19 RI (22 DI) at Maissin, having swiftly and successfully crossed a two–hundred–metre open zone into the village, again fought courageously house–to–house without faltering. Their leader, Colonel Chapès, was described as 'a superb soldier' by his commanding officer's biographer.[12] His charismatic leadership was evident and contributed heavily to the good performance of his regiment: 'There was a moment's hesitation. But Colonel Chapès threw himself forward chanting the *Marseillaise* and to the sound of that triumphal hymn the eastern part of the barrier was broken'.[13]

The lack of consistency in French infantry performance in the encounter battles of the Ardennes can be seen to have been heavily influenced by the lack of training given to the young conscripts of the classes of 1912 and 1913 because of the Three Year Law and by the random application of Clauswitzian 'friction' through variables such as officer casualties, weather and terrain.

Second only in importance was the issue of training camps. French long–term funding constraints and bureaucratic obstacles had significantly delayed their 1897 building programme. Had that programme been delivered, France would have had, by 1909 at a cost of 40 million francs, three new very large camps (6–7000 hectares each) and a 2000 hectare camp for each corps.[14] The programme, proposed by CSG, was approved by the War Minister, so only the Finance Ministry and Parliament stood in the way of delivery. But between 1897 and 1909, France had twelve changes of War Minister, five of them in 1898.[15] That year the Dreyfus Affair was in full swing; priorities were changing; each new Government would set its own budget (if it had time); the Training Camp programme got lost somewhere in the political morass. A second programme was announced in 1908, but that too foundered through bureaucratic lethargy.

9   AFGG I/1 (1936), p.374; and AAT 22N213/8/1: *État des pertes, août 1914.*
10   AFFG I/1 (1936), p.370; and Grasset, *Virton*, pp.51–62; and Bircher, *Ethe-Virton*, pp.47–51.
11   AFGG I/1 (1936), pp.372–3; and Grasset, *Ethe*, pp.113–118; and General de Trentinian, *Ethe: La 7e Division du 4e Corps dans la Bataille des Frontièrs (10 août au 22 septembre 1914)* (Imprimérie L. Fournier, Paris, 1937), passim.
12   AFGG I/1 (1936), p.410; Bujac, *Eydoux*, p.70.
13   Bujac, op. cit., p.72.
14   AAT 1N8: *Process Verbaux du CSG Dec 1897.*
15   www.wikipedia.org/Minister_of_Defence (France), accessed 26 March 2008.

The comparative lack of long–term facilities for combat exercises had a huge adverse consequence for the French in August 1914. This was particularly true for junior officers and NCOs, with the Germans being able to practice doctrine and improve their command skills much more frequently, which in turn would improve the quality of training given during each three-year conscript cycle. Regular high–quality training over a sustained period – the nature of mass armies incorporating large numbers of reservists requires solid basic training with effective refresher courses over subsequent years – was the bedrock of a successful early twentieth century European army.

By 1911, when Joffre renewed the French programme of building training camps, the Germans possessed twenty–eight large camps, twenty–six of at least 5625 hectares each. There was one camp per corps region and three artillery camps, one being an extra–large range at Grafenwöhr.[16] At this same moment in time France had only two large (corps) camps and two smaller (divisional) camps, one of which was still being completed.[17] These four camps – Châlons, Coëtquidan, Courtine and Mailly – ranged from 2000 to 3000 hectares, but Châlons was badly organised and in need of renovation and Mailly was considered virtually unusable. There were in addition three small, brigade–sized camps, but their scope for combat exercises was severely limited.[18]

Châlons had been in existence since before 1870, and post–Sedan reforms had only called for the building of small camps capable of taking regimental exercises and firing–ranges of five to six kilometres length for the artillery.[19] The Commissions in 1897 and 1907 which recommended the building of more large camps for mixed–arms manoeuvre were never followed through. Thus the initial decision to build only small camps shows a lack of vision; the later decisions show a lack of political will. The Germans had vision, money and political will, and they gained a twenty–year advantage over their enemy.

As a result of the very significant delays in the French building programme, units were subjected to strict allocation schedules for time to practice brigade and divisional combat and mixed–arms exercises. Joffre later wrote that barely a third of regular troops spent fifteen days each year at a camp, the rest had no large unit or mixed–arms exercises at all.[20] By implication many two–year conscripts might have missed out altogether if their unit was not allocated a slot during their two summers in barracks, something which would contribute to the explanation of French inconsistent performance.

Furthermore, Joffre himself highlighted how there was an uneven treatment between French formations. Those furthest away from the few available camps might receive no large–unit training at all, the implication being that the extra cost and logistical difficulty of transporting those large units from longer distances was prohibitive.[21] With the bulk of the camps in the north, it has been suggested that units from the southern military regions (which included Roques's 12 CA and Poline's 17 CA) would have been less well prepared than, for example, Gérard's 2 CA. Sarrail's 6 CA, as part of the north–eastern permanent frontier defence force was an exception, having a generally higher state of preparation. But other than the 1913 schedule, records have not been found to corroborate Joffre's assertion.

The programme for 1913 proposed a series of events at their seven camps during which 'most corps' would be able to practice some sort of larger–scale manoeuvre and combined–arms operation, depending on the size of the camp allocated.[22] It should be noted that the culminating

16   Joffre, *Mémoires*, pp.79–80; Porch, *Marne*, p.200; Zuber, *Ardennes 1914*, p.68.
17   Joffre, op. cit., pp 79–80.
18   Porch, *Marne*, p.200.
19   Goya, *La Chair et l'Acier*, pp.126–127.
20   Joffre, *Mémoires*, p.80.
21   Ibid.
22   AAT 7N1929, *Instruction générale de l'armée Nr 78*, published on 7 December 1912 by *L'État major de l'armée*.

annual autumn Grand Manoeuvre was held in open country. At the camps a strict central allocation system was in place. For example, the units of 3 and 6 CAs were to share the facilities at Châlons during the year, while the smaller (brigade) camps at Souges and Le Valdahon accommodated the units of one corps each – 18 and 7 CAs respectively. Special credits had been voted for these combined–arms exercises, the details of which are missing from the archives. So one is unable to assess how long or how effective each event was, although, as will be seen below, there was a severe constraint on how much blank ammunition could be used at such events. Thirteen metropolitan army corps plus the Colonials were accommodated in this part of the 1913 programme; notable by their exclusion were Roques's 12 CA and Poline's 17 CA which were to feature respectively in the lost opportunity at Neufchâteau and the disaster at Bertrix.[23] However, those two corps both took part in the autumn 1913 Grand Manoeuvre, where they performed badly, attracting severe criticism from Joffre himself.[24] One can only speculate how much an opportunity to practice in the summer of 1913 might have improved those two corps' performance in the autumn of 1913 or indeed in August 1914.

Under Joffre's regime there were serious attempts to improve the amount of field training given. The 1913 Schedule proposed a second set of events: *manoeuvres progressives*, at which three chosen corps – 3, 8 and 20 – were each allocated funds for a fifteen–day event, either brigade or divisional, at the end of which the two divisions of the corps were given three days to manoeuvre against each other. But none of the major units of either Ruffey's Third or de Langle's Fourth Army were included in this part of the programme.

The third leg of the programme was a series of brigade manoeuvres – five days of activity spread over a ten day period. Eleven of the metropolitan corps were allocated funds for this; notably again 12 and 17 CAs were omitted, although 11 and 2 CAs of Fourth Army took part, as did 4 and 5 CAs of Third Army. A brief analysis of the split of corps between those going to camps in 1913 and those omitted from the programme tends to support the thesis that the 'cost and distance' issue was at least one key factor in the choice: 12, 17, 14 and 15 CAs (none of which attended a camp at all that year) were all from the southern military regions.

The cavalry were not overlooked in the 1913 programme: General Sordet (then commanding 10 CA but earmarked to have the Cavalry Corps as his wartime command) was allocated funds for an event at Camp Sissonne in early September involving 3, 4 and 5 DCs; and a few other cavalry divisional and brigade events were scheduled. There were also some special manoeuvres in the Alps, the Vosges and in Tunisia.[25] But Joffre's efforts, while they must have improved upon a previously dire situation, were too little, too late and could not compare with the continuous long–term commitment of the Germans.

The French 1913 Schedule has been described in great detail because it illustrates the way French units were rationed in their combat training, even at a time when Joffre's regime was attempting to breathe new life into the French army. There is no corresponding schedule on the German side because their activity – being decentralised and 'business–as–usual' – needed no rationing or allocation. A German regional corps commander had exclusive access to his own facility all year, giving each of his two divisions a theoretical maximum of thirteen weeks (up to sixty–five days) on large–scale and mixed–arms exercises assuming a twenty–six week window for outdoor exercises between April and the end

---

23   Interestingly, both 14 and 15 CAs, which were routed at Morhange on 20 August 1914, were also omitted from the 1913 combined arms exercises.

24   Joffre, *Mémoires*, p.38.

25   The full 1913 programme can be found in AAT 7N1929: *Instruction générale de l'armée nr.78 (Paris, 7 décembre 1912).*

of September each year. Even before one considers the quality of instruction and the professionalism of execution, it is clear that the Germans had at least a four–fold advantage in available time to practice in the field. And this advantage had applied for most of the decade before the war, so that the German reservists of 1914 in both the active and reserve divisions had enjoyed an equal superiority of available training facilities during their initial conscript period as well as during refresher–training. The question remains as to what detail there is to substantiate the actual as opposed to the theoretical use of these relatively abundant German facilities.

The destruction of the German archives has left little relevant pre–1914 source material, but there is some evidence to support Zuber's conclusion that the German army 'spared no pains to ensure that the troops were trained to perform their simple combat tasks in the exceptionally difficult environment of the modern high-intensity battlefield'.[26] Reflecting the difficulty of reconstituting a dismembered archive, a file on 5 AK's 1896 manoeuvres contains only irrelevant material about Fusilier Regiment 37's mobilisation *Bestimmung* between 1869 and 1870.[27] But a few pertinent files exist. A typed mimeo book records nineteen tactical exercises performed in 1891 by 33 and 34 ID for General Graf von Häseler. A report on 16 AK's August 1902 cavalry–infantry combined–arms exercise criticises a 'Blue' cavalry brigade for attempting to turn the refused right flank of a 'Red' infantry brigade.[28] Records of cavalry exercises in 13 AK's region during August–September 1904 remain: three brigades and six divisions attended, each having a full day's exercise over a twelve–day period.[29] An interesting exercise took place in August 1912 between 13 AK and 18 AK: the purpose was to practice reconnaissance skills, with two opposing cavalry divisions advancing into contact in front of the following infantry and artillery columns. The scope included testing the efficacy of both aeroplanes and field telephony.[30] A seventy–five page report on 16 AK's September 1910 corps manoeuvre details what happened, what orders were given, and so on, and contains their own commanding general's analysis and criticisms.[31] The report is an attractive printed and bound A5 book which gives the impression of being intended for military libraries, for wider dissemination outside the corps and for use in on–going training. It would have formed useful reading for officers in the winter months, alongside their map exercises and war games.

This surviving German material gives the impression of being a small part of a large corpus of organised recording, reporting, analysis and feedback, designed to cumulatively inform the future as well as improve the present and illuminate the past. It takes its place in the heart of the German Army's quality–management system, and it accounts for much of what can be observed on the battlefields of 22 August. The German unit which drove the French 113 RI from the field at Longwy was III/125 IR whose officers and NCOs led their men through the fog using compasses to find the direction of their designated objective.[32] A young Lieutenant Erwin Rommel led his company through the early morning fog and on through a day of aggressive fighting at Bleid (part of the encounter battle at Ethe), and his account bears witness to the quality of the German tactical training regime.[33] Walther Bloem, novelist and reserve officer, who fought at Mons, writes evocatively and in detail of his and his men's execution of tactics learned on the training grounds.[34]

26   Zuber, *Ardennes 1914*, p.79 and (for his own analysis of the issue) pp.12–79, passim.
27   BA/MA PH10/II/67: 5 AK manoeuvres, 1896.
28   BA–MA PH9/I/1: Cavalry manoeuvres, 1902.
29   BA–MA PH9/I/3: Cavalry exercises in 13 AK region, August–September 1904.
30   BA–MA PH6/I/200: *Die Aufklärungs Uebung zwischen dem XIII und XVIII Armeekorps am 1, 2, 3 August 1912.*
31   BA–MA PH6/I/80: XVI Korps manoeuvre September 1910.
32   Stühmke, *IR 125*, p.10.
33   E. Rommel, *Infantry Attacks* (transl. Lt-Colonel Kiddé & publ. US Army War College, Fort Leavenworth, 1937), pp.6–10.
34   W. Bloem, *The Advance from Mons 1914: The Experiences of a German Infantry Officer* (transl. G. C. Wynne, publ.

And above all, there is the example of 88 RIR at Neufchâteau, described in detail in Chapter 3 above, an example which highlights how the quality of German training extended equally to their reserve formations.

When one looks at the human raw material (eligible conscripts) on each side, for whom these training exercises were devised, another qualitative differentiator is revealed. The average French recruit arguably required more rather than less training than his German counterpart. Because of their larger population, the Germans could afford to be much more selective in their choice of conscript than the French, needing only a proportion of each year's intake to fill the ranks of their standing army.[35] In 1910 only 52% of eligible men were selected for active service, the rest being placed on the muster rolls of the Ersatz Reserve.[36] Over that period France took 80% of her annual intake to fill the requirements of the standing army.[37] This meant that the Germans had much more scope to select on physical fitness, intelligence, motivation, political reliability and other appropriate characteristics.

One important dimension in which the larger population, and selection, favoured the Germans was in demographics: they had a larger pool of rural, rather than urban conscripts. This was important when choosing both physical and political attributes. And the evidence shows that such choices were made; even in 1911 and despite increasing urbanisation, 64% of conscripts came from rural areas and only 6% from areas of high urban intensity.[38] Following the Europe–wide revolution of 1848, both France and Germany experienced an upsurge in left–wing activists who found the close–packed intense industrial environment a more fruitful seedbed for dissent than the slower, open pace of rural life. In France, 'anti–militaristic demonstrations accompanied the annual departure of conscript classes in large cities.'[39] Douglas Porch linked this urban political unrest to the indiscipline increasingly encountered in many regiments after 1900 which in his view 'was seen as a direct result of growing anti–militaristic influence in the ranks,' although he goes on to claim that specific revolts by French regiments were much less political than about bad conditions such as poor food, accommodation and lack of leave.[40] But there is no doubt that the growth of active socialism was an underlying factor adversely affecting morale and discipline and that Germany's ability to select from a pool of conscripts allowed her to minimise the effect on the army.

As well as having a larger and wider pool from which to select its recruits, the German army possessed several other advantages over the French. First Prussia then the German Reich managed the difficult trick of setting the army as an institution apart from civilian life and at the same time retaining a high degree of public support and approbation.[41] A notable feature was the absorption of middle–class men into the officer corps while getting them to fit in and adopt the mores of that elitist body.[42] 'In Imperial Germany the possession of a commission was an important sign of social acceptability, and it was eagerly sought after'.[43] This unique status helped recruitment and maintained the required level of high quality cadres.

Helion & Co., Solihull, 2004), pp.38–51.

35 Snyder, *The Ideology of the Offensive*, p.42.
36 Nash, *Imperial German Army*, p.23.
37 P. Kennedy, *The Rise and Fall of the Great Powers* (Unwin Hyman, London, 1988), p.223.
38 Nash, *Imperial German Army*, pp.13–20.
39 Porch, op. cit.,p.114.
40 Ibid., p.130.
41 For a detailed analysis of this issue, see: G.A. Craig, *The Politics of the Prussian Army 1640-1945* (Clarendon Press, Oxford, 1955), especially Chapter VI *The State within the State 1871-1914, pp.217–254*; and Kitchen, *The German Officer Corps*, especially Chapter VI *The army and the civilians, pp.115–121*.
42 Craig, op. cit., p.238.
43 Ibid., p.237.

France managed to engender the opposite effect, actively seeking during the 'republicanisation' period to make her officers good citizens at the expense of military virtues, whilst at the same time lowering their social status.[44] Porch summed it up thus: 'Radical calls for civic spirit to replace, rather than reinforce, the military spirit dear to post–1870 reformers did not announce that the Left had at last hit upon a coherent philosophy of military organisation, but rather betrayed a lack of appreciation of the profession of arms of which the Left had long been secretly proud'.[45]

With an average of only fifteen days of field exercises each in a full year of national service, and despite route marches, square drills and small–unit exercises, French recruits had plenty of idle time in barracks during which boredom and frustration were natural consequences and issues such as food and leave took on great importance.[46] Poor leadership from both NCOs and officers could only exacerbate the situation.[47] Add to this potent cocktail of ingredients the fact that conscripts were assigned to a regiment in their own local region,[48] surrounded by a civilian community of which they had only recently been part, and an environment was created in which poor morale, indiscipline and worse flourished.

The record of indiscipline, riot and even mutiny within the French army, particularly in the key period from 1900 to 1913, is well documented. By 1906, the general lack of discipline was acknowledged by the then War Minister, Étienne, as having 'reached worrying levels'.[49] However the situation varied from region to region. In Normandy, 3 CA's region, 'signs of antimilitarism were almost trivial',[50] whereas in 1907 the viticole crisis in the Midi erupted in riots and open mutiny. At least nine regiments were involved, one of them a supposedly elite unit, *13 chasseurs à pied*. There were further riots right up to 1913.[51] Once again it is noticeable that all the regiments cited by Porch in the 1907 crisis were from the southern military districts.

The same sort of socialist pressures were evident in Germany: in the 1912 elections the Socialist Party (SPD) – 'the Germany of the organised working class, the most electorally successful party of the pre–war period' – won 34.8% of the vote.[52] But it was balanced by a strong and 'profoundly conservative' section of society that was exemplified by the Veterans' Association which, with 2.8 million members, had a larger membership than the SPD.[53] For complex reasons which cannot be adequately covered here, the line between political debate and activism was not crossed in Germany, though the tension undoubtedly existed. Living with that tension, the army managed to avoid the worst consequences through selective recruitment, insulation from everyday civilian life and a high level of activity including combat exercises.

This necessarily brief overview of the quality of the average conscript called up to be trained for war once again leads to the conclusion that Germany enjoyed a considerable advantage. And when one looks at the quality of the trainers – the company, battalion and regimental officers and NCOs, the pattern of German advantage continues.

---

44   Smith, op. cit., pp.22–27; and Porch, op. cit., pp.73–104; and Rolston op. cit., pp.285–288.
45   Porch, op. cit., p.74.
46   Ibid., p.201.
47   Ibid., pp.131–2.
48   Ibid., p.31.
49   Ibid., p.116.
50   Smith, op. cit., p.26, citing Jean–Jaques Becker's survey of antimilitarism in the Calvados, *Le Carnet B: les pouvoirs publics et l'antimilitarisme avant la guerre de 1914* (Paris: Éditions Klinksieck, 1973), pp.93-102.
51   Porch, op. cit., pp.114–116.
52   Ibid.
53   Ibid., p.17.

The higher social status of the German officer corps fed its exclusivity and made it a desirable profession.[54] Even reserve officer status was something to aspire to and, once gained, something to be proudly preserved.[55] War games and map exercises in winter, staff rides and field exercises in spring and summer were the standard fare of the German cadre.[56] In France by 1911, a demoralised, under–paid and under–valued cadre was undermanned and spent far too much time on office administration and public social duty.[57] The disparity in the attractiveness of the military as a career led to a shortage of French officers. From 1897 to 1907, applications for Saint Cyr dropped by 49%.[58] On 31 December 1911 there was an overall shortfall of 12% of lieutenants and sub–lieutenants (5499 compared to an official complement of 6252) and some 300 more were on detached duties which took them away from the leadership and training of their companies. Ideas for closing the gap included promoting more NCOs (shifting the problem downwards) and shortening the officer training course (lowering the quality).[59] The same situation applied to NCOs: by 1914, Germany had 112,000 well-trained NCOs compared to France's 48,000 although the size of their mobilised armies was broadly comparable.[60] The overall result of these shortages was that in France 'training personnel were in short supply',[61] which impacted on the quality and quantity of small–unit combat training (company, battalion and regiment), the only type of preparation which could have been done given the lack of large training camps.

The ongoing French political debate as to how much to spend on the military, and in what areas, was not confined to long–term capital investment programmes like the building of camps. The reluctance to send troops long distances to get to the camps points to an annual budgetary issue regarding day–to–day running costs. And there is evidence that there were severe budgetary restrictions on 'consumables'. According to a table setting out blank ammunition allocations for 1913 (when Joffre was attempting to increase the effectiveness of training), infantry on 'army' exercises were allowed 60 shots, cavalry 25. A further 40 bullets each were allocated to the infantry for 'brigade' exercises (cavalry were allowed 12). The field artillery were given 565 75mm blank shells per battery to expend at 'army' exercises and 250 more for brigade exercises during the year. Joffre's *Instruction générale* for the Autumn 1913 army manoeuvre contains an order to both sides to conserve the bulk of their munitions for the second half of the event, a pragmatic response to a budgetary constraint which nevertheless would have decreased the realism of the training. The participating 17 CA's general instruction for the event includes a note that there were 4000 blank 75mm shells in the corps' artillery park for resupply during the event – roughly 30 shells per gun if the full complement of corps artillery was deployed.[62] In an artillery exercise inspected by General Ruffey on 24 April 1914, three artillery regiments (25, 46 and 61 RACs) practiced the three doctrinal steps taken during combat – engagement of the artillery of the advance guard, engagement of the main body including corps artillery, and thirdly the task of supporting the decisive attack – each battery of four guns was given forty–eight shells.[63] If final proof were needed of the degree of central control over

54   Stone, *Fighting for the Fatherland*, p.223 & pp.234–244.
55   Kitchen, *German Officer Corps*, pp.120–123.
56   Bucholz, *Moltke*, pp.18–57.
57   Smith, op. cit., pp.37–38; Porch, op. cit., pp.19–22, 27,37–44, 92–104, 121–133, 169–190.
58   Porch, op. cit., p.82.
59   AAT 7N109: miscellaneous papers of the War Ministry, 1912: A report to the Minister by the colonel in charge of 1e Bureau, April 1912.
60   Kennedy, op. cit., p.223.
61   Porch, op. cit.,p.193.
62   AAT 7N1929: *Manoeuvres du sud–ouest en 1913*.
63   AAT 1N14: Inspections, 1914.

the minutiae of expenditure, it is apparent from a note from the Ministry to the commander of 17 CA, issued 3 June 1913 in advance of the September Grand Manoeuvre. It authorised General Grellet (commander of the Blue force's provisional cavalry brigade) to perform a reconnaissance 'between Gers and Blaise, near Lectoure and Condom. He has a car allocated to him and his budget allocation is confirmed.'[64]

Whereas the limitations imposed on the French by their lack of facilities and of money forced them to adopt a centralist approach, the Germans had no such problems. Their system of funding a seven–year cycle based on a set amount per man ensured a guaranteed sum of money per region free from political interference.[65] Their decentralised approach devolved authority down to corps regional level. An added advantage and cost saving came from their superior facilities; the cost of sending a division to its camp for a field exercise was minimal – the camps were local and they marched there, gaining additional experience in route march and deployment. By comparison with the French, this was a better position to be in when preparing for war; nevertheless, Storz argues that there were still deficiencies on the German side, in the size and number of the smaller German *Exerzierplätze*, leading to unrealistic exercises.[66]

In the German Army, the standard application of doctrine and the maintenance of a relatively high level of efficiency were ensured by the system of inspection. There were technical inspectorates, for example one for the cavalry arm, one for engineers, significantly one for foot (heavy) artillery and even one for communications. In a classic matrix organisation, there were simultaneously Inspectors–General with responsibility for the corps regions. These senior officers, eight of them, each owning a group of corps, were the designated army–commanders, backed by a permanent staff organisation.[67] In addition to giving feedback to those commanders whom they inspected, the Inspectors–General sent an annual report to the Chief of General Staff, intended to promote best practice across the whole army. Von Moltke personally read and acted upon these reports, for example in respect of improving the use of aeroplanes for artillery spotting:

> The annual reports of the Inspector–General of Foot Artillery (III,62375/12 of 8/11/1912) and the Inspector of Field Artillery (I.3740/12, Secret, of 26/10/1912), which I have now received, both show plainly that officers controlling artillery fire will be very materially assisted by spotting and observation from aircraft... I can only emphatically support the proposals in both reports that aircraft sections shall be assigned to artillery practice schools. During the training year which has just begun [1913] we must come to some definite conclusions in this matter in order that we may start the system of equipping our artillery with the means of air reconnaissance...it is essential that obstacles be overcome.[68]

Von Moltke's dominant position in the German decision–making process was crucial to success of implementing improvements as a result of inspection, as is made clear by a similar note on aviation:

---

64   Ibid.
65   Dupuy, op. cit.,p.92 & p.125; and E.D. Brose, *German History 1789–1871* (Berghahn Books, Oxford 1997), pp.351–354.
66   D. Storz, *Kriegsbild und Rüstung vor 1914: Europäische Landstreitkräfte vor dem Erstemn* Weltkrieg (Verlag E.S. Mittler & Sohn, Berlin, 1992), p.106.
67   Nash, *Imperial German Army*, p.26.
68   Quoted in: General Ludendorff, *The General Staff and its Problems, Vol. 1* (transl. F.A.Holt, publ. Hutchinson & Co., London, 1920), p.47.

But first of all I will send the Ministry of War the memorandum on the condition of French aviation to which I have already referred. On 1 April 1914, the assumption of 450 military aeroplanes and somewhere about 350 aviators will not be too high. For that time I consider we should require 324 aeroplanes...In my view the obstacles to the realisation of my programme are not the objections urged above, but simply the question of money and *personnel*. ... I therefore adhere to my former standpoint, that my programme must be carried into effect by 1 April 1914. Please see that this is done.[69]

When one seeks reasons for the way that Germany overtook France's dominant position in the sphere of military aviation between 1911 and 1914, the examples above highlight the key role of the inspection system linked to a strong focussed command structure. Moltke's position at the top of the inspection organisation and process ensured a powerful application of quality improvement as well as a standardisation of approach within the German army.

In France, as has been previously mentioned, inspections were abolished by War Minister General André in 1901 'in the conviction that local commanders could best judge their own troops'.[70] They were reinstated by General Joffre after his appointment as 'generalissimo' in July 1911[71] and thereafter there was a flurry of activity, evidence of the French Army's belated but genuine attempts to catch up for lost time. Every member of CSG launched himself into a full schedule of inspections of his designated corps, and records exist for every year from 1911 onwards.[72]

Joffre's plans for 1914 were ambitious; a confidential memo of 5 January 1914 outlines proposed special exercises for the commanders of large units (the necessary follow-on from Grandmaison's teachings and the October 1913 Regulation), based on map exercises and staff rides.[73] He also planned a special staff ride for members of the Army General Staff, accompanied by students of the *Centre des hautes études militaires* (the third year course at the ESG set up by Foch for the training of the best students as prospective army staff officers) directed by General Belin, head of his Operations Bureau. This event was scheduled for 20–25 July 1914 and was presumably overtaken by events. Members of CSG held their own exercises: de Langle de Cary and his chief of staff, Maistre, set up a map exercise for 26–29 May 1914, but it is not clear whether it took place.[74] The return of members of CSG to inspection duties undoubtedly started to improve the French Army's training regime. But this last–minute ramping up of serious activity was no substitute for the long and continuous process which can be traced on the German side.

Overall, General Ludendorff was in no doubt as to the superior quality of Germany's training regime:

Discipline, to which officer and private alike were subjected, was in my opinion the only basis on which an army could be effectively trained for war. Such training could only be acquired through long service. It is only what discipline makes second nature in a man that is lasting, and survives even the demoralizing impressions of the battlefield and psychological changes wrought by a long campaign. It was our thorough discipline and training in peacetime which was to make up for our inferiority in numbers in the coming war.[75]

69   Ibid., p.43.
70   Porch, *Marne*, p.176.
71   Ibid.
72   AAT 1N13–15: Inspections 1888–1914; and 6N42: *Fonds Gallieni, observations sur les manoeuvres en 1911*; and 6N43: ibid., *manoeuvres d'armée de 1912*.
73   AAT 7N/1930: *Instruction sur les exercices des Grandes Unités en 1914*.
74   Ibid.
75   General Ludendorff, *My War Memories 1914–1918 Volume 1* (Hutchinson & Co., London, 1919), p.28.

If the inspection reports and consequent improvement projects were the day–to–day signs of a sound training process, then the annual autumn Grand Manoeuvre was the end–of–term exam. It was the opportunity for two chosen army commanders to show off their skills and for four or more corps commanders to demonstrate the proficiency which they had drilled into their units. Except that it did not actually happen that way. Both sides descended into artificially stage–managed events, with the French as might be expected descending further.

In Germany the *Kaisermanöver* was, even after von Moltke the Younger had persuaded the Emperor to stop ruining it by taking part,[76] first and foremost a spectacle and showcase rather than a realistic combat simulation.[77] But at least the German Army took pride in the opportunity to show off its discipline, ardour and professionalism.[78] And, in 1909, the Germans took a big step towards greater realism by stopping their practice of taking breaks during the exercise, and instead conducting a continuous four day manoeuvre.[79]

In France, the Autumn Manoeuvre merely showed up the ongoing deficiencies in the French Army, even in 1913. Joffre himself testifies to the poor quality of the 1911, 1912 and 1913 manoeuvres.[80] German official observers of those of 1908, 1910 and 1912 corroborate Joffre's overall opinion.[81] And General Bonnal's comprehensive analysis of the 1908 manoeuvre simply reinforces the point that the French problem was deeply engrained, while implicitly pointing to the fact that many of the brigade and divisional commanders of 1908 would be the corps and army commanders of 1914.[82]

It is difficult to sum up this brief analysis of the comparative state of the French and German training regimes without seeming totally critical of the French. Joffre and his staff made significant efforts to improve French training from 1911 onwards, and there are signs that improvements were being made. But the legacy of the past and the wasted years between 1897 and 1911 could not be overcome in the short few years before the war. Germany had put in place a quality system and process which stood the test of time, and backed it consistently with funding and facilities. Even under Joffre's regime, political issues and social pressures took precedence over military necessity, as the passing of the 1913 Three Year Law tellingly demonstrated.

In Germany, despite similar underlying social and political pressures, the army – genuinely a state within the state – was to a large extent insulated from outside influence. With guaranteed funding and strong autocratic support from their Supreme War Leader, the War Minister and the Great General Staff, the decentralised but generally efficient regional corps commanders were able to concentrate on preparing the army for war.

---

76   Bucholz, *Moltke*, pp.242–3.
77   Storz, *Kriegsbild*, pp.107–111.
78   Bucholz, op. cit., p.246.
79   Stolz, op. cit., p.107.
80   Joffre, *Mémoires*, pp.33, 37, 38.
81   BA–MA PH3/–/655: Reports on French manoeuvres.
82   H. Bonnal, *Les Grandes Manoeuvres en 1908* (Elibron Classics, 2005, an unabridged facsimile of the edition published by R. Chapelot & Cie, Paris, 1909), pp. 3–67.

9

Armaments and Equipment

This chapter will examine the extent to which the comparative quality, numbers or usage of key items of equipment affected the outcome of the Battle of the Ardennes, testing what has so far been written on each subject against what has been observed in the analysis of the encounter battles. In order to set this examination into context, a very brief review of the state of pre–war build-up of armaments on each side from 1900 to 1914 will first be undertaken. In this review, the definition of the term 'armaments' put forward by David Stevenson – 'which in its Edwardian English usage, like that of its Continental synonyms (*Rüstungen, armements*), might embrace organisation, manpower, and deployments' –will be adopted.[1]

The period 1904–1914 showed two distinct characteristics in armaments growth. On the one hand there was the long–and medium–term growth needed to keep pace with technological change and industrial production techniques; and on the other hand there were the short–term peaks of armament activity associated with various international diplomatic crises. Underlying both was an endemic sense of 'competition in military preparedness'[2] between nations, leading at times to an outright arms race – 'intense competition between Powers or groups of Powers, each trying to achieve an advantage in military power by increasing the quantity or improving the quality of its armaments or armed forces'.[3] David Herrmann, writing in 'The arming of Europe', highlights 'the relationship between the means available and the way they were to be used', something which this chapter seeks to emphasise, drawing examples from the studies of specific encounters.[4] Dieter Storz has studied the pre-war preconceptions of modern war as well as preparation for it, in order to highlight the transition from preconception to reality, but without reference to actual battlefield events, something which this study adds to the overall consideration of armament and the coming of war.[5]

The underlying long–and medium–term growth experienced between 1904 and 1914 was driven by the need to adopt new weapons such as the machine gun and the quick–firing field gun, new products such as the telephone, wireless and field kitchen, and new inventions such as the aeroplane.[6] All such preparation was constrained by limitations in finance and political will.[7]

The short–term 'arms race' between Germany and France took place in specific periods of political and diplomatic tension, involving 'a series of diplomatic confrontations ... war scares,

1   Stevenson, *Armaments and the Coming of War* p.10.
2   Ibid., Prologue, p.(v).
3   Ibid., p.9, citing H. Bull, *The Control of the Arms Race: Disarmament and Arms Control in the Missile Age* (London, 1961), p.4.
4   Herrmann, *The Arming of Europe and the Making of the First World War*, Preface, p.(xiii).
5   Storz, *Kriegsbild und Rüstung vor 1914*.
6   Herrmann, op. cit., p.5.
7   Ibid., pp.29–35.

the threat of war used as a tool of diplomacy, and in some cases even the partial mobilization of forces.'[8] These short–term arms races were chiefly defined by key political events, notably 'the first and second Moroccan crises, the Bosnia and Herzegovina annexation crisis, and the moves for intervention in the Balkan Wars of 1912 and 1913'.[9] During these crises, threats of war and increases in numbers in the light of other Powers' real or imagined expansion became a particular concern; then and in the immediate aftermath, questions of finance and budgets took second place to military necessity.

When it came to funding both long– and short–term armaments improvement, France was at a considerable disadvantage throughout the period. Using Stevenson's figures, French annual defence expenditure in 1913 was 145% of its 1901 level at current prices, Germany's was 207%;[10] Stevenson also shows that at no time between 1901 and 1913 did Germany spend less than 50% more than France per annum, the gap being 50% more in 1902, rising to a peak of 79% more in 1913.[11] In 1906 in response to the Moroccan crises,the French Government gave the Ministry of War an increase of 4.4% while the German military budget remained flat (at constant prices); but France only managed to reduce Germany's superior defence budget from 162.1% to 161.2%. Of course, Germany was spending considerable sums on her naval ambitions, so overall defence spending does not necessarily reflect commitment to land armaments. But the figures do demonstrate that when, as in the immediate aftermath of the second Moroccan crisis, Germany's naval expenditure took a lower priority, land armament expenditure could be considerably increased.

The step–increments driven by shifts from medium–term to short–term development show a different pattern from the underlying trend of expenditure. Stevenson has shown how, in the medium–term, expenditure was directed mainly towards *matériel*, with some modest increases in manpower; during short–term crises, however, the impetus was towards larger increases to manpower.

During the period leading up to 1904, all armies had achieved a 'steady state of development' without resorting to an arms race. And from 1904–1908 'land armaments remained in approximate equilibrium.' This was the period when France, relying for too long on the superior rate of fire of the 75mm field gun, allowed numbers of field guns to drop. Germany hastened to produce a quick-firing version of their 77mm cannon, after which numbers became important again, and France found herself with too few pieces. Overall during this period 'the German army made considerable strides', adopting a new rifle, cartridge, and uniform, the 15cm heavy howitzer 02 and starting to distribute the M08 machine gun and the light field howitzer.[12]

It was also the period in which France produced the 155mm Rimailho heavy howitzer, albeit in small numbers, and decided (in September 1907) to provide every metropolitan infantry regiment with a machine gun company.[13] France's attitude to long–term development, described by Joffre as 'half–asleep', is further exemplified by the October 1906 new long–term programme for *matériel*, which although approved in principle by parliament, was subject to annual votes for actual funding. Given France's political instability and the rapid fall and rise of successive governments, approval in principle by a previous administration became irrelevant and short-term funding decisions were regularly overturned by the next administration.

---

8   Herrmann, op. cit., p.3.
9   Ibid.
10   Stevenson, *Armaments*, p.2, Table 1.
11   Ibid., p.4, Table 2.
12   Stevenson, *Armaments*, pp.64–303 passim; Herrmann, *Arming of Europe*, pp.35–47.
13   Herrmann, *Arming of Europe*, pp.69 & 91.

The next period, from 1908 to 1912, has been described by Stevenson as a 'breakdown of equilibrium' in both the East and West, triggered by the Agadir crisis of 1911 and resulting in 'Germany's reorientation of priorities from the naval to the land race, which became manifest in 1911–12 although its origins dated back further.' But it was also a period that saw the restructuring of the French High Command and the emergence of Joffre as commander–in–chief designate. He immediately set to work lobbying for, inter alia, a new field howitzer and a new long-range field gun.[14] The French completed the delivery of the 1907 long–term programme – distribution of machine guns, work on fortresses – and also set out on a new programme of military aviation, after Blériot's successful channel crossing in 1909. But France's main preoccupation was to restore parity in field gun numbers and achieve a marginal superiority from the qualitative edge of the 75mm.[15]

1911 was the year of the next German Quinquennat, the five-yearly review of military budgets by the Reichstag, but such was the power of the Treasury Secretary that it contained only modest measures. Then came 'Agadir', resulting in 'short–term measures all over Europe'.[16] By October 1911 there was a German perception that they were not militarily strong enough to face up to an alliance of the other Great Powers, and an Army Bill was prepared for 1912 calling for a huge one–off increase in expenditure, equivalent to the sum of all the annual increases since 1893.[17] At the same time, France also perceived herself to be 'not sufficiently prepared for war'.[18] This was the time of *réveil nationale*, (national revival) although 'there was no one turning-point as dramatic as in Germany', more an acceleration in intensity of preparation.[19]

But it was 1912 which proved to be the year in which the short–term arms race took off. Plans laid then by Germany resulted in the 1913 Army Bill, and in France in the new Three Year Service Law. These were primarily measures directed at huge increases in manpower, and in direct preparation for war. Since the purpose of this chapter is to examine aspects of *matériel* rather manpower, this important step on the road to war must be passed over in favour of the developments in equipment. For the French, a great deal of time and energy was put into the new aviation arm, following the success of aeroplanes in the 1910 and 1911 manoeuvres. So too, Germany belatedly sought to catch up with France with regard to heavier–than–air craft. The 1913 Army Bill provided 79m marks for aviation, compared to 71m for artillery. It is interesting, too, that alongside the enormous increases in manpower, the bill sought to achieve two other vital things: firstly it sought to provide long–term infrastructure (230m marks for accommodation for the extra troops) – something which the French struggled and failed to resolve in relation to their Three Year Law; and secondly it provided for the early completion of previously authorised programmes. As Stevenson has put it: 'the speed of implementation of Germany's bill and its opponents' delays' pointed to 'a window of opportunity opening after all for Germany in 1914'.[20]

This brief resume of the comparative development of armaments in the decade before the war has raised some key issues which provide a framework for the following examination of individual topics. Germany had the higher level of available funds and hence the flexibility to choose between major land and naval programmes. Germany had the long–term stability and commitment (compared to the French at least) to invest in infrastructure and large capital programmes such as training grounds. Germany had the funds and commitment to accelerate programmes for early

---

14   Joffre, *Mémoires*, pp.60–70.
15   Stevenson, *Armaments*, pp.94–177.
16   Stevenson, *Armaments*, pp.178–203.
17   F. Fischer, *War of Illusions: German Policies from 1911 to 1914* (translated by Marian Jackson, Chatto & Windus, London, 1975), pp.116–121; and Stevenson, *Armaments*, pp.202–210.
18   G. Krumeich, *Armaments and Politics in France on the eve of the First World War* (Berg, Leamington Spa, 1984) p.21.
19   Stevenson, *Armaments*, p.216.
20   Stevenson, *Armaments*, pp.293–298.

completion. France, on the other hand, placed short–term constraints on long–term investment, in the form of annual parliamentary votes and frequent changes of government. France also lacked the internal mechanisms – possibly even the will – to push to completion even those things which were authorised, as will be seen in the discussions below, particularly on the key question of artillery.

There is a perception amongst many historians that France entered the war in August 1914 both completely outclassed and completely outnumbered by the Germans in terms of heavy field artillery.[21] Douglas Porch says categorically: 'The French army's most glaring deficiency in 1914 was its almost total lack of heavy artillery'.[22] Michel Goya has written that such heavy artillery as the French did possess was ancient and introduced into the field army only at the last minute.[23] And David Stevenson wrote in 2004 that 'the heavy artillery service that Joffre knocked together after 1913 comprised only about 300 guns mostly pre–quick–firing weapons pirated from fortresses, and held at army group rather than at divisional level.'[24] Dieter Storz comes to the conclusion that France's refusal over many years to adopt heavy artillery in greater numbers compelled her field artillery to take up much more dangerous firing positions than was necessary, whereas German artillerymen had more willingly adopted heavy guns because of their aversion to firing from concealed positions.[25] Even the French High Command at the time subscribed to this perception of weakness. Robert Doughty quotes French War Minister Messimy writing immediately after the war: 'responsibility for the French army's not having heavy artillery at the declaration of war falls principally on the artillery's technical services'.[26]

Joffre too in his memoirs writes of France being half–asleep between 1905 and 1911, during which time France lost her previous advantage in the sphere of artillery, and Germany introduced both the heavy but mobile 150mm and the lighter 105mm field howitzers. Joffre's assertion that France had held but then lost her pre–eminent position in this arm in the early years of the twentieth century is corroborated by historian Eric Dorn Brose (studying the German army) and by contemporary French General Baquet, who was a key figure in French artillery development.[27] At the turn of the century, France possessed a range of heavy guns such Baquet's *obusier de 155 court modèle 1890*, de Bange's 1880 220mm, 240mm and 270mm mortars, as well as his 1879 120mm howitzer; but they were all even then obsolete or obsolescent, they were relatively immobile, and they were in the main intended for the reduction of fortresses. When in 1900 Germany 'adopted a wheeled 150mm howitzer for general service and began converting its carriage to a recoil–absorbing version in 1903'[28], two factors initially prevented the French from following their lead. Firstly, there was a general belief that the superior mobility and rate of fire of the 75mm field gun would obviate the need for a heavy howitzer in the field. Secondly, France's then war plans, versions XIV and XV, were still essentially defensive in character and did not (as did the Schlieffen Plan) envisage the reduction of fortresses while on the march. When in 1904 it was eventually decided to replace the 120mm–155mm range with a modern, mobile field piece, the French chose Captain Emile Rimailho's newly designed 155mm heavy howitzer. After testing and trials it went into full production between 1904 and 1908,[29] but, despite the production line being still available in 1909, barely one hundred guns were produced

21   For example, Doughty, *Pyrrhic Victory*, pp.29–33 and Clayton, *Paths of Glory*, pp.33–34.
22   Porch, *Marne*, p.232.
23   Goya, *La Chair et l'Acier*, p.155.
24   Stevenson, *Cataclysm.*
25   Storz, p.264.
26   Doughty, op. cit.,p.33, citing: Messimy, *Mes souvenirs,* p.88.
27   Brose, *Kaiser's Army,* op. cit., pp.108–111; and Baquet, *Souvenirs,* p.18.
28   Herrmann, op. cit., p.90.
29   Herrmann, op. cit., p.91.

over the whole of its production cycle, based on a standard of six guns per corps.[30] Actual production was slow and when in July 1909 a new Artillery bill became law, there was only provision for an extra three batteries (twelve guns) of heavy howitzers, which still only raised the available total to twenty-one batteries (eighty–four guns).[31] In 1911 General Dubail called for more heavy artillery, a force of 216 guns made up of more Rimailhos plus some new 120mm cannon.[32] This was the moment, the last real opportunity before the war, for France to have committed to the production of large enough numbers of heavy mobile guns to at least match the Germans, but they did not take it. Whether it was because there were difficult choices to be made between different arms competing for limited funds is not entirely clear. But Stevenson, highlighting the reluctance of the French High Command to embrace the heavy weapon, writes that the Rimailho 'was a failure, with insufficient range and mobility to be an answer to the German 10.5 cm field howitzer'.[33] Stevenson cites a note by General Villemajane, dated 2 September 1905, in support of this argument, and it is interesting to note that Villemajane went on to command 33 DI at Bertrix in August 1914; there, as has been shown, he held responsibility for the debacle which left all his field artillery blocked on a forest path to be destroyed by the Germans. He was sent to Limoges on 31 August 1914. This of itself does not rule him out as a credible source; however by comparing the 155mm Rimailho on the one hand with the more mobile 105mm German light howitzer (with which it had a comparable range of about 6,000 metres) and on the other hand criticising it for lacking the 8,000 metre range of the German 150mm heavy howitzer (with which it had a comparable lack of mobility), Villejamine was being very selective in his argument.[34] This supports other evidence that suggests that a majority of French staff and senior officers simply saw no role for either the light field howitzer or the heavy mobile howitzer – at least until it was too late.[35] It suffices to record that the French had the opportunity to produce many more Rimailhos in time to equip their corps to a comparable level to the Germans, but chose not to take it.

Over the same period, Germany produced enough of their 15cm sFH 02 howitzers to allow every army corps its own integral heavy artillery battery, and increase numbers until each corps had sixteen heavy guns. Furthermore, when the French ceased even their meagre production of Rimailhos, Germany was preparing for production of an upgrade, the 15cm sFH 13, so that a continuous output was sustained into the first winter of the war, and beyond. The French lack of production numbers despite considerable production capability was matched by a lack of field organisation. Only in the months immediately before they war did the French General Staff organise their Rimailhos into regiments. All the evidence supports the argument that it was indifference on the part of the French command that led to the decline in their heavy artillery capability.

It is possible that the heavy artillery was another victim of the 'republicanisation' of the army during the post–Dreyfus period. Baquet wrote that if France had had a powerful and competent Director of Artillery between 1901 and 1912, there would have been enough heavy guns. But the last such Director, General Deloge, responsible for the adoption and roll–out programme of the 75mm field gun, was dismissed in 1901 and replaced by a series of less competent but more politically acceptable officers.[36]

---

30   Ibid.
31   Stevenson, *Armaments*, p.177.
32   Stevenson, *Armaments*, p.217.
33   Stevenson, *Armaments*, p.95.
34   For artillery facts, see: D. Nash, *German Artillery 1914–18* (Altmark Publications, London, 1970), passim; and I.V. Hogg, *Twentieth Century Artillery* (Amber Books, Rochester, 2000) p.60.
35   Herrmann, op. cit., pp.91–92, citing Generals Hagron and Langlois.
36   Baquet, op. cit.,p.41 and pp.33–34.

Turning to the situation at the beginning of the war, there is some confusion as to exactly how many heavy guns there were on each side. Joffre wrote that 'to sum up, at the beginning of August 1914, a French army corps had 120 75mm field guns firing a 7.3kg shell, and that was all; a German army corps had 108 77mm field guns, 36 105mm howitzers firing a 15kg projectile, and 16 150mm heavy howitzers firing a 42kg shell'.[37] However on the issue of heavy guns he was disingenuous; whilst his facts are strictly correct, Joffre used the narrow point that his own heavy guns – 105 155mm heavy howitzers, 96 120mm howitzers and 20 batteries [108 pieces] of 120mm field guns, 308 in all – were held at army level to argue that they should therefore be compared not with the German corps artillery but with the 848 heavy guns in the German armies' siege trains, most of which were not mobile enough for use in the field;[38] he then compounded his obfuscation by ignoring the 2700 heavy guns in French fortresses designed to resist siege.[39] There was, for example, a battery of 155mm Rimailhos in the small fortress at Longwy, which Joffre does not acknowledge. Furthermore both de Langle de Cary and Ruffey delegated command of their heavy guns to one or more of their corps commanders, so the supposed organisational difference between the two sides cannot be used to confuse the issue of how many mobile heavy pieces each side put into the field.[40] The true comparison relevant to the battles is this: there were only 404 German mobile heavy pieces with their seven field armies on the Western front (excluding those in the siege trains), whilst Joffre's 308 mobile heavy pieces were supplemented by 16 British 60pdrs.[41]

The real issue, that Joffre in his memoires was probably trying to put the best gloss on, was that by October 1914, with the onset of trench warfare, heavy field artillery came into its own, and the lack of production facilities with which France commenced the war came into sharp focus; this argument is supported by a near–contemporary source: in 1920 Colonel Aublet wrote that from 14 October 1914, GQG formalised a programme for the use of obsolete heavy fortress artillery to augment the few mobile heavy guns in the field; one hundred batteries of 90mm guns were deployed, together with groups of 95mm, 120mm and 155mm short and long guns; all had poor mobility, range and rate of fire, but they were all France possessed.[42]

By contrast, from 1902 onwards, German mobile heavy gun production had been a continuous process and in 1914 the factories were rolling new 1913–type 150mm heavy howitzers off her production lines. The Rimailho production line was still operating in 1909, when twelve extra guns were commissioned; but presumably it was then closed and dismantled, otherwise one would expect Joffre to have commissioned a fresh production run in addition to stripping the fortresses of obsolete 19th century weapons; perhaps the lines were being geared up for the new guns ordered by Joffre in 1911–13; in any case, it would be many months before any new French guns came off new production lines and arrived at the front. But this is a separate issue from that of the number or quality of guns in field during the war of movement in August 1914, when the situation was very different from what Joffre claimed and from what has so far been written into history.

The number of heavy mobile pieces with the two opposing field armies was much closer than has been claimed; and in the Ardennes it was even closer, indeed in sheer numbers the French had

37 Joffre, *Mémoires*, p.71.
38 The German Army siege train included many 210mm mortars and the 305mm and 420mm pieces which demolished the Liège forts. See: Cron, *Imperial German Army*, p.142 .
39 Joffre, *Mémoires*, p.61; and Contamine, *Marne*, pp.88–89.
40 *AFGG I/1*, Annex 746: *III armée, Verdun, 21 août, 17.30: Ordre générald'opérations nr.17 pour la journée du 22 août, V, elements d'armée*: for the attack on 22 August, Ruffey put AL 2 [*artillerie lour de groupe 2*] under 5 CA's command and AL4C under command of 6 CA.
41 Contamine, op. cit., p.87.
42 Lieutenant–Colonel Aublet, *L'artillerie française de 1914 à 1918* (*Revue Militaire Française nr.98*, August 1929), p.240.

more heavy pieces. De Langle and Ruffey between them had been given 108 of Joffre's mobile heavy guns;[43] whilst Duke Albrecht and Crown Prince William had 96 150mm mobile guns, 16 with each of six regular army corps.[44] Following Joffre's tenuous argument, it is true that the German Fourth and Fifth Armies' siege trains had between them 48 210mm mortars,[45] but these needed 18 horses and three travelling carriages each, took many hours to assemble, and sat on a platform of heavy planks.[46] They were totally unsuitable for the field and were not intended for any role except the reduction of fortresses. In fact 8 of these great guns were with Kaempffer's detachment besieging Longwy and fortuitously were in a position to intervene in the fighting on 22 August around that place, although no specific evidence for such intervention has yet to be found.[47]

Nor were the qualitative differences anywhere near as great as has been suggested. In August 1914 at least 40%, possibly more, of the German 150mm howitzers were still of the 1902–type, heavier, slower and without shields.[48] They were not modern quick–firing guns, and had to be repositioned after each shot.[49] All of Joffre's 105 Rimailho 155mm howitzers, on the other hand, were of a 1904–type with a modern quick–fire capability similar to that of the French 75mm field gun of 1897. It was capable of firing an average 5 shots per minute, rising to a maximum of an astonishing 15 aimed shots per minute by a well–trained detachment. It has been reported that 'war experience showed it to be fool–proof and robust'.[50] Baquet considered the Rimailho to have had great mobility.[51] In short, Joffre's Rimailhos were as mobile and much faster-firing than many of the German guns, if lacking the extra 2,000 metres range.

Admittedly, the other two types of French guns were inferior, but were still serviceable. There was Baquet's 120mm short gun (howitzer), 84 guns of 1890–vintage with a range of 5.8km and a 20kg high explosive shell.[52] This was the field howitzer introduced at the zenith of France's military recovery but not followed through thereafter. The remaining 120 guns were de Bange 120mm long guns, 1878–vintage, with a range of 8km. It was a heavy piece (4000kg) but could be pulled by six horses or a tractor, and 84 of them had been modified for field use.[53] De Langle's twelve guns were all Rimailhos; Ruffey had been given twelve 155mm Rimailhos, twelve 120mm Baquets and seventy-two 120mm de Banges.[54] The de Banges were intended for the defence of the Meuse Heights and, by implication, of Ruffey's vulnerable right–rear flank.[55]

The remaining argument in favour of German superiority in heavy artillery rests not with numbers, nor with the qualitative difference between the Rimailho and the Krupp howitzer, but

43   *AFGGI/1* (1936), Appendix iii, p.519, 522, 532 & 540–567.
44   Cron, op. cit., pp.311–317.
45   Ibid., pp.311 & 314.
46   *Handbook of the German Army 1914* (War Office, 1914, The Imperial War Museum Department of Printed Books, 1912), pp. 156–7.
47   See: *Weltkrieg 1*, p.230, and p.304 for composition and location of Kaempffer's detachment.
48   Of the 10 German Foot Artillery regimental histories in the Imperial War Museum collection (ie : 10 out of 24 regiments, a statistically accurate 42% sample size) 4 claim that their regiment was equipped with the 150mm sFH '02, 3 with the 21cm mortar, 1 with an unspecified model of 150mm howitzer and 2 are not specific as to type or model.
49   Nash, *German Artillery*, p.30.
50   I.V. Hogg, *Allied Artillery of World War One* (The Crowood Press, Marlborough, 1998), pp. 89–93; and Hogg, *Twentieth-Century Artillery*, pp.52, 60; and Nash, *German Artillery*, pp. 30–35.
51   Baquet, op. cit.,p.30.
52   Nash, *German Artillery*, p.95.
53   The original de Bange 1878 had to be mounted on a platform before firing, and was therefore only suitable for static defence, siege or fortress work. The modified version was fitted with wheels from which the gun could be fired in the field.
54   AFGG I/1 (1936), Appendix iii, p.556.
55   AFGG I/1, Annex 8: *Directives pour la concentration, Directive particulière pour la IIIe armée, 3° Mission;* and Annex 323: *III armée, Verdun, 15 août, 17.00: Ordre général d'opérations nr.10 pour la journée du 16 août, D. Artillerie lourde.*

with the technical superiority of the standard 1902 150mm Krupp over the modified 120mm de Bange. But beyond the technical aspects, the true key issue was the use made of them during the encounter battles. The question about heavy artillery is inextricably bound up with doctrine, training and implementation.

On the planning and organisational front, the Germans had established a clear advantage. The Foot (heavy) Artillery battalions allocated to their regular army corps had been embedded in their respective units and military districts for over a decade.[56] They had their own technical inspectorate to ensure technical competence as well as coming under the general inspection of the army commander–designate for proficiency and combined–arms work.[57] The General Staff had ensured over the years that resistance to their use, from senior commanders complaining about restrictions to the mobility of their columns, was overcome by both persuasion and regulation.[58] Their staff preparations had even extended to pre–war reconnaissance trips to assess whether roads and bridges would hold the weight of the heavy cannon. One such report on a trip through the Ardennes, produced in August 1912, was signed off by a certain Oberst Ludendorff of the General Staff.[59] There was however one organisational problem; on the march the Foot Artillery battalion travelled at the back of one of the two divisional columns. Under the conditions which pertained in the Ardennes in August 1914 – a series of unconnected encounters by divisional columns separated by bands of forest – it meant that one divisional column per corps had heavy artillery support, the other did not. And (given that German reserve corps played key roles in both Fourth and Fifth Army's fighting) it is most relevant that there were no heavy guns in any reserve corps in those armies.[60]

The French, as Goya has said, above, had the guns – albeit not as ancient as he has inferred – but did not incorporate them into regiments for the field army until early 1914. This was a doctrinal issue. The French had not revised their doctrine since the 1890s, when they restricted their role to the reduction of fortresses. German thinking had started at the same point, but Schlieffen foresaw that his envelopment strategy required him to reduce minor fortresses and field fortifications while on the move, requiring more mobility.

In 1904 Fayolle's lectures on artillery at ESG dismissed the role of heavy howitzers in the field.[61] But in the 21 July 1911 session of CSG, France's senior generals discussed a paper which reviewed the effect of Germany's new military law ('the biggest increase in effort since 1871') and concluded that, inter alia, there was a need to create special firing ranges for heavy artillery.[62] War Minister Messimy authorised on 2 October 1911 the formation of a mobile heavy artillery organisation, which resulted in forty-two 120L [de Bange] guns being mounted on 155 CTR carriages in 1912. The same instruction acknowledged that the Rimailho 155 CTR was classified as a 'modern' weapon but contained no suggestion that it should be mass–produced.[63] There was on the French side a clear acknowledgement that they faced a potential problem with German heavy mobile artillery; there was a lot of debate and, clearly, a little action around the periphery of a solution. But in 1911 the big issue, funding, confounded the proper solution, which was the urgent construction of new

56   Brose, *Kaiser's Army*, pp.151, 156, 165–166.
57   Ibid., p.170.
58   Ibid., p.75 and p.100.
59   BA–MA PH3/–/538: Reconnaissance of the Semoy, August 1912.
60   Cron, op. cit., pp. 313–316.
61   AAT 1N016: *École supérieure de la Guerre: Fayolle's, cours d'artillerie 1904*: *Notonsen passant que les obus à grande capacité, lancés par des canons de gros calibre, ne donnèrent pas d'avantage.*
62   AAT 7N108: op. cit., Ministry of War, staff papers, 1911: a secret note regarding Germany's new military law.
63   Ibid.

production lines and a new generation of modern heavy guns.

It was on 26 September 1913 that Messimy authorised the War Ministry's Third (Operations) Bureau to set up heavy artillery field regiments, with effect from 1 April 1914. A secret note in the Operations Bureau's files shows how, as late as January 1914, they were rushing to put in place arrangements for the heavy artillery to join the ranks of the artillery normally employed on the field of battle. The same report contains a very realistic and sombre assessment of the potential damage to be expected from the German heavy howitzers, and examines ways of countering this.[64] But there was no time left for the formulation of doctrine and the dissemination of regulations for the use of heavy artillery in a war of manoeuvre, let alone any chance to practice with the newly–formed regiments. General Chomer wrote a note to the War Ministry in February 1914 which stated that the Germans were much better armed and prepared for the artillery battle, which he found infinitely regrettable. In the margin, someone has written in pencil: 'True, but what can we do?'[65]

So in the absence of doctrine and training, it comes as no surprise to find that the twelve 155mm Rimailho howitzers delegated to General Brochin's 5 CA by Third Army command were left tantalizingly just ten kilometres behind the front on 22 August, just out of range of the improvised German fieldworks which the infantry were to attack.[66] Similarly, the twelve Rimailhos allocated to Fourth Army were delegated to General Roques's 12 CA on 17 August.[67] Their orders for 22 August were to gather in the Florenville clearing, some twenty–three kilometres behind the actual fighting.[68]

Sarrail's 6 CA had been given the more mobile 120mm Baquet guns, and the remainder – the de Bange 120mm guns – were with Third Group of reserve divisions, in strong defensive positions protecting the Meuse Heights with their longer range.[69] At least Sarrail attempted to make use of his heavy artillery on 22 August, the only French general to do so. But he was frustrated by the length of time which the guns took to get to their allocated position. More than six hours after the 10.00 deadline for their deployment at Cutry, five kilometres south of Longwy from where they could and should have played a vital role in breaking up the attacks of 6 RAK, Sarrail was still impatiently waiting for them to open fire.[70] On the morning of 23 August Sarrail demonstrated the important French ability to learn 'on their feet' and ordered his 120mm heavy cannons to open fire at dawn in order to prepare the way for his attempt to continue the offensive.[71]

But even though the French use of the heavy guns put at their disposal was so poor, the influence of the 48 German heavy howitzers in Fourth Army also seems to have been very limited. The sixteen guns of 8 AK remained silent on 22 August as they were too far away from the battle zone. The sixteen guns of 6 AK are not mentioned as having taken part in the battles at Rossignol and Tintigny, indeed Rocolle asserts that they were not engaged,[72] and the outcome of that encounter

64 AAT 7N50/4: Papers of *Cabinet du Ministre* on heavy artillery: a secret note *sur l'emploi de l'artillerie loured de champagne (état–major de l'armée, 3e Bureau, Janvier, 1914).*

65 Ibid., 'vrai, mais que faire?'.

66 AFGG I/1, Annex 746: *III armée, Verdun, 21 août, 17.30: Ordre générald'opérations nr.17 pour la journée du 22 août*; and Annex 773: *5 CA, Longuyon, 21 août: Ordre générald'opérations nr.17 pour la journée du 22 août.*

67 AFGG I/1, Annex 425: [Fourth Army] *Armée de Varennes,17 août, 14.00: Ordre général nr.15, concernant les mouvements du 18.*

68 AFGG I/1, Annex 780: *12e Corps d'armée, 21 août, 23.00: Ordre général nr.13 pour les Opérations du 23 août* [sic] – referring to 22 August despite clerical error.

69 AFGG I/1, Annex 365: *III armée, Verdun, 16 août: Ordre générald'opérations nr.11 pour la journée du 17 août*; and Annex 423: *III armée, Verdun, 17 août, 16.00: Ordre générald'opérations nr.12 pour la journée du 18 août*; and Annex 743:*III armée, Verdun, 21 août, 02.00: Ordre générald'opérations nr.16 pour la journée du 21 août.*

70 AFGG I/1, Annex 743: op. cit.; and Annex 912: *6 CA à armée Beuville, 22 août, 16.25.*

71 AFGG I/1, Annex 913: *Général commandant 6e CA à général commandant la 12e division, Arrancy, le 22 août, à 21.30;* and Annex 1088: *22e division, Ordre, 22 août.*

72 Rocolle, *Hécatombe*, p.14, note 21.

shows they were not needed. Only the sixteen guns of 18 AK at Bertrix were in action, supporting 21 ID's action which destroyed the French 33 DI in the forest of Luchy. Analysis of that encounter battle suggests that they were arguably less influential than the 77mm field guns which destroyed the limbered French artillery at close range. Because of the organisational issue discussed above, 21 ID's sister division, 25 ID, fighting at Maissin and Anloy, had no heavy gun support.

On the German Fifth Army front, there was a similar story. On the right, it was the massed ranks of 77mm field guns that supported 5 AK's initial attacks during the fighting at Virton and Ethe,[73] although Grasset records that General von Below, commanding 9 ID, called for and received support from ten or twelve of 5 AK's 150mm howitzers at Virton (the other four or so may have been held in reserve or taken to Ethe, the situation is unclear).[74] In any case, at Virton the facts show that by the end of the day the French had achieved artillery dominance,[75] whilst at Ethe, where one might have expected high–trajectory heavy howitzers to destroy the French troops trapped in the village and the valley, they actually held out until nightfall and marched away under the cover of darkness.[76] On the left, 16 AK's Foot Artillery battalion had been allocated to Kaempffer's siege detachment along with 13 AK's heavy howitzer battalion and therefore took no part in the manoeuvre around Ruffey's right flank.

When on 22 August 5 CA attacked the German centre around Longwy, 16 AK's heavy artillery – 1st Battalion, 10th Foot Artillery regiment armed with the older SfH '02 model howitzer – was temporarily placed under the command of the nearest corps, 6 RAK, and they marched towards the fighting around Huffigny where they played an important role in preventing that reserve corps from breaking under the pressure from Sarrail's powerful and experienced regular troops.[77] Similarly, 13 AK's guns were diverted to support the battle against Brochin's 5 CA. Reports on the French side of their infantry streaming back over the Tellancourt plateau pursued by German artillery strongly suggests that the 150mm guns, with their longer range, their high explosive shells and their terrifying noise, were instrumental in keeping the French running. It is fair to say that in the defence of the centre of Crown Prince William's line, either side of Longwy, two battalions of 150mm howitzers performed a valuable supporting role, although the key moments in the fighting took place under cover of thick fog and were conducted by infantry alone.

But despite the contribution of two battalions of foot artillery around Longwy, the overall balance of evidence suggests that the heavy field howitzer did not play a significant role in the Ardennes on 22 August. Only one–third of the German heavy guns came into action, and only at Longwy can they be seen to have made an appreciable difference to the result. None of the French heavy guns were used, although Sarrail did intend to use his. The Rimailhos attached to 5 CA might have made a difference if they had been used to support the attack west of Longwy, but only if it had been postponed until the fog lifted. The French could and should have made better use of the resources allocated to them, but were lacking in both doctrine and training for their use.

The next piece of equipment which features high in the list of reasons given by historians for French failure is the light field howitzer. The prevailing opinion is very straight–forward: in August 1914 the Germans had them, the French did not, which gave the former a key battlefield advantage, particularly in the Ardennes where the higher trajectory was useful for bombarding the dead

73   Grasset, *Ethe, croquis 9*, opposite p.82; and Grasset, *Virton, croquis 5*; and Bircher, *Ethe-Virton, Karte 4, Gefechtbei Ethe*, end papers.
74   Grasset, *Virton*, p.83.
75   Ibid., pp.176–177.
76   Grasset, *Ethe*, pp.116–118.
77   H. Wendlandt, *Das 1 hannoversche Bataillon des Niedersächsischen Füssartillerie-Regiments Nr.10* (Gerhard Stalling, Oldenburg, 1922), pp.20–22.

ground behind hills and in valleys. Stevenson for example wrote of the French: 'Their 75mm field guns were ineffective in the hilly terrain…they were no answer to the German machineguns and field howitzers, which wreaked havoc.'[78]

By 1914 each German regular division had a three–battery battalion (18 guns) of 1909–vintage 105mm light field howitzers per division.[79] But within each division, only one group (*Abteilung*) in one of the two artillery regiments held all the howitzers; in the Ardennes campaign with its multiple small columns and individual encounters, it was a matter of random chance as to where the German howitzers would be found. So for example the German 49 Brigade fighting at Anloy had the support of howitzers but its sister 50 Brigade at Maissin did not.[80] Furthermore the German reserve divisions had only one regiment of field guns, without howitzers, so that there were no German howitzers present at the key encounter at Neufchâteau.[81]

The French infantry divisions, both regular and reserve, were armed exclusively with 75mm field guns. Such was the technical superiority of this weapon that a consensus of opinion within the Artillery Directorate of the War Ministry opted for its exclusive and universal use at the expense of the 120mm and 155mm pieces which had been in use up until 1903. Only in 1911, when the post–Agadir military revival began under Joffre, did the search for a new light howitzer really start.[82] And even then, the army faced bureaucratic resistance from the Artillery Directorate at the War Ministry, which frustrated any chance of a swift decision and implementation.

Immediately upon his appointment Joffre commissioned a report which concluded that there was an urgent need for two new pieces, one being a light howitzer. But discussions with the Artillery Directorate took eight months before a test battery of Schneider's existing 105mm howitzer – produced for export to the Bulgarian army – was requisitioned for field trials.[83] Despite technical opposition, Joffre finally persuaded War Minister Miller and to buy 200 customised light howitzers, but it took many more months of further discussions and protracted testing (until early 1913) for the order to be placed, half from Schneider's Creusot factory and half from the Ministry's own factory at Bourges.[84] Baquet wrote that in France at this time there were political difficulties in giving work to private firms instead of state factories. Schneider got few orders, despite being the best manufacturer and having production lines exporting to several other nations. Then the field howitzer programme became one of the casualties of the cuts in the 1912 budget,[85] and the order was reduced to 36 pieces, the first of which were delivered in the autumn of 1914, too late for the battles on the frontiers.

In place of the cancelled howitzers, 'the Chamber Budget Commission decided in March 1913 to save 80 million francs by rejecting the development of a light field howitzer and adopting the *plaquette Malandrin*',[86] a specially designed metal collar, sometimes referred to as 'fins', which when fitted to a 75mm shell gave it a howitzer–like high trajectory.[87] This option was not only considerably cheaper than building new guns, it also appealed to those who wanted to simplify the supply train by minimising the different sizes of munitions. It lacked the range and the weight of shell of the German 105mm, and it reduced mobility – it has been argued that the French device

78   Stevenson, *1914–18.*, p.53.
79   Brose, op. cit., p.151.
80   FAR 61, op. cit., Introduction, unnumbered page for specification and p.12 for location.
81   Brose, op. cit., p.110; and Cron, op. cit., p.313.
82   Stevenson, *Armaments*, p.217.
83   Joffre, op. cit., p.66.
84   Baquet, op. cit.p.38.
85   Joffre, op. cit., pp.52–5.
86   Stevenson, *Armaments*, p.314.
87   Joffre, op. cit., p.69; Herrmann, op. cit., p.203.

'required the gun to be dug in and therefore militated against the mobility and speed which had become the artillery's watchwords'[88]– but there were arguments in its favour. General Baquet wrote that the *plaquette*'s trajectory was higher than that of the German piece and that factor, combined with a shrapnel shell, meant it could hunt out and kill soldiers in dead ground, the implication being that increased range and weight of projectile were not key issues for a battlefield weapon.[89] On the internal politics surrounding this issue, Baquet also wrote that there were too many opinions spread over the *État-major* and Artillery Directorate and no one individual sufficiently powerful and convincing to impose his opinion within the sceptical *milieu* of 1912.[90]

But the Germans had had their difficulties too. Contrary to what one might believe, given the popular view of the Prussian army as a centre of excellence, the German development and adoption of the light howitzer was not a straight–forward issue. During the 1880s there was considerable resistance from traditionalists: there were for example suspicions that test firing trials were rigged to show howitzers in a poor light.[91] Only in 1896, when Schlieffen became personally convinced that flat–trajectory cannons were ineffective against field emplacements, did the introduction of the L.FH-98 105mm howitzer get forced through, albeit still in the face of strong opposition. Schlieffen was opposed in particular by General Ernst Hoffbauer, inspector–general of field artillery from 1891 to 1899. At one stage of the debate, Schlieffen even believed that he might lose the argument, but decided to press on, and eventually got his way. The gun was first introduced in 1900.[92]

Having taken the decision to include 105mm howitzers in their line of battle, the Germans stuck to it, allocated funding and swiftly executed delivery of the programme. Within two years of Schlieffen's intervention, the 1898 howitzer was rolling off the production line. And in 1910 they introduced a more modern version, L.FH9809, which had genuine modern quick–firing capability, a shield, delayed fuse shells for use against field fortifications and an extended range of 6300 metres. In 1911, just as the French reopened their debate about such a weapon, the Germans added a three–battery battalion of the new 105mms to each of its then twenty–three army corps.

But did the German howitzers give them a battlefield advantage in the Ardennes on 22 August 1914? The first point to make is that the terrain over which the encounter battles were fought was not universally inimical to the French field guns. The whole southern half of the battlefield, from Metz to Longwy, is open with flat plateaux and rolling slopes; the Maginot Line fort at Fermont, with its excellent field of fire, is proof of that. At Virton and Ethe, the battlefields were natural amphitheatres in which two German divisional commanders separately set up old–fashioned gun lines on open ground in front of the forests, and field guns operated at relatively close range (up to 4000 metres).[93] Here, on the French Third and German Fifth Army fronts, there was no glaring need for a high–trajectory weapon. On the other half of the front there was a further variety of terrain. At Rossignol and Tintigny the battle ground was the Semoy river valley, narrow, with low water meadows overlooked by ridges; at Neufchâteau it was arguably howitzer country, with ridges and hollows, copses and clearings – but the German reserve division there had no howitzers. At Bertrix the significant fighting was on flat ground covered with either trees or high gorse. At Anloy and at Maissin the German artillery held the high ground firing down on their enemy, which gave them extra trajectory and less dead ground. The terrain disputed by the German and French

88   Strachan, *To Arms*, p.229.
89   Baquet, op. cit., p.30.
90   Baquet, op. cit., pp.27, 41.
91   Brose, *Kaiser's Army*, pp.62–63.
92   Ibid.,p.66.
93   See note 43, above.

Fourth Armies was not, overall, such that the absence of a light field howitzer would significantly disadvantage one side.

On the French side, there has not yet been found a single direct reference to the use of the French *Plaquette Malandrin* in the Ardennes. But there are perhaps hints: the German accounts of the fight for Neufchâteau town refer to French artillery chasing their infantry through the folds and hollows of the hills, which suggests a high–trajectory weapon reaching dead ground;[94] and at Bellefontaine, where Cordonnier's brigade held off the attacks of the German 9 ID, Cordonnier wrote: 'Our shells [*obus*] with their high–angle fire made light of the changes of slope and continued their ravages behind the crests where the enemy had previously found shelter'.[95]

The light howitzer story really becomes pertinent, as with the heavy artillery, with the onset of trench warfare in October 1914. Then the superior German ability to lob high–trajectory shells into trenches and to destroy field earthworks (the purpose Schlieffen originally chose for this weapon) would give them a clear advantage until belatedly the guns ordered by Joffre in 1911 arrived on the battlefield.

From the earliest to the latest writing, historians make much of French infantry throwing themselves against entrenched Germans protected by barbed wire and armed with machine guns. In 1930 Liddell Hart wrote that 'the French attacked blindly with the bayonet and were mown down by machine guns'.[96] In 2004 David Stevenson wrote that the French 75mm field guns 'were no answer to the German machine guns and field howitzers, which wreaked havoc.'[97] Although this 'machine gun' issue is contextual to the overall *offensive à outrance* debate, it nevertheless requires clarification.

The fact is that each side had exactly the same number of machine guns per regiment – six. The Germans organised theirs into one six–gun company per infantry regiment.[98] The French, on the other hand, allocated a two–gun section to each infantry battalion.[99] This gave the German regimental commander speed and flexibility during battle, to move all six guns to a critical location or to split them up to support various different parts of the engagement. With hindsight this is a firepower issue: the French regarded two guns per battalion as a way of increasing average weight of fire without extra men; the Germans saw merit in using massed fire according to particular circumstances.

But rather than an inspired doctrinal decision, the German organisation may have been more chance than judgement. Germany lagged behind the French in the distribution of the machine gun to all its infantry regiments. In the early years of the 20th century there was considerable resistance from the infantry on grounds of weight, reliability and lack of manoeuvrability, and from the artillery, perhaps on grounds of competition.[100] Experiments between 1899 and the early 1900s with machine gun detachments in sixteen Jaeger battalions were not a success and 'initial plans for integrating the guns into their battalions were jettisoned in favour of independent detachments stationed with the Jaeger in peacetime but marching with the cavalry at manoeuvres and during wartime.'[101] In 1904 not a single German infantry regiment had a machine gun detachment, and the persistence with experimentation owed a lot to the Kaiser's personal fixation with things

94   *Weltkrieg 1*, p.337.
95   General Cordonnier, *Une Brigade au Feu (Potins de Guerre)* (Henri Charles-Lavauzelle, Paris, 1921), p.269.
96   Liddell Hart, *First World War*, p.82.
97   Stevenson, *1914-1918*, p.53.
98   Handbook of the German Army 1914, p.120.
99   Handbook of the French Army, pp.317–319.
100 Brose, op. cit., p.94.
101 Brose, op. cit., p.95.

British and with the British cavalry's use of machine guns with their cavalry and mounted infantry during the South African War.[102] Indeed in 1901 draft machine gun regulations, infantry officers had stipulated that the weapon should remain at least 800 metres behind the firing line.[103] It was only when the first Moroccan crisis convinced the Kaiser that the army was not ready to fight and win a major European war that the question of machine guns was properly addressed as part of the overall German military improvement drive.[104] Germany had only ninety-one machine guns at that time outside its fortress detachments, grouped in thirteen cavalry detachments. As a result of the Russo-Japanese war, four experimental infantry machine gun detachments were formed.[105] Tests by these units in 1906 and 1907 of the new lightweight Maxim MG.08[106] were successful, and distribution of the new MG.08 started towards the end of von Einem's Ministry.[107] But full roll–out was delayed by the 1908 German financial situation and by Treasury Minister Adolf Wermuth's 'formidable' hold on the purse strings.[108] So the 1911 Quinquennat provided funding for only a small increase in machine guns;[109] enough to fund one new detachment (six guns) per regular infantry brigade.

Already by this time France had twice that strength, with six guns per regiment. France had been an early adopter of the guns produced by the Hotchkiss company, starting with the purchase in 1897 of a small batch of the successful Hotchkiss M1897, 'the first gun to combine simplicity with reliability', and over 200 M1900s soon afterwards.[110] But the Technical Directorate within the War Ministry was not content to buy 'off the shelf', and made two unsuccessful attempts to 'improve' on Hotchkiss' original design. The Puteaux M1905 was introduced as part of the medium–term measures for which 200m francs were voted in the winter of 1905.[111] But they were 'troublesome' and were rapidly withdrawn from the field army and relegated to static use in fortresses and strong-points, where the drawbacks were not so obvious.[112] It was replaced by the Saint-Etienne M1907, which was better, if still with shortcomings and with weaknesses inherited from the Puteaux.[113] In 1907, in an apparent response to the successful tests, and planned roll out, of the German MG.08, France decided urgently to provide the entire metropolitan infantry with machine–guns, and this was implemented between 1908 and 1911.[114] But the Saint–Etienne M1907 was not a success and despite being radically modified in 1915 and 1916, it was finally replaced by the original Hotchkiss design.[115]

But initial German reluctance to fully embrace this new technology was reversed when Moltke and the General Staff absorbed the lessons of the Russo–Japanese war.[116] Their original plan to give each brigade a machine gun company starting in 1911 was accelerated, and in 1909, two years ahead of schedule, extraordinary funding was found to fit out the first four brigades with their six–gun detachment. In the 1910 Kaiser Manoeuvre, machine gun detachments were integrated

102 Storz, *Kriegsbild*, p.339; Brose, op. cit., pp.94, 96, 121.
103 Ibid., pp.94–97.
104 Ibid., pp.141–142.
105 Brose, p.142.
106 J. Walter, *Machine guns of two World Wars* (Greenhill, London, 2005), pp.78-81.
107 Stevenson, *Armaments*, p.103.
108 Ibid., p.178.
109 Ibid.
110 Walter, op. cit., p.60.
111 Stevenson, *Armaments*, p.71.
112 Walter, op. cit., p.62.
113 Walter, op. cit., pp.63–64.
114 Stevenson, pp.95, 176.
115 I.V. Hogg and J. Weeks, *Military Small Arms of the 20th Century*, (Arms and Armour Press, London, 1977), pp. 205-206.
116 Brose, op. cit., pp.143–144.

into a 'mixed brigade' structure within General Alexander von Kluck's Red Army. In the 1911 Manoeuvre, 'regular infantry brigades on both sides had a machine gun detachment'. Doctrinal issues were resolved; Brose argues that 'with only six maxims to deploy, brigade commanders were forced to hold their detachments in reserve'[117]. On the other hand, Storz's analysis concludes that it was kept organisationally separate from regular infantry units quite deliberately on the grounds of its weight, complexity and of the difficulty integrating it into existing infantry tactics; however it was increasingly used in combination with the rifles in the firing line and therefore became part of the infantry fire fight, so that the armies which took the field in 1914 no longer regarded it as an exotic piece of special equipment but as a regular infantry support weapon.[118] Whatever the reason, German machine guns were retained in separate machine gun companies, to be used 'in a trouble–shooting role that brought the guns to the spot where they were most needed.'[119] Finally, as a response to the stimulus of the second Moroccan crisis, Germany rushed into a military expansion which gave a machine gun detachment to each regiment.[120] Only a number of reserve regiments were still lacking in machine guns in August 1914 (as has been shown in the analysis of 21 RID's fight at Neufchâteau).

To summarise the pre–war status of the machine gun, it is fair to say that the two sides were more or less at the same stage of development. In implementing their machine gun programme, the Germans had started later but caught up fast; they chose a robust and reliable product and they fell into an organisational structure that fortuitously proved to be the model for the future. The French rolled out their guns to infantry battalions earlier, but lost qualitative advantage by trying unsuccessfully to adapt the original Hotchkiss design. The French chose to use two machine guns per battalion for additional fire-power, the Germans retained the tactical flexibility of the six–gun machine gun company. But how were these weapons used in battle?

Little has been written about French machine guns' contribution to the battles in the Ardennes but they were there nevertheless. At Maissin, I/19 RI advanced across the valley separating them from the village accompanied by its two machine guns, which augmented firepower from the flanks.[121] At nearby Anloy, the author of the regimental history of the German 116 IR noted how they were fired upon at a range of barely 400m by hidden riflemen and machine gunners.[122] At Bertrix the Germans needed artillery to suppress French resistance, using direct fire at 400m at the French, whose machine guns were hidden behind bushes and hedges.[123] At Neufchâteau, where a German reserve division was fighting for its life, it was the French machine guns which did the damage: 'It was well into 1:30 pm and the firing–lines lay only 300–400m from the enemy in a deliberate fire–fight, which the French strengthened from time to time with their machineguns, while the Regiment in those days as a Reserve formation still had no machineguns.'[124]

The role of the French machine gun in August 1914 has been greatly understated, primarily it seems because it was used simply as an augmentation to battalion fire-power rather than as a regimental tactical differentiator. There is also, of course, the powerful influence of the myth of *offensive à outrance*, under which it would be unthinkable that the French also used their machine guns effectively. And it is true that the six–gun German company was used very flexibly and to great

---

117   Brose, p.144.
118   Storz, op. cit., pp.344-345.
119   Ibid., p.145.
120   Herrmann, op. cit., p.168.
121   Bujac, *Eydoux*, p.72.
122   IR 116, op. cit., p.24.
123   See Chapter 5, p.217, note 26, above.
124   Jordon, *RIR 81*, p.9.

tactical advantage. A classic example was during the fighting at Ochamps, part of the encounter battle at Bertrix, where the machine gun company of 87 RI was split into three sections; two were placed on the heights around the chapel and the third at the southern exit from the village.[125]

Given the evidence, it is fair to say that the only times that the German machine guns played the stereotypical role attributed to them was when, as with 95 RI at Maissin, a tactically inept French attack was launched from too far out with too little preparation.

Aeroplanes were a very new weapon of war in August 1914. The rate of technological innovation and development since the first powered flight in 1903 had been astonishing. In 1910 alone, twenty or more significant milestones were broken, some in the United States, some in Europe, including the first machine gun in an aircraft, the first bomb dropped and the first air–to–ground wireless communication.[126]

The catalyst for this explosion of activity was Blériot's channel crossing on 25 July 1909. That seminal event was swiftly followed by another, the world's first International Air Show of 22–29 August 1909, at Reims. From a military perspective, this event was crucial to the development of French air power. General Pierre Roques (then Director of Engineers at the War Ministry)[127] attended, and subsequently built a new career around the establishment of an independent French Air Force, beating off a strong bid by the Artillery Directorate for control of the new instrument of war.[128] By 1914 France was recognised as the pre–eminent nation in civil aviation, with the best power units (the proven lightweight Antoinette aero engine in production and the world class Gnôme rotary engine in development), the best craft and arguably the best pilots.[129] However events on the battlefields of the Ardennes in August 1914 seem to show a degree of German superiority in the use of this arm, as will be demonstrated below. This difference between a perception of French superiority ('only in aeroplanes were the French universally judged superior', writes David Herrmann of the balance of military power in 1914)[130] and contrary evidence from this study requires examination.

Following the events of 1909 and 1910, the French GQG made military aviation the predominant theme of its 1910 autumn manoeuvres, where it proved its worth in reconnaissance and artillery spotting.[131] Ten aircraft were involved, four for each army corps and two for the GQG umpires and observers.[132] By comparison, German manoeuvres as late as August 1912 between 13 AK and 18 AK and involving a *staffel* of aeroplanes on each side, concluded that the fliers did not prove themselves; the Blue side's aircraft did not put in an appearance, and those on the Red side suffered eight defective motors on 1 and 2 August before they got near the enemy.[133]

Germany had started later than France down the heavier–than–air development path, concentrating too long on the alternative Zeppelin lighter–than–air technology, and was clearly behind her enemy in terms of aerial technology[134]:

125 Kaiser, *Bertrix*, p.6.
126 www.century-of-flight.freeola.com/Aviation history/aviation timeline/1910.htm, accessed 2 September 2009.
127 This is the same Pierre Roques who was commander of 12 CA at Neufchâteau on 22 August 1914. See Chapter 3.
128 C. Carlier, *Sera maître du monde, qui sera maître de l'air*, pp.129–192.
129 J.H. Morrow, *The Great War in the Air* (Smithsonian Institution Press, Washington, 1993), pp.6–8; and W. Raleigh, *The War in the Air, Volume 1* (OUP, Oxford, 1922), p.177; Carlier, *maître de l'air*, passim.
130 Herrmann, op. cit,, p.201.
131 Carlier, *sera maître de l'air*, pp.181–191.
132 AAT 7N1927: Manoeuvres de Picardie (1910).
133 BA–MA PH6 I/200: *Die Aufklärungs Uebung zwischen dem XIII und XVIII Armeekorps am 1,2,3 August 1912*.
134 www.airships.net/zeppelins; accessed 2 September 2009; and Morrow, op. cit., pp.8–9, 15; and Raleigh, op.cit., p.177; and Carlier, op. cit., pp.328–329.

Although Germany had the edge in dirigibles, in heavier–than–air flight the French secured a lead in pilot training and in airframe and engine manufacture that inspired great national enthusiasm. In 1911 the Germans thought the French had over a hundred aircraft and seventy–seven military pilots, although both sides were still uncertain about the new invention's utility.[135]

But starting after the success of the French 1910 autumn manoeuvres, Germany made a significant and ultimately successful effort to catch up with France, in numbers of aircraft and pilots if not necessarily in quality.[136] They first used aeroplanes in their 1911 *Kaisermanöver*, and immediately afterwards (November 1911) decided to increase funds for military aviation.[137] Included in the 1912 Army Bill was funding for 'specialized troops, including the aviation units'.[138] And the drive to catch up was led from the top; Moltke himself wrote on 3 December 1912 that:

> The annual reports of the Inspector–General of Foot Artillery (III.62375/12 of 8/11/1912) and the Inspector of Field Artillery (I.3740/12, Secret, of 26/10/1912), which I have now received, both show plainly that officers controlling artillery fire will be very materially assisted by spotting and observation from aircraft.[139]

Moltke had already made plain his determination to match France in this area. In a note to the War Ministry dated 6 November 1912, he wrote that he assumed that France would have at least 450 military aeroplanes and 350 aviators by 1 April 1914. He called for an increase in Germany from the 156 aircraft planned by the Ministry to a total of at least 324, concluding: 'I therefore adhere to my former standpoint, that my programme must be carried into effect by 1 April 1914. Please see that this is done.'[140] It seems that Moltke got his way; the German 1913 Law included provision for an extra 79 million marks for aviation, to be fully implemented by 1916,[141] and in the 1913 Prussian army estimates a sum of 23 million marks (about 6.8% of the total non-recurrent spending) was allocated to 'aircraft, airships, and ground infrastructure', compared with 3.5% of capital spending on aviation in France.[142] It would seem that on the French side the hard decisions on where to spend limited funds provoked budget owners in the traditional arms to resist cuts in order to fund the aviation arm, unproven as it was in combat.[143] Germany's financial flexibility, on the other hand, allowed it to create on 1 October 1913 five new aviation battalions under a new Aviation Inspectorate (part of Generalleutnant Ernst von Hoeppner's Inspectorate of Military Communications).[144] Germany grew, France stagnated; and as a result, the French army failed to field the numbers of aeroplanes (450) and pilots (350) predicted by Moltke, although they clearly had the capacity and opportunity to do so, whereas the German army substantially met Moltke's targets. In 1914 the French army fielded 23 *escadrilles* (138 aeroplanes) compared to thirty-three for Germany (220 aeroplanes).[145]

135 Stevenson, *Armaments*, p.176.
136 Storz, *Kriegsbild*, pp.345–352; Raleigh, op. cit., p.180; M. Cooper, *The Birth of Independent Air Power* (Allen & Unwin, London, 1986), p.9.
137 Storz, op. cit., p.348.
138 Stevenson, *Armaments*, p.204.
139 Ludendorff, *The General Staff and its Problems, Vol I*, p.47.
140 Ibid., p.43.
141 Stevenson, *Armaments*, p.295.
142 Ibid., p.330.
143 C. Carlier, 'Observations de la 3e dimension' (La Revue Historique des Armées, Nr.234/2004) p.51.
144 Carlier, *sera maître de l'air*, p.328.
145 P-M.de la Gorce, *The French Army: A military–political history* (transl. K. Douglas, publ. Weidenfeld & Nicolson,

The way in which France and Germany used their respective new air forces was rooted in the way their respective organisations had developed. As has been shown above, the leadership of Chief of General Staff Moltke was critical in getting the numbers of aeroplanes considered necessary, and Moltke was heavily influenced by reports from his two artillery Inspectors that the aeroplane should be used for spotting and directing artillery fire. So it is no co-incidence that each corps commander was given his own squadron of aeroplanes to spot for the 16 heavy howitzers, leaving but a single squadron under the direct command of each army – and none at OHL level.[146] In France, there were not enough squadrons to allow one per corps, so Joffre placed them at army command level. There is an observable tendency in large bureaucracies for ownership to define usage based on personal objectives: devolve to army corps level and the aircraft will be used for tactical purposes; hold them at army level or above and they will be used for operational and even strategic tasks. The evidence from this study, summarised and analysed below, shows that such was the way it turned out in August 1914.

Pre–war developments contributed to the outcome described above. In October 1911 a British report on the state of French military air power during the summer of 1911 said that the French War Ministry 'had at its disposal, so far as could be ascertained, something between two hundred and two hundred and twenty aeroplanes'– many more than were deployed in August 1914. The report concluded that their methods of training were elaborate and complete, and that 'the air corps was continually practiced in co-operation with all other arms – infantry, cavalry, and artillery.'[147] Had Colonel Estienne won for the Artillery Directorate the political battle over ownership of the air arm, one can legitimately speculate that greater use of aeroplanes for artillery spotting and battlefield observation would have been made, based on the ground–breaking aeronautical exercises carried out by the French air corps with infantry, artillery and cavalry at the Camp de Châlons. But ownership by the Engineering Directorate almost inevitably focused development in a different direction:

> The artillery needed to spot targets hidden behind crests, and direct and control fire on those targets. For that they needed fast, short–range aeroplanes capable of flying about a hundred metres above the ground for about an hour. The Engineers hoped to provide long–range reconnaissance for the infantry and cavalry, using an aeroplane capable of seeking out enemy reserve forces at least a hundred kilometres behind the front, flying high enough to avoid risk, that is to say at about a thousand metres for both legs of the journey. In 1909, the aircraft were capable of meeting the demands of the Artillery, but not those of the Engineers'.[148]

But by 1914, as will be shown below, evidence suggests that the Engineers had achieved their objectives for the new air arm at the expense of the artillery.

One final organisational feature influenced the comparative use of air power during the Ardennes campaign. Having decided to allocate his available squadrons to his army commanders, Joffre then gave Fourth Army just two squadrons (twelve aeroplanes) compared to four for Third Army and five for Fifth Army.[149] There is no explanation to be found for this decision; perhaps, again like the

London, 1963) p.83; and Carlier, *sera maître de l'air*, pp.249–330; and Cooper, *Air Power*, p.9.

146   Cron, *Imperial German Army*, pp.299–329, Appendix 1, The Field Army 17 August 1914.
147   Raleigh, *The War in the Air, Vol 1*, p.177.
148   Carlier, *sera maître de l'air*, p.136.
149   AFGG I/1, Appendix III, pp.556, 563, 567.

heavy artillery of which he gave de Langle just twelve guns, he was guided by a preconceived notion of limited usefulness in the difficult Ardennes terrain, or perhaps it was because Fourth Army was originally in reserve and could rely on reports from the front; but there is no evidence to support either hypothesis. The result, however, was that de Langle had limited resources compared to his opponent, and made limited use of them, especially in the tactical arena. Ruffey, too, seems to have limited the use of his more plentiful aerial resource to operational reconnaissance, which was of course an army commander's prime concern.[150] The needs of the French corps commanders do not seem to have been considered, despite effective pre–war practice at the tactical level during manoeuvres.[151]

And so on the battlefields of the Ardennes on 22 August 1914, it seems that Germany achieved a decided battlefield advantage in the practical use of aircraft in warfare. German reconnaissance aircraft, taking off as soon as the fog lifted, had identified the advance of de Langle's army at the earliest opportunity and alerted corps commanders and army commander Duke Albrecht to the impending crisis.[152] At Bertrix a German aeroplane was scouting ahead of 21 ID as it advanced towards 33 DI, and the shooting down of that machine by French infantry – cutting short its flow of battlefield intelligence – indirectly caused the final contact to come as something of a surprise to the Germans as well as the French.[153] The aeroplane almost certainly belonged to 18 AK's integral support squadron.[154]

On the French side, de Langle's flyers were only asked to perform operational missions under his direct control, and then quite late in the day. They seem to have delivered their first reports on the situation as late as 17.00, and even then gave little useful intelligence.[155]

At an operational level, the quality of intelligence gained by observing marching columns from the air has been shown in this study to have been overrated, since flights were severely limited by the weather and both sides had rapidly developed the ability to hide large bodies of troops in woods and villages, and march at night.[156] The failure of Ruffy's airmen to spot and report the movements of the German Fifth Army immediately preceding their attack exemplifies this point. On the other hand the tactical application - where the enemy was deployed for battle and could not hide - seems to have been a factor in German superiority, compensating for the cavalry's inability to penetrate security screens with their modern firepower.

In short, the use to which each side put the new arm, air power, shows once again that the key issues were organisation and process driven; that small but important doctrinal differences arose and that German pragmatism triumphed over French bureaucracy. Here, as elsewhere, France squandered an initial technical advantage and suffered as a result on the battlefield.

Although a relatively insignificant item of equipment, albeit very important to the troops, the question of the French lack of field kitchens is important in its own right but also perfectly exemplifies one of the worst traits of French military preparation. The Germans had introduced

150 *AFGG I/1*, Annex 739: *III Armée, Compterendu de renseignements nr.35: 'Trois reconnaissances aériennesdans zone Longuyon, Virton, Étalle, Arlon, Pétange, Capellen, Luxembourg, Rémich, Bettembourg, Audun–le–Roman, Briey'.*
151 H. C. Johnson, *Breakthrough: Tactics, Technology and the search for victory on the Western Front in WW1* (Presidio, Novato CA,1994), p.18; and Carlier, op. cit., pp.206–208, 257–259.
152 *Weltkrieg 1*, pp.315–316.
153 A.G.M., *Bertrix 1914*, op. cit., pp.245–247; and Kaiser, *Bertrix*, op. cit., pp.6–7.
154 FAR 25, op. cit., p.27.
155 *AFGG I/1*, Annex 867: *Aviateur lieutenant Gouin à Monsieur le général commandant l'armée. Le 22 août 1914, 17h.20.*
156 See: General Armengaud, *Renseignement Aérien* (Librarie Aéronautique, Paris, 1931), passim, for a general discussion of French use of their fledgling airforce in 1914.

field kitchens about the time of the Bosnian crisis, an 'expensive innovation'.[157] Hot food the night before a battle and even coffee in the morning before the fighting started became a normal but important part of the routine of the German soldier.[158] On the other hand, there are several instances of French soldiers going into action on 22 August cold, tired and hungry, not having had hot food for sometimes as long as a whole day.[159]

Charles Humbert was senator for the Meuse region, member of the *commission sénatoriale de l'armée*, and renowned for asking awkward questions about French military preparation. In a parliamentary session on 31 October 1913, he asked about the status of field kitchens.[160] The answers provided to him illuminate the French army's way of effecting change. Field kitchens had first been tested in 1905, and annually thereafter. In 1908 there were large–scale experiments of kitchens of different types. During the winter of 1911–1912 the War Ministry conducted a formal trial between the three leading competing systems. Between 1905 and 1913 the Ministry spent 274,800 francs on these tests and trials, ranging from 5,600 francs in 1905 to a peak of 129,000 francs in 1910. The status in October 1913 (about the time that the Germans were rapidly introducing them) was that there would be further tests pitting the three 2–wheeled systems against some new 4–wheel types, some with ovens and some without ovens, to find the best choice. The intention was to take a decision (in 1913), fit out four or five corps with the chosen model during 1914 and then equip the rest of the army during 1915 and 1916 with annual programmes within the limits of the budget. It seems that no decision was actually taken in 1913, and there is no evidence found yet that any French corps went into action in 1914 equipped with field kitchens.

For nine years the bureaucrats in the War Ministry struggled with the issue of finding the perfect field kitchen, unable to choose between the number of wheels needed or decide on the relative merit of an oven. Budgetary constraints would ensure that, if and when a type was chosen, it would take at least three years to equip just the regular army corps. War overtook the process and French troops went into battle on 22 August 1914 all too often deprived of their last meal.

Perhaps the least significant but most widely–known French equipment issue was that of the red trousers worn ·by their infantrymen, leading to unfavourable comparisons to anachronistic Napoleonic warfare. The British had had khaki for more than a decade, the Germans their field grey since 1909.[161] If final proof were needed of the rationale for change, it was provided by the Russo–Japanese war.[162] Typically, given the pattern emerging from evidence above about the nature of French bureaucracy, the French army in their autumn manoeuvres of 1911 had experimented with camouflage of a *réséda* colour (which is apparently a shade of green), following a recommendation by a Committee led by General Dubail, but no decision had been taken.[163] Traditionalists resisted change;[164] and the uniform had taken on a political dimension. The issue had got caught up in Miller and's attempts to boost Army and officer prestige in the post 'republican' period of military revival, between 1911 and 1914. He had banned officers from wearing civilian clothes, and the traditional colourful uniform was thus deemed important for morale.[165] Although the now

157 Stevenson, *Armaments*, p.330.
158 For example, see: Zuber, *Ardennes*, pp. 185, 250.
159 For example, 3 DIC: Moreau, *Rossignol*, p.54.
160 AAT 7N53 – Ministry of War papers containing all questions received from Charles Humbert, Senator for the Meuse, and the Ministry's written responses.
161 Hermann, op. cit., p.10; Stevenson, *Armaments*, p.103.
162 Herrmann, op. cit., p.71.
163 Storz, op. cit., pp.289-292; Ralston, *Army of the Republic*, pp.323–324; Herrmann, op. cit., p.204.
164 Herrmann, op. cit., pp.71–73.
165 Porch, op. cit., pp.184–185.

notorious phrase *le pantaloon rouge, c'est la France* (red trousers symbolise France) was uttered by War Minister Étienne in 1906, it does exemplify the 'original patriotic tradition' of the Radical party and of parliamentarian Étienne Clémentel, who was responsible for the Army budget when the question of credits for camouflage uniforms was considered, and his advocacy of the red trousers was crucial to the postponement of any change.[166] It was only at the eleventh hour –on 9 July 1914– that a law was passed to provide the French infantry with new *bleu horizon* uniforms, which became available in 1915, too late for the early battles.[167]

But was the French uniform the significant drawback that it has sometimes been taken to be? It was, perhaps, symbolic of an attitude within military and political French circles that mistook show for substance and which failed to comprehend the impending realities of modern warfare. But there is little evidence that it significantly worsened French chances of success in the Ardennes battles. Indeed if the 'friendly fire incident' evidenced at Neufchâteau is anything to go by, French artillery did not find the red trousers sufficiently noticeable to stop them firing on their own side.[168] Contemporary pictures show that the dark blue overcoat worn by the *poilu* (private soldier) covered fully two–thirds of their body, although officers with their short blue tunics were more colourfully exposed, and the cavalry dragoons' metal cuirasses frankly ridiculous. But there is a case to be answered: a young Lieutenant Rommel, fighting with 53 Brigade at the village of Bleid near Ethe on 22 August, wrote of leading his men into contact with an enemy distinguishable by their red breeches showing up amongst the yellow corn in the fields, but then he also refers to the bright reflection of their cooking gear attached to the top of their tall packs, so the question of French attention to camouflage is clearly more wide–ranging.[169] What is important about the French uniform issue is how it informs us of the comparative weight of military need as opposed to socio–political bias in French preparations for war.

Finally, an issue which is made relevant by the doctrinal issue, associated with *offensive à outrance*, of whether to dig temporary battlefield trenches or not: the question of entrenching and other field tools. Contrary to what one might expect, the French units were just as well endowed with such tools as their German counterparts. Each French infantry company of about 250 men was allocated 80 spades, 80 picks, 16 wire cutters, 8 hand axes and 1 jointed hand saw, all to be carried with their packs; further heavier tools travelled with the first and second line transport.[170] Despite this official allocation, Major Burne (using Grasset as his source) records an incident at the battle at Virton where 124 RI, under artillery fire on exposed hillside, 'proceeded to dig in as best they could with the lids of their mess–tins and even with their fingers, for they had few entrenching tools'.[171] However, Grasset himself said: 'But everyone was driven by the urge to get forward and close with the enemy; nobody thought to dig for shelter and their tools remained on their packs and they simply used furrows and stacks of straw as they could be found'.[172] Burne through his erroneous interpretation contributed to the building of a myth, whereas Grasset points to a training issue and an unfettered offensive attitude, rather than an equipment issue. The impression gained by Edward Spears during his liaison work with Lanrezac's Fifth Army reinforces this conclusion: 'somewhat to my surprise, I saw no attempt being made anywhere to dig entrenchments...The whole pre–war

166   Ralston, op. cit., pp.323–324.
167   Herrmann, op. cit., p.204.
168   See: Chapter 3, note 72, above.
169   Rommel, *Infantry Attacks*, p.10.
170   *Handbook of the French Army 1914*, op. cit., p.219, Table VI.
171   Burne, *Virton*, op. cit., p.46.
172   Grasset, *Virton*, p.121.

training, or lack of training in this respect, was telling'.[173] So the French had the tools but not the inclination (or doctrine or training) to use them.

By comparison, a German infantry company carried 100 spades, 10 pickaxes and 5 hatchets with them, with heavier tools in the regimental first line transport and more in the second line transport.[174] And they had been trained over a long period to use them. As Spears said:

> I for one was soon to learn that you apply in time of war the lessons you have learned in peace; you may do less than you did in peacetime, you will certainly not do more. In war it is too late to remember theories and axioms which are all very well for officers on Staff rides; the soldier is either too tired or has no time to think; he will only do what comes to him naturally and instinctively, through long usage.[175]

A specific German instruction manual on digging and building field emplacements was already in use in 1893, and was translated into English by the Corps of Royal Engineers. Amongst its guiding principles, it states that: 'Field defences have acquired additional importance from the effect of modern firearms ... they make it possible to offer a stout resistance even with comparatively weak forces, or else, by economising men, they enable a sufficient force to be reserved for an effective counter–attack at the decisive points.'[176] One sees at Maissin proof of the application of the defensive doctrine, and at Rossignol that of the counter–attack. And linking the 1893 doctrine with the 1914 application in the field lay two decades of instruction and practice on Germany's abundant training grounds. The lessons of the Russo-Japanese War were taken onboard: at the end of 1905 an anonymous article in *Militärwochenblatt* called for the regulations on giving protection to the infantry to be properly implemented after years of theoretical observance.[177] The call seems to have been heeded, for Zuber observes that 'in 1911 the new regulation *Feld-Pionierdienst aller Waffen* (Combat Engineer Tasks for all Arms) integrated engineer training, principally digging in, river crossing and clearing obstacles, into the training of all combat arms', and that (keeping one step ahead) 'the 1st Foot Guard regimental history reported practicing attacks on field fortifications in September 1912 and 1913'.[178]

The 1893 Instruction stated that 'one pace per rifle should be reckoned for shelter trenches', although this may well have widened by the time the war started, in accordance with development of infantry doctrine on dispersal. 'Intervals of a few paces may be conveniently left between the trenches of different companies', indicating that initial shallow scrapes for individuals were intended to be enlarged into continuous 'company' lines.[179] If there was time, the troops were expected to 'prepare the foreground (clear the field of fire) and mark out distances'.[180] Wire entanglements and *abatis* (felled trees or thick branches) were to be sited 150 feet in front of the line of the defence and the *abatis* would conceal the wire.[181] According to doctrine, a practised workman [a pioneer] should in one hour be able to excavate 35–42 cubic feet of light soil, 26 cubic feet of medium and 14 cubic

173   Edward Spears, *Liaison 1914* (Cassell, London, 1999), p.107.
174   *Handbook of the German Army 1914*, op. cit., p.320, Appendix XI.
175   Spiers, op.cit., p.108.
176   *Instruction in Field Fortification. A Translation of the German "Feld–Befestigungs Vorschrift" of 1893* (Professional papers of the Corps of Royal Engineers (Foreign Translation Series), Royal Engineers Institute, Chatham, 1895), p.3, Article V.
177   Storz, op. cit., pp.173-174.
178   Zuber, *Ardennes*, pp.58-61.
179   *Instruction in Field Fortification*, op. cit., p.19, Article 32.
180   Ibid., p.9.
181   Ibid., pp.33–36, Articles 103–107, and figures 41 & 42.

feet of heavy soil; infantry using entrenching tools should accomplish the same in no more than twice the time.[182] Using these figures, and the measurements given for a standard kneeling shelter trench[183], the calculation shows that a German infantryman was trained to dig his initial shelter trench - which we would call a foxhole - with a three foot depth in just over half–an–hour. It is little wonder that the French were amazed by evidence of such achievement, nor that they misinterpreted what they saw.

At Maissin, the French recorded that there were enemy trenches, barbed wire, and dummy soldiers whose helmets were cunningly disguised turnips.[184] General Eydoux and his men could not envisage these works having been constructed during the long hours of the fire-fight and concluded that they had been prepared in advance. This is plainly nonsense; the German infantry had only arrived at Maissin at the same time as the French, and if an advance party were to have made such preparation the trenches would have faced west, from where the French attack was expected rather than south where the French achieved surprise by their unexpected advance. So too at Rossignol, an experienced Colonel of the Colonial Army, Lieutenant–colonel Vitart, mistakenly reported that the enemy positions facing him had been prepared in advance.[185] This common mistake stemmed from a total lack of understanding on the French side about what could be achieved by training, practice and the effective application of doctrine, and contributed in no small part to the myth that the Germans were lying in ambush positions in the forests on 22 August.

One is therefore drawn to the conclusion that the issue of German trenches and barbed wire is one of doctrine and training rather than of equipment. It is instructive insofar as so many French soldiers saw what they wanted to see in order to seek explanations for their defeat, and it informs us as to how inaccurate pictures of ambush and preparation have coloured many previous accounts of the Battle of the Ardennes.

In conclusion on the various armament and equipment issues, one is drawn on the French side to underlying themes of insufficient funding, of delay due to excessive bureaucracy and of a lack of genuine public and military will to prepare, rather than practical issues of technology and production. It is clear, too, that the initial technological advantage of the French 75mm field gun left them for too long with an ultimately false sense of security, and for a crucial period they traded numbers of guns for rate of fire. When their potential adversaries caught up in the qualitative race, France had to divert precious funds to make up the numbers again, instead of (say) investing in heavy artillery. The French army's greater reliance on State–owned industry not only limited their capacity for production, but introduced delay while customised designs of standard private industry models were planned and created and (in the case of the Hotchkiss machine gun) ended up with an inferior product.

On the German side, one sees conversely a swifter response, based in no small part on greater funds and political will, and less convoluted bureaucratic rules, processes and systems. One sees that the medium–term improvements in equipment taken by Germany after the first Moroccan crisis laid better foundations for later expansion than in France. In Germany, once a weapon (such as the heavy field howitzer) was introduced into the arsenal, it was produced in both sufficient numbers and with appropriate upgrades; there is an observable degree of continuity which was absent in the more volatile French political – military environment. When the arms race moved into the last pre–war short–term cycle, Germany was able not only to expand manpower but also

---

182   Ibid., pp.7–9, Articles 26 & 29.
183   Ibid., p.10.
184   Bujac, op. cit., pp.72–73.
185   Moreau, op. cit., p.61.

to bring forward and complete vital equipment programmes. Storz's conclusion is that Germany's initial success stemmed less from superior technology than from the methodical, thorough hard work with which they prepared to use that technology; work which allowed for fewer significant weaknesses in performance, compared to the French, whose last-minute energies were focussed on overcoming all the issues arising from the questions of uniform, of field equipment and of heavy artillery.[186] Ultimately it would seem that slow French progress in all aspects of preparation during the period between 1900 and 1911 gave Germany a window of opportunity that she exploited when she went to war in August 1914.

---

186 Storz, op. cit., p.370 & pp.369-373, passim.

Conclusions

In this book I have set out to achieve three things: to present the first operational study of the August 1914 Ardennes campaign and uniquely as seen from both sides; to demonstrate that in two particular encounter battles (at Maissin and at Neufchâteau) the French had the opportunity to inflict a tactical, possibly an operational, defeat upon their opponents but in both cases failed to do so; and to explore the reasons for that French failure by setting what happened into the context of previous explanations - particularly the myths propagated in early literature and carried forward without further consideration - and against a brief survey of each side's pre–war preparations.

The operational study has concluded that Joffre's strategy for an offensive through the Ardennes was not the foolish venture that some historians have claimed; on the contrary, despite the flaws in French intelligence and analysis, Joffre delivered superior forces at the weakest point in the German deployment. Contamine defined a strategic triumph as one in which you put sufficient superior strength at a decisive point, but conversely suggests that if neither of the opposing forces has more than a 25% – 30% advantage over the other, then strategy gives way to tactics.[1] On a thirty–five kilometre front between Maissin and Neufchâteau, Joffre managed to commit ninety–six battalions of regular infantry against twenty–four regular and twelve reserve German battalions – a 60% advantage; he did so under the cover of thick fog and achieved total surprise; and he gave his battlefield commanders at least half–a–day to achieve a result before the first enemy reinforcements could intervene. Moreover, in specific places the odds in France's favour were simply overwhelming. This, it can be argued, was strategic success. Tactical failure in the encounter-battles that followed have overshadowed the role of the commander-in-chief.

German strategy on the Ardennes front was essentially defensive but deliberately full of risk. OHL preferred to deploy maximum force at their proposed decisive point on their right wing; for lack of overall resources, Duke Albrecht was given insufficient forces to cover his expanding front and was denied the security of a HKK (independent cavalry corps) on his southern flank. Those risks nearly brought Fourth Army to disaster and only the tactical competence of their divisional, brigade and regimental units bought them victory from the jaws of defeat.

At the army operational planning level, both de Langle de Cary and Ruffey underestimated the challenges they faced in accomplishing their respective missions and failed to anticipate and plan to overcome or avoid key obstacles to success. The failure to order strong mixed–arms advance guards to secure the exits of forests through which their columns had to march was a significant error by both Third and Fourth Army staff; this was a failure to apply doctrine and was contrary to the fundamental principle of *sûreté* embedded in both the 1895 and 1913 regulations. The failure

---

1   Contamine, *Revanche*, p.222.

to co–ordinate 5 CA's assault on German trenches with the advance of the rest of the army – even if in the event extraneous factors made the problem irrelevant – was another operational planning error. This too was an error not of doctrine but of execution. Briefing by both armies' intelligence and operations staff was deficient, Fourth Army's particularly so, and subordinate units marched into contact in an unnecessary state of ignorance.

Both Duke Albrecht and Crown Prince William discharged their simpler operational missions with greater competence than their opponents. Duke Albrecht's daily orders reflect his awareness of and preparation for a turn southwards whilst pursuing his westerly march, even if he was taken unawares by the timing and direction of the French attack because of the fog. And there were elements of luck – Clausewitz's principle of 'friction' – all of which worked in Germany's favour at the operational level. Crown Prince William's unilateral decision to turn south on the night of 21–22 August meant that Ruffey would have to fight through to his objectives rather than undertake a peaceful march. And the German Fifth Army's advance could have opened up a thirty–kilometre gap between them and Duke Albrecht's Fourth Army, a gap which, given the French Plan and actual movements, would have been filled by the French 2 CA occupying the operationally important Étalle corridor, a move that would threaten to split the two German armies. Instead, and as a result of ingrained staff training, German staff officers of 5 AK, 6 AK and Fourth Army combined to highlight a potential operational weakness and deliver a solution. As a direct result of this excellent staff work, 6 AK marched southwards and serendipitously met the French Colonial Corps at Rossignol.

Turning to the respective conduct of combat operations, this study has revealed crucial differences between the two sides. The issue of communications in August 1914 was always going to be one of explaining varying degrees of imperfection. Radio technology was in its infancy and telephone and telegraph apparatus relatively slow and cumbersome to set up; neither was suited to large armies engaged in mobile warfare. And the size of the modern battlefield meant that physical means of communication had decreased dramatically in effectiveness. The motor–car was limited by the state and scale of the road network, the horse by its lack of speed. On the battlefield itself, all types of courier, even pedestrian, were vulnerable to long–range rifle, machine gun and artillery fire in an extended 'killing zone'.

The communications within the German Fourth Army have been shown to be of high quality, yet even with that advantage Duke Albrecht was able to exert only a partial control over events. Orders that he gave had already been overtaken by events by the time they were received, and his subordinates had to use their best judgement to apply the spirit of those orders to the changing situation. Crown Prince William's communications were good enough to have been cited by the official historian as a significant factor in his success;[2] but were not necessarily of the excellence achieved by Duke Albrecht's staff given the longer distances Fourth Army had to cover. On the other hand, reporting discipline and communications within the French Fourth Army were so poor that army commander General de Langle de Cary was left largely ignorant of what was occurring and unable to exercise any degree of control over events in the crucial centre and left–wing actions of his army .

Command and control also left much to be desired within the subordinate units of de Langle's Army. General Eydoux was unable to accelerate the slow and ponderous approach and deployment of his left–hand 21 DI at Maissin despite his desire to do so; General Radiguet of that division, together with his brigadiers and colonels, was unable to prevent an unauthorised and costly premature infantry attack led by one of his headstrong battalion commanders. Conversely at Neufchâteau the untimely wounding of Colonel Descoings seems to have been the cause of a potentially victorious pursuit grinding to a halt; too much seems to have depended on the personal ability and charisma of individual officers rather than the corporate culture of the army.

That corporate culture existed within the German army. One sees in the performance of Duke Albrecht's subordinates a high standard of command and some of the best features of German doctrine in action. At Bertrix General von Schenk (18 AK) exercised his discretion under the doctrine of *Auftragstaktik* (mission tactics) to alter the orders he had been given to suit what he felt were the conditions at the front. At Rossignol General de Beaulieu of 12 ID executed an exemplary attack using 'fix, hold and envelop' tactics; the degree of his success was very much enhanced by the poor quality of command demonstrated by his opponent.

General Ruffey of the French Third Army has generally been underrated as a commander; he had placed liaison officers with his corps commanders and this together with good communications enabled him, unlike de Langle, to intervene in the actions of his various corps at several critical moments. But he was unable to control the slow speed with which his heavy artillery executed his orders. Furthermore the transfer of Third Group of reserve divisions from his command may have contributed to that unit's failure to intervene in the battle on his right wing.

Crown Prince William's release of 16 AK from defensive duties around the *Moselstellung* to attempt a flanking movement of Sarrail's right wing exemplifies his - or his chief-of-staff's - firm control of his army's battle; it was a question of assessing risk and opportunity, and it was well taken. So too the release of troops and guns from the siege of Longwy to support the battle against Brochin's 5 CA demonstrates positive command characteristics and a timely ability to respond to requests from the front with appropriate decisions.

In the battle chapters of this book, the encounter battles at Neufchâteau and at Maissin–Anloy were analysed from the perspective of both sides, to demonstrate that the French lost two major opportunities to break through the German line. It is only by comparing the records of each side that the inevitable human 'gloss' or 'spin', or understandable ignorance of what lay on the other side of the line, can be assessed, and a balanced account of the battle presented. Using this methodology, it has been made clear that the French records of the two battles have provided a distorted historical perspective, and that the extent of the opportunity given to Generals Eydoux and Roques was never understood. Subsequent histories reflect this initial distortion.

Some historians, starting with Henry Contamine in 1970 and echoed by Pierre Rocolle and others, have noted that Roques's corps faced weak opposition and might have done better. There is indeed a hint in the immediate aftermath of 22 August that senior officers within Fourth Army dimly perceived that an opportunity had been lost, and two divisional commanders became both the necessary victims of Joffre's drive to eradicate sub–standard performers and also sacrifices at the altar of Roques's ambition. But the scale of the lost opportunity could only come to light from a comparative analysis of the German side. At Neufchâteau the orientation of the opposing forces was as important as the numbers and quality of troops, and the open right (westerly) flank of the German 21 RID at Nevraumont was the key to carrying out an operational manoeuvre, which Roques and his men missed.

Similarly at Maissin, there is no record at all that General Eydoux and his men appreciated at the time or afterwards what an opportunity they had missed. The vast gap in width and depth which extended beyond the final rifleman on the German 117 IR's right wing offered at the tactical level the opportunity for 21 DI to overlap and overwhelm its opponent's flank with superior numbers;

General Eydoux's failure to make proper use of his corps cavalry regiment to discover the gap was reprehensible. At the operational level there was the prospect of de Langle de Cary pushing his cavalry corps through the gap, followed by the infantry of 9 CA, on a march to the north to threaten 8 AK and von Hausen's Third Army. At Maissin above all the other encounter battles, the poor quality of French communications – both technically and in terms of lack of disciplined feedback – proved to be one of the decisive factors which robbed France of her opportunity.

The Germans were in no doubt as to the potential consequences of a successful French attack. Commenting on the surprise and shock experienced by Duke Albrecht when he received news of de Langle's advance, it has been noted in the German official history: 'Now the priority task for Fourth Army was the protection of the left flank of Third Army, and only when this was guaranteed could Third Army cross the Maas [Meuse] in order to seek to bring about the decisive action as part of the Right Wing of the Armies'.[3] After the battle, when Duke Albrecht's success in rebuffing de Langle became clear, 'the serious crisis which had threatened not only the [Fourth] Army but also the whole front of the German wheeling Right Wing was seen to have been favourably overcome... somewhat later news came in from Third Army that it would assault across the Meuse on 23 August'.[4] There can be no clearer indication of the operational potential of a French victory than this admission that von Hausen's crossing of the Meuse on 23 August might have been delayed. It is ironic that the French did not even know what an opportunity they had missed.

The analysis of the other battles on Fourth Army front is important because it shows how in the crucible of war, the relative impact of different events influences the overall course of the operation. The overwhelming (and arguably unnecessary) tactical defeat of the French 33 DI in the Forest of Luchy north of Bertrix had knock–on effects which swamped any appreciation of the potential for success delivered at Neufchâteau and Maissin. The French disaster at Bertrix adversely affected the whole of 17 CA almost immediately and news of the defeat spread rapidly to the units either side; the precipitate retreat of 17 CA was the key event which wrested the last vestiges of operational control from de Langle de Cary and made an overall French withdrawal inevitable. Together with the disaster at Rossignol it focussed French command attention away from its lost opportunities.

Rossignol was significant at the time not only because of the casualties but also because of the psychological impact of the decimation of France's supposedly elite colonial corps. Operationally it had a huge impact on de Langle's plan which was predicated upon CAC getting safely through the forests onto the more open ground north of Neufchâteau. With hindsight this is important because of the light it shines on weaknesses in French corps and divisional command and control and because of the conclusions which can be drawn from the failure of Gerard's 2 CA to even attempt to fulfil its mission.

This study has shown that French Fourth Army had two clear opportunities to achieve both tactical and operational victory in the Ardennes on 22 August; but that their commanders were not up to the task of achieving tactical success and were incapable of recognising operational manoeuvre opportunities. These events reinforce our understanding of why Joffre felt compelled to remove so many of his brigade, divisional and corps commanders in the first weeks of the war.

In comparing the detailed action in the Battle of the Ardennes against official doctrine and regulations, reasons have been found to explain why the French Third and Fourth Armies failed at both operational and tactical levels and why, conversely, the German Fourth and Fifth Armies succeeded. The disparity between doctrine and performance on the French side can be traced to

3   *Weltkrieg 1*, p.316.
4   *Weltkrieg 1*, pp.333–335.

weaknesses in pre-war preparation, especially in training.

Before the war the German army was given the resources needed to pursue a long–term programme of continuous improvement of her military machine, and she had the political and popular will to devote the resources necessary over the long–term to support the military's needs. She also used her greater resources during periods of medium–term armaments growth to improve the *matériel* of her forces, so that when the short–term crises came and the arms race became a question of numbers of men, fewer hard choices had to be made between men and machinery. This was the case particularly during the period between the first and second Moroccan crises. Many of the improvements which strengthened the German Army in time for action in August 1914 – the 150mm heavy howitzers, the 105mm field howitzers, the second artillery regiment per regular division, the machine gun companies attached to every regular infantry regiment – started to be delivered from 1905 onwards.

French preparation was virtually the converse of that of the Germans. The French compounded their natural disadvantages of low population and weaker industrial capacity by placing political issues above military ones. They may have had no option, given the volatility of the French political scene and the perceived fragility of the Third Republic, but from a narrow military perspective, the effect was to dilute the energy and focus of the nation away from preparation for war. When France did eventually wake up to the danger, she had left herself too little time to effect the major changes needed. Between 1870 and 1892, France had made significant improvements in the armed forces, and her army at the turn of the century, well–trained, endowed with heavy and light howitzers and with the world's best field gun, was impressive. But the Dreyfus affair and its aftermath led to a decade of military stagnation from which the French army did not fully recover. Most if not all of the individual issues examined in this book, in which the French demonstrated their lack of progress, were rooted in the malaise stemming from the Dreyfus affair and its aftermath.

Between 1905 and 1911, France could have mass–produced the Rimhailo 155mm heavy howitzer, a weapon superior to the German 1902 150mm gun; France could have settled the long debate about adopting a light field howitzer, and mass–produced the Schneider 106.7mm gun built for the Russians in 1907 which instead was subsequently modified into the 105mm Schneider field howitzer of 1913 which first appeared - too late - in the autumn of 1914; or in March 1912, the new Schneider 105mm howitzer produced for Bulgaria and admired by Joffre could have been rushed into service; French field kitchens could have been provided to all units immediately after the comprehensive trials of 1908; camouflage uniforms could have been issued in 1911 after the trials of the *réséda* coloured kit. In all these instances it was bureaucracy, indecision, departmental in–fighting and political interference as much as issues of funding which prevented the French from at least narrowing the gap between them and their future adversary.

This study has shown that doctrine was not the significant issue that it has generally been taken to be. In fact, despite differences in detail, the two sides' tactical doctrines were very similar; the evidence presented shows that, in the Ardennes at least, the key difference was that the two German armies performed in a manner reflecting the doctrine they had been taught but the French did not.

At the tactical level there is no evidence of a French doctrine of *offensive à outrance*: rather the predominant impression of French performance in the Ardennes is one of slow and ponderous deployment, slack security and caution under fire. There is, however, at least one instance (at Maissin) where the unofficial 'cult of the offensive' might be seen as the cause of a rash and costly (and unauthorised) infantry attack. But France's operational and strategic doctrines have been shown to have been in a state of flux, caught when war broke out between the 1895 Regulations and those recently issued in October and December 1913. The confusion caused by this change of doctrine was compounded by confusion within the French officer corps about the difference between operational and tactical levels.

On the German side, tactical doctrine was as offensively–minded as the French; everywhere across the Ardennes front units sought to press forward using fire and movement, even when engaged in a defensive mission. But it is equally clear that German doctrine concerning combined–arms cooperation was put into practice very effectively and enabled them to achieve fire superiority on several key battlefields. So too, German doctrine on the use of temporary field fortifications lessened the impact of French fire. But the German infantry still suffered high casualties as a result of their aggressive fire and movement tactics – at Neufchâteau in particular losses were heavier than the French; German casualties were a key factor in the failure to aggressively follow up on 23 August the victories won the day before.

While doctrine can be shown to have been a less important issue than has hitherto been thought, then training – or on the French side, lack of training – appears to be much more important. The evidence from the battles combines with the comparative analysis of pre–war preparations to show Germany's advantage at every level. Facilities, funds, choice of conscript, quality and number of officers and NCOs, the amount of field exercise, inspection, feedback – in all these it has been shown that Germany had the advantage and that this worked itself out in Germany's favour during the fighting.

On the question of whether particular items of equipment gave a decisive advantage in battle, the overall conclusion is that these were much less important to the result than has previously been thought. German heavy artillery, while contributing to the rout of 5 CA at Longwy, was otherwise only a minor factor; French heavy artillery was present in the field under certain corps's control, but doctrine and training in its use were deficient, and this important asset remained unused. Field howitzers do not figure as key weapons, whereas surprisingly massed German field–guns have been shown to have been important at Maissin–Anloy, Neufchâteau, Bertrix, Rossignol, Virton and Ethe. It was speed of deployment and firing first rather than precision accuracy which gave German gunners their initial advantage. However, at those same places, massed French field–guns, while invariably slower to enter action, were also more effective than has been recognised; although poor combined–arms cooperation did lessen their contribution.

The legend of pre–prepared German trenches, machine guns and wire in ambush positions has been shown to be just that: legend. Testimony from contemporary French witnesses such as Lieutenant–Colonel Vitart at Rossignol suggests that this legend has its roots on the battlefield, where French soldiers made false deductions from the speed and efficiency with which German infantry dug temporary field fortifications during the fire–fight.[5]

Some of the smaller equipment issues illuminate differences between French and German efficiency in preparation. The absence of French field kitchens is a case study in bureaucratic inefficiency, while the infamous issue of *les pantaloons rouges* (red trousers) evidences how political interference limited the ability of the army to determine its future even in the smallest detail.

Of all the issues examined above which led to a disparity between French and German performance on the battlefield in August 1914, three in particular stand out: the French Three Year law passed in 1913; the issue of large training camps; and the importance of an inspection regime. The French

5   Moreau, *Rossignol*, p.61.

politicians' decision not to retain the fully–trained conscripts of the class of 1910 for an extra year but to call up the twenty–year–olds of the class of 1913 meant that nearly two–thirds of the men in each regular unit that went into battle on 22 August 1914 were young untrained recruits. The French failure to fund and build sufficient large training camps meant that the opportunities for general officers to exercise large units of brigade–size and over, and practice their operational and tactical skills including combined–arms, were few and far between. General André's cancellation of the inspection regime in 1905 removed a key component of France's quality control and improvement process, making it impossible to impose standard practice upon trainers and trainees or to increase the overall standard. In 1911, with Joffre's promotion to 'generalissimo', steps were taken to rectify the problems with training facilities and with inspection, but there was insufficient time for the changes to take effect before war broke out. In Germany, the decisions taken regarding all three of these key issues during the period 1894–1914 led to a significant long–term advantage the results of which were shown on the battlefield.

The encounter battles of 22 August 1914 which together constitute the Battle of the Ardennes have been shown to have been significant events in the opening stages of the war. Germany took risks in the way it chose to link Fifth Army and the *Moselstellung* with Third Army and the Meuse; and with Joffre's achievement of strategic and operational surprise in the central Ardennes, those risks looked for a time to have been foolhardy. The potential for disruption of the German timetable for the advance of the *Schwenkungsflügel* has been clearly demonstrated, whether the French knew it at the time or not. A tactical victory on 22 August at Maissin, Anloy or at Neufchâteau, driving the Germans early from the battlefield, might arguably have revealed to de Langle the possibility of several fruitful operational manoeuvres during the following days, especially if better application of the doctrine of *sûreté* by 17 CA had mitigated the harmful effect of the German attack at Bertrix. And judging by German testimony, a further French advance on 23 August would probably have prevented von Hausen's Third Army from crossing the Meuse. Beyond that one enters the realm of speculation; it is enough to prove that the opportunity was there, and to demonstrate why the French, through poor operational and tactical capability, were not capable of seizing it.

On 23 August, Joffre's attention was drawn to events in Belgium west of the river Meuse, which was from then on to become the main theatre of operations. He had tried, and failed, to get de Langle and Ruffey to continue their offensive; instead he had to settle for a stout defence of his own centre while he developed his plans for a counter–attack on his left. But even in defeat, de Langle and Ruffey achieved one important result: their armies withdrew bloodied but unbroken, and lived to fight another day. Despite the large numbers of casualties on the French side on 22 August – 27,000 killed according to Contamine – the Germans had not achieved a decisive result. Schlieffen might have called it an ordinary victory. Brochin's 5 CA, for example, was routed at Longwy and in running suffered far fewer casualties than did CAC which stood firm at Rossignol, was enveloped and decimated. Once reformed, under new leadership and with replacements from arguably better–trained reservists, 5 CA was able to join the defence of the new French line within twenty–four hours. Within CAC, the casualties were almost exclusively incurred by 3 DIC, and the defensive line on 23 August was built around 2 DIC and the survivors. On 23 August, the French defence was supported by the heavy artillery which had lain idle the day before; the six reserve divisions of Maunoury's Army of Lorraine (built around Third Group of reserve divisions and endowed with substantial heavy artillery considered too immobile to join the Ardennes offensive) formed a strong barrier along the Meuse heights south–east of Verdun, enabling Ruffey's Third Army to link with them in the new defensive line. Joffre was even able to move Maunoury himself and some of his troops to join the build–up around Paris. The French losses on 22 August came from regular divisions which contained two classes of raw recruits; their replacements, and the men of the reserve divisions were, fortunately for France, probably more experienced. And the French learned their lessons fast.

On the German side, the failure of Duke Albrecht to organise a swift and decisive follow–up to his tactical success was due to the heavy casualties incurred on 22 August, and the German losses were from the most recently and best trained troops. 18 AK in particular was unable to march until after midday on 23 August, enabling de Langle's divisions to break contact and giving them time to regroup. Crown Prince William had been forbidden to cross the line of the Chiers–Crusnes rivers, and when that order was rescinded by OHL, Ruffey too had had time to regroup.

All of these factors combined to improve the overall French position, despite the setbacks and tactical defeats on 22 August. German success in the Ardennes was limited to having avoided defeat; they were not able to capitalise on that success, and, with the French defensive line intact, with the French advantage of henceforth being the defender in the Ardennes, supported by heavy artillery and with the infantry encouraged to dig defensive works, there was less pressure on Joffre on that part of his front. He was able to devote his energies to organising his successful counter–attack on the Marne.

The central conclusion of this book is that, as Contamine suggested in *La Revanche*, poor French execution arising from inadequate pre–war military training was the main cause of French failure and German success in the Ardennes. It is therefore particularly surprising that only fourteen days later Joffre achieved victory on the Marne. This apparent dichotomy requires some brief explanation.

At the strategic level, the campaign of the Marne exhibited several significant differences from the Ardennes. Thanks to Joffre's use of railways and interior lines, transferring units from his right to left wing, the Anglo-French forces outnumbered the Germans by 41 infantry and 8½ cavalry divisions to 23½ and 5 divisions across the chosen front.[6] And the French units had been brought up to strength by reservists from the depots, whereas German losses on the long march and in battle meant that, for example, in von Kluck's I Army 'most corps were down to half of their full strength by early September'.[7] The long German supply lines, stretching back to Namur and even Liège, caused grave difficulties; the troops were exhausted by three weeks of constant marching and fighting. Many French troops were relatively fresh, brought up by train, and those from the depots were reservists of the older classes, all of whom had received their full two year's training, rather than the twenty– and twenty–one year olds whose training had been measured in months. Even those who had taken part in the great retreat were now more experienced, and reinvigorated by the prospect of attacking at last.[8] In the more open terrain east of Paris, and with better communications, Joffre exerted close personal control over his army commanders, in contrast to the remote and out of touch von Moltke, who to a great extent allowed his individual army commanders to act as they saw fit.[9] Moltke's telecommunications network linking him to his two key army commanders was fragile;[10] and those two commanders were lax in their reporting.[11]

In fact, and this leads to a generic point regarding the differences in performance on the Marne compared to the Ardennes, many of the faults and weaknesses observed on the French

6   Tyng, *Campaign of the Marne*, p.189; Herwig, op. cit., pp.219, 231, 244.
7   Herwig, op. cit., p.219.
8   Doughty, *Pyrrhic Victory*, p.82.
9   Tyng, op. cit., pp.267–269; Herwig, op. cit., pp.220–221.
10   Herwig, op. cit., p.246.
11   Herwig, op. cit., p.220.

side at strategic and operational levels in the Ardennes can be observed on the German side on the Marne. For example, allied operational use of their air reconnaissance units improved rapidly and dramatically in early September 1914, not least perhaps because their reports were now believed and used.[12] German movements were observed, and operational plans laid as a result. In the Ardennes, the twenty-kilometre gap in the centre of the German line at Neufchâteau went unobserved, and an opportunity was lost. On the Marne, the fifty-kilometre gap between von Kluck and von Bulow was found, and exploited.[13] German air reconnaissance, so much better than the French at the tactical level in the Ardennes, was now found wanting. The very strength offered by aeroplanes under corps commander's control now became a weakness, as reconnaissance concentrated on what was directly in front of each corps, rather than on the wider operational vista. Von Kluck inexplicably 'neglected what seemed in retrospect rudimentary precautions, for he caused no serious aerial reconnaissances to be made of the region of Paris';[14] and when the aircraft of the one squadron under his direct control reported French troops marching north, the intelligence was dismissed as being only French rear guards.[15]

From the very beginning of the war, Joffre had been improving the quality of his senior commanders by ruthlessly weeding out the old, weak and inefficient.[16] On the Marne, his key army commanders were the excellent Maunoury, Franchet d'Esperey and Foch rather than the average to poor Lanrezac, de Langle de Cary and Ruffey.[17] Similar changes had taken place for the better at corps and divisional levels. The opposite is true on the German side: where Duke Albrecht had fought an excellent battle in the Ardennes on 22 August, co–operating well with Crown Prince William, von Kluck and von Bülow were seemingly at odds with each other; and von Hausen, deciding to rest his men on 5 September, 'lost a splendid opportunity to exploit a twenty–five–kilometre gap that had developed between Foch's Ninth Army and Langle de Cary's Fourth Army'.[18] So the French performed comparatively better at the strategic and operational levels on the Marne. However it was not necessarily the case that all French tactical weaknesses were eliminated overnight. Some gradual improvements can be noted; for example an innovative night bombardment on 7–8 September led to the capture – 'brilliant in tactical execution' – of the key village of Marchais–en–Brie, which unhinged the German defence on the Ourcq.[19] But there were still a great many poor French tactical performances: on 5 September a French reserve cavalry brigade scouting ahead of Maunoury's advance failed to locate Gronou's corps whose artillery then disrupted a marching column of 14 DI.[20] The opposing German cavalry, Otto von Garnier's 4 KD, had only 1200 horsemen left, but still kept up vigilant patrols and detected Maunoury's columns marching on the Ourcq. Also on 5 September Gronau's 4 RAK fought and won an important tactical encounter against superior numbers.[21] But fresh French troops were brought up to attack again on the following day; in open battle with deep reserves, tactical failure on the Marne was not as significant as it had been in the Ardennes. So again, on 7 September yet another fresh unit (63 RID) was thrown into this engagement and, using massed infantry charges, failed. Only a brilliant

12 Goya, *La chair et l'acier*, pp.195–196; Tyng, op. cit., p.211; Herwig, op. cit., p.253; Doughty, op. cit., pp.85–86 and p.93.
13 Tyng, op. cit., pp.211–220; Herwig, op. cit., p.254.
14 Tyng, op. cit., p.207.
15 Herwig, op. cit., pp. 223–224.
16 Herwig, op. cit., p.195.
17 See: Doughty, op. cit., p.85.
18 Tyng, op. cit., pp.231–243; Herwig, op. cit., p.237.
19 Tyng, op. cit., p.251.
20 Herwig, op. cit., p.241.
21 Tyng, op. cit., pp.226–230.

and bold intervention by Colonel Robert Nivelle's artillery regiment, galloping into the firing line and shooting over open sights, saved another rout.[22] On 8 September, Eydoux's 11 CA (now part of Foch's Detachment) was routed by von Hausen's Saxons - 'one French artillery battery after another fled' – but unlike in the Ardennes, reserves were available to come up to shore up the line.[23]

These examples show that the tactical advantage held by the Germans during the Ardennes encounters generally continued into the Marne campaign. But on the one hand it was outweighed by French operational advantages and superior forces and on the other hand, an accumulation of small random events – 'this tremendous friction, which cannot, as in mechanics, be reduced to a few points, is everywhere in contact with chance, and brings about effects that cannot be measured'[24] – now seemed to start to work in France's favour. In the Ardennes, German field guns dragged into the firing line by individual initiative brought about favourable results on several occasions; on the Marne, Nivelle's guns performed a similar feat. In the Ardennes, a French divisional commander at Bellefontaine and a regimental commander at Maissin decided that their men were too tired to obey orders, with detrimental results; on the Marne, German Army commander von Hausen did the same thing and lost an opportunity to beat Foch. In the Ardennes, vital intelligence was ignored or misinterpreted by some French commanders; on the Marne it was the Germans who ignored or misinterpreted reported French movements. In the Ardennes, de Langle de Cary's corps commanders failed to communicate with army HQ and with each other; on the Marne, a similar fault lay at the door of von Kluck and von Bülow.

Tactical improvement within French units had been under way since 16 August, when Joffre issued the first of several directives (a second came out on 24 August) to correct specific faults.[25] But the issue of centralised directives – 'it is important ... to await the support of the artillery and to stop the troops from exposing themselves too early to enemy fire'[26] – can only achieve so much; equally important was the spontaneous low-level learning from mistakes, a process identified and described by Goya as 'a capacity within the French army for adapting which, after the bloody reverses since the beginning of the war, wrested a decisive success on the Marne.' This adaptability manifested itself not just in pressure upwards for change based on experience, but also on the lateral diffusion of best practice between peers.[27]

In short, the beginnings of tactical improvement within French units can be seen to have started even in the short span of time between the Ardennes battles and the Marne, but not enough either to account for the French success or to challenge the conclusion that poor French training lay at the heart of their poor tactical performances on 22 August 1914. Success on the Marne was due primarily to operational improvements and to superior resources and conditions on the French side.

This necessarily brief comparison between French failure in the Ardennes and success on the Marne only fourteen days later highlights some of the key conclusions arrived at in this book. Joffre achieved strategic surprise in the Ardennes, only to have two fleeting chances for operational manoeuvre denied him by poor performance of certain corps and divisional commanders. One can only speculate what might have happened if Foch had commanded 12 CA and not 20 CA, or

22   Herwig, op. cit., p.242, 247.
23   Herwig., pp.257–260.
24   Clausewitz, On War, p.139.
25   Goya, La Chair et l'Acier, p.234.
26   AFGG I, Annex 352: GQG le 16 août 14: Communication secrète aux commandants d'armée. (Suite à la communication du 11 août 1914).
27   Goya, op. cit., p.197.

Franchet d'Esperey 11 CA rather than 1 CA. Joffre's recognition of the need to improve the quality of his senior commanders was, like his identification of key generic tactical errors, evident from the very first days of his appointment to supreme command. He took immediate corrective action on both counts, but there was insufficient time for improvement before the Ardennes offensive was launched.

The operational study and battle analysis in this book has shown that the hitherto relatively unknown Battle of the Ardennes deserves greater attention from historians. The two French missed opportunities will forever testify to the unfortunate necessity for the French army of August 1914 to learn its lessons in action rather than on the training ground. And the Germans, relying upon the tactical superiority of its troops, would continue to the Marne before their own operational and strategic weaknesses would be revealed.

Appendix

Orders of Battle

Note 1:   Sources are: France = AFGG Tome I, Volume 1, Appendice III, pp.535–585 and Tome X, vols I & II; Germany = Weltkrieg 1, pp.664–687 and Cron, op. cit., pp.299–329.

Note 2:   On the French side, generals who were relieved of their post (*limogés*) before 31 August 1914, that is as an immediate consequence of the battles in the Ardennes and their aftermath, are shown with their successors.

A: Army Operations

French 3 Army

Commander:	General Ruffey (then General Sarrail from 30 August)
Chief of Staff:	General Grossetti (then Colonel Lebouc from 30 August)
4 Corps	General Boelle
7 DI	General de Trentinian
8 DI	General de Lartigue
5 Corps	General Brochin (then General Micheler from 23 August)
9 DI	General Martin
10 DI	General Auger (then General Charles Roques from 26 August)
6 Corps	General Sarrail (promoted to 3 Army on 30 August), succeeded by General Verraux (42 DI)
12 DI	General Souchier
40 DI	General Hache (then General Leconte from 25 August)
42 DI	General Verraux (then General Grossetti from 30 August)
3 GDR	General Paul-Durand
54 DR	General Chailley
55 DR	General Leguay
56 DR	General Micheler (then General de Dartein from 23 August)
7 DC	General Gillain (then General d'Urbal from 25 August)

*   *   *

French 4 Army

Commander:	General de Langle de Cary
Chief of Staff:	General Maistre
11 CA	General Eydoux
21 DI	General Radiguet
22 DI	General Pambet
12 CA	General Pierre Roques
23 DI	General Leblond (then General Bapst from 22 August)
24 DI	General du Garreau de la Méchenie (then General Deffontaines from 22 August, then General Descoings from 26 August)
17 CA	General Poline (then General J.B.Dumas from 22 August)
33 DI	General de Villemejane (then General Guillaumont from 31 August)
34 DI	General Alby
CAC	General Lefèvre
2 DIC	General Leblois
3 DIC	General Raffenel (killed 22 August, succeeded by General Leblond then permanently by General Goullet on 12 September)
5 Colonial Brigade	General Goullet
Provisional Cavalry Corps	(General Abonneau)
4 DC	General Abonneau
9 DC	General de l'Éspée

* * *

German 4 Army

Commander:	Generaloberst Archduke Albrecht von Württemberg
Chief of Staff	Generalleutnant Freiherr von Luttwitz
6 AK	General von Pritzelwitz
11 ID	Generalleutnant von Webern
12 ID	Generalleutnant de Beaulieu [sic]
8 AK	Generalleutnant von Schepe und Weidenbach
15 ID	Generalleutnant Riemann
16 ID	Generalleutnant Fuchs
18 AK	General von Schenk
21 ID	Generalmajor von Oven
25 ID	Generalmajor Kuhne
8 RAK	General von und zu Egloffstein
15 RID	Generalleutnant von Kurowski
16 RID	Generalleutnant Mootz
18 RAK	Generalleutnant von Steuben
21 RID	Generalleutnant von Rampacher
25 RID	Generalleutnant Torgany

* * *

German 5 Army

Commander:	Generalmajor Crown Prince Wilhelm of Prussia, Crown Prince of Germany
Chief of Staff:	Generalleutnant von Knobelsdorf
5 AK	General von Strantz
9 ID	Generalleutnant von Below
10 ID	Generalleutnant Kosch
13 AK	General von Fabeck
26 ID	Generalleutnant Wilhelm Herzog von Urach
27 ID	Generalleutnant Graf von pfeil und Klein-Ellguth
16 AK	General von Mudra
33 ID	Generalleutnant Reitzenstein
34 ID	Generalleutnant von Heinemann
5 RAK	General von Gundell
9 RID	Generalleutnant von Suretzky-Sornitz
10 RID	Generalleutnant von Wartenberg
6 RAK	General von Gossler
11 RID	Generalmajor Suren
12 RID	Generalleutnant von Lutwitz
4 HKK	Generalleutnant von Hollen
3 KD	Generalmajor von Unger
6 KD	Generalleutnant Graf von Schmettow

*   *   *   *   *   *   *

B: Lost Opportunities

Neufchâteau

France

12 CA	General Roques
Corps troops:	300 RI, 326 RI; 21 Chasseurs; 52 RAC
23 DI	General Leblond
45 Brigade	General Masnou
63 RI	
78 RI	
46 Brigade	Colonel Chéré
107 RI	
138 RI	
A.D.23: 21 RAC	
5° escadron, 21 chasseurs	

*

24 DI   General du Garreau de la Méchenie

    47 Brigade   Colonel Descoings

        50 RI

        108 RI

    48 Brigade   General Sorin

        100 RI

        126 RI

    A.D.24:   34 RAC

    6° escadron, 21 chasseurs

*

5 Colonial Brigade   General Goullet

    21 RIC   Colonel Aubé

    23 RIC   Colonel Nèple

    3 RACC

    3 Chasseurs d'Afrique

*   *   *

Germany

21 RID   Generalleutnant von Rampacher

    41 Reserve Infantry Brigade   Generalleutnant von Mey

        80 RIR

        87 RIR* [no mgs]

    42 Reserve Infantry Brigade   Generalleutnant von Quidtman

        81 RIR* [no mgs]

        88 RIR

    21 Reserve Artillery Regiment

    7 Reserve Dragoon Regiment

25 RID   Generalleutnant Torgany

    49 Reserve Infantry Brigade   Oberst von Helldorf

        116 RIR

        118 RIR*[no mgs]

    50 Reserve Infantry Brigade   Oberst von Bassewitz

        168 IR (active unit)

        83 RIR

    25 Reserve Field Artillery Brigade

    4 Reserve Dragoon Regiment

*   *   *

Maissin-Anloy

France

11 CA	General Eydoux

Corps troops: 293 RI, 337 RI, 28 RAC, 2 Chasseurs

21 DI	General Radiguet
41 Brigade	Colonel de Teyssière
64 RI	
65 RI	
42 Brigade	Colonel Laméy
93 RI	
137 RI	
A.D.21	Colonel Morizot
51 RAC	

5 squadron, 2 Chasseurs

*

22 DI	General Pambert
43 Brigade	General Duroisel
62 RI	
116 RI	
44 Brigade	General Chaplain
19 RI	
118 RI	
A.D.22	Colonel Ely
35 RAC	

6 squadron, 2 Chasseurs

*

17 CA (elements)	General Poline
34 DI	General Alby
67 Brigade	General Dupuis
14 RI	
83 RI	
68 Brigade	General Berteaux
59 RI	
88 RI	
A.D.34	Colonel Delmotte
23 RAC	

6 squadron, 9 Chasseurs

*   *   *

Germany

25 ID   General Kühne

    49 Brigade   Generalmajor von Uthmann

        115 Leib Guard IR

        116 IR

    50 Brigade   Generalmajor Freiherr von Spesshardt

        117 Leib IR

        118 IR

    25 Field Artillery Brigade

        25 FAR

        61 FAR

    6 Dragoon Regiment

* * * * * * *

C: Other Battles

Bertrix

France

33 DI   General de Villemejane

    65 Brigade   Colonel Huc

        7 RI

        9 RI

    66 Brigade   General Fraisse

        11 RI

        20 RI

    A.D.33   Colonel Paloque

        18 RAC

    5 squadron, 9 Chasseurs

* * *

Germany

21 ID   Generalmajor von Oven

    41 Brigade   Generalmajor von Esch

        87 IR

        88 IR

    42 Brigade   Generalmajor von Elster

        80 Füs.R

        81 IR

    21 Feldartillerie Brigade Generalmajor von Scherbening

        27 FAR

        63 FAR

(attached corps troops)

        Fussartillerie I/3

        Feld–Flieger Abteilung 27

* * *

Rossignol

France

CAC   General Lefèvre

    Corps troops (excluding 5 Colonial Brigade): 3 RACC, 3 Chasseurs d'Afrique

2 DIC   General Leblois

    4 Colonial Brigade   General Boudonnet

        4 RIC

        8 RIC

    6 Colonial Brigade   General Caudrelier

        22 RIC

        24 RIC

    1 RACC

    5 squadron, 6 Dragoons

*

3 DIC   General Raffenel

    Commandant Moreau

    1 Colonial Brigade   General Montignault

        1 RIC

        2 RIC

    3 Colonial Brigade   General Rondony

        3 RIC

        7 RIC

    2 RACC

    6 squadron, 6 Dragoons

*   *   *

Germany

6 AK   General von Pritzelwitz

    Corps troops: Fussartillerie III/6. Feld–Flieger Abtl. 13

11 ID   Generalleutnant von Webern

    21 Brigade   Generalmajor von Drabich–Waechter

        10 Gren. R.

        38 IR

    22 Brigade   Oberst Sendel

        11 Gren. R.

        51 IR

    12 Feldartillerie Brigade   Generalmajor von Bischoffshausen

        6 FAR

        42 FAR

    11 Jaeger zu pferd

*

12 ID	Generalleutnant de Beaulieu
24 Brigade	Generalmajor von der Hende
23 IR	
62 IR	
78 Brigade	Generalmajor Vollbrecht
63 IR	
157 IR	
12 Feldartillerie Brigade	Generalmajor Zietlow
21 FAR	
57 FAR	
2 Uhlans	

*   *   *   *   *   *   *

Bibliography

A. Archival Sources

1. *Ministère de la Défense/Etat-Major de l'Armée de Terre/ Service Historique*, Vincennes
Direction du Service de Santé; Étude de Statistique Chirurgicale: Guerre de 1914-1918:

> *Les Blessées Hospitalisés à l'intérieur du Territoire, Tome Premier* (Imprimerie Nationale, Paris,1924)

École Supérieure de Guerre:

> Cours d'Histoire de La Guerre de 1914-1918 par le Colonel Duffour, Tome 1 (1923), Ch.II La Bataille des Frontières

Les Archives de la Guerre Série N 1872-1919:

Inventaire Sommaire	pp.98-213
1N08	*Procès-Verbaux du CSG, decèmbre 1897-fèvrier 1902*
1N011	Miscellanoeus papers of *Conseil Supérieur de la Guerre*, 1905-1913
1N013-15	Inspections, 1888-1914
1N016	*École supérieure de la Guerre: Fayolle's cours d'artillerie 1904: Notonsen passant que les obus à grande capacité, lances par des canons de gros calibre, ne donnèrent pas d'avantage.*
6N042	*Fonds Gallieni: Observations sur les Manoeuvres en 1911*
6N043	*Fonds Gallieni: Manoeuvres d'armée de 1912*
7N033	*Lois Militaires, 1872-1914*
7N050	Miscellaneous notes on the use of artillery, 1913-1914
7N053	Parliamentary questions from Charles Humbert, Senator for the Meuse.
7N108	Miscellaneous staff papers on heavy artillery, June 1911-June 1912
7N109	Miscellaneous staff papers on officer & NCO shortages, April 1912
7N1927	*Manoeuvres de Picardie en 1910*
7N1928	*Dossiers des Manoeuvres d'Ouest en 1912*
7N1929	*Manoeuvres du Sud-ouest en 1913*
7N1930	*Instruction sur les exercices des Grandes Unités en 1914*
19N656	*Renseignements divers du 2e Bureau de 4e Armée*
19N674	*4e Armée: Ordres Généraux 1914*
19N753	*4e Armée: Comptes rendus*
22N207	*Ordres, Opérations, Pertes, 5e CA*

22N213	*État des Pertes du 5e CA*
22N788	Miscellaneous papers of 1Bureau, 12 CA
22N795	*Etat des Pertes du 12e CA*
22N816	Papers of 1 Bureau, 12 CA
22N816	Papers of 3 (Operations) Bureau, 12 CA
22N817	Notes & Orders of 3 (Operations) Bureau, 12 CA
24N153	*EM de la 9e Division, Contrôle des Pertes*
24N187	Miscellanoeus papers of 10 DI:
	Sorties du 8 août 1914 au 17 janvier 1915
24N420	21 DI Orders 1914
24N428	Miscellaneous documents of 3rd Bureau, 22 DI
24N468	Miscellanoeus papers of 3e Bureau, 24e DI
24N3009-3010	Miscellanoeus papers of 5 Colonial Brigade
25N083	*Etat des Pertes du 100e RI*
25N118	*Etat des Pertes du 126e RI*
25N123	Miscellaneous papers of 131 RI
25N593	Miscellaneous papers of *22e Chasseurs à Cheval*
26N033	*Journal de Marche et des Opérations* (JMO) *4e Armée*
26N118	JMO 6 CA
26N136	JMO12 CA
26N285	JMO 9 DI
26N287	JMO 10 DI
26N289	JMO 11 DI
26N290	JMO 12 DI
26N302	JMO 21 DI
26N307	JMO 23 DI
26N309	JMO24 DI
26N324	JMO 33 DI
26N326	JMO 34 DI
26N342	JMO 42 DI
26N509	JMO 47 Brigade
26N509	JMO 48 Brigade Vol 1: 8/8/14-23/9/15
26N509	JMO 49 Brigade
26N586	JMO 14 RI
26N640	JMO 50 RI
26N650	JMO 59 RI
26N665	JMO 83 RI
26N685	*Dossier de la Service de Santé du 126e RI:* (JMO is missing)
26N673	JMO 100 RI
26N678	JMO 108 RI
26N889	JMO *9e Chasseurs à cheval*

***Les Armées Françaises d'Outre-mer* (Histoire Militaire de Madagascar, Imprimérie Nationale, Paris, 1931), pp.129-159:**

Opérations de la colonne légèreet prise de Tananarive, 14-30 Septembre 1895

Annuaire Officiel de l'armée de France pour l'année... (Berger-Levrault, Paris):

1887-1912:	Entries for:	_Roques, P.A._
		Joffre, J.J.C.
1912:	Entries for:	_Leblond, C.G._

           Bapst, E.A.
           Masnou, J.G.A.
           Garreau de la Mèchenie,
           Deffontaines
           Descoings
           Peslin, P.
           Martin, E.
           Auger, M.A
           Roques, C.
           Brochin,
           Micheler, F.

2. Bundesarchiv, Militärarchiv, Freiburg-im-Breisgau

PH2-/024	Miscellanoeus papers on Field Artillery Regulations, 1906
PH3 -/251	4&5 Army organisations 1914
PH3-/350	Reports and miscellanoeus papers on German manoeuvres 1912-1914
PH3-/530	OHL _Denkschrift_ 1913 on French and German army strength in peace and war
PH3-/538	Intelligence report on a Reconnaissance of the Semoy river, August 1912
PH3-/539	Intelligence notes on French mobilisation
PH3-/629	Intelligence Briefings on the French fortress at Longwy, 1907-1914
PH3-/641	Standing Orders for Army General Staff Officers, HKK & Cavalry Divisions
PH3-/650	Miscellaneous documents pertaining to German manoeuvres 1912-1914
PH3-/651	Inspections, January-July 1914
PH3-/655	German reports on French manoeuvres, 1908-11
PH3-/657	German reports on French military developments 1911-1912
PH5-II/238 & 239	4 Army, _Aufmarsch West_
PH5-II/240	4 Army Rail & March Tables
PH5-II/241	Intelligence about Belgian & Dutch armies 1914
PH6-I/080	16AK manoeuvres 1910
PH6-I/083	18AK Service Instructions
PH6-I/084	18AK Orders 1-9 August 1914
PH6-I/200	13AK & 18 AK reconnaissance exercises, 1-3 August 1912
PH6-I/210	8AK Staff Orders, 1899
	Report on an 8AK General Staff Ride, 1899
PH6-I/261	16AK, Tactical Exercises 1891

PH6-I/213	8AK miscellaneous papers on mobilisation, August 1914
PH6-I/301	War plans of 6 AK 1914-1918
PH9-I/001	16AK Cavalry Exercises 1902
PH9-I/003	Cavalry Exercises in 13AK's region, August-September 1904
PH10-II/067	5AK 1896 manoeuvres
PH16-/017	War Diary of 8AK's Telephone Group 8, 1914-1915

B. Unit Histories

1. German Infantry

80 IR: *Das Königlich Preussische Füsilier Regt. Nr 80 im Weltkriege 1914-18, Teil 1* (Oldenburg, Berlin, 1925)

81 IR: *Das Königlich Preussische Infanterie Regt. Nr 81 im Weltkriege 1914-8* (Oldenburg, Berlin, 1932)

81 RIR: Generalmajor a D von Jordon, *Das Reserve Infanterie Regiment Nr 81 im Weltkrieg* (Hans Druner, Osnabrück, 1933)

83 RIR: Hauptmann a. D. Wahrenburg, *Reserve Infanterie-Regiment Nr 83* (Oldenburg i. D., Berlin, 1924)

88 IR: Walter Rogge *Das Königlich Preussische 2 Nassauische Infanterie Regt. Nr 88 im Weltkriege 1914-18* (Bernard und Graefe, Berlin, 1936)

114 IR: *Geschichte des 6 Badischen Infanterie-Regiments 'Kaiser Friedrich III' Nr.114 im Weltkrieg 1914 bis 1918* (Sporn, Zeulenroda, 1932)

116 IR: A. Hiss *Infanterie-Regiment Kaiser Wilhelm (2 Grossherzoglich Hessisches) nr.116* (Oldenburg, Stalling, 1924)

117 IR: K. Offenbacher, *Die geschichte des Infanterie-Leibregiments Grossherzogin (3. Grossherzoglich Hessisches) Nr. 117* (Oldenburg, Stalling, 1931)

118 IR: H. Freund, *Geschichte des Infanterie-Regiments Prinz Karl (4.Grossh. Hess) Nr 118 im Weltkrieg* (Fink, Gross-Gerau, 1930)

119 IR: Oberst Freiherr v Semmingen-Guttenberg-Fürfeld, *Das Grenadier-Regiment Königin Olga (1 Württ.) Nr 119 im Weltkrieg 1914-1918* (Ehr. Belser AG, Stuttgart, 1927)

120 IR: Oberst a D. Simon, *Das Infanterie-Regiment 'Kaiser Wilhelm, König von Preussen' (2 Württemb.) Nr 120 im Weltkrieg 1914-1918* (Ehr. Belsersche Verlagsbuchhandlung, Stuttgart, 1922)

125 IR: General Stühmke, *Das Infanterie-Regiment 'Kaiser Friedrich König von Preussen' (7 Württ.) Nr 125 im Weltkrieg 1914-1918* (Ehr. Belser AG, Stuttgart, 1923)

127 IR: Oberstleutnant U. Schwab, *Das neunte württembergische Infanterie-Regiment Nr 127 im Weltkrieg 1914-1918* (Ehr. Belsersche Verlagsbuchhandlung, Stuttgart, 1920)

2. German Field Artillery

10 FAR: H. Wendlandt, *Das 1 hannoversche Bataillon des Niedersächsischen Füssartillerie-Regiments Nr.10* (Gerhard Stalling, Oldenburg, 1922)

13 FAR: Dr H. Pantlen, *Das Württembergische Feldartillerie-Regiment König Karl Nr 13 im Weltkrieg 1914-1918* (Ehr. Belser AG, Stuttgart, 1928)

25 FAR: *Grossherzogliches Artilleriekorps, 1 Grossherzoglich Hessisches Feldartillerie-Regiment Nr 25 im Weltkrieg 1914-1918 [FAR 25]* (Verlag Rolf & Co., Berlin, 1935)

29 FAR: Hauptmann Gerof, *Das 2 Württ. Feldartillerie-Regiment Nr 29 'Prinzregent Luitpold von Bayern' im Weltkrieg 1914-1918* (Ehr. Belsersche Verlagsbuchhandlung, Stuttgart, 1921)

49 FAR: Major E. Zimmerle, *Das 3 Württembergische Feldartillerie-Regiment Nr 49 im Weltkrieg 1914-1918* (Ehr. Belsersche Verlagsbuchhandlung, Stuttgart, 1922)

50 FAR: *3. Badisches Feldartillerie-regiment Nr.50* (Oldenburg, Berlin, 1929)

61 FAR: *Das 2. Grossherzoglich Hessische Feldartillerie Regiment Nr 61 im Weltkrieg 1914/1918* (Stalling, Oldenburg / Berlin, 1927)

63 FAR: H. Hecht, *Das 2 Nass. Feldartillerie-Regiment Nr 63, Frankfurt, im Weltkriege (Erster Teil: Bis zu Sommerschlacht 1916)* (C. Adelmann, Frankfurt a. M., 1924)

65 FAR: H. Neeff, *Das 4 Württ. Feldartillerie-Regiment Nr 65 im Weltkrieg 1914-1918* (Ehr. Belser AG, Stuttgart, 1925)

3. German Foot Artillery

General R. Landauer, *Württembergs Füssartillerie* (Bergers Literar. Büro und Verlangsanstalt, Stuttgart, 1930)

Dr H. Wetzel, *Kriegserlebnisse der 9 Batterie des niedersächsischen Fuss-Artillerie-Regiments Nr 10* (Drück der Union Deutsche Verlagsgesellschaft, Stuttgart, 1921)

E. Pieper, *Der Regimentstab und das II Bataillon (Mörser) des Thür. Fussartillerie-Regiments Nr 18* (Bernhard Sporn, Zeulenroda-Thür., 1930)

M. Schöne, *Das 1 Bataillon des 2 Rgl. Sächs. Fussartillerie-Regiments Nr 9* (Verlag der Buchdruckerei der Wilhelm und Bertha v. Baensch Stiftung, Dresden, 1925)

K. Boëtticher, *Fussartillerie-Bataillon Nr 35 (unter Einschluss der Stammbatterie 6 Batterie des Thüring. Fussartillerie-Regiments Nr 18)* (Gerhard Stalling, Oldenburg, Berlin, 1924)

W. Schmoeckel, *Geschichte des I Bataillons 2 Garde-Fussartillerie-Regiments* (Bernhard Sporn, Zeulenroda (Thüringen), 1931)

R. v. Berendt, *Das 1 Garde-Fussartillerie-Regiment im Weltkrieg* (Gerhard Stalling, Oldenburg/Berlin, 1928)

Das Westfälische Fussartillerie-Regiment Nr 7 im Weltkriege 1914/18 (Gerhard Stalling, Oldenburg, 1932)

K. Hendemann, *Schleswig-Holsteinsches Fussartillerie-Regiment Nr 9* (Gerhard Stalling, Oldenburg/Berlin, 1921)

P. Bansi, *Niedersächsisches Fussartillerie-Regiment Nr 10* (Gerhard Stalling, Oldenburg/Berlin, 1928)

Die 2 Reserve-Batterie des Niedersächsisches Fussartillerie-Regiments Nr 10 (Gerhard Stalling, Oldenburg/Berlin, 1936)

H. Wendlandt, *Das 1 hannoversche Bataillion des Niedersächsischen Fussartillerie-Regiments Nr 10* (Gerhard Stalling, Oldenburg, 1922)

4. German Cavalry

5 Horse Jaeger: P. Creuzinger, *Königlich Preussischen Jaeger Regiments zu pferde nr. 5* (Sporn, Zeulenroda, 1932)

6 Uhlans: Herman Freiherr Hillier von Gaertringen, *Geschichte des Thüringischen Ulanen-Regiments Nr 6 von 1813 bis 1919* (Wilhelm Rolf, Berlin, 1930)

7 Hussars: F.K. von Zitzewitz, *Das Husaren-Regiment 'König Wilhelm I' (1 Rheinisches) Nr.7 vom Jahre 1902 bis zum ende des Krieges 1914-18* (Bernhard Sporn, Zeulenroda [1930])

9 Uhlans: E. Von Etzel, *Geschichte des 2 Pommerschen Ulanen-Regiments Nr 9* (Wilhelm Rolf, Berlin, 1931)

13 Horse Jaeger: W. Guenther, *Geschichte des Jäger-Regiment zu Pferde Nr 13, 1913-1920* (Gerhard Stalling, Oldenburg und Dortmund, 1926)

20 Uhlans: *Bilder aus der Geschichte des Ulanen-Regiments 'König Wilhelm 1' (2 Württ.) Nr 20* (Ehr. Belser AG, Stuttgart, 1934)

5. French Cavalry

2 Chasseurs: *Historique du 2e Régiment de Chasseurs* (Henri Charles-Lavauzelle, Paris, 1920)

6. French Field Artillery

34 RAC: *34° Régiment d'artillerie, Historique du Régiment* (Henri Charles-Lavauzelle, Paris, 1920)

30 RAC: *Historique du 30e Régiment d'Artillerie de Campagne, 1914-1918* (Librarie Chapelot, Paris, n.d.)

21 RAC: *21e Régiment d'artillerie, Historique du P.A.D. 23* (Henri Charles-Lavauzelle, Paris, 1920)

C. Primary Published Material
1. Authors

General Armengaud, *Renseignement Aérien* (Librarie Aéronautique, Paris, 1931)

Von Balck, *Taktische Studien* (Verlag von A. Bath, Berlin, 1911)

General Baquet, *Souvenirs d'un Directeur de l'Artillerie* (Henri Charles-Lavauzelle, Paris, 1921)

General Berthaut, *L'Erreur de 1914* (N.p., Paris, 1919)

Dr. E. Bircher (Oberst und Kommandant der Schweizerischen Infanterie-Brigade 12), *Die Schlacht bei Ethe-Virton am 22. August 1914* (Verlag R. Eisenschmidt, Berlin, 1930)

W. Bloem, *The Advance from Mons, 1914: the experiences of a German infantry officer* (transl. G.C. Wynne, reprinted Helion & Company, Solihull, 2004)

General Boichut, *La Bataille des Frontiers à la 42e Division* (Berger-Levrault, Paris, 1936)

General Boëlle, *Le 4e Corps d'Armée sur l'Ourcq* (Berger-Levrault, Paris, 1924)

H. Bonnal, *L'Art Nouveau en Tactique* (LibraireMilitaire R. Chapelot et Cie., Paris, 1904)

H. Bonnal, *Les Grandes Manoeuvres en 1908* (Elibron Classics, 2005, an unabridged facsimile of the edition published by R. Chapelot & Cie, Paris, 1909)

Colonel Bujac, *Le Général Eydoux et le XIe Corps d'Armée au début de la grande Guerre (Août-Septembre 1914) d'après les Notes du Général* (Nantes, Rue de la Fosse, 1924)

General de Castelli, *Le 8e Corps en Lorraine* (Berger-Levrault, Paris, 1925)

General de Castelli, *Cinq Journées au 8e Corps* (Berger-Levrault, Paris, 1930)

C. von Clausewitz, *On War* (Edited and translated by Michael Howard and Peter Paret, Everyman's Library, London, 1993)

General Cordonnier, *Une Brigade au Feu (Potins de Guerre)* (Henri Charles-Lavauzelle, Paris, 1921)

Capitaine breveté F. Culmann, *L'armée allemande en 1910 et l'armée française d'après le projet de loi des cadres* (Berger-Levrault et Cie., Paris 1908)

L. Dauby, *Jours de Sang, de Larmes et de Gloire. 1914-1918* (A. Gillet, Bertix, 1918)

B. Delabeye, *Avant la Ligne Maginot* (Causse, Graille et Astelnau, Montpellier, 1939)

General Dubail, *Quatre Années de Commandement, Tome 1* (Le Fournier, Paris, 1920)

Captain E. Dupuy, *La Guerre dans les Vosges: 41e division d'infanterie, 1 août 1914 – 16 juin 1916* (Payot, Paris, 1936)

General E. Von Falkenhayn, *General Headquarters 1914-1916* (transl., & publ. Hutchinson & Co., London, 1919)

Maréchal Fayolle, *Cahiers Secrets de la Grande Guerre* (Plon, Paris, 1964)

R. Freiherr von Gleichen-Russwarm [Hauptmann und Leiter der Feldpressestelle des Gr. Haupt-Quartiers] und E. Zuborn [Hauptmann im Grossen Generalstab], *Die Schlacht bei Mons* (Verlag von Gerhard Stalling, Oldenburg, 1919)

Captain Gluck, *Obusiers de Campagne de l'artillerie Lourde* (Librarie Chapelot, Paris, 1913)

Colonel de Grandmaison, *Deux Conférences faites aux officiers de l' État-Major de l'Armée (février 1911)* (Berger-Levrault, Paris, 1911)

Colonel de Grandmaison, *Dressage de l'Infanterie en vue du Combat Offensif* (Berger–Levrault, Paris, 1912)

Sir I. Hamilton, *The Soul and Body of an Army* (Edward Arnold & Co., London, 1921)

J. Joffre, *Mémoires du Maréchal Joffre (1910-1917), Tome 1* (Librarie Plon, Paris, 1932)

H. Kaiser, *Deutsche und französische artillerie in der Schlacht bei Bertrix – 22 August 1914* (Waisenhaus-Buchdruckerie, Hanau, 1937)

General de Langle de Cary, *Souvenirs de Commandement 1914-16* (N.p., Paris, 1935)

General H. Langlois, *Conséquences Tactiques des Progrès de l'armement: Étude sur le terrain* (Henri Charles-Lavauzelle, Paris, 1905)

General Lanrezac, *Le Plan de Campagne Français, et le premier mois de la guerre (2 août – 3 Septembre 1914)* (Payot, Paris, 1920)

General Legrand-Girarde, *Opérations du 21e corps d'Armée (1 août-13 Septembre 1914* (Plon, Paris, 1922)

General Ludendorff, *The General Staff and its Problems, Vol. 1* (transl. F.A. Holt, Publ. Hutchinson & Co., London, 1920)

General Ludendorff, *My War Memories 1914-1918 Volume 1* (Hutchinson & Co., London, 1919)

G. von Mutius, *Die Schlacht bei Longwy* (Verlag von Gerhard Stalling, Oldenburg, 1919)

J. Moreau, *Rossignol, 22 août 1914, Journal du commandant Jean Moreau, chef d'état-major de la 3e Division Coloniale,* (retranscribed and with commentary by Éric Labayle et Jean-Louis Philippart, Anvoi, Parçay-sur-Vienne, 2002)

Commandant breveté Niessel, *Enseignements Tactiques dé coulant de la Guerre Russo-Japonaise* (3e Édition, Henri Charles-Lavauzelle, Paris, 1909)

B.G.O'Rorke, Chaplain to the Forces, *In the Hands of the Enemy* (Longman, Green & Co, London 1916)

General Palat, *Le Combat de Toutes Armes* (Berger-Levrault& Cie., Paris, 1909)

Colonel J. Paloque, *L'Artillerie dans la Bataille* (O. Doin et Fils, Paris, 1912)

General J. Paloque, *1914, Bertrix* (Charles-Lavauzelle & Cie., Paris, 1932)

Commandant de Pardieu, *Étude Critique de la tactiqueet des nouveaux Règlements allemands* (Henri Charles-Lavauzelle, Paris, 1910)

General Pichot-Duclos, *Au GQG de Joffre: Réflexions sur ma vie militaire* (Arthaud, Grenoble, 1947)

J. de Pierrefeu, *French Headquarters 1915-1918* (transl. Major C.J.C. Street, publ. Geoffrey Blas, London, n.d.)

General Pierron, *La Stratégie et la Tactique Allemande au Début du XXe Siècle* (Henri Charles-Lavauzelle, Paris, c. 1905)

General Pupéraux, *La 3me Division Coloniale dans la Grande Guerre* (L. Fournier, Paris, 1919)

Reuters, *The French Official Review of the War* (Constable & Co., London, 1915)

E. Rommel, *Infantry Attacks* (transl. Lt-Colonel Kiddé & publ. US Army War College, Fort Leavenworth, 1937)

Count A. von Schlieffen, *Cannae* (Transl. & publ. US Army War College, Fort Leavenworth, 1931)

J. Simonin, *De Verdun à Mannheim* (Pierre Vitet, Paris, 1917)

Edward Spears, *Liaison 1914* (Cassell, London, 1999)

General de Trentinian, *Ethe: La 7e Division du 4e Corps dans la Bataille des Frontières (10 août au 22 septembre 1914)* (Imprimérie L. Fournier, Paris, 1937)

General V. D'Urbal, *Souvenirs et Anecdotes de Guerre 1914-1916* (Berger-Levrault, Paris, 1939)

Weygand, *Mémoires, Tome 1* (Flammarion, Paris, 1953)

2. Regulations

The Operations of Large Formations (conduite des grandes unite):(translated from the Field Service Regulations of the French Army, dated 28th October, 1913, by the General Staff, War Office and published by HMSO, London, 1914)

Manuel sur le service en campagne de l'infanterie (Librarie Militaire de Berger–Levrault et cie, Paris, 1899)

The Field Service Regulations (Feld Dienstordnung 1900) of the German Army 1900 (translated by Colonel H.S. Brownrigg, Intelligence Dept. at the War Office & published by HMSO, London, 1900) and *The Field Service Regulations of the German Army 1908* (translated by the General Staff, War Office and published by HMSO, London, 1908)

Feld-Befestigungs Vorschrift 1893 (translated and published for the Corps of Royal Engineers by The Royal Engineers Institute, Chatham, 1895)

D. Memoirs and Contemporary Accounts

General Armengaud, *Renseignements Aérien* (Librarie Aéronautique, Paris, 1931)

General Baquet, *Souvenirs d'un directeur de l'artillerie* (Henri Charles–Lavauzelle, Paris, 1921)

Colonel Bujac, *le Général Eydouxet le 11e Corps d'Armée, août – sept 1914* (Nantes, Rue de la Fosse, 1924)

General Cordonnier, *Une brigade au feu (Potins de Guerre)* (Henri Charles–Lavauzelle, Paris, 1921)

L. Dauby, *Jours de Sang, de Larmes et de Gloire. 1914-1918* (A. Gillet, Bertrix)

J.Didier, *Echec à Morhange: août 1914 La bataille de Lorraine* (Ysec éditions, Louviers, 2003)

F. Engerand, *Les Frontières et La Force Allemande* (Perrin et Cie., Paris, 1916)

Fernand Engerand, *Le Secret de La Frontière 1815-1871-1914 Charleroi* (Éditions Bossard, Paris, 1918)

F. Engerand, *La Bataille de la Frontière, aôut 1914* (Brossard, Paris, 1920)

A. Grasset, *Vingt Jours de Guerre aux Temps Héroïques* (Berger-Levrault, Paris-Nancy, 1918)

A. Grasset, *Précepts et Jugements du Maréchal Foch* (Berger-Levrault, Paris, 1919)

A. Grasset, *La Guerre en Action* (Berger-Levrault, Paris): *Neufchâteau* (1923), *Virton* (1925), *Ethe* (1925)

Mémoires du Maréchal Joffre (1910–1917) Tome Premier (Plon, Paris, 1932)

H. Kaiser, *Deutsche und Französische Artillerie in der Schlacht bei Bertrix, 22 August 1914* (Waisenhaus–Buchdruckerei, Hanau, 1937)

De Langle de Cary, *Souvenirs de Commandement, 1914-1916* (Paris, 1935)

General Lanrezac, *Le plan de campagne francais et le premier mois de la guerre* (Payot, Paris, 1929)

General Erich von Ludendorff, *The General Staff and its Problems* (transl. F.A.Holt, Hutchinson & Co, London, 1920)

General Erich von Ludendorff, *My War Memories 1914-1918 Volume 1* (Hutchinson & Co, London, 1919)

J. Moreau, Rossignol, *22 août 1914, Journal du commandant Jean Moreau, chef d'état-major de la 3e division Coloniale*, (retranscribed and with commentary by Éric Labayle et Jean-Louis Philippart, Anvoi, Parçay-sur-Vienne, 2002)

B.G.O'Rorke, Chaplain to the Forces, *In the Hands of the Enemy* (Longman, Green & Co, London 1916)

Colonel J. Paloque, *L'Artillerie dans la bataille* (O. Doin et Fils, Paris, 1912)

Général Paloque, *Bertrix 1914* (Charles-Lavauzelle & Cie, Paris, 1932)

General Pichot-Duclos, *Au GQG de Joffre* (Arthaud, Grenoble, 1947)

P. Puccini, *En Avant! Capitaine Lionel Lemoël 1914-1916* (Alan Sutton, Saint-Cyr-sur-Loire, 2004)

E. Rommel, *Infantry Attacks* (transl. Lt-Col Kiddé, publ. US Army, 1937)

Le Chanoine Jean Schmitz et Dom Norbert Nieuwland, *L'Invasion Allemande dans les provinces de Namur et de Luxembourg: Sixième Partie (Tome VII) La bataille de Neufchâteau et de Maissin* (G. Van Oest & Cie, Librarie Nationale d'Art et d'Histoire, Bruxelles/Paris, 1924)

J Simonin, *De Verdun à Mannheim: Ethe et Gomery (22, 23, 24 Août 1914)* (Pierre Vitet, Paris, 1917)

Edward Spears, *Liaison 1914* (Cassell, London, 1999)

General V. D'Urbal, *Souvenirs et Anecdotes de Guerre 1914-1916* (Berger-Levrault, Paris, 1939)

Colonel E. Valarche, *La Bataille des Frontieres* (Berger–Levrault, Paris, 1932)

E. Secondary Works: Published
1. Official Histories

Les armées françaises dans la grande guerre,
- Tome I, premier volume & Annexes 1-1006
- Tome X, premier etdeuxième volumes
(Ministère de la Guerre, État-major de l'armée, service historique, Imprimerie Nationale, Paris, 1923 and 1936)

Reichsarchiv,Der Weltkrieg 1914 bis 1918 (Reichsarchiv, E.S.Mittler & Sohn, Berlin, 1925):
Die militärischen Operationen zu Lande, Erster Band
Das deutsche Feldeisenbahnwesen I

History of the Great War: Military Operations, France and Belgium, 1914
(Brigadier-General Sir James E. Edmunds, Macmillan & Co., London, 1937)

2. Authors

L.H. Addington, *The Blitzkrieg era and the German General Staff, 1865-1941* (Rutgers University Press, New Brunswick, New Jersey, 1971)

T.J. Adriance, *The Last Gaiter Button: a study of the mobilization and concentration of the French Army in the War of 1870* (Greenwood Press, Connecticut, 1987)

L. Albertini, *The Origins of the War of 1914, Volume II* (transl. I.M. Massey, publ. Oxford University Press, 1953)

R.B. Asprey, *The German High Command at War: Hindenberg and Ludendorff and the First World War* (London, 1993)

J-J. Becker, *les Français dans la Grande Guerre* (Robert Laffont, Paris, 1980)

I.F.W. Beckett, *The Great War 1914-1918* (Pearson Education Limited, 2001)

S. Berstein & P. Milza, *Histoire de la France au XXe siècle* (Bibliothèque Complexe, Paris, 1995)

Dr E. Bircher, *Die Schlacht bei Ethe–Virton am 22. August 1914* (Verlag R. Eisenschmidt, Berlin, 1930)

D. Blackbourn, *The Long Nineteenth Century: A History of Germany, 1780-1918* (London: Fontana Press, 1997)

W. Bloem, *The Advance from Mons 1914: The Experiences of a German Infantry Officer* (transl. G.C. Wynne, reprinted Helion & Company, Solihull, 2004)

B. Bond, *The Pursuit of Victory, from Napoleon to Saddam Hussein* (OUP, Oxford, 1996)

B. Bond (ed.), *Look to your front'* (BCMH, Spellmount, Staplehurst, 1999)

E. D. Brose, *German History 1789-1871* (Berghahn Books, Oxford, 1997)

E. D. Brose, *The Kaiser's Army: The Politics of Military Technology in Germany during the Machine Age, 1870-1918* (Oxford University Press, Oxford, 2001)

A. Bucholz, *Moltke, Schlieffen and Prussian War Planning* (Berg, Oxford, 1991)

H. Bull, *The Control of the Arms Race: Disarmament and Arms Control in the Missile Age* (Institute for Strategic Studies, London, 1961)

Claude Carlier, *Sera maître du monde, qui sera maître de l'air; la création de l'aviation militaire Française* (Economica, Paris, 2004)

William Carr, *A History of Germany 1815–1990* (Edward Arnold, London, 1969)

R. Chickering, *Imperial Germany and the Great War 1914-18* (Cambridge University Press, Cambridge, 1998)

R. Chickering & S. Förster, *Great War, Total War* (Cambridge University Press, Cambridge, 2000)

M. Christian-Forge, *1914-1918 La Grande Guerre* (Librarie Aristide Quillet, Paris, 1922)

W.S. Churchill, *The World Crisis* (Thornton Butterworth Ltd., 1923) and (Odhams, Watford, 1938)

R. M. Citino, *The German Way of War* (University of Kansas Press, Lawrence KS, 2005)

Anthony Clayton, *Paths of Glory: The French Army 1914-1918* (Cassell, London, 2003)

R. Connaughton, *Rising Sun and Tumbling Bear: Russia's War with Japan* (Cassell, London, 2003)

H. Contamine, *La Revanche 1871-1914* (Berger-Levrault, Paris, 1957)

H. Contamine, *La Victoire de la Marne* (Eds Gallimard. Paris, 1970)

M. Cooper, *The Birth of Independent Air Power* (Allen & Unwin, London, 1986)

G.A. Craig, *The Battle of Königgratz* (Weidenfeld & Nicolson, London, 1965)

G.A. Craig, *The Politics of the Prussian Army 1640-1945* (Clarendon Press, Oxford, 1955)

G.A. Craig, 'Hans Delbrück: The Military Historian', published in *Makers of Modern Strategy* (ed. Peter Paret, Princeton University Press, 1986)

C.R.M.F. Cruttwell, *A History of the Great War 1914-1918* (Oxford, Clarendon Press, 1934)

K. Demeter, *The German Officer-Corps in Society and State 1650-1945* (transl. A. Malcolm, Weidenfeld and Nicholson, London, 1965)

J. Desmarest, *La Grande Guerre 1914-1919* (Hachette, Paris, 1978)

J. Didier, *Echec à Morhange, août 1914: La bataille de Lorraine* (Ysec éditions, Louviers, 2003)

R.A. Doughty, *Pyrrhic Victory: French strategy and Operations in the Great War* (Harvard University Press, Harvard MA, 2005)

Colonel T.N. Dupuy, *A Genius for War, The German Army and General Staff 1807-1945* (Macdonald and Jane's, London, 1977)

A.J. Echevarria II, *After Clausewitz* (University of Kansas, Lawrence KS, 2000)

Brigadier–General Sir J.E. Edmonds, *History of the Great War, Military Operations, France and Belgium, 1914* (Macmillan and Co., Ltd., London, 1937)

F. Engerand, *La Bataille de la Fronrier, août 1914* (Brossard, Paris, 1920)

Cyril Falls, *The First World War* (Longmans, London, 1960)

N. Ferguson, *The Pity of War* (Allen Lane, London, 1998)

M. Ferro, *The Great War* (transl. N. Stone, publ. Routledge, London and New York, 1973)

M. Ferro, *Pétain* (Fayard, Paris, 1987)

Fritz Fischer, *War of Illusions: German Policies from 1911 to 1914* (translated by Marian Jackson, publ. Chatto & Windus, London, 1975)

R.T. Foley, *German Strategy and the Path to Verdun* (Cambridge University Press, Cambridge, 2005)

R. Fraenkel, *Joffre, L'âne qui commandait des lions* (Éditions Italiques, Paris, 2004)

Field Marshal Viscount French, *1914* (Constable & Co., London, 1919)

D. Fromkin, *Europe's Last Summer* (William Heinemann, London, 2004)

M. Fulbrook, *German History since 1800* (Arnold, London, 1997)

E. Gabory, *Les Enfants du Pays Nantois et le XIe corps d'Armée* (Perrin, Nantes & Paris,1923)

Nikolas Gardner, *Trial by Fire* (Praeger, London, 2003)

A. Gat, *A History of Military Thought from the Enlightenment to the Cold War* (Oxford University Press, Oxford, 2001)

M. Genevoix, *'Neath Verdun, August-October 1914* (transl. H. Grahame Richards, publ. Hutchinson & Co., London, 1916)

R. Gildea, *Barricades and Borders: Europe 1800-1914* (Oxford University Press, Oxford, 1987)

W. Goerlitz, *The German General Staff: its history and structure* (Transl. Brian Battershaw, Hollis and Carter, London, 1953)

P-M.de la Gorce, *The French Army: A military-political history* (transl. K. Douglas, publ. Weidenfeld and Nicolson, London, 1963)

M. Goya, *La Chair et l'Acier: l'invention de la guerre moderne (1914-1918)* (Tallandier, Paris, 2004)

Commandant A. Grasset, *Un combat de rencontre, Neufchâteau, 22 août 1914* (Berger-Lavrault, Paris, 1923)

Commandant A. Grasset, *La Guerre en Action: le 22 août 1914 au 4e Corps d'Armée: Ethe* (Berger-Levrault, Paris, 1924)

Commandant A. Grasset, *La Guerre en Action: le 22 août 1914 au 4e Corps d'Armée: Virton* (Berger-Levrault, Paris, 1925)

Commandant A. Grasset, *Précepts et Jugements du Maréchal Foch* (Berger-Levrault, Paris, 1919)

Y. Gras, *Castelnau* (Editions Denoël, 1990)

P. Griffith, *Forward into Battle* (The Crowood Press, Swindon, 1990)

R. Griffith, *Marshal Petain* (Constable, London, 1970)

B. I. Gudmundsson, 'Unexpected Encounter at Bertrix' (in *The Great War*,ed. Robert Cowley, Pimlico, London, 2004)

G. Le Hallé, *Le système Séré de Rivières, ou le Témoignage des Pierres* (Ysec Editions, Louviers, 2001)

Ed. R.F. Hamilton & H.H. Herwig, *War Planning 1914* (Cambridge University Press, Cambridge, 2010)

J. Harding, *Boulanger* (W.H. Allen, London, 1971)

G. Hartcup, *The War of Invention: Scientific Developments 1914-18* (Brassey's Defence Publications, London, 1988)

G.F.R. Henderson, *The Science of War* (Longmans & Co., London, 1908)

D. Herrmann, *The Arming of Europe and the Making of the First World War* (Princeton University Press, Princeton NJ, 1996)

H.H. Herwig, *The First World War, Germany and Austria-Hungary 1914-1918* (Arnold, London, 1997)

H. H. Herwig, *The Marne, 1914* (Random House, New York, 2009)

B. Heuser, *The Evolution of Strategy: Thinking war from Antiquity to the Present* (Cambridge University Press, Cambridge, 2010)

Generalleutnant z D. Von Hofacker, *Der Weltkrieg* (Verlag von W. Kohlhammer, Stuttgart, 1928)

M. Howard, 'Men Against Fire: The Doctrine of the Offensive in 1914', published in *Makers of Modern Strategy* (ed. Peter Paret, Princeton University Press, Princeton MJ, 1986)

J.M. House, *Combined Arms Warfare in the Twentieth Century* (University Press of Kansas, Lawrence KS, 2001)

M. Howard, *The Franco–Prussian War* (Routledge, London, 2001)

Ed. M. Hughes & M. Seligmann, *Leadership in Conflict 1914-1918* (Leo Cooper, Barnsley, 2000)

I.V. Hull, *Absolute destruction: military culture and the practices of war in Imperial Germany* (Cornell University Press, London, 2005)

Lt-Colonel T.M. Hunter, *Marshal Foch – a Study in Leadership* (Historical Section, Army Headquarters, Ottowa, Canada, 1961)

J-C.Jauffret, *Parlement, Gouvernement, Commandement: L'armée de métier sous la 3e République* (Service Historique de l'armée de Terre, Vincennes, 1987)

C.H.L. Johnson, *Famous Generals of the Great War* (Little, Brown & Company, Boston, 1919)

D. Johnson, *France and the Dreyfus Affair* (Blandford Press, London, 1966)

H. C. Johnson, *Breakthrough: Tactics, Technology and the search for victory on the Western Front in WW1* (Presidio, Novato CA, 1994)

O. Johnson, *The Spirit of France* (Little, Brown & Company, Boston, 1916)

J. Keegan, *The First World War* (Hutchinson, London, 1998)

A. Kemp, *The Maginot Line* (Frederick Warne, London, 1981)

P. Kennedy, *The Rise and Fall of the Great Powers* (Unwin Hyman, London, 1988)

Martin Kitchen, *The German Officer Corps 1890-1914* (Clarendon Press, Oxford, 1968)

G. Krumeich, *Armaments and Politics in France on the eve of the First World War* (transl. Stephen Conn, Berg Publishers, Leamington Spa, 1984)

Jean Lacouture, *De Gaulle: the Rebel, 1890–1944* (trans. Patrick O'Brian, Collins Harvill, London, 1990)

J-C.Laparra, *La machine à vaincre: l'armée allemande 1914-1918* (Imprimerie France Quercy, Mercuès, 2006)

B.H. Liddell Hart, *A History of the World War* (Faber & Faber, London, 1930)

B.H. Liddell Hart, *Foch: the Man of Orleans* (Eyre and Spottiswoode, London, 1931)

B.H. Liddell Hart, The Real War 1914-1918 (Faber & Faber, London, 1930)

H. Linnenkohl, *Vom Einzelschuss zur Feuer-Walze: Der Wettlauf zwischen Technik und Taktik im Ersten Weltkrieg* (Bernard & Graefe Verlag, Koblenz, 1990)

General Ludendorff, *My War Memories 1914-1918, Vol 1* (transl. F.A. Holt, Publ. Hutchinson & Co., London, 1919)

J. Marshall-Cornwall, *Foch as Military Commander* (Batsford, London, 1972)

J. Maurin, *Armée-Guerre-Société, Soldats Languedociens (1889-1919)* (Publications de la Sorbonne, Paris, 1982)

R. Magraw, *France 1914-1915* (Oxford University Press, Oxford, 1983)

J.F. McMillan, *Dreyfus to De Gaulle: Politics and Society in France 1898–1969* (Edward Arnold, London, 1985)

C. Messenger, *The Last Prussian: A Biography of Field Marshal Gerd von Rundstedt 1875-1953* (Brasseys UK, London, 1991)

A.R. Millett & W. Murray, *Military Effectiveness: Volume 1, The First World War* (Cambridge University Press, Cambridge, 1988)

P. Miquel, *La Grande Guerre* (Librarie Arthème Fayard, Paris, 1983)

A. Mombauer, *Helmuth von Moltke and the Origins of the First World War* (Cambridge University Press, Cambridge, 2001)

J.H. Morgan, *The German War Book: a literal and integral translation of the 'Kriegsbrauch im Landkriege', issued and reissued by the German General Staff for the instruction of German Officers* (London, 1915)

J.H. Morrow, *The Great War in the Air* (Smithsonian Institution Press, Washington, 1993)

J. Mosier, *The Myth of the Great War* (Profile Books, London, 2001)

L.M. Moyer, *Victory must be Ours: Germany in the Great War, 1914-18* (Leo Cooper, London, 1995)

S. Naveh, *In Pursuit of Military Excellence: the evolution of operational theory* (Frank Cass, London, 1997)

General Niox, *La Grande Guerre* (De Gigord, Paris, 1921)

Ed. John Andreas Olsen & Martin van Creveld, *The Evolution of Operational Art from Napoleon to the Present* (Oxford University Press, Oxford, 2011)

H. Otto & K. Schmiedel, *Der Erste Weltkrieg* (DMV, Berlin, 1983)

I. Ousby, *The Road to Verdun* (Jonathan Cape, London, 2002)

Général Palat, *La Grande Guerre sur le Front Occidental* (Librairie Chapelot, Paris): *I Les élements du conflit* (1917), *II Liége, Mulhouse, Sarrebourg, Morhange* (1917), *III Batailles des Ardennes et de la Sambre* (1918)

L. Patry, *The Reality of War: A Memoir of the Franco-Prussian War 1870-1871* (transl. D. Fermer, publ. Cassell, London, 2001)

W. Paul, *Entscheidung im September: Das Wunder an der Marne 1914* (Heyne, München, 1974)

W.J. Philpott, *Anglo-French Relations and Strategy on the Western Front, 1914-1918* (Macmillan Press, Basingstoke, 1996)

D. Porch, *The March to the Marne: The French Army 1871-1914* (Cambridge University Press, Cambridge, 1981)

M. von Poseck, *The German Cavalry in Belgium and France, 1914* (E.S. Mittler & Sohn, Berlin, 1923, translated by Captain Alexander C. Strecker, US Cavalry and printed by US War Office)

Barry R. Posen, *The Sources of Military Doctrine: France, Britain and Germany between the World Wars* (Cornell University Press, London, 1984)

R. A. Prete, *Strategy and Command: the Anglo-French Coalition on the Western Front, 1914* (McGill-Queen's University Press, Canada, 2009)

P. Puccini, *En Avant! Capitaine Lionel Lemoël 1914-1916* (Editions Alan Sutton, Saint-Cyr-sur-Loire, 2004)

D. Queloz, *De la manoeuvre Napoléonienne à l'offensive à outrance* (Economica, Paris, 2009)

Walter Raleigh, *The War in the Air, Volume 1* (OUP, Oxford, 1922)

David B. Ralston, *The Army of the Republic* (The M.I.T. Press, Cambridge MA, 1967)

R. Recouly, *General Joffre and His Battles* (Charles Scribner, New York, 1917)

Colonel Repington, *The First World War 1914-1918 Vol 1* (Constable & Co., London, 1920)

G. Ritter, *The Sword and the Sceptre, Volume III* (transl. University of Miami Press, Florida, 1970)

P. Rocolle, *L'Hécatombe des Généraux* (Editions Laranzelle, Paris-Limoges, 1980)

H. Rosinski, *The German Army* (Pall Mall Press, London, 1966)

M. Samuels, *Doctrine and Dogma : German and British infantry tactics in the First World War* (Greenwood Press, New York, 1992)

D.E. Showalter, *Railroads and Rifles : soldiers, technology and the unification of Germany* (Archon Books, Connecticut, 1976)

B. Simonet, *Franchise Militaire : de la Bataille des Frontières aux combats de Champagne 1914-1915* (Gallimard, Paris, 1986)

Leonard V. Smith, *Between Mutiny and Obedience: The Case of the French Fifth Infantry Division* (Princeton University Press, Princeton MJ, 1994)

J. Snyder, *The Ideology of the Offensive: Military Decision making and the disasters of 1914* (Cornell University Press, London, 1984)

D. Stevenson, *Armaments and the Coming of War, Europe 1904-1914* (Clarendon Press, Oxford, 1996)

D. Stevenson, *1914–1918* (Allen Lane, London, 2004)

D. Stevenson, *Cataclysm* (Basic Books, New York, 2004)

D. Storz, *Kriegsbild und Rüstung vor 1914: Europäische Landstreitkräfte vor dem Ersten Weltkrieg* (Verlag E.S. Mittler & Sohn, Berlin, 1992)

D. Stone, *Fighting for the Fatherland* (Conway, London, 2006)

H. Strachan, *The First World War Volume 1: To Arms* (Oxford University Press, Oxford, 2001)

Sun Tzu, *Master Sun's Art of War* (transl. P.J. Ivanhoe, publ. Hackett Publishing Company, Indianapolis/Cambridge, 2011)

J.K. Tanenbaum, *General Maurice Sarrail 1856-1929* (University of North Carolina Press, Chapel Hill NC, 1974)

C. Telp, *The Evolution of Operational Art 1740–1813* (Frank Cass, London & New York, 2005)

J. Terraine, *The Western Front 1914-18* (Hutchinson & Co., London, 1964)

J. Terraine, *White Heat: The New Warfare 1914-18* (Sidgwick & Jackson, London, 1982)

T. Travers, *The Killing Ground* (Allen & Unwin, London, 1987)

B. Tuchman, *August 1914* (Constable & Co., London, 1962)

B. Tuchman, The Guns of August (Ballantine, New York, 1994)

S. Tyng, *The Campaign of the Marne* (Longmans, Green & Co., 1935)

Colonel E. Valarché, *La Bataille des Frontières* (Editions Berger-Levrault, Paris, 1932)

J. Verhay, *The Spirit of 1914: Militarism, Myth and Mobilisation in Germany* (Cambridge University Press, Cambridge, 2000)

J.L. Wallach, *The Dogma of the Battle of Annihilation* (Greenwood Press, Westport Connecticut and London, 1986)

E. Weber, *The Nationalist Revival in France, 1905-1914* (University of California Press, Berkeley CA, 1968)

General Weygand, *Histoire de l'Armée Française* (Ernest Flammarion, Paris, 1953)

J.F.Williams, *Corporal Hitler and the Great War 1914-1918: The List Regiment* (Frank Cass, London & New York, 2005)

Ed. K. Wilson, *Decisions for War, 1914* (UCL, London, 1995)

P.H. Wilson, *German Armies, War and Politics 1648-1806* (UCL Press, London, 1998)

J. Winter & B. Baggett, *The Great War and the Shaping of the 20th Century* (Penguin Studio, New York, 1996)

D. Zabecki, *Steel Wind: Colonel Georg Bruchmüller and the birth of modern artillery* (Praeger, Westport CT, 1994)

T. Zuber, *Inventing the Schlieffen Plan* (Oxford University Press, Oxford, 2002)

T. Zuber, *The Battle of the Frontiers: Ardennes, 1914* (Tempus, Stroud, 2007)

T. Zuber, *The Real German War Plan 1904-14* (The History Press, Stroud, 2011)

F. Secondary Works : Journals

1. *Revue Historique des Armées*

C. Carlier, 'Observations de la 3e dimension' (Nr.234, 2004)

2. *Revue Historique de l'Armée*

'La Division de Paris au Feu: 10e Division d'Infanterie 1914-1915' (Vol. VIII, Annéenr. 1)

3. *Revue Militaire Française*

Commandant Padovani, 'A la droite de la 5e Armée Française' (Nrs. 74 & 75, July-September 1927)

Colonel H. Rozet, 'Une Journée de crise à la IIIe Armée Allemande: Combats de Signy-L'Abbaye, la Fosse-à-l'Eau (28 août 1914)' (Nr 92, 1929)

Capitaine C-J. Marchal, 'La VII° Armée Allemande en couverture en Août 1914' (Nr.95 May 1929)

Lt-Colonel de Nerciat, 'A propos du Cinquantenaire de l'École Supérieuere de Guerre' (Nr. 96A, Vol.21, 1926)

Lt-Colonel du genie Baills, 'Évolution des idées sur l'emploitactique de l'organisation de terrain de Napoléon à nosjours' (Nr.96, Vol.22, 1926)

Commandant A. Pugens, 'The Genesis of Neufchâteau' (Nrs.96 & 97, 1929)

Lieutenant-Colonel Aublet, 'L'artillerie française de 1914 à 1918' (Nr.98, August 1929)

Lieutenant-Colonel A. Pugens, 'Rossignol' (Nrs.105 & 106, March-April 1930)

Commandant Lefranc, 'Morhange' (Nr.112, October 1930)

4. *War In History*

T. Holmes. 'A reluctant March on Paris' (Vol.2, 2001)

R.T. Foley, 'The Origins of the Schlieffen Plan' (Vol.10, Nr.2, 2003)

R.T. Foley, 'The Real Schlieffen Plan' (Vol.13, Nr.1, 2006)

T. Hippler, 'Conscription in the French Restoration: The 1818 Debate on Military Service' (Vol. 13, Nr. 3, 2006)

5. *Journal of the Royal Artillery*

Lt-Colonel A.H. Burne, 'The French Guns at Bertrix, 1914' (Vol.LXIII, 1936-37)

'AGM', 'Bertrix 1914, seen from the German side' (Vol. LXIV 1937-8)

6. *Journal of Military History*

Lieutenant–Colonel A.H. Burne, 'The French Guns at Bertrix 1914' (Vol. LXIII, 1936–37)

T.M. Holmes, 'Schlieffen and the Avoidance of Tactics: A Reinvestigation' (Vol.27 Nr.4, December 2004)

J. McRanole & J.Quirk, 'The Blood Test Revisited:A new look at German Casualty counts in the First World War' (Vol. 70, Nr. 3, July 2006)

7. *The Army Quarterly*

'The Battle of Morhange: Foch & XX Corps' (Vol.XVIII, April-July 1929)

'Operations in the Bruche Valley' (Vol.XVIII, April-July 1929)

AFPC & FASC, 'The Battle of Sarrebourg-Vosges' (Vol.XIX, October 1929-January 1930)

Major R.L. Bond, 'The Mulhouse campaign, August 7th 1914' (Vol. XXI, October 1930)

Major E.W.N. Wade MC, 'From Maxim to Vickers: some reminiscences of an Infantry Machine Gun Officer' (Vol.XXVIII, April-July 1934)

8. *Military Affairs*

J.C. Arnold, 'French Tactical Doctrine 1870-1914' (Vol.42, Nr.2. April 1978)

9. *The Army Review*

'A Report on the French Manoeuvres in the South-West' (Vol.VI, Nr.1)

10. *The Fighting Forces*

'France's African Armies' (Vol.II, Nr.4, 1925)

Major A.H. Burne, 'The Battle of Ethe' (Vol.VI, 1929)

Major A.H. Burne, 'The Battle of Virton' (Vol. VIII, 1931

Major A.H. Burne, 'The Battle of Rossignol' (Vol. VIII Nr.3, October 1931)

Major A.H. Burne, 'Bertrix' (Vol. VIII Nr.4, January 1932)

G. Reference Works

B.L. Dastrup, *The Field Artillery History and Source Book* (Greenwood Press, Westport CT, 1994)

P. Chamberlain & T. Gander, *World War Two Fact Files: Heavy Artillery* (MacDonald & Jane's, London, 1975)

Herman Cron, *Imperial German Army 1914-18* (transl. C.F.Colton, Helion & Company, Solihull, 2001)

C.E. Crutchley, *Machine Gunner 1914-1918* (Machine Gun Corps & Mercury Press, n.p., 1973)

J. Ellis, *The Social History of the Machine Gun* (Pimlico, London, 1976)

Handbook of the French Army 1914 (War Office, 1914, The Imperial War Museum Department of Printed Books, 1912 [Amended to August 1914])

Handbook of the German Army 1914 (War Office, 1914, The Imperial War Museum Department of Printed Books, 1912 [Amended to August 1914])

Major F.W.A. Hobart, *Pictorial History of the machine Gun* (Ian Allan, London, 1971)

I.V. Hogg, *Allied Artillery of World War One* (The Crowood Press, Marlborough, 1998)

I.V. Hogg, *Twentieth-Century Artillery* (Amber Books, Rochester, 2000)

I.V. Hogg and J. Weeks, *Military Small Arms of the 20th Century*, (Arms and Armour Press, London, 1977)

Lieutenant-Colonel Hutchison, *Machine Guns: Their history and tactical employment* (Macmillan, London, 1938)

F. Kosar, *A Pocket History of Artillery: Light Field Guns* (Ian Allan, London, 1971)

D.B. Nash, *Imperial German Army Handbook 1914–1918* (Ian Allan Ltd, London, 1980)

D. Nash, *German Artillery 1914-1918* (Almark Publications, London, 1970)

F.J. Stephens & G.J. Maddocks, *Uniforms and Organisation of the Imperial German Army 1900-1918* (Almark, London, 1975)

J. Walter, *Machine guns of two World Wars* (Greenhill, London, 2005)

The War Office, *The Development of Artillery Tactics and Equipment* (HMSO, London, 1951)

H. Theses and Other Unpublished Works

R.H. Cole, 'Forward with the Bayonet: the French Army prepares for offensive warfare, 1911-1914' (University of Maryland PhD, 1975)

W. Sanders Marble, ''The Infantry cannot do with a gun less': The Place of the Artillery in the British Expeditionary Force 1914-1980 (Kings College London PhD, 1998)

M. Buck, 'French Artillery Doctrine before the First World War' (A paper presented to the Royal Artillery Historical Society, 16 January, 2002)

J. Dauphin, '22 août 1914: Bataille des Frontières, Virton, Ethe, Signeulx, Rossignol, Neufchâteau' (A collection of witness statements and memories compiled by the local schoolmaster at Latour, Belgian Ardennes)

Index

Index of People

Alby, General 109, 113–114, 121, 223, 226
André, War Minister General 144, 175, 185

Baquet, General 145, 190, 198
Boelle, General vi, 55, 60, 65–66, 68, 71, 82, 164, 222
Brochin, General 40, 65–68, 168, 173, 195–196, 213, 217, 222

Chapès, Colonel 112, 169, 177
von Clausewitz, C. 150–151, 166, 172, 212, 220
Contamine, Henry xv, xvii, xxiii, 85, 87–88, 106, 144, 157, 159, 192, 211, 213, 217–218
Cordonnier, General xxiv, 41, 130, 199

D'Urbal, General V. 58–59, 222
de Langle de Cary, General vi, viii, xxi, xxv, 31, 33–34, 37–42, 44–50, 52–60, 62–65, 67–68, 70–71, 74, 89, 105, 109, 111, 120, 124–125, 130, 136–138, 153, 162–164, 166–167, 171, 179, 185, 192–193, 205, 211–214, 217–220, 223
Descoings, Colonel 95–97, 99–101, 105, 169, 213, 225

Étienne, War Minister 142–144, 155, 165, 175, 177, 182, 185–186, 190, 194, 197, 207
Eydoux, General vi, 45, 57, 59, 72, 108–109, 111–112, 116–118, 120–122, 133, 163–164, 168, 177, 201, 209, 212–214, 220, 223, 226

Foch, Marshal 105, 116, 120, 185, 219–220
Fraisse, General 126–127, 158, 227

Garreau, General 91, 96–99, 101, 104–105, 223, 225
Gérard, General xxi, 55, 58, 60, 130, 178
Goullet, General 88, 90, 92–93, 223, 225

von Hausen, General xvi, 36, 39, 44, 163, 214, 217, 219–220

Joffre, General xix, xxii, 30, 32, 35–37, 39, 42–43, 48, 53, 55–56, 63–64, 66, 68, 106, 109, 115, 124, 137, 141, 146, 150, 153–154, 156, 159, 167, 174, 176, 178–179, 183, 185–186, 190, 192–193, 211, 213, 217–218, 221

von Jordon, Major–General 87, 94, 96–98, 101

Kaempffer, General 39–40, 61, 63–64, 66, 193, 196
von Knobelsdorf, Lieutenant-General xvii, xx, 48, 55, 62, 131–133, 185, 222–224

Lanrezac, General 34, 37, 207, 219
Leblois, General 136–137, 223, 228
Leblond, General 91–94, 97, 101, 104–106, 223–224
Lefèvre, General 42, 59, 90, 136–137, 223, 228

Maistre, General 47, 55, 223
Maunoury, General xviii, 43, 48, 68–69, 217–219
von Moltke, Helmuth vi, 33, 62, 77, 143, 147, 184, 186, 218
Montignault, General 134, 136, 228
Moreau, Commandant Jean xx, 55, 131–136, 206, 209, 216, 228

Poline, General 108, 125–126, 164, 223, 226
von Pritzelwitz, General 51, 223, 228

Radiguet, General 116–117, 120, 212, 223, 226
Raffenel, General 131–133, 135, 223, 228
von Richthofen, General 31, 33–34, 163
Rocolle, Pierre xxiv, 51, 66, 68–69, 85, 101, 106, 126, 132, 134, 137, 195, 213
Roques, General Pierre i, vi, xiii, xxi, xxiv–xxv, 41, 46, 52, 57, 59, 73, 85–88, 90–93, 96–99, 101–107, 109, 125, 168, 178–179, 195, 202, 213, 222–224
Ruffey, General vi, ix, xviii, 31–32, 36–37, 39–44, 47–49, 60, 63–70, 74, 161, 164, 167, 171, 173, 179, 183, 192–193, 196, 205, 211–213, 217–219, 222

von Schenk, General 51–52, 99, 120, 213, 223
von Schlieffen, Count A. i, xi, xv, xviii, 29, 143, 147, 151, 154, 166, 168, 174, 190, 194, 198–199, 217
von Steuben, General 51, 88–89, 92, 223

Vitart, Colonel 133, 136, 209, 216

William, Crown Prince vi, 32–33, 38, 40–43, 48–50, 60–63, 66, 69–70, 75, 161, 193, 196, 212–213, 218–219, 224
von Württemberg, Duke Albrecht vi, xvi–xvii, 34, 36–42, 44, 46–48, 50–53, 62, 67, 70, 76, 85, 101,

Index of French Military Units & Formations

Index of German Military Units & Formations

Index of General & Miscellaneous Terms